British Social
Attitudes
the
14th report

Social and Community Planning Research (SCPR) is an independent, non-profit social research institute. It has a large professional staff together with its own interviewing and coding resources. Some of SCPR's work - such as the survey reported in this book - is initiated by the institute itself and grant-funded by research councils or foundations. Other work is initiated by government departments, local authorities or quasi-government organisations to provide information on aspects of social or economic policy. SCPR also works frequently with other institutes and academics. Founded in 1969 and now Britain's largest social research institute, SCPR has a high reputation for the standard of its work in both qualitative and quantitative research. SCPR has a Survey Methods Centre and, with Nuffield College Oxford, houses the Centre for Research into Elections and Social Trends (CREST), which is an ESRC Research Centre. It also houses, with Southampton University, the Centre for Applied Social Surveys (CASS), an ESRC Resource Centre, two main functions of which are to run courses in survey methods and to establish and administer an electronic social survey question bank.

The contributors

Steven Barnett
Senior Lecturer at the Centre for Communication and Information Studies, University of Westminster

Lindsay Brook
Research Director at SCPR and Co-director of the *British Social Attitudes* survey series

Alex Bryson
Senior Research Fellow at the Policy Studies Institute

Caroline Bryson
Senior Researcher at SCPR and Co-director of the *British Social Attitudes* survey series

John Curtice
Senior Lecturer in Politics and Director of the Social Statistics Laboratory, University of Strathclyde

Lizanne Dowds
Research Affiliate at The Centre for Social Research, Queen's University, Belfast

Anthony Heath
Professor of Sociology at the University of Oxford, a fellow of Nuffield College, and Co-director of the ESRC Centre for Research into Elections and Social Trends based at SCPR and Nuffield College

Roger Jowell
Director of SCPR and Co-director of the *British Social Attitudes* survey series; Visiting Professor at the London School of Economics and Political Science

Ken Judge
Professor of Social Policy, University of Kent

Jo-Ann Mulligan
Research Officer at the King's Fund Policy Institute

Stephen McKay
Research Fellow at the Centre for Research in Social Policy, Loughborough University

Alan Murie
Professor and Director of the Centre for Urban and Regional Studies, University of Birmingham

Bill New
Senior Research Officer at the King's Fund Policy Institute

Kenneth Newton
Professor of Government at the University of Essex and Executive Director of the European Consortium for Political Research

Alison Park
Research Director at SCPR and Co-director of the *British Social Attitudes* survey series

Roger Tarling
Professor of Social Research at the Institute of Social Research, University of Surrey

Bridget Taylor
Research Officer at Nuffield College, Oxford

Katarina Thomson
Research Director at SCPR and Co-director of the *British Social Attitudes* survey series

British Social Attitudes

the
14th report

The end of Conservative values?

Editors
Roger Jowell
John Curtice
Alison Park
Lindsay Brook
Katarina Thomson &
Caroline Bryson

Ashgate

Aldershot • Brookfield USA • Singapore • Sydney

SOCIAL & COMMUNITY
SCPR
PLANNING RESEARCH

Published by
Ashgate Publishing Limited
Gower House
Croft Road
Aldershot
Hants GU11 3HR
England

Ashgate Publishing Company
Old Post Road
Brookfield
Vermont 05036
USA

ISSN 0267 6869
ISBN 1 84014 043 7

Printed and bound by Athenaeum Press, Ltd., Gateshead, Tyne & Wear.

Contents

CHAPTER 3.   THE NHS: NEW PRESCRIPTIONS NEEDED?

by Ken Judge, Jo-Ann Mulligan and Bill New **49**

CHAPTER 4.   BENEFIT CLAIMANTS: VILLAINS OR VICTIMS?

by Caroline Bryson **73**

Introduction

This Report, like its thirteen predecessors, presents the first analyses and interpretations of the latest in SCPR's *British Social Attitudes* survey series. But, as always, it also tries to take a longer view. In particular, we take stock of the attitudes and values that characterised the 1980s and early 1990s while the Conservative party was enjoying a record period in office. We try to find out whether and to what extent the public at large ever really adopted Conservative values and - if so - when and how they began to reject them. Alternatively, we examine whether these sorts of links between government policy and public opinion exist at all.

The *British Social Attitudes* series, started in 1983, is designed to chart, describe and analyse trends in public attitudes over the years. It is therefore uniquely able to provide the source material for understanding the ebbs and flows of value changes in Britain over the last two decades of the twentieth century.

It was, after all, always Mrs. Thatcher's aim not just fundamentally to change the direction of British public policy, but also to transform the way the public viewed the world, themselves and the role of government in their lives. At the heart of her vision was an 'enterprise society' in which the public believed in, and lived by, the market, adopting the principles of competition and appreciating the virtues of a flexible, unfettered market for jobs. In view of the Conservatives' remarkable electoral successes during the period, it is intriguing to find out how far they actually succeeded in winning over the hearts and minds of the electorate as well as collecting their votes.

For the most part our evidence suggests they failed in this larger task. In the two chapters here that address two of the subjects most central to the Conservatives' reform programme - work and housing respectively - the

public attitudes we uncover are hardly consistent with what had been hoped for under the 'Thatcher revolution'.

First, in Chapter 2, on attitudes to work, Alex Bryson and Stephen McKay find little enthusiasm among the public for the virtues of a flexible labour market. True, they find that attitudes towards work are partly cyclical so that concerns about job security, for instance, rise and fall with unemployment levels. But, after allowing for this tendency, they find nonetheless that people are even more concerned now about job security than they were in the 1980s. Although strikes may have become less common, workers have become more critical than ever about the relationship between management and workers. Moreover, in sharp contrast to the notion of an 'enterprise society', or for that matter a 'classless society', hostility towards income inequality has risen rather than fallen.

Perhaps one of the most imaginative ways in which the Conservative government attempted to foster belief in the market was through its promotion of owner-occupation. In a 'property-owning democracy', they reasoned, most people would have a stake in the market through owning their own homes. The government encouraged council tenants to buy their homes by offering them highly favourable terms and in the 1980s presided over one of the biggest booms in the housing market ever experienced. At the turn of the decade, however, the housing market slumped, and - as Alan Murie shows in Chapter 7 - the shockwaves of this appear to have had a long-term impact on attitudes towards owner-occupation, outliving the worst period of the slump itself. Although a clear majority of the population would still prefer to own their home rather than rent it, they are much more sceptical than before about the automatic advantages of ownership and more aware than ever of its risks. Moreover, as Murie argues, it is probably no longer sensible to think of owner-occupiers as a single social group with a clear stake in the market. Both in terms of social experience and political values, those in low-value owner-occupied housing turn out to have much more in common with those in council housing than with those in high-value properties.

In Chapter 4, Caroline Bryson looks at changes in attitudes towards the welfare state. Having found some comfort for the Conservatives from the fact that public support for more welfare spending has declined over the period, she finds nonetheless that only a minority of the public seems to be at all concerned about 'scrounging on the welfare', or persuaded by the view that too much welfare makes people less willing to work. Certainly there is no widespread perception of a debilitating 'dependency culture', a spectre evoked at Conservative Party conferences.

The National Health Service emerged as a policy priority for the Conservatives only in the late 1980s, following mounting public concern about its effectiveness in responding to the increasing demands made of it. A number of measures were introduced, designed to improve the performance of the NHS within existing resources, once again largely by means of market mechanisms. As a result, it was hoped, waiting lists would be reduced and patient choice increased. But, in Chapter 3, Ken Judge and his colleagues

suggest that these reforms have hardly had their desired effect on public attitudes. On the contrary, dissatisfaction remains as strong as ever, as do concerns about the inadequacy of funding for the NHS. Moreover, there appears to be a close link between the level of public satisfaction with the service and increases in government spending on it.

Another area where government policy changed during its tenure, indeed perhaps even more so on than on the NHS, was the environment and transport. Early in its life, the Conservative government was widely believed to be in favour of allowing people the unfettered freedom to own and use a motor car. But towards the end of the 1980s, evidence emerged about a number of environmental problems such as the 'greenhouse effect', the growth of a hole in the ozone layer, and rising levels of asthma. Mrs. Thatcher herself expressed concern about the future of the environment, and the government began to increase fuel taxes and cut road building programmes.

In Chapter 6 Bridget Taylor shows that this change of policy matched a change in public mood. There has been growing concern about the environment in general (albeit tempered somewhat by economic recession) and about the motor car in particular. Yet she also demonstrates that there is still considerable reluctance to change behaviour. Car owners may be happy to see city centres pedestrianised but they are not willing to pay more to use their cars. In contrast to the philosophy of Thatcherism, people seem to hope that governments can solve the problem, rather than individuals have to change their lifestyles.

There is, however, one major policy area in which the Conservative government, in its final years, was clearly more in tune with public opinion. As Roger Tarling and Lizanne Dowds show in Chapter 10, the government's response from 1993 onwards to apparently ever-rising levels of crime, was to adopt noticeably less liberal policies that tilted the balance away from the protection of suspects in favour of helping the police and courts both to improve their rate of conviction and to make sentencing stricter. Meanwhile, public opinion - never very liberal on these matters in the first place - became even less liberal over the period, possibly in response to these changes in official policy. Even here, however, there is some room for doubt about the causal chain of events, since the opposition Labour party moved in a similar direction on law and order over the period. It could be that this bipartisan switch of policy may have been particularly influential.

A new consensus may have emerged on law and order during the final few years of the Conservative administration. But these years also saw a new division between the two main parties on how Britain should be governed. During its 18 years in opposition, the Labour party had slowly become committed to a wide range of constitutional changes including reform of the House of Lords, devolution for Scotland and Wales, and the introduction of a Bill of Rights. It also promised a referendum on the future of the first-past-the-post electoral system for Westminster elections. All of these measures were opposed by the Conservatives. In Chapter 5, John Curtice and Roger

Jowell conclude that Labour's, as opposed to the Conservatives', solutions appear to hold sway with the public. With the important exception of electoral reform, there is widespread support for many of the changes on the new government's constitutional agenda.

Though there has in the same period been a sharp decline in public confidence in politicians and the political system, this does not in itself explain the rise in support for constitutional change. Nor, as Kenneth Newton shows in Chapter 8, can the decline in political trust or political participation in turn be blamed, as it often is, on the public's growing reliance on television for news. As always, the real relationship is more complex, but the evidence certainly suggests that watching a lot of television may, after all, make us a better informed, rather than a more apathetic, society.

If the Conservative government had indeed succeeded in making an impact on values, we might have anticipated that it would be particularly influential on those who had little or no adult experience of anything but Conservative governments. In Chapter 1, Anthony Heath and Alison Park examine the attitudes of 'Thatcher's Children' across a wide range of issues, and find that people who 'came of age' since the Conservatives came to power turn out to differ little in their values from the rest of society. And such generational differences as do exist - for instance, lower support for the monarchy and greater enthusiasm for the European Union - are at the very opposite end of the spectrum to those encouraged by Mrs. Thatcher.

This conclusion is bolstered in Chapter 9 by Steven Barnett and Katarina Thomson, who analyse attitudes towards censorship of television and cinema violence. Not only are younger generations more liberal than their elders, as might be expected, but evidence of any return to 'Victorian values' is certainly hard to find.

None of these findings suggests, however, that the new Labour government will be any more successful in bringing public opinion into line with public policy. Indeed, in many respects, there already appears to be a distinct gap between public preferences and the new government's policy priorities. For instance, most people, increasingly concerned about reducing inequality, insistently want to see more public spending on services such as health and education even if it means higher taxes - a policy the new government is very unlikely to adopt, at least in the short-term. Still, it may be that *all* governments nowadays are destined to suffer from an adverse public reaction when the realities of economic stringency, among other things, lead to unfulfilled public expectations. Either way, with the future of the *British Social Attitudes* series secure until almost the end of the new government's first term in office, public attitudes will, over the next few years, be particularly interesting to chart.

The longevity of the series owes everything to its many generous funders, in particular the Sainsbury Family Charitable Trusts, whose commitment to core-funding has now extended to fourteen years, with at least another three years promised. But others too have made substantial, and in many cases long-term commitments, to the design and inclusion of particular modules of

questions.   The Department for Education and Employment, the Home Office, the Department of Health, the Department of the Environment, the Department of Transport, the Department for Trade and Industry, and the Department of Social Security are all among these, as is the Economic and Social Research Council (ESRC), the Countryside Commission, the Charities Aid Foundation, the Nuffield Foundation, the Leverhulme Trust, the British Board of Film Classification and the Broadcasting Standards Commission. This year we are also able to add for the first time to our list of funders the BBC, the Independent Television Commission and the Office of the National Lottery.

The ESRC also finances our participation in the *International Social Survey Programme* (ISSP), now comprising nearly 30 countries and bringing an important cross-national perspective to the series. Next year's volume, *The 15th Report*, will be devoted largely to reporting cross-national differences in attitudes.

The *British Social Attitudes* series also continues to have close links with the *British Election Study* and the *British Election Panel Study*, both of which have been conducted by SCPR for many years and are now carried out within the *Centre for Research into Elections and Social Trends (CREST)* - an ESRC Research Centre linking SCPR and Nuffield College, Oxford. Indeed, with funding from the ESRC, the 1996 *British Social Attitudes* survey was deployed to serve also as the first round of the *British Election Campaign Panel*. By including a module of questions on political attitudes and voting intention a year before the general election, and then by reinterviewing respondents twice more (over the telephone) during the election campaign proper and once more immediately after the election, we were able to track changes in both attitudes and voting intentions (and the relationship between them) in the year leading up to the election.

As in previous years, a survey in the *Northern Ireland Social Attitudes* (NISA) series, funded by the Northern Ireland Departments, also took place in 1996. The fieldwork was carried out by our colleagues at the Central Survey Unit of the Northern Ireland Statistics and Research Agency (NISRA), using substantially the same questionnaire as in Britain, but with the addition of a section on community relations in Northern Ireland. Findings from the NISA series are reported separately (the last volume to appear being Dowds *et al.*, 1997).

The number of colleagues who contribute critically to the success of *British Social Attitudes* grows larger each year. Within SCPR we are particularly indebted to our interviewers and their area managers for their skills, endurance and persistence in coping with an ever more complicated survey, and to our colleagues in other parts of the institute who supervise fieldwork, data preparation and data processing. As we go to press we wish to record our appreciation to Sheila Vioche for producing the camera-ready copy from our numerous messy drafts and to Sarah-Jane Lilley for her help with data preparation and analysis.

Outside SCPR we owe an immense debt to Ann Mair of the Social Statistics Laboratory at the University of Strathclyde for her annual efforts in producing a meticulous SPSS system file for use initially by the authors, but also later by the whole research community through the Data Archive at the University of Essex. We also wish to thank the staff at Ashgate Publishing - especially Sonia Hubbard and Ann Newell - for their help and patience in getting this Report - plus its recent companion volume (Taylor and Thomson, 1996) - to press with ever-shrinking deadlines.

As always we reserve our special and most heartfelt thanks to the 3,600 or so anonymous respondents in England, Scotland and Wales, and a further 750 or so in Northern Ireland, who gave their time without reward save for making their voices heard. We hope they feel that their efforts were justified.

The Editors

References

Dowds, L., Devine, P. and Breen, R. (eds.) (1997), *Social Attitudes in Northern Ireland: the 6th Report*, Belfast: Appletree Press.

Taylor, B. and Thomson, K. (eds.) (1996), *Understanding Change in Social Attitudes*, Aldershot: Dartmouth.

1 Thatcher's children?

Anthony Heath and Alison Park [*]

Like some nations, particular generations are associated with certain stereotypes. The one that came of age during the recent eighteen years of Conservative rule - 'Thatcher's children', as they are often called - is attributed with a range of characteristics that are not necessarily consistent with one another. On the one hand they are supposed to be a materialistic and grasping generation, reared on conspicuous consumption and instant gratification, and on the other, a disaffected generation, disinterested and disengaged from many aspects of civil society. This generation is, of course, not alone in attracting such stereotypes. Their immediate predecessors, who grew up during the 1960s and 1970s, are also frequently seen as a generation apart, characterised for instance by liberalism towards moral matters and little respect for 'traditional' forms of authority.

Our aim in this chapter is to examine the evidence behind these generational stereotypes, focusing particularly on whether the attitudes of the generation who grew up and reached adulthood during the Thatcher years differ markedly from those of earlier generations. In other words, does the notion of 'Thatcher's children' have any substance?

---

[*] Anthony Heath is Professor of Sociology at the University of Oxford, a fellow of Nuffield College, and Co-director of the ESRC Centre for Research into Elections and Social Trends based at SCPR and Nuffield College. Alison Park is a Research Director at SCPR and Co-director of the *British Social Attitudes* survey series.

The values of a generation

Why might values differ?

How likely is it that young people's attitudes could have been particularly shaped by 18 years of Conservative rule? One theory of social change holds that adolescence and young adulthood is a critical period for the development of values, attitudes and beliefs. During these impressionable years, young people are particularly receptive not only to new ideas and viewpoints, but also to the prevailing social climate and philosophy. Once established, these beliefs and values will tend to crystallise and stabilise, in many cases persisting throughout people's lives (Mannheim, 1928). So, when a particular generation experiences a distinctive slice of history in its youth, it may well leave a lasting imprint on its social and political consciousness. This process can create stark generational differences in values, since different generations grow up with different sets of historical circumstances. So, as older generations die and are replaced by younger cohorts, the overall balance of values in the population will change.

Even according to this theory of social change, some slices of history will naturally have a greater impact than others. For instance, the experience of growing up during the second world war would be likely to have made a powerful impression just as, in a very different way, might have coming of age during the sixties. It is also possible that the Thatcher years will have had a considerable impact.[1] During this period large-scale privatisation and deregulation of the economy took place, offering new opportunities for high salaries and conspicuous consumption within a newly individualistic and materialistic economy. Among the most popular and enduring images to emerge during that time was a stereotypical group known as 'yuppies' (young, upwardly-mobile professionals) with their expensive cars and expense-account lifestyles.

According to the theory then, such a distinctive political and economic atmosphere is surely likely to have made a lasting impact on the values of young people who were developing their political consciousness at the time. True, the actual experience of life for the majority of young people, particularly among those in the growing ranks of the unemployed and among others dependent on social security, was not nearly so glamorous. But even if their experiences might have been different, they too, according to the theory, would be likely to have been exposed to the same materialistic ethos and been affected by it.

A diametrically opposed set of expectations about the attitudes and values of 'Thatcher's children' is derived from the theory of 'postmaterialism' (Inglehart, 1977). Also based on the notion of distinctive generations, this theory emphasises the role of 'formative affluence' rather than focusing on the particular political era during which a generation grew up. Inglehart's argument is that young people who grew up during a period of relative economic affluence and stability will be *less* materialistic than previous

generations, not more so. This is because they will take affluence and stability for granted, unlike, say, those who grew up during the war and experienced rationing and privation in addition to direct physical danger. On this account, the wartime generation will give priority to overcoming economic and physical privation and will thus place an emphasis on material security for themselves and their families. In contrast, the post-war generations, who have experienced formative affluence, will place their priorities on other needs - such as quality of life, freedom of expression and the like.

Underpinning Ingelhart's theory is the notion of an implicit hierarchy of human needs, with physical security at the bottom and 'luxuries' such as self-expression and creativity at the top. Once these lower-level needs have been satisfied, individuals will inevitably turn their priorities to the higher-level needs. By this account, then, we can expect those who grew up during the affluence of the Thatcher years, when North Sea Oil and the proceeds of privatisation permitted a long period of rising living standards, to display 'postmaterialistic values' which emphasise freedom of expression, quality of life, protection of the environment and so on, as opposed to starkly materialistic values emphasising success in terms of monetary and other economic achievements.

Examining generational differences

While these two theories - 'political eras' and 'formative affluence' - differ markedly in their predictions about the values of the Thatcher generation, both are based on the notion that some attitudes are formed early in one's life and are relatively stable over time (see Alwin and Scott, 1996). However, many attitudes clearly *do* change over an individual's lifetime. Attitudes towards crime and punishment, for instance, may well evolve gradually, with intolerance increasing as one acquires property, has children and so on. This process confounds our ability to identify 'true' generational differences which, by definition, should persist over time. Rather, an apparent 'generation gap' may simply reflect the different stages of the life-cycle that each generation has reached. In these circumstances, each generation's characteristics will change as it ages, becoming more like the generation before it. We can never definitively disentangle life-cycle and generational interpretations. This is largely because of what is technically known as an 'identification problem', which is discussed in more detail in the appendix to this chapter.

In this chapter we investigate whether any observable differences between generations exist and, where they do, whether they are attributable to 'life-cycle' or 'generation'. We focus on attitudes towards four broad topics. The first and second - politics and attitudes towards economic life - allow us specifically to address the notion of 'Thatcher's children'. The third - attitudes to freedom of expression - allows us to assess Inglehart's theory of

postmaterialism and 'formative affluence'. And the final set of attitudes we examine here are towards the monarchy and Britain's place in the world - subjects which are likely to throw light on the relationship between historical context and generational differences in attitudes.

We divide respondents to the survey series into four different 'generations', according to when they were likely to have achieved political consciousness, as follows[2]:

- An 'eighties' generation of young people, born after 1960 and mostly socialised during the late 1970s and 1980s;
- A 'sixties' generation, born between 1946 and 1960 and mostly socialised during the 1960s and early 1970s;
- A 'post-war' generation, born between 1927 and 1945 and mostly socialised during the 1940s and early 1950s;
- A 'pre-war' generation, born before 1926 and mostly socialised during the 1920s and early 1930s.

Party identification and political interest

To what extent then are the political attitudes of Thatcher's children, the 'eighties' generation, distinctive? We begin with party preferences. The natural hypothesis is that during this era of Conservative power, young people, impressed by the party's success and 'surrounded' by its distinctive philosophy, would be more likely to identify with it than with the 'failed' opposition parties. If so, there is considerable American (and some British) evidence that this early attachment to a party - or party identification - would tend to endure through their lives, providing a very long term advantage for the Conservatives.

Although our data certainly suggest generational differences in identification with different parties, they clearly contradict the notion that those who grew up during the Conservative years are more likely than average to identify with the Conservatives. On the contrary, they are the generation *least* likely to do so - and have always been so throughout our survey's lifetime. Among the two youngest of our generations there is a Labour lead of 20 points, compared with a lead of only 7 points among the post-war generation and a Conservative lead of one point among the pre-war generation.

Party identification (1996)

	All	Eighties	Sixties	Post-war	Pre-war
	%	%	%	%	%
Conservative	28	23	25	33	36
Labour	42	43	45	40	35
Liberal	11	8	12	12	13
Other party	3	4	3	3	3
None	10	16	9	6	5
Labour lead	+14	+20	+20	+7	-1
Base	*3605*	*1117*	*962*	*896*	*630*

As the table shows, there are undeniable age-related differences in party identification. But it is much more questionable whether these reflect the distinctive experiences of successive generations of young people. It may well be, for instance, that the attitudes of the young towards these issues evolve gradually as they get older, adapting to changing circumstances and life-cycle changes. There is certainly evidence that young people tend to be somewhat more left-wing than average, and then move slightly to the right during their twenties and early thirties (Brown, 1992).

To explore whether these age differences are indeed the result of life-cycle processes, we need to compare the patterns for the various generations *over time*. What we want to discover is whether each generation retains its distinct characteristics as it ages (which would suggest a 'generational' difference) or whether its values change over time (which would suggest a 'life-cycle' difference). To do this, we compare data from the 1983 and 1996 *British Social Attitudes* surveys.[3] In order to ensure that we are comparing 'like with like' we have subdivided our oldest and youngest generations to take account of 'entrants' and 'exits'. Otherwise our 1996 'eighties' generation would include people who were not old enough to have been interviewed as part of the 1983 survey, and we would not have been able to tell if a difference between our 1983 and 1996 findings reflected the distinct views of these new 'entrants' or a change among the entire 'eighties' generation. Similarly, among our oldest generation we need to take account of 'exits' through death. So, within this generation we have distinguished those birth cohorts born before and after 1917.

As the next table shows, *all* our birth cohorts clearly moved away from the Conservatives over the period from 1983-1996 - no more than what we would expect, given the changing political complexion of the years in question. Thus, in 1983 the Conservatives were riding high after the British victory in the Falklands War and the split in the Labour Party that had led to the formation of the Social Democratic Party. At the time of the fieldwork for the 1983 *British Social Attitudes* survey, the Conservatives were heading for their landslide election victory. The situation was, of course, wholly different in 1996, when the Conservatives had endured a record period of unpopularity in the opinion polls and were heading for an historic landslide defeat in the 1997 election.

Per cent identifying with the Conservative Party

	1983	Base	1996	Base	Change
All	39	*1755*	28	*3605*	-11
Eighties					
1966 and later	-	-	21	*710*	n/a
1961-65	30	*149*	27	*407*	-3
Sixties					
1946-60	36	*506*	25	*962*	-11
Post-war					
1927-45	43	*543*	33	*896*	-10
Pre-war					
1917-26	35	*268*	33	*433*	-3
1916 and earlier	43	*289*	-	-	n/a

n/a = not applicable

As the table shows, the fall in Conservative popularity affected different birth cohorts differently. The overall fall in support between 1983 and 1996 was 11 percentage points. But among both our youngest and oldest generations the fall in identification with the Conservative party was much *lower* than this average fall - at around three points. Among the young this may be explained by their tendency to start off with left-wing leanings, and move towards the right over time. This tendency to become more right-wing with age may have partially counteracted any overall shift among the young away from the Conservatives over the period. Alternatively, perhaps, Thatcherism *did* appeal more to the young than to older generations (or did not *put off* the young as much). Even so, this 'eighties' generation remained the least likely of all to identify with the Conservative party in 1996. The relatively small fall in support for the Conservatives among the old is likely to reflect nothing more than their simply being less inclined than younger generations to change their partisanship, something that many will have held onto for fifty years or more.

Of course, party identification is not the only measure of how growing up under Conservatism might affect one's political attitudes. One of the most commonly expressed concerns about the 'youth of today' is their apparent disengagement from, and disinterest, in civil society. For this generation, it is said, "politics has become a dirty word" (Wilkinson and Mulgan, 1995). Certainly, young people are less likely than older cohorts to be registered to vote. Turnout at the recent general election was, at 71 per cent, the lowest since 1931 and seems to have been lower still among first-time voters. This points towards an age-group who are largely distinctive in their *lack* of interest in traditional politics (Park, 1995). And our findings appear to back this up. As the next table shows, the eighties' generation are the least likely to be interested in politics. In fact, nearly half profess little or no interest in politics, a much higher proportion than among other cohorts.

Interest in politics (1996)

	All	Eighties	Sixties	Post-war	Pre-war
	%	%	%	%	%
"A great deal" or "quite a lot"	31	22	31	37	37
"Some"	33	32	38	31	26
"Not very much" or "none at all"	37	46	31	31	37
Base	*3605*	*1117*	*962*	*896*	*630*

Although we know from previous research that interest in politics is age-related, increasing over the life-cycle of an individual, there is also evidence that the 'gap' between the interest expressed by 18-24 year olds and older cohorts has been growing - in other words, that generational differences may also be at play (Park, 1995).

As the next table shows, however, our findings here give more credence to 'life-cycle' explanations of political interest than to ones based upon a fundamental generation gap. As we look along the rows of the next table, we see that interest in politics increases among all our birth cohorts between 1986 (when we first began to ask this question) and 1996. So, levels of political interest, rather than being enduring and stable characteristics of particular generations, do seem instead to increase with age. As each generation gets older, its level of political interest increases; the overall population average remains static, however, as younger, relatively uninterested people enter the scene and older, more interested ones depart.

Per cent with "a great deal" or "quite a lot" of interest in politics

	1986	Base	1996	Base	Change
All	29	*1545*	31	*3605*	+ 2
Eighties					
- 1966 and later	-	-	21	*710*	n/a
- 1961-65	22	*269*	25	*407*	+ 3
Sixties					
- 1946-60	26	*435*	31	*962*	+ 5
Post-war					
- 1927-45	34	*486*	37	*896*	+ 3
Pre-war					
- 1917-26	32	*178*	38	*433*	+ 6
- 1916 and earlier	30	*177*	-	-	n/a

n/a = not applicable

In summary, there is little evidence here to support the notion that the ascendancy of the Conservatives under Mrs Thatcher left a particular political

imprint on the generation referred to as 'Thatcher's children'. They remain
less likely to identify with the Conservative party than any other generation
and, though they are less interested than average in politics, in this respect
they simply mirror their predecessor generations at a similar age. In all
likelihood this generation's interest in politics, like that of those before them,
will develop with age.

Attitudes towards economic issues

Another way in which our youngest generation might differ from its
predecessors is in its attitudes towards economic issues - surely the most
distinctive and salient part of the Thatcherite philosophy. This group grew up
in a prevailing atmosphere of individualism and materialism not experienced
to the same extent by previous cohorts (Walker, 1996). How then do they
compare with other generations in their attitudes?

  Throughout the survey series' life we have asked about the different factors
that might influence a person's choice of job - such as pay, job security,
promotional opportunities and so on. If the 'political era' in which one lives
were the key influence on attitudes, then material concerns such as pay and
promotion should figure more prominently than average among the eighties'
generation. If, on the other hand, the 'formative affluence' thesis were the
key influence, then the two younger generations (the sixties' generation as
well as the eighties) will tend to favour, say, interesting work rather than
more material concerns.

  In fact our findings do not quite bear out either of these expectations. As the
next table shows, all four generations turn out to place the greatest emphasis
on job security and in this respect they differ little. In each case over seven in
ten choose this factor as one of the two most important features of a job.
Next in overall importance is interesting work, but here there are some
intriguing generational differences. The sixties generation is the most likely
to give high priority to interesting work, with 57 per cent naming it as either
their first or second choice, compared to only 46 per cent of the youngest
(eighties) generation. The youngest generation gives relatively high priority
to pay.

Suppose you were advising a young person who was looking for his or her first job. Which one of these would you say is the most important, and which next? (1993)

% choosing as "most" or "next most" important	All	Eighties	Sixties	Post-war	Pre-war
Secure job	71	72	71	71	71
Interesting work	50	46	57	52	45
Promotion opportunities	32	34	29	32	32
Good conditions	31	27	31	32	38
Good starting pay	14	20	12	13	12
Base	*2931*	*754*	*850*	*718*	*609*

Note: each figure shows the proportion of people choosing this answer as a first or second choice, thus numbers sum to 200%.

So these findings do indeed fit the notion that those who grew up in 'Thatcher's Britain' are more materialistic than their predecessors. True, the differences are not that large, and the priority they give to pay is not that high in itself - only relatively high in comparison with other generations - but at least the differences are in the expected direction. This does seem to be a generation that is more likely than average to place an emphasis on money. Once again, however, this difference could quite conceivably reflect life-cycle differences rather than generational ones. For instance, an integral part of most career structures is that young people are paid less than their older colleagues. They might correspondingly be more acutely aware of income disparities and for that reason place more emphasis on this aspect of a job than would others. Some of the difference may thus simply be a function of life-cycle circumstances. And certainly, when we compare answers to these questions over the years, there turns out to be little to support the notion that the generation who grew up in the 1980s and 1990s are significantly more materialistic than their predecessors.[4] Either way, the 'formative affluence' model seems to be in trouble.

One distinctive characteristic of the Conservative era was a considerable increase in social inequality. Since coming to power in 1979 a primary government objective was the liberalisation of the labour market and introduction of greater 'flexibility'. Providing incentives for high-performing individuals was thought to encourage higher rates of economic growth, and was thus part and parcel of the economic ethos of the time. Is our youngest generation, who reached adulthood during this period, thus more likely than any other generation to see a degree of social inequality as an acceptable price of economic progress? We asked first:

*Thinking of income levels generally in Britain today, would you say that the **gap** between those with high incomes and those with low incomes is too large, about right, or too small?*

In 1995 nearly nine in ten people (87 per cent) took the view that the income gap was 'too large', an increase of 15 points since we first asked this question in 1983 (Spencer, 1996). In any event there was no difference in this respect between our four generations. 'Thatcher's children' are just as opposed to income inequality as are other generations.

We also ask a more specific question of employees, this time about pay levels in their own workplace:

> *Thinking about the **highest** and **lowest** paid people at your place of work, how would you describe the **gap** between their pay, as far as you know?*

As the next table shows, these findings also contradict the notion that those who grew up in the eighties are more inured to inequality. In fact, the two youngest generations (who are probably themselves among the lower paid on average) are the *most* critical of the gap between the highest and lowest paid at their workplace. Thus 22 per cent of the Thatcher generation say this gap is "much too big", compared with 13 per cent of the pre-war generation. Once again, however, the generational differences are relatively small, and the dominant impression from the table is of the similarity between the generations. And when we examine how the attitudes of these generations have changed between 1983 and 1996 we find no evidence whatsoever of any generational trends.

Employee's perception of gap between highest and lowest paid at work (1996)

	All	Eighties	Sixties	Pre-war
	%	%	%	%
Much too big	20	22	20	13
Too big	25	27	25	24
About right	44	43	42	48
Too small	3	2	3	3
Base	*1531*	*665*	*590*	*267*

Note: This question was asked only of employees, hence the absence of data for the pre-war generation, who are largely retired from work.

What then of attitudes towards 'big business' and its relationship with workers? Is the 'Thatcher generation', who grew up amidst an ethos stressing free-market enterprise and profit, more likely than a generation who came of age when more collectivist principles were rife, to be supportive of business? We asked all respondents how much they agreed or disagreed with the statement that "big business benefits owners at the expense of workers". And, sure enough, this time the youngest generation *is* marginally less likely than other generations to believe that business exploits workers, while the sixties generation is the most likely to take the opposite view.

Big business benefits owners at the expense of workers (1996)

	All	Eighties	Sixties	Post-war	Pre-war
	%	%	%	%	%
Agree	59	55	63	58	59
Neither agree nor disagree	25	31	22	22	21
Disagree	14	12	14	17	16
Base	*3077*	*942*	*846*	*797*	*492*

Responses to this question have, in fact, changed substantially over time. As the next table shows, both the eighties' and sixties' generations have become much more critical of big business over the last thirteen years. While in 1983, one half of each of these generations regarded big business as inherently exploitative, by 1996 over 60 per cent took this view. Changes of this magnitude have not occurred among either of the other two generations. Cynicism about business appears to increase with age and work experience, peaking in late middle age and then levelling off. We can only speculate as to the reasons for such shifts, but it would clearly be implausible to conclude that those who grew up during the 1980s are in general any more accepting than average of economic inequality and income disparities.

Per cent agreeing "big business benefits owners at the expense of workers"

	1986	*Base*	1996	*Base*	Change
All	54	*1318*	59	*3077*	+ 4
Eighties					
- 1966 and later	-	-	52	*594*	n/a
- 1961-65	50	*224*	61	*348*	+ 11
Sixties					
- 1946-60	50	*391*	63	*846*	+ 13
Post-war					
1927-45	60	*417*	58	*797*	- 2
Pre-war					
- 1917-26	56	*145*	62	*357*	+ 6
- 1916 and earlier	52	*141*	-	-	n/a

n/a = not applicable

So, nowhere have we been able to find clear cut evidence that 'Thatcher's children' are more likely than others to have adopted the much-heralded political and economic values of that period. Rather, when it comes to the aspects of political and economic life we have examined, there is precious little evidence of any true generational differences at all. Instead, the few age differences we found seem much more likely to reflect the different life-cycle stages reached by each group.

Attitudes to freedom of expression

We turn now to the Inglehart theory that post-war generations are more inclined to adopt 'postmaterialist' values such as freedom of expression, quality of life and so on, than to be motivated by more basic 'materialist' concerns such as physical and material security. We start by focusing on freedom of expression, as expressed by attitudes towards the legitimacy of different forms of protest - public protest meetings, marches and demonstrations, and national strikes. As the next table shows, support for these forms of protest clearly does differ among generations. In each case the two youngest generations are the most likely to believe that each type of protest should "definitely" be allowed, and the oldest the least likely to take this view.

Should different forms of protest be allowed? (1996)

	All	Eighties	Sixties	Post-war	Pre-war
	%	%	%	%	%
% saying "definitely" should be allowed					
Public protest meetings	54	59	60	51	30
Marches and demonstrations	31	41	36	24	11
National strikes	12	16	14	11	5
Base:	987	295	282	261	149

These findings appear encouraging for the theory of formative affluence. People who grew up in the relative affluence of the 1960s and beyond seem to place a higher value on the right to protest than those who grew up before then. However, an examination of change over time shows that, once again, life-cycle influences are more evident than any deep-rooted gulfs between the generations. 'Liberalism', on this measure, clearly tends to decrease with age. As the next table shows, the post-war generation was in 1985 much more 'liberal' in its attitudes than the pre-war generation (with 64 per cent and 54 per cent respectively thinking that public protest meetings should definitely be allowed). In this respect, the post-war generation resembled the sixties generation. But by 1996 support among the same post-war generation had fallen to 51 per cent - a large drop of thirteen percentage points - bringing it down to the level expressed *in 1985* by the older pre-war generation. And, although support among the 1961-65 cohort increased, this simply brought it up to the level expressed *in 1985* by the sixties' generation.

Per cent saying public protest meetings should "definitely" be allowed

	1985	Base	1996	Base	Change
All	59	*1530*	54	*987*	- 5
Eighties					
- 1966 and later	-	-	56	*195*	n/a
- 1961-65	58	*235*	66	*100*	+ 8
Sixties					
- 1946-60	64	*467*	60	*282*	- 4
Post-war					
- 1927-45	64	*451*	51	*261*	- 13
Pre-war					
- 1917-26	54	*208*	31	*108*	- 23
- 1916 and earlier	43	*169*	-	-	n/a

n/a = not applicable

It also seems at face value that the sixties and eighties generations are much more accepting of the claims of conscience over law. We asked:

Are there any circumstances in which you might break a law to which you were very strongly opposed? (1994)

	All	**Eighties**	**Sixties**	**Post-war**	**Pre-war**
	%	%	%	%	%
Yes	30	39	36	24	13
No	66	56	59	72	83
Base	*1132*	*317*	*273*	*307*	*235*

On this issue, the four generations divide broadly into two camps, with the two youngest being much more likely than the two oldest to downgrade automatic adherence to the law - a division which survives in response to a more normative question:

In general, would you say that people should obey the law without exception, or are there exceptional occasions on which people should follow their consciences, even if it means breaking the law? (1996)

	All	Eighties	Sixties	Post-war	Pre-war
	%	%	%	%	%
People should ...					
... obey law without exception	41	28	39	54	49
... follow conscience on occasion	56	68	60	43	41
Base	*1175*	*258*	*319*	*300*	*198*

So, in terms of attitudes relating to freedom of expression there does seem to be a division between the generations which conforms to the theory of 'formative affluence'. But if these were indeed values that had crystallised early in life, influenced by the political and economic environment in which the two youngest and two oldest generations grew up, then they would be relatively stable over time *within generations*. And once again this turns out not to be the case, at least not in response to our first question about people's *individual* propensities to break a law ("Would *you* break a law...?"). As the next table shows, the apparent generational variations appear to reflect no more than the different life-cycle stages reached by each of the generational groups. In each group, the proportion of people who say they would *never* break the law increases between 1983 and 1996. So, in this respect at least, age appears to breed conformity.

Per cent saying there are no circumstances under which they might break a law

	1983	Base	1994	Base	Change
All	62	*1755*	66	*1132*	+4
Eighties					
- 1966 and later	-	-	57	*171*	n/a
- 1961-65	48	*149*	54	*146*	+6
Sixties					
- 1946-60	55	*506*	59	*273*	+4
Post-war					
- 1927-45	58	*543*	72	*307*	+14
Pre-war					
- 1917-26	74	*268*	81	*146*	+7
- 1916 and earlier	76	*289*	-	-	n/a

n/a = not applicable

However, we at last obtain a quite different picture when we look at people's attitudes towards the *principle* involved in the issue of conscience *versus* law.

Here the changes over time *within* each cohort tend to be smaller than the overall change among the population as a whole, suggesting relative stability within generations. The large amount of change in the population as a whole - an increase of 10 points in support of the claims of conscience over law - is thus more likely to be attributable to a process of generational replacement than life-cycle changes within each generation.

Per cent saying people "should follow conscience"

	1983	Base	1996	Base	Change
All	46	*1755*	56	*1175*	+10
Eighties					
- 1966 and later	-	-	68	*234*	n/a
- 1961-65	65	*149*	68	*124*	+3
Sixties					
- 1946-60	56	*506*	60	*319*	+4
Post-war					
- 1927-45	48	*543*	43	*300*	-3
Pre-war					
- 1917-26	30	*268*	43	*135*	+11
- 1916 and earlier	30	*289*	-	-	n/a

n/a = not applicable

So, on the normative or symbolic question about the respective claims of conscience and law, as opposed to the behavioural question about one's own willingness to take a conscientious stand, generational differences do seem to come into their own.

Attitudes to the monarchy and Britain's place in the world

Perhaps the most obvious areas in which to look for generational differences are those dealing with attitudes towards traditional British institutions and Britain's place in the world. In these respects, the world within which our youngest generation has grown up differs radically from the one in which our older generations did - during the times of the British Empire and the war years. Here then, surely, is an easy test for theories of generational change to pass.

In many respects, the monarchy is one of Britain's most distinctive institutions and has always been closely associated with the Empire and its successor, the Commonwealth. Moreover, attitudes towards the monarchy are likely to be symbolic ones, crystallising early in life and being relatively resistant to change over time. Although our findings do show that overall public support for the monarchy has plummeted over the last 13 years - from nearly two-thirds of people (65 per cent) in 1983 who thought it was "very important" to less than one third (32 per cent) who took that view in 1996 - we might still expect to find substantial generational differences. After all,

since our youngest generation grew up during a period of hitherto unknown scrutiny and criticism of the royal family, they will inevitably be the least supportive of the monarchy. And, as the next table shows, this proves to be the case. Belief in the importance of the monarchy is highest of all among the oldest generation, with 43 per cent saying that the monarchy is "very important", and then falls within each subsequent generation, to only 23 per cent among the youngest group.

How important or unimportant do you think it is for Britain to continue to have a monarchy? (1996)

	All	Eighties	Sixties	Post-war	Pre-war
	%	%	%	%	%
Very important	32	23	32	37	43
Quite important	35	33	39	35	30
Not very/not at all important	22	29	18	19	16
Monarchy should be abolished	11	14	11	8	8
Base	*1175*	*358*	*319*	*300*	*198*

When we compare the 1983 and 1996 responses among our generations we find that the fall in support for the monarchy turns out to have affected all generations alike. This is a classic example of what is termed a 'period effect' - an historical change whose impact is roughly the same on all parts of the population. Thus, even the pre-war generation, 90 per cent of whom felt in 1983 that it was "important" for Britain to continue to have a monarchy, have lost quite a bit of their former enthusiasm. Nonetheless, there also turn out to be clear signs of persisting generational differences. Among three of our cohorts the fall in support is lower than the overall fall of 19 percentage points, indicating that, alongside a general fall in support for the monarchy, a process of generational replacement is also at work. Older, more supportive, generations are being replaced as they die by younger generations who are less supportive (though this process explains only a small amount of the overall change compared with the period effect).[5]

**Per cent saying "very" or "quite" important that Britain
continues to have a monarchy**

	1983	Base	1996	Base	Change
All	86	*1755*	67	*1175*	- 19
Eighties					
- 1966 and later	-	-	52	*234*	n/a
- 1961-65	75	*149*	64	*124*	- 11
Sixties					
- 1946-60	84	*506*	71	*319*	- 13
Post-war					
- 1927-45	87	*543*	72	*300*	- 15
Pre-war					
- 1917-26	90	*268*	70	*135*	- 20
- 1916 and earlier	90	*289*	-	-	n/a

n/a = not applicable

What of Britain's role in Europe? Here we might expect to find that the older
generations - whose view of the world would have been formed during
Britain's pre-war imperial role or by their own experiences in the war - would
have the greatest ambivalence about Europe and be the most reluctant to give
up aspects of Britain's national sovereignty. And our findings back up this
hypothesis. Between 1983 and 1991 we asked annually whether Britain
should continue within the European Community, or withdraw, during a
period when public acceptance of membership was increasing. When we first
asked the question just over half said Britain should remain a member, and by
1991 over three-quarters took this view (Evans, 1995). As the next table
shows, however, support for continued membership varied sharply across the
generations, splitting them neatly in half - with the two youngest significantly
more likely than the two oldest to argue for a continuing British role in
Europe.[6]

*Do you think Britain should continue to be a member of the European
Community or should it withdraw? (1991)*

	All	Eighties	Sixties	Post-war	Pre-war
	%	%	%	%	%
Britain should continue	77	83	84	72	67
Britain should withdraw	17	9	13	23	23
Don't know	6	8	3	5	9
Base	*1436*	*323*	*404*	*412*	*297*

As noted, public enthusiasm for Europe increased markedly over the 1980s
and, as the next table shows, this holds true for all four generations (another
example of a 'period effect'). However, the increase in support was greatest

among the eighties and sixties generations. Consequently, while in 1983 no clear generation gap in attitudes could be found, a divide had certainly become apparent by 1991. Now, those who grew up in the eighties and sixties are more likely than those who grew up either in the aftermath of the Second World War or before it to favour a closer relationship with Europe.

Per cent saying Britain should "continue" to be a member of the European Community

	1983	Base	1991	Base	Change
All	53	*1755*	77	*1436*	+ 24
Eighties					
- 1966 and later	-	-	87	*198*	n/a
- 1961-65	53	*149*	76	*125*	+ 23
Sixties					
- 1946-60	55	*506*	84	*404*	+ 29
Post-war					
- 1927-45	53	*543*	72	*412*	+ 19
Pre-war					
- 1917-26	54	*268*	69	*181*	+ 15
- 1916 and earlier	48	*289*	-	-	n/a

n/a = not applicable

So, there are indeed marked generational differences in respect of Britain's role in the world and the perceived importance of the monarchy. There is an apparent 'fault-line' between those who grew up before the 1960s and those who came of age afterwards.

Conclusion

We have examined both whether there are distinct generational differences in attitudes towards a range of social phenomena and, specifically, whether the generation of so-called 'Thatcher's children' who came of age during the 1980s has a unique 'imprint' of social, economic and moral values.

The simple answer to the latter question appears to be 'no'. The eighties generation is, if anything, *less* inclined to identify with the Conservative party than any older generation. On the other hand, there are suggestions in the data that, in certain respects, it is a somewhat more materialistic generation than its predecessor generations were. In keeping with its tag of 'Thatcher's children', its members tend, for instance, to place more emphasis on pay *per se* than on other aspects of a job than do those of older generations. Overall, however, the abiding impression from our data is that such differences as can be found between the generations in their attitudes to work are small and could well be due to life-cycle processes rather than generational replacement. In any event, our findings hardly provide any ringing endorsement of the theory that the Thatcherite values of the eighties had any

profound influence on the generation who formed its political and social values during that period. Rather, they substantiate previous findings that Thatcher's crusade for a fundamental change in values spectacularly failed to hit the mark (see for example Crewe, 1988; Jowell and Topf, 1988; Gershuny, 1994).

An alternative hypothesis is that the experience of growing up under Conservatism actually *disenchanted* this generation, leaving them with a more negative view than average of Conservative philosophy and a greater tendency towards political apathy. At first glance, there appears to be some truth in this notion. The eighties' generation turns out to be less rather than more tolerant of income inequality, and more rather than less suspicious of the motives of 'big business'. And they *are* the least interested in politics of all the generations. However, most - if not all - of these apparent differences reflect the different stages each generation has reached in their life-cycle. There is thus every reason to expect that, over time, the eighties generation will develop an interest in politics and modify their views so that they begin to resemble more the interest in politics and the political preferences of previous generations.

So, the notion of a generation of 'Thatcher's children' finds little support here, despite the real generational differences we found, for instance, in support for the monarchy, in attitudes towards Europe and in the principle of freedom of expression. But such differences are implausibly attributable to Thatcherism.   Rather, they reflect 'period effects' (historical changes affecting all generations alike) and, to a limited extent, they are also more in keeping with the theory of 'postmaterialism' and 'formative affluence'. Thus a generation that can take needs such as physical security for granted will be more likely to give priority to other goals such as quality of life and freedom of expression.

But by far the clearest message to emerge from our analysis is the relative rarity of true generational differences. Many of the apparent gulfs between the attitudes of different generations appear to be transient, reflecting their different ages and experience, rather than the unique circumstances during which they grew up.

Notes

1. For instance, Alwin and Krosnick (1991) suggest that the unique political characteristics of certain eras "provide a basis for the assumption that birth cohorts achieving political awareness during the ascendancy of one particular political party will be affected by that differential popularity of parties and candidates" (171). The Thatcher years were, of course, notable for marking a long period of Conservative ascendancy.
2. We use a very wide definition for each of our generations in order that we can carry more detailed analyses discussed later in this chapter.
3. The ideal way to do this would be to conduct a panel study, in which the same people were re-interviewed over time. We do not have a suitable panel study, but we can do almost as well by comparing different surveys in which members of the same birth cohort have been sampled on different occasions. If we have used appropriate random sampling

methods, then we can trace the attitudes and values of the birth cohort in question over time, even though we have not actually re-interviewed the same individuals. Of course, we must be sure that the same wording and procedures were used in the different surveys that are to be compared. We must also remember that migration and death will mean that we are not sampling exactly the same original population of individuals in our two surveys. For example, people who died between 1983 and 1996 will have been potential members of the sample in 1983 but not in 1996. This is likely to be a particular problem when looking at the changing attitudes of older generations. For this reason we divide our youngest and oldest generation in two in order to allow for 'entrants' and 'exits'.

4. Unfortunately, because our earliest (1986) and latest (1993) readings on these questions are relatively close together it is not possible to examine in any more detail whether the variations we have found are reflections of the life-cycle or of deeper generational differences.

5. A simple method for calculating how much overall change can be explained by generational replacement is to compare the average within-cohort change with the overall change. In the case of the monarchy the overall change of 19 points can be compared with an average within-cohort change of 14 points (that is 11+14+15+19+10 divided by 5). If we assume that the within-cohort change is due to period factors, and that life-cycle processes have not been at work, then it follows that what is left must be due to generational replacement. This therefore suggests that roughly one quarter of the overall change (5 out of 19 points) can be explained by generational replacement. It is interesting that rather similar conclusions about the contribution of generational replacement have been reached by Heath and Martin (1996), who found that replacement explained slightly less than quarter of the overall change in attitudes towards abortion (see also Alwin and Scott, 1996).

6. Our questions on Europe have changed over the years to reflect the different issues at stake. We focus here on a question last asked in 1991 which we can compare with data from 1983. However, the generational differences we find are also clearly evident in more detailed questions concerning Britain's relationship with Europe which were asked from 1993 onwards.

References

Alwin, D. F. and Krosnick, J. A. (1991), 'Aging, cohorts and the stability of sociopolitical orientations over the life span', *American Journal of Sociology*, **97**: 169-95.

Alwin, D. F. and Scott, J. (1996), 'Attitude change: its measurement and interpretation using longitudinal surveys', in Taylor, B. and Thomson, K., *Understanding Change in Social Attitudes*, Aldershot: Dartmouth.

Brown, A. (1992), 'Thatcherism and the death of the Left?', *CREST Working Paper, No. 12.*, London: SCPR.

Crewe, I. (1988), 'Has the electorate become Thatcherite?' In Skidelsky, R. (ed.), *Thatcherism*, London: Chatto and Windus.

Evans, G. (1995), 'The state of the Union: attitudes towards Europe', in Jowell, R., Curtice, J., Park, A., Brook, L. and Ahrendt, D. (eds.), *British Social Attitudes: the 12th Report*, Aldershot: Dartmouth.

Gershuny, J. (1994), 'British economic values in Mrs Thatcher's laboratory', in Gottlieb, A., Yuchtman-Yaar, E. and Strumpel, B. (eds.), *Socio-economic change and individual adaptation: comparing East and West*, Greenwich, Connecticut: JAI Press.

Glenn, N. (1977), *Cohort Analysis*, Sage University Paper series on Quantitative Applications in the Social Sciences, Beverly Hills: Sage.

Heath, A. and Martin, J. (1996), 'Changing attitudes towards abortion: life-cycle, period and cohort effects' in Taylor, B. and Thomson, K. (eds.), *Understanding Change in Social Attitudes*, Aldershot: Dartmouth.

Inglehart, R. (1977), *The Silent Revolution: Changing Values and Political Styles among Western Publics,* Princeton: Princeton University Press.

Jowell, R. and Topf, R. (1988), 'Trust in the Establishment', in Jowell, R., Witherspoon, S. and Brook, L. (eds.), *British Social Attitudes: the 5th Report,* Aldershot: Gower.

Mannheim, K. (1928), *Essays in the Sociology of Knowledge,* London: RKP.

Mason, W.M. and Fienberg, S.E. (eds.) (1985), *Cohort Analysis in Social Research: Beyond the Identification Problem,* New York: Springer-Verlag.

Park, A. (1995), 'Teenagers and their politics', in Jowell, R., Curtice, J., Park, A., Brook, L. and Ahrendt, D. (eds.), *British Social Attitudes: the 12th Report,* Aldershot: Dartmouth.

Spencer, P. (1996), 'Reactions to a flexible labour market', in Jowell, R. Curtice, J., Park, A., Brook, L. and Thomson, K. (eds.), *British Social Attitudes: the 13th Report,* Aldershot: Dartmouth.

Walker, D. (1996), 'Young people, politics and the media', in Roberts, H. and Sachdev, D. (eds.), *Having their say: the views of 12 to 19 year olds,* Barkingside: Barnardo's.

Wilkinson, H. and Mulgan, G. (1995), *Freedom's Children,* Demos Paper No. 17, London: Demos.

Appendix

The 'identification problem'

In comparing birth cohorts in different surveys we face what is termed an 'identification problem'. This simply means that the patterns we observe may reflect period, life-cycle and/or generational processes, and that it is not possible to identify the three processes simultaneously.

- Period effects are historical changes which take place over time and can be thought of as affecting all individuals alike. They would generally be measured by observing differences between survey years.
- Life-cycle effects are those which take place as people age, and can be measured by the chronological age of different survey respondents.
- Generational effects are those which distinguish people brought up in different eras, and can be measured by the year of birth of survey respondents.

However, once we know the period (survey year) and someone's year of birth, we naturally also know their age. Thus, if we know that someone is in the 1961-65 birth cohort and that the survey year is 1983, it follows that he or she was aged 18-22 at the time of the survey.

This produces an identification problem. If we have already measured, say, period and birth cohort, then we cannot independently identify age since it is already logically implied by the measures of period and birth cohort. We cannot therefore simultaneously include all three variables in an analysis. Only two can be entered at a time. (For further details see Glenn 1977; Mason and Fienberg 1985).

There may however be external theory or evidence to suggests that one of the three variables can be assumed to be constant, or we may be able to include direct measures of, say, life-cycle stage rather than inferring it directly from age. In the present chapter, we note that theory and evidence strongly point to the existence of period effects on some variables. After all, the *British Social Attitudes* series has itself documented many changes in attitudes that have demonstrably taken place 'across-the-board', affecting all age-groups alike. We have not therefore not taken seriously the notion that the observed patterns in the data could be due to a combination of birth cohort and life-cycle processes *alone*. The complete absence of period effects may be a logical possibility, but it would be far too implausible a thesis to rely on.

Instead we have concentrated on exploring whether the observed pattern can more plausibly be explained by a combination of period and life-cycle effects, or by a combination of period and generational effects. Either way, we assume that period effects are present. We then adopt the rule of thumb that, if the intra-cohort changes are larger than the overall period change, life cycle processes are likely to have been at work. Conversely, if the intra-cohort changes are smaller than the overall period change (that is, if the birth cohorts exhibit relative stability in their attitudes), then we conclude that generational processes are likely to have been at work.

2 What about the workers?

Alex Bryson and Stephen McKay [*]

The world of employment has fundamentally changed since Margaret Thatcher first entered 10 Downing Street in 1979. There have been structural changes to the economy, in particular a shift towards the service sector and private ownership, away from the manufacturing sector and public ownership. Over this period Britain has experienced historically high levels of unemployment. The composition of the workforce has also changed. Now there are almost as many women working as men, largely due to an increase in the participation of married women (Sly *et al.*, 1997). The age profile of the workforce has altered, with the young often delaying their entry into work, and older men in particular being more likely than before not to be in work at all (Bryson and McKay, 1994).

The types of job available have also changed. A rise in professional and managerial positions has led to increasing demand for highly qualified workers, while the demand for manual workers - particularly in semi-skilled and unskilled occupations - has declined. There has been substantial growth in part-time jobs and some increase in 'flexible' forms of work (Beatson, 1995). There is an increasing perception that employment has become less secure, with the much heralded demise of the 'job for life'. And the rewards from working have changed; while there was an unprecedented growth in real earnings during the 1980s, this accompanied a widening gap between top earners and low earners (Machin, 1996).

Change has been equally evident within the workplace. Union membership

[*] Alex Bryson is a Senior Fellow at the Policy Studies Institute. Stephen McKay is a Research Fellow at the Centre for Research In Social Policy at Loughborough University.

and union recognition have declined inexorably, as has the proportion of workers covered by collective bargaining (Millward *et al.*, 1992). There has been a shift away from overt industrial conflict. Media commentators view this trend as evidence that managers possess the whip hand; academics point to the growth in 'individualisation', an environment in which only those with portable skills will continue to command good wages and remain employable.

Many of these changes are evident in other western industrialised countries. Nevertheless, Britain's experience remains distinctive. Margaret Thatcher's government in 1979 was the first to be committed government to a vigorous programme of labour market deregulation in the name of economic growth and prosperity. Although it can be difficult to establish causality, many of the changes that subsequently occurred were explicit goals of government policy, or else attendant upon them. Government sought to effect them directly through legislation, through the setting of a monetary and fiscal framework, or through other means such as public pronouncements. The liberalisation of markets and capital flows, the privatisation programme, the removal of statutory minimum wages in those areas of the economy previously covered by Wages Councils, and a legislative programme targeted at what were perceived as special legal privileges that allowed trades unions to initiate industrial action, were all elements in a programme which sought to establish the pre-eminence of the market and of capital.[1]

But what have *employees* made of these changes? What impact have they had upon their experience of, and attitudes towards, work? There is a growing literature on this subject (Gallie and White, 1993; Spencer, 1996). In this chapter we assess the extent to which employees have perceived a deterioration in their working environment and examine some of the possible consequences, not only for employees, but also for government, employers and trades unions. We use the expression 'working environment' not to mean the physical environment (such as noise, pollution or the speed of the production line), but in the wider sense of the 'quality of working' - akin to the 'quality of life'.

Examining time trends

One of our aims is to examine trends over time in employees' attitudes towards work and the workplace.[2] In doing this we must distinguish between three possible explanations for such change. The first stems from *changes in the composition of the workforce* (for example, a rise in the proportion of women working, or a change in the age-profile of employees). For example, if women are more likely than men to hold a particular view and if the proportion of employees who are women is growing, then - all things being equal - the proportion of employees holding this view would grow. A second possible reason for change is linked to *the business cycle*. It may be, for example, that some attitudes vary depending on whether the economy is in a period of upturn or downturn - so some changes may simply reflect the

fluctuations of the economy. This leaves a third possible reason for change - an **underlying** *time trend*, that is, a change over time which can not be accounted for by these other types of change. These different possible trends not only have very different implications for policy, but may also counteract and mask one another - making simple year-on-year data difficult to interpret. The regression models we report on explicitly account for changes in the business cycle over time by including the level of unemployment and the changes in unemployment levels.[3] They also measure the extent to which attitude change has occurred over time *above and beyond* what would be expected as a result of economic change.[4] The models include a number of other factors, such as: age; sex; ethnicity; qualifications; social class; region; hours worked; having dependent children; whether a spouse or partner works; industrial sector; and size of the workplace. Thus, although estimating the impact of these 'controls' over time is beyond the scope of this chapter, the analysis does provide indication as to whether time trends may be due to changes in workforce composition.[5]

A more detailed account of the statistical technique of regression can be found in Appendix I of this Report.

Perceptions of the working environment

Is there any evidence that increasing proportions of employees are dissatisfied with their working environment? We begin by examining employees' attitudes towards four different aspects of work: pay; job security; management of the workplace; and the influence they have at work.

Pay

The gap between the pay of high and low earners has widened considerably since the late 1970s. By the 1990s this gap was wider than at any time since figures began to be compiled in 1886 (Gosling *et al.*, 1994). And there is now near unanimity that the gap between those with high incomes and low incomes is "too large", with 87 per cent taking this view in 1994 (Spencer, 1996).

However, an increased gap between the pay of high and low earners in the economy as a whole does not automatically imply that a similar increase over time has occurred in existing workplaces. It may be that the perception of an increasing gap between the high and low paid within the economy as a whole simply reflects the changing nature of the economy - the move from manufacturing to service industries, for instance. So, in order to gauge people's attitudes to their own working environment we ask:

*Thinking of the **highest** and the **lowest** paid people at your place of work, how would you describe the **gap** between their pay, as far as you know?*

In fact, a substantial proportion of employees think the pay gap at their own workplace is "too big" - albeit a lower proportion than takes this view about the gap between those on high and low incomes in Britain as a whole. Attitudes to this issue have fluctuated over time. In the early to mid 1980s, four in ten thought the pay gap at their workplace was too large. By the late 1980s this proportion was growing - by 1994 a half of all employees considered the pay gap at their workplace to be too big. Now the proportion has fallen to 45 per cent, but is still well above the average for the 1980s.

Employees' perception of the gap between highest and lowest paid at work

	1983	1984	1985	1986	1987	1989	1990	1991	1993	1994	1995	1996
% saying												
Gap "too big"	40	38	39	39	41	45	47	44	46	52	50	45
Base	*817*	*778*	*857*	*1532*	*1381*	*1462*	*1307*	*1236*	*1114*	*1447*	*1448*	*1542*

We must be wary of reading too much into these data. Perhaps the changes we have commented on simply reflect changes in the composition of the workforce - or, perhaps they are linked to cyclical fluctuation in the labour market. And, when we use more sophisticated modelling techniques, we find that there *is* indeed a cyclical trend - employees are less likely to see the gap as too big in times of high unemployment. The model also shows that changes in the composition of the workforce may also make a difference. For example, women are more likely than men to say that the gap between the highest and lowest paid at their place of work is too big, and as the proportion of women in the workforce has grown considerably over this period this may account for the changes we have found. On the other hand, part-time workers are less likely to think the pay gap is too big, and the proportion of part-time workers has also grown. But, taking these factors into account, there appears to have been a significant *underlying* increase over time in the proportion of employees who feel that the gap between the highest and lowest paid at their workplace is too great (see model A in the appendix to this chapter).

Asked to say if the wages they themselves received for the job they did were "on the low side, reasonable or on the high side?", a different story emerges. Employees in the 1990s were *less* likely than employees in the 1980s to say their wages were on the low side. As the next table shows, the proportion in this camp fell from 42 per cent in 1987 to just 28 per cent five years later. However, since 1991 the percentage who say their wages are on the low side has been rising and shows signs of returning to the levels prevailing throughout the 1980s.

Employees' perception of own pay

% saying	1983	1984	1985	1986	1987	1989	1990	1991	1993	1994	1995	1996
Pay "on the low side"	41	41	40	40	42	40	35	28	31	35	35	39
Base		817	778	857	1532	1381	1462	1307	1236	1114	1447	1448	1542

Our statistical model shows that, even once we take other factors into account, the proportion of employees who feel their pay is low has fallen significantly since the early 1980s. This is despite the fact that there has been a growing gap between the pay of high and low earners. Of course, this may simply reflect the fact that, with the exception of the lowest paid, employees have seen their earnings rise by considerably more than the rate of inflation during this period (Gosling et al., 1994). Indeed, we know that middle and higher income groups have become less dissatisfied about their pay, while low income employees have remained disgruntled (Spencer 1996). This leads to a further possible explanation - that, during times of employment restructuring and high unemployment, employees may simply be thankful to have a job at all, and hence less inclined to feel dissatisfied with their pay. There is some evidence for this in our model as it shows employees to be less likely to say they are low paid in times of rising unemployment, even when we take variations in job insecurity into account (see model B in the appendix to this chapter).

Overall, then the last two decades have been marked by increased dissatisfaction with income inequalities, both in the country as a whole and in the individual workplace. But this has not fed through into individual dissatisfaction with one's own pay. This may be because employees are becoming more aware that many earn much less (as well as much more) than themselves.

Job security

In the on-going debate as to whether jobs are becoming less secure commentators have often focused their attention on how long employees remain in a job (Burgess and Rees, 1996; Gregg and Wadsworth, 1995; Booth et al., 1996). Very few have taken account of more subjective measures, such as employees' expectations regarding future expansion or contraction at their workplace (Spencer, 1996).

In order to examine job security in detail, we have constructed an 'index of security' which is based upon people's answers to a number of questions measuring their *subjective* perceptions of their jobs. The scale runs from minus 10 (which denotes maximum job *in*security) to plus 8 (maximum job security). The construction of the index and the questions included in it are described in more detail in the appendix to this chapter.

As the next table shows, there is no clear trend in the overall level of job

security over the period. However, it appears that job insecurity is higher during periods of high unemployment (for instance, 1983 and 1984) and then falls when unemployment levels are lower (such as 1989 to 1990).

An index of job security

	1983	1984	1985	1986	1989	1990	1991	1993	1994	1995	1996
Job security index	.03	-.07	.18	.37	.96	1.42	1.16	-.37	-.34	.22	.35
Base	*817*	*778*	*857*	*1532*	*1462*	*1307*	*1236*	*1114*	*1447*	*1448*	*1542*

Our model confirms that insecurity is greater when unemployment is high. As the previous table shows, job security rose in the late 1980s during the Lawson boom. However, our model also shows that in the 1993/96 period the average level of job security is significantly lower than it was in the early 1980s. So, the underlying trend since 1993 is for employees to have become more concerned about job insecurity, once the effect of the economic recovery is taken into account, providing clear evidence of a deterioration in perceptions of the working environment (see model C in the appendix to this chapter).[6]

The quality of workplace governance

The 1990s have been marked by historically low levels of industrial conflict.[7] The Conservative government took this as evidence that their legislative programmes had contributed to better workplace relations. Yet although the number of working days lost through stoppages may be at its lowest, it does not necessarily follow that relations between management and employees are harmonious. We ask:

> In general how would you describe relations between management and other employees at your workplace: very good, quite good, not very good, or, not at all good?

In fact, there has been a slight increase over the period in employees' dissatisfaction with workplace relations. Whereas in the early 1980s just over a sixth took the view that management and employee relations were not good, in the 1990s between a quarter and a fifth of employees felt this way.

Employees' perceptions of management-employee relations

	1983	1984	1985	1986	1987	1989	1990	1991	1993	1994	1995	1996
% saying												
Relations "not very" or "not at all" good	15	16	17	19	18	19	17	21	20	24	24	20
Base	*817*	*778*	*857*	*1532*	*1381*	*1462*	*1307*	*1236*	*1114*	*1447*	*1448*	*1542*

The statistical model confirms that there has been a significant underlying deterioration over time in employees' perception of workplace relations, even when other factors have been taken into account (see model D in the appendix to this chapter).

The trend is even clearer when we examine whether employees generally trust management not to try to get the better of them "if it gets the chance". In the mid-1980s just over half (53 per cent) thought management would try to get the better of them - but during the 1990s the proportion taking this view has never been lower than 61 per cent, peaking at 66 per cent in 1995.

Management will always try to get the better of employees if it gets the chance

	1985	1986	1987	1989	1990	1991	1993	1994	1995	1996
% agreeing	53	53	63	58	62	61	61	64	66	62
Base	*743*	*673*	*1246*	*1280*	*1167*	*1160*	*532*	*1271*	*1275*	*1351*

The statistical model indicates that the odds of holding this view were greater during the mid-1990s than they were in the mid-1980s even once other factors are taken into account (see model E in the appendix to this chapter).

We can also look at whether employees think that their workplace is well managed:

> *In general, would you say your workplace was very well managed, quite well managed, or, not well managed?*

The majority of workers do consider their workplaces to be managed well. But, on average throughout the period, roughly one-fifth of employees thought their workplace was *not* well managed. At first sight there is no strong trend over time.

Employees' perceptions of how well their workplace is managed

% saying	1983	1984	1985	1986	1987	1989	1990	1991	1993	1994	1995	1996
Workplace "not well managed"	20	19	18	20	20	18	19	20	21	23	23	22
Base	*817*	*778*	*857*	*1532*	*1381*	*1462*	*1307*	*1236*	*1114*	*1447*	*1448*	*1542*

But, having controlled for other factors, it becomes apparent that there is an *underlying* trend over time albeit not a very strong one. Since the late 1980s employees have become *less* likely to think their workplace is well managed.[8] And employees' views on this subject were not related to the business cycle: unemployment levels and changes in unemployment were not related to whether employees thought their workplace was well managed (see model F in the appendix to this chapter).

Influence at work

Do employees feel their views at work matter? We ask:

> *Suppose there was going to be some decision made at your place of work that changed the way you do your job. Do you think that **you personally** would have any say in the decision about the change, or not?*

We then ask those who think they *would* have a say:

> *How much say or chance to influence the decision do you think you would have: a great deal, quite a lot, or, just a little?*

As the next table shows, the proportion of employees who thought they would have influence fell sharply in the late 1980s. True, since then confidence has increased - but certainly not to the level of the mid-1980s. By 1996 just over a half of employees felt they would "have any say", and one-third thought they would have "quite a lot" or "a great deal" of say.

Employees' perceptions of their influence over decisions at work

	1985	1987	1989	1991	1993	1996
% thinking						
Would have "any say"	62	51	50	54	52	55
Would have "quite a lot" or "a great deal" of say	37	29	30	35	33	35
Base	*857*	*1381*	*1462*	*1236*	*1114*	*1542*

Regression models confirm that there was an underlying fall during the late 1980s in employees' confidence that they would have influence over decisions at work, even when other factors are taken into account (see model G in the appendix to this chapter).

Responses to disillusionment: 'exit' or 'voice'?

Our look at employees' perceptions of their working environment suggests that some deterioration has taken place since the early 1980s. Employees are more likely to think that the gap between the best and worst paid at their workplace has increased (but are no more likely than they were to feel that their own pay is "too low"). Perceptions of job insecurity have risen, and faith in management fallen. And employees are less likely to feel that they would have any influence over decisions affecting their own work. But how do people react to these sorts of changes? We now explore two competing theses. One argues that employees in this situation have become less

committed to paid work, perhaps raising the likelihood that they will leave their job voluntarily. And the alternative states that there will be an increased demand for having a greater say in the workplace, perhaps - though not necessarily - through union representation. To summarise, the issue becomes whether employees respond to disillusionment with strategies of 'exit' or 'voice'?[9]

'Exit' strategies

In the original literature on 'exit' and 'voice', the terms were used to discuss 'consumer' strategies towards public goods such as education. In these cases, there is often a clear 'exit' strategy, usually in terms of buying private services. Of course, in the case of employment, 'exit' strategies are not so easy - opting out of work altogether without an alternative source of income is not something that most employees would relish. However, there are other exit strategies open to the disillusioned employee. He or she *can* leave her present employment for another job (in the hope that it will be better) or leave employee status for self-employment.

Leaving one's job

We ask:

> How likely or unlikely is it that you will leave this employer over the next year for any reason? Is it very likely, quite likely, not very likely, or not at all likely?

Those who say they are "very" or "quite likely" to leave are then asked why. From the many possible responses we have constructed two definitions of voluntary 'exits'. The first, and narrowest, includes only those who say they will leave to join another employer or to become self-employed; the second, wider definition, also includes those who say they will leave to look after the home, children or relatives, or to return to education.

At first glance, the voluntary exit rate appears to have doubled between 1983 and 1996. Those exits which conform to our narrow definition rose from eight per cent to 17 per cent over the period. However, the increase largely occurred between 1983 and 1984; since then the rate has only marginally increased.

Likelihood of leaving current employer over the next year, and reason given

% saying	1983	1984	1985	1986	1989	1990	1991	1993	1994	1995	1996
Will leave for another job or self-employment	8	13	12	12	15	15	12	12	14	16	17
Will leave for another job, self-employment, family or education	8	15	14	14	17	17	13	14	16	19	18
Base	*817*	*778*	*857*	*1532*	*1462*	*1307*	*1236*	*1114*	*1447*	*1448*	*1542*

In fact, statistical models show that there is *no* underlying trend towards more employees leaving their jobs voluntarily once other factors are taken into account.[10] Voluntary exits are 'procyclical' in their relation to the business cycle, that is, they are more likely when unemployment is low and when the unemployment rate is falling. Furthermore, it is possible that other changes in the labour market have cancelled out any underlying trend over time. One possible candidate is the increased participation of women in the workforce who, as the model shows, are less likely than men to leave their jobs. Of course, there are other possible changes over time which we have not taken account of - for instance, increasing rates of *in*voluntary job exits such as redundancy or early retirement among disgruntled employees who may otherwise have left voluntarily. These can make it difficult to assess whether or not 'exit' strategies have increased or not.

While no trend over time may exist, employees' expectations about leaving their current job voluntarily *are* strongly associated with negative feelings about their working environment. Not surprisingly perhaps, once we take other factors into account, voluntary exits are much more likely among those who feel they are low paid, that their workplace is poorly managed, that management and employee relations are poor, and among those who feel higher than average job insecurity.

Whether or not employees feel they have a say in how their work is organised is another important influence - those desiring more say are also more likely to expect to leave voluntarily. It is unlikely that the expectation of a new job increases the desire for a say: it is more likely that the desire for more say at work, if frustrated, increases the likelihood that an employee will leave (see models H and I in the appendix to this chapter).

Whether an employee leaves his or her job voluntarily is also related to a number of other factors (Theodossiou, 1996). As our models show, voluntary exits are more likely in smaller establishments, among employees in higher occupational classes, and with higher qualifications, and among those with recent experience of unemployment. They tend to be lower among women, those with children and partners, and older workers. Exit rates also vary by region, the rate being particularly high in Greater London.

This suggests that employers should not be lulled into a sense of security by the lack of any underlying trend towards more voluntary exits. The data are clear: dissatisfied employees want to leave their jobs. Given a chance (such

as an upturn in the business cycle) they may well do so.

Work and job commitment

Leaving one's job may seem a drastic step for many employees. There are many external factors (financial commitments such as a mortgage, lack of suitable alternative employment and so on) which make it an unrealistic option for many people. So we need to look at what we can call 'softer' forms of exit - declining work and job commitment.
  We start by looking at commitment to working in general. Our traditional measure of work commitment (see, for example, Hedges, 1994) is:

> *If without having to work, you had what you would regard as a reasonable living income, do you think you would still prefer to have a paid job or wouldn't you bother?*

There is no clear trend here over time. Throughout the period between 25 and 30 per cent of employees said they would not work if they had an alternative living income. This is confirmed by statistical models. However, there *is* a link to the business cycle: in times of rising unemployment fewer employees say they would not bother to work. And there is a strong link to negative perceptions of one's working environment[11] (see model J in appendix to this chapter).

Employees' commitment to work

	1984	1985	1986	1989	1993	1994	1995	1996
	%	%	%	%	%	%	%	%
% saying								
Would not bother to work if had reasonable income	29	27	26	25	24	29	29	30
Base	*778*	*857*	*1532*	*1462*	*1114*	*1447*	*1448*	*1542*

If we look at commitment to one's *own* job, rather than to work in general, we obtain similar findings. We ask:

> *For some people their job is simply something they do in order to earn a living. For others it is much more than that. On balance, is your present job just a means of earning a living, or, does it mean much more to you than that?*

Roughly one-third of employees view paid work as "just a means of earning a living". The proportion taking this view rose marginally in the early to mid-1990s.

Employees' commitment to their job

% saying	1985	1989	1991	1993	1994	1995	1996
Work is "just a means of earning a living"	30	31	32	36	38	35	33
Base	*857*	*1462*	*1236*	*1114*	*1447*	*1448*	*1542*

Models confirm that, once other factors are taken into account, there is a clear underlying trend over time, with stronger support for this view in the period 1987 to 1991 compared to 1985, and still stronger support between 1993 and 1996. Changes in the business cycle had no effect on commitment to one's job.

The models also show a relationship between job commitment and other attitudes towards one's job. Those most likely to see their jobs as simply a way of earning a living are also those employees who perceive the relationship between management and employees to be poor, who are dissatisfied with the way in which management are running the workplace, and who consider the gap between the pay of the highest and lowest paid at work to be "too big". This group are also more likely to feel they are paid "on the low side" and to have above average job insecurity. In fact, with the exception of occupational class, these factors have the strongest relationship with job commitment of all those we examined. Of course, this association does not tell us the *direction* of the relationship. It may be, for instance, that decreased job commitment stems from increased dissatisfaction with various elements of one's job (this is the interpretation that best fits our 'exit' theory). But, alternatively, it could be that those with low job commitment are more likely to be dissatisfied with these sorts of things in the first place (see model K in the appendix to this chapter).

'Voice' strategies

An alternative approach for the disgruntled employee is 'voice': increased protest or demands to have one's views heard. Yet the traditional means for a collective voice at the workplace - the trade union - has been in steady decline over the period. Far from workers flocking to unions in order to gain a voice, union membership has plummeted - from one-half of employees in 1983 to one-third in 1996.[12] This fall in membership reflects the dramatic decline in the proportion of workplaces which have recognised unions for collective bargaining purposes: the proportion of employees with a recognised union at their workplace fell from two-thirds in 1983 to less than one-half in 1996.

Union membership and recognition

% employees who...	1983	1984	1985	1986	1987	1989	1990	1991	1993	1994	1995	1996
... are union members	49	47	43	42	40	39	36	37	35	35	32	31
... are in workplaces with union recognition	66	63	63	62	63	53	58	58	51	49	51	46
Base		*817*	*778*	*857*	*1532*	*1381*	*1462*	*1307*	*1236*	*1114*	*1447*	*1448* *1542*

The demise of unionisation is reflected in the fact that, whereas over a half of employees (54 per cent) thought that unions had "too much power" in 1983, this had fallen to 15 per cent by 1996.

Employees' attitudes towards unions

	1985	1986	1987	1989	1990	1994	1996
	%	%	%	%	%	%	%
Unions have ...							
... too much power	54	47	43	38	28	10	15
... too little power	10	13	15	18	14	33	23
Base	*743*	*673*	*636*	*633*	*573*	*410*	*422*

We already know that there has been a fall in the proportion of employees who think they would have influence over decisions that might change the way they work. Not surprisingly, there has been an equivalent rise in the proportion of employees who feel they *should* have more say in work decisions. This is backed up by statistical models. We asked:

> *Do you think you should have **more** say in decisions affecting your work, or are you satisfied with the way things are?*

	1985	1987	1989	1991	1993	1996
% saying						
Should have "more say"	36	46	44	45	52	46
Base	*857*	*1381*	*1462*	*1236*	*1114*	*1542*

Perhaps not surprisingly, employees who are in a relatively poor position at work are the most eager to have a greater say. In fact, whether or not an employee wants more influence is closely associated with other measures of the working environment (such as attitudes towards management and feelings of job insecurity). Demand for "more say" is highest among those employees who are the *least* satisfied with their working environment. And employees who see their jobs simply as a means of earning a living are also more likely than average to want more say.

   Those who already feel they have a chance to influence decisions at work, such as those higher up the occupational hierarchy, are the least interested in

having a greater say (see model L in the appendix to this chapter).

The role of trade unions

True, union membership and union recognition have declined throughout the 1980s and 1990s. But, given the demand we have seen among employees for an increased 'voice' in the workplace, we need to examine the role trade unions have been playing. After all, they are the traditional voice for workers. What part do they play in satisfying employees' wishes for a greater say at work? What impact do they have on attitudes towards the working environment?

We included union membership and union recognition in all the models we have referred to so far. Although they are closely associated, union membership and union recognition are two quite distinct phenomena. Union membership is an *individual* decision, perhaps reflecting particular political beliefs or a more pragmatic belief that membership of a union offers the opportunity to voice concerns effectively. Union recognition, on the other hand, is a *workplace* characteristic, signifying that an employer has voluntarily agreed to recognise one or more unions for collective bargaining purposes. Of course, the employee's likelihood of being in a unionised workplace is related to a number of the characteristics of that workplace - such as the industrial sector it operates within, its size, and the composition of its workforce. In our statistical models we take these factors into account. Consequently, we can see whether, say, union membership is really associated with particular attitudes, or whether the difference that seems to exist merely stems from the particular characteristics of those who are in certain types of workplaces.

There are a number of areas where union membership and/or union recognition do seem to matter. For example, employees in workplaces with recognised unions are *less* likely than average to feel their pay is "on the low side". However, they are *more* likely to think the gap between the pay of the highest and lowest paid at their workplace is "too big". This is likely to reflect the politicisation of unionised workplaces.

Although union members are more likely than other employees to hold the view that "management will always try to get the better of employees if it gets the chance", employees in firms with a recognised union (but who are not necessarily members) are *less* likely than average to hold this view. This may be because the presence of a recognised union precludes management from behaving in particular ways, or else that employers who voluntarily recognise unions are also the least likely to want to take advantage of their workers.

Union members are more likely to think that the relationship between management and employees is poor, and that their workplace is poorly managed. Here union recognition did not prove important. Perhaps union members are more critical than other employees of the way workplaces are run. Or, alternatively, they may possess information which puts them in a

better position to make critical judgements.

Despite this, in many ways trade unions are a good thing from an employer's point of view. Union members are significantly *less* likely than other employees to say that they will leave a job voluntarily (even once we have controlled for other factors), suggesting that the voice trade unions provide for employees may reduce the demand for 'exit' (Theodossiou, 1996, presents similar findings). And simply working in a workplace with a recognised union (irrespective of whether one belongs to it) reduces the likelihood of a voluntary exit still further.

Paradoxically, being in a workplace with a recognised union does *not* feed into greater satisfaction with the voice that employees have at work.[13] Our models show that both union membership and union recognition are actually associated with employees thinking they have *less* of a say. This is likely to reflect the expectations that unionised workers have, rather than the 'real' level of voice workers have in unionised workplaces.

It seems, then, that while union recognition may be linked to a more positive view of the working environment, it may also raise the expectations employees have about that same environment.

The data also point to a dilemma for trade unions when it comes to the issues of most importance to their members. We ask all those employed in workplaces with recognised unions what they felt was the most important thing that trades unions should try to do at *their* workplace. In 1989, "improving pay" and "protecting existing jobs" were joint first choices - with "improving working conditions" a close second. But, by 1993, 42 per cent cited "protecting existing jobs", double the percentage opting for "improving working conditions" (21 per cent) and nearly four times the percentage choosing "improving pay" (12 per cent). In 1996, job security remained the top priority, being cited by one-third of those covered by recognised unions. And yet statistical models indicate that union membership and union recognition are strongly associated with employees feeling *less* secure in their jobs (once we take into account other factors which could affect job security, such as the size of the establishment, industrial sector, the business cycle and so on). This tendency for greater feelings of insecurity among unionised workplaces and employees could, of course, simply reflect a greater politicisation and awareness of the issue of job security. But it is also possible that there is a trade off between unions meeting other goals, such as tackling low pay, and delivering job security.[14]

Despite the growing demand for a greater say in the workplace, this is not identified as being a major priority for *trade union* action. Between 1989 and 1996 an average of 13 per cent of union members cited "having more say" (either over how day to day work is done or over management's long-term plans) as the *main* priority for their union. In 1996 only 10 per cent cited this as the priority.

Conclusion

In the eyes of employees, the working environment has clearly deteriorated since the early 1980s. Nowadays employees are more likely to feel that the gap between the high and low paid at their workplace is too large, that management and employee relations are poor, that their jobs are insecure, that their workplaces are not being managed as well as they could be, and that they do not have much say over how their work is organised. It has been suggested that employees could respond to such trends with either 'voice' or 'exit' strategies. In the event, the chapter has shown there to be evidence supporting both. For instance, employees are more likely to demand a say at work in the 1990s, but they are also more likely to see their jobs simply as a means of earning a living, rather than as something more fulfilling.

Having said this, employees now are no more likely than those in the 1980s to pursue more extreme 'exit' strategies. There has been no underlying increase in the likelihood of someone giving up their job voluntarily, nor in the proportion of employees who would be willing to give up work if they had a reasonable income to live on. Clearly, employees are prepared to 'tough it out', even if their commitment to the job is waning, although there may be other adverse consequences such as greater stress.

Nevertheless, there are warnings here both for employers and government. Negative perceptions of the workplace have grown over the last 13 years. These are linked to lower work and job commitment and demands for a greater say at work. Although this has not so far resulted in more people actually leaving their jobs voluntarily, it *is* linked to the wish to do so, and this could easily be a future trend, over and above what would in any case be expected during a period of economic upturn. If employers are to maintain employee commitment, and prevent employees 'voting with their feet' (either by searching for work elsewhere or leaving the labour market entirely), then they will need to consider new ways of accommodating employees' desire for a greater voice. The 'employee involvement' agenda of the 1980s and early 1990s, based largely on employers' terms and with little or no concern for employees' individual and collective rights, appears to have failed.

It is not particularly surprising that employees are increasingly likely to think the gap between the high and low paid at their workplace is too big. These perceptions reflect a reality which employers and governments have been aware of for some time. But it might come as a bit of a surprise to find that employees perceive a deterioration in employment relations, managerial performance, job security and their own involvement in decision-making. Tackling these issues will require concerted effort and new thinking from the government in collaboration with the trades unions and employers.

The new government is committed to introduce legislation requiring employers to recognise trade unions when a majority of workers vote for recognition. This legislation will mark a significant break from the 'voluntarism' which has characterised collective labour relations for most of the post-war period. But alone it does not guarantee a reversal in the decline

of unions. Similar legislation exists in the United States where union density is - at around 15 per cent - lower still. Moreover, unions will have to respond to the agenda of potential new union members. This will mean tackling job insecurity alongside other, more traditional, areas like pay and conditions. Also, they may need to do more to pursue employees' demand for a greater say in the workplace. In doing so they may need to make use of new structures, such as the Works Councils proposed under European Union legislation and perhaps even revisit the debates about 'industrial democracy' last aired in the 1970s.

Notes

1. The extent to which this programme had its intended effects is disputed. See, for example, Brown *et al.* (1997) for a discussion of how industrial relations legislation affected the UK economy and Elgar and Simpson (1993) for the impact of legislation on the conduct of industrial disputes.
2. All analysis in this chapter focuses on *employees* only. Some of the questions were also asked of the self-employed and those not in work. The self-employed are a rather special group, likely to have a very different experience of their working life from employees. The small numbers in the *British Social Attitudes* samples makes separate analysis difficult. Those not in work are also likely to have very different attitudes. For a discussion of the development of attitudes of the unemployed, see Spencer (1996).
3. A graph showing changes in the unemployment rate over the period 1983-96 is shown in the appendix to this chapter.
4. We also include in our models the chronological time period (for which we have chosen the periods 1983-86, 1987-91 and 1993-96). Because our three chronological time periods straddle the various stages of the business cycle, the two are independent of each other. This means that when we interpret our statistical models, we can estimate the separate effects of time and the business cycle on attitudinal change by examining whether either of the two sets of factors attain significance in the model. There are a number of ways of specifying the chronological time periods. However, diagnostic analysis suggests that our findings are relatively robust to different specifications.
5. For example, the part-time variable measures the average effect of being a part-time worker on our dependent variables for the whole period. If its coefficient is consistent with the time trend, it is possible that at least some of the time effect may be accounted for by the growth in part-time working. To test this hypothesis formally it would be necessary to interact part-time working with time period.
6. The coefficient for the period 1993-96 is the *average* for that period. As the descriptive data show, the job security index was much lower in 1993-94 than in 1995-96. But to test whether perceptions of job security have improved *after controlling for other factors*, it would be necessary to decompose the time periods in the model still further. This is not technically possible without removing the unemployment variables from the model because of collinearity between the unemployment variables and the time period variables.
7. Working days lost through stoppages have been lower in the 1990s than for any period since records began in 1891 (ONS, 1997).
8. The significant deterioration is between 1987-91 and 1993-96. A comparison of these periods with the base period (1983-86) shows no significant difference.

9. Hirshman (1970) was the first to explore these concepts of 'voice' and 'exit'. More recently Crouch (1995) has applied these concepts more broadly in exploring the possibilities for labour in a (post-) modern world.

10. Strictly speaking, voluntary 'exit' forms part of the calculation of the insecurity index and so is both an independent and a dependent variable in this model. However, voluntary 'exit' is only part of the insecurity index and alternative specifications of this model confirm that the results are robust to its inclusion or exclusion.

11. Feelings of job insecurity, the pay gap being too large and that the workplace is poorly managed all increase employees' willingness to be without a job if they had a reasonable income. However, feeling low-paid and believing management/employee relations were poor had no significant effect.

12. Official trade union membership statistics presented in the Certification Office Annual Reports, 1983-1996, show that membership decline began in 1979/80, declining each year thereafter.

13. Freeman and Medoff (1984) argue that unions can become 'voice activators' for employees, articulating issues of collective concern.

14. In recent years a number of unions have negotiated job security pacts with employers, sometimes at the expense of other competing interests such as higher pay deals. Nevertheless, these deals remain rare (IRS, 1997).

References

Beatson, M. (1995), *Labour Market Flexibility*, Employment Department Research Series No. 48.

Booth, A. L., Francesconi, M. and Garcia-Serrano, C. (1996), *Job Tenure: Does History Matter?*, ESRC Research Centre on Micro-social Change, Paper Number 96-12, University of Essex.

Brown, W., Deakin, S. and Ryan, P. (1997), 'The effects of British Industrial Relations Legislation, 1979-97', National Economic Review, **161**.

Bryson, A. and McKay, S. (1994), 'Is it worth working? An introduction to some of the issues' in Bryson, A. and McKay, S. (eds.) *Is it worth working?*, London: Policy Studies Institute.

Burgess, S. and Rees, H. (1996), 'Job tenure in Britain 1975-1991', *The Economic Journal*, 106, 334-45.

Certification Office for Trade Unions and Employers' Associations (1983-1996), *Annual Reports*.

Crouch, C. (1995), 'Exit or Voice: two paradigms for European industrial relations after the Keynesian welfare state', *European Journal of Industrial Relations*, Vol. 1, No. 1, 63-81.

Elgar, J. and Simpson, R. (1993), 'The impact of the law on industrial disputes in the 1980s' in Metcalf, D. and Milner, S., *New perspectives on industrial disputes*, London: Routledge.

Freeman, R. and Medoff, J. (1984), *What do trade unions do?*, New York: Basic Books.

Gallie, D. and White, M. (1993), *Employee commitment and the skills revolution*, London: Policy Studies Institute.

Gosling, A., Machin, S. and Meghir, C. (1994), *What has happened to wages?*, Institute for Fiscal Studies, Commentary No. 43.

Gregg, P. and Wadsworth, J. (1995), 'A short history of labour turnover, job tenure and job security, 1975-93', *Oxford Review of Economic Policy*, 11:1, 73-90.

Hedges, B. (1994), 'Work in a changing environment' in Jowell, R., Curtice, J., Brook, L. and Ahrendt, D. (eds.) *British Social Attitudes; the 11th Report*, Aldershot: Dartmouth.

Hirshman, A. O. (1970), *Exit, Voice and Loyalty*, Cambridge, MA: Harvard University Press.

Industrial Relations Services (1997), 'From here to security', IRS Employment Trends 631, May 1997.

Machin, S. (1996), 'Wage inequality in the UK', Oxford Review of Economic Policy, **12** 47-64.

Millward, N., Stevens, M., Smart, D. and Hawes, W.R. (1992), *Workplace industrial relations in transition*, Aldershot: Dartmouth.

Office of National Statistics (1997), official statistics on industrial stoppages, 1891-1996, as provided by Jackie Davies at the ONS.

Sly, F., Price, A. and Risdon, A. (1997), 'Women in the labour market: results from the spring 1996 Labour Force Survey', Labour Market Trends, July.

Spencer, P. (1996), 'Reactions to a flexible labour market', in Jowell, R., Curtice, J., Park, A., Brook, L. and Thomson, K. (eds.), *British Social Attitudes: the 13th Report*, Aldershot: Dartmouth.

Theodossiou, I. (1996), *A Model of the Causes of Leaving Unemployment: or who experiences the highest risk of job termination?*, Department of Economics Discussion Paper 96-20, University of Aberdeen.

Acknowledgement

SCPR is grateful to the Department for Education and Employment and to the Department for Trade and Industry for their financial support for the survey which has enabled us to ask questions on labour market, workplace and education issues since 1984.

Appendix

The rate of unemployment 1983-1996, per cent

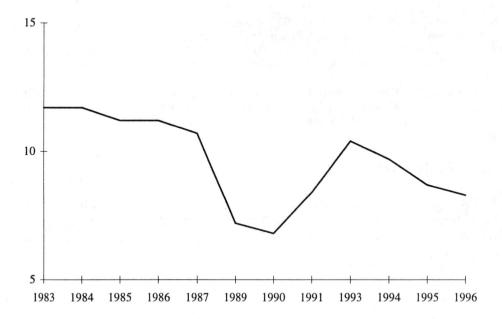

Note: the unemployment rate is derived from the *Labour Force Surveys* in the spring of each year. The rate is calculated by dividing the number of unemployed according to the *International Labour Organisation (ILO)* definition by the total number of economically active. The 1983 figure is adjusted to account for the use of the old *Labour Force Survey* definition.

Construction of the insecurity index

There are advantages to constructing a composite scale measuring insecurity, rather than individual questions. The index of employee security was derived using the following variables, and the allocation of the following weights to particular codes. The index was available for all *British Social Attitudes* years apart from 1987. (*British Social Attitudes* was not conducted in 1988 and 1992) These variables attempt to capture the likelihood of remaining in employment, whether exits are voluntary or forced, respondents' action in the event of job loss, and so on.

Preliminary factor analysis confirmed the importance of these variables, but was not pursued further given the limited number of variables consistently present in the range of survey years. Of course, the purpose of constructing such an index lies in its usefulness, hopefully as demonstrated in this chapter; it is not an end in itself.

Variable in BSA dataset	Range of codes	Contribution to index of employee security
LEAVEJOB [likely to leave job]	1 [very likely]	-2
	2 [quite likely]	-1
	3 [not very likely]	+1
	4 [not at all likely]	+2
ELOOKJOB [action if lost job]	1 [start looking]	-2
	2 [wait]	0
	3 [not start looking]	+2
EFINDJOB [months to find a job]	1-4	+2
	5+	-2
NUMEMP [workplace employment next year]	1 [increase]	+2
	2 [reduce]	-2
	3 [stay the same]	0
If expecting to leave job: **WHYGO1, WHYGO2, WHYGO4**	Through redundancy, contract expiry or closure of firm	-2
WHYGO7, WHYGO3, WHYGO6	Through going self-employed, retiring, or starting a new job	+2
If not expecting to leave job: **WAGEXPCT** [expected wages next year]	1 [increase above prices]	+2
	2 [increase with prices]	+1
	3 [increase below prices]	-1
	4 [no increase]	-2

Logistic regression models

Not all models include data from all years, partly because the *British Social Attitudes* survey was not conducted in 1988 and 1992 and partly because not all questions were asked in all survey years. In particular, 1987 is excluded from many of the models.

The models presented are final models and do not include variables used in earlier exploratory modelling, either because they had no significant impact or because similar variables proved more robust in alternative specifications. These included marital status, age of youngest child, number of children in the household, alternative measures of social class and socio-economic group, earnings levels, public and private sector employment, and alternative specifications of time trends.

Variables used in final models

Reference category for independent variables is as shown unless otherwise specified.

Business cycle

URise	Unemployment rate rose over previous year; Reference: unemployment rate did not rise.
UHigh	Unemployment rate above 9.7%; Reference: unemployment rate 9.7% or below.

Chronological time

Yr8386,Yr8791,Yr9396	Year of BSA survey, grouped; Reference: Yr8386.

Demographics

Fem	Woman; Reference: man.
Age1824,Age2534,Age3544, Age4554,Age5564,Age65pls, Agedk	Respondent's age, grouped. Agedk=data missing Reference: Age2534.
Ethnic	Non-white; Reference: white.
Highqual, Alev, Olev, CSE, Othqual, Noqual	Highest educational qualification: Highqual = above 'A' level; Reference: Model E - has qualifications; Model G - no qualifications.
AnyOwnKd	Respondent is living with dependent children; Reference: not living with dependent children.
Partner	Respondent has a partner; Reference: no partner.
PnrWking	Partner in paid work; Reference: no partner/partner not working.
SocRent, DKTenur	Tenure: respondent in social rented accommodation; DKTenur = data missing; Reference: all other forms of housing tenure.
South, GtrLon, Mids, North, Wales, Scotland	Region respondent lives in; Reference: South.

Type of worker

Und30hrs	Works under 30 hours per week; Reference: 30+ hours per week.
AnyU	Respondent has experienced unemployment in the last five years; Reference: no experience of unemployment.
Salatar, Routnm WkClass, OtherHG	Hope-Goldthorpe class schema: Salariat, Routine non-manual, Working class, OtherHG = Petty bourgeousie/ manual/ foremen/ supervisors; Reference: salariat.
UnionMem	Member of a trade union; Reference: not a member.

Type of workplace

UnionRec

Recognised union at respondent's workplace;
Reference: no recognised union.

Manufac, Services
Constru, Othersec

Sector of workplace; Reference:
Models A, B: Manuf/Constru/Othersec;
Models C, G, H, I, J, K, L: Services;
Models D, E, F: Manuf.

Sizu25,Siz2599,Si100499,
Sizov499,Sizmis

Banded number of employees at the respondent's
workplace. Sizmis=data missing; Reference:
Models B - G:- Sizu25;
Models H - L: size under 100.

Attitudes

PGap2Big

Gap between pay of highest and lowest paid people at
workplace is too big/much too big; Reference: any other
answer.

LowWage

Own wage is low/very low for the job I do; Reference: any
other answer.

ManPoor

Workplace is not well managed; Reference: any other answer.

PoorIR

Management/employee relations at workplace are not very
good,not at all good; Reference: any other answer.

Secure

Index of job security (-10 to +8).

Insecure

Scoring -1 or less on the job security index.

GetBettr

Agree/strongly agree with the statement that: 'Management will
always try to get the better of employees if it gets the chance'.

SayALot

Have a great deal of say/ quite a lot of say in decisions made at
work which change the way my job is done.

MoreSay2

Should have more say in decisions affecting my work.

VolExit

Very/quite likely will leave for another job/self-employment
over the next year.

VolExit3

Very/quite likely will leave for another job/ self-
employment/full-time education/family reasons over the next
year.

EarnLiv

Work is just a means of earning a living.

NotBothr

Wouldn't bother to work if had a reasonable living income
without having to work.

Model :	A		B		C		D	
Dep. var.:	PGap2Big		LowWage		Insecure		PoorIR	
Yrs excluded:	87		83, 87		83, 87		83, 87	
Indep. vars:								
URISE	-0.11	*	-0.35	**	0.00		-0.02	
UHIGH	0.09		-0.09		0.35	**	-0.05	
YR8791	0.47	**	-0.13		-0.34	**	0.15	
YR9396	0.52	**	-0.22	**	0.41	**	0.30	**
FEM	0.15	**	-0.01		0.13	*	-0.21	**
AGE1824	0.05		0.23	**	-0.15		0.00	
AGE3544	-0.09		0.06		0.05		-0.23	**
AGE4554	-0.07		0.14	*	0.21	**	-0.35	**
AGE5564	-0.14		0.21	**	0.21	*	-0.36	**
AGE65PLS	-0.75	**	0.03		-0.77	*	-0.72	*
AGEDK	0.01		0.69		-1.16		-0.36	
ETHNIC	0.21	*	0.30	**	0.10		-0.08	
ANYOWNKD	-0.02		-0.10	*	0.13	*	0.00	
PARTNER	-0.01		n.i.		-0.15	*	0.12	*
PNRWKING	n.i.		-0.10	*	n.i.		n.i.	
SOCRENT	0.17	**	0.31	**	n.i.		n.i.	
DKTENUR	0.07		-0.56		n.i.		n.i.	
GTRLON	0.01		-0.08		-0.01		0.09	
MIDS	0.17	**	0.03		-0.05		0.01	
NORTH	0.07		0.14	**	0.08		-0.10	
SCOTLAND	0.22	**	0.07		-0.01		-0.25	**
WALES	-0.07		0.06		0.23	*	-0.15	
UND30HRS	-0.53	**	-0.22	**	-0.04		-0.28	**
ANYU	n.i.		n.i.		0.35	**	n.i.	
ROUTNM	0.21	**	0.12	*	-0.03		0.04	
WKCLASS	0.13	*	0.46	**	0.02		0.24	**
OTHERHG	0.08		0.20	**	-0.05		0.11	
UNIONMEM	0.25	**	n.i.		0.17	**	0.29	**
UNIONREC	0.33	**	-0.14	**	0.44	**	0.00	
SERVICES	0.03		0.20	**	n.i.		-0.05	
MANUFAC	n.i.		n.i.		-0.26	**	n.i.	
CONSTRU	n.i.		n.i.		0.05		-0.51	**
OTHERSEC	n.i.		n.i.		0.25	**	-0.01	
SIZ2599	n.i.		-0.17	**	0.11		0.29	**
SI100499	n.i.		-0.49	**	0.23	**	0.54	**
SIZOV499	n.i.		-0.53	**	0.24	**	0.68	**
SIZMIS	n.i.		-0.45	*	0.70	**	-0.40	
MANPOOR	0.35	**	0.43	**	0.52	**	n.i.	
POORIR	0.64	**	0.36	**	0.29	**	n.i.	
PGAP2BIG	n.i.		n.i.		0.14	**	0.69	**
LOWWAGE	n.i.		n.i.		0.43	**	0.46	**
SECURE	-0.04	**	-0.09	**	n.i.		-0.11	**
Constant	-1.17	**	-0.54	**	-2.41	**	-2.36	**
Degree of freedom	31		34		37		35	
Model chi-square	1124		942		1087		1187	
-2 log likelihood	17033		15324		12891		11213	
Base	*12893*		*12077*		*12095*		*12077*	

Model :	E		F		G		H	
Dep. var.:	GetBettr		ManPoor		SayALot		VolExit	
Yrs excluded	83, 84, 87		83, 87		83, 86, 90 94, 95		83, 87	
Indep. vars:								
URISE	0.00		0.00		0.08		-0.25	**
UHIGH	-0.09		-0.10		-0.12		-0.24	**
YR8791	0.35	**	-0.01		-0.42	**	0.07	
YR9396	0.58	**	0.13		-0.34	**	-0.04	
FEM	-0.35	**	-0.42	**	-0.08		-0.26	**
AGE1824	0.15		-0.37	**	-0.23	*	0.13	
AGE3544	0.02		-0.12		0.20	*	-0.44	**
AGE4554	-0.08		-0.33	**	0.02		-1.18	**
AGE5564	0.01		-0.38	**	-0.02		-2.47	**
AGE65PLS	0.24		-1.03	**	0.33		-1.47	**
AGEDK	-1.14		-0.20		1.49	*	-0.33	
ETHNIC	0.63	**	-0.16		-0.05		0.19	
NOQUAL	0.40	**	n.i.		n.i.		n.i.	
HIGHQUAL	n.i.		n.i.		0.29	**	n.i.	
ALEV	n.i.		n.i.		0.44	**	n.i.	
OLEV	n.i.		n.i.		0.19	*	n.i.	
CSE	n.i.		n.i.		-0.01		n.i.	
OTHQUAL	n.i.		n.i.		-0.17		n.i.	
ANYOWNKD	0.05		-0.02		0.07		-0.31	**
PARTNER	0.08		0.07		0.17	*	-0.22	**
GTRLON	0.14		0.15		0.03		0.22	*
MIDS	0.18	**	-0.10		0.00		-0.07	
NORTH	0.13	*	-0.13	*	-0.06		-0.20	**
SCOTLAND	0.09		0.25	**	-0.42	**	-0.20	*
WALES	0.23		-0.10		-0.18		-0.21	
UND30HRS	0.04		-0.31	**	-0.43	**	0.15	
ANYU	n.i.		n.i.		-0.21	**	0.52	**
ROUTNM	0.51	**	0.07		-0.76	**	0.00	
WKCLASS	1.01	**	0.15	*	-1.07	**	-0.19	*
OTHERHG	0.54	**	0.19	*	-0.33	**	-0.21	
UNIONMEM	0.55	**	0.23	**	-0.24	**	-0.36	**
UNIONREC	-0.23	**	0.06		-0.18	*	-0.43	**
SERVICES	-0.12		-0.14	*	n.i.		n.i.	
MANUFAC	n.i.		n.i.		0.18	*	-0.02	
CONSTRU	-0.20		-0.36	**	0.09		-0.31	*
OTHERSEC	-0.11		-0.19		-0.11		-0.34	*
SIZ2599	0.11		0.22	**	-0.48	**	n.i.	
SI100499	0.14	*	0.28	**	-0.51	**	-0.15	*
SIZOV499	0.09		0.49	**	-0.69	**	-0.30	**
SIZMIS	-0.12		-0.18		-1.60	**	0.13	
MANPOOR	n.i.		n.i.		-0.50	**	0.62	**
POORIR	n.i.		n.i.		-0.73	**	0.52	**
PGAP2BIG	0.41	**	0.55	**	-0.36	**	0.09	
LOWWAGE	0.23	**	0.52	**	-0.27	**	0.60	**
SECURE	-0.06	**	-0.13	**	n.i.		-0.07	**
Constant	-0.81	**	-1.71	**	0.99	**	-1.05	**
Degree of freedom	36		35		42		37	
Model chi-square	1050		1181		1102		1588	
-2 log likelihood	11073		11428		7884		8477	
Base	*8793*		*12077*		*6958*		*12726*	

Model :	I		J		K		L	
Dep. var.:	VolExit3		NotBothr		EarnLiv		MoreSay2	
Yrs excluded	83, 87		83, 87, 90, 91		83, 84, 86, 87, 90		83, 84, 86, 90, 94, 95	
Indep. vars:								
URISE	-0.20	*	-0.26	**	0.01		0.13	
UHIGH	-0.27	**	-0.04		0.07		0.10	
YR8791	0.04		-0.12		0.25	*	0.48	**
YR9396	-0.07		0.10		0.43	**	0.65	**
FEM	-0.02		-0.11	*	-0.16	**	0.06	
AGE1824	0.19	*	-0.29	**	0.10		0.08	
AGE3544	-0.64	**	0.07		-0.21	**	-0.30	**
AGE4554	-1.40	**	0.37	**	-0.14		-0.22	**
AGE5564	-2.43	**	0.46	**	0.02		-0.43	**
AGE65PLS	-1.06	**	0.59	**	-1.66	**	-1.51	**
AGEDK	-0.64		-0.42		0.55		-0.26	
ETHNIC	0.18		-0.53	**	0.19		0.00	
ANYOWNKD	-0.33	**	-0.19	**	-0.06		0.08	
PARTNER	0.00		0.11		0.07		-0.02	
GTRLON	0.21	*	0.09		0.19	*	-0.01	
MIDS	-0.07		0.00		0.03		-0.01	
NORTH	-0.23	**	0.22	**	0.24	**	-0.01	
SCOTLAND	-0.28	*	0.15		0.19	*	0.13	
WALES	-0.28		0.29	**	0.07		0.11	
UND30HRS	0.28	**	0.34	**	0.02		-0.34	**
ANYU	0.49	**	0.01		0.19	**	-0.03	
ROUTNM	0.02		0.10		1.23	**	0.18	*
WKCLASS	-0.15	*	0.04		1.66	**	0.14	
OTHERHG	-0.24	*	0.03		1.13	**	0.07	
UNIONMEM	-0.38	**	0.07		-0.06		0.38	**
UNIONREC	-0.46	**	0.09		-0.06		0.44	**
MANUFAC	0.01		0.10		0.44	**	-0.06	
CONSTRU	-0.38	*	0.08		-0.03		-0.46	**
OTHERSEC	-0.36	**	0.13		0.01		-0.15	
SI100499	-0.10		0.06		0.19	**	-0.02	
SIZOV499	-0.28	**	0.03		0.13		0.06	
SIZMIS	0.07		0.07		0.37		0.35	
MANPOOR	0.52	**	0.25	**	0.44	**	0.91	**
POORIR	0.52	**	0.09		0.44	**	1.12	**
PGAP2BIG	0.10		0.17	**	0.16	**	0.73	**
LOWWAGE	0.54	**	0.00		0.13	*	0.45	**
SECURE	-0.10	**	-0.02	*	-0.07	**	n.i.	
Constant	-1.01		-1.52		-2.55	**	-1.89	
Degree of freedom	37		37		37		36	
Model chi-square	1773		355		1477		1608	
-2 log likelihood	9083		12014		9877		8182	
Base	*12077*		*10152*		*8480*		*6968*	

*   significant at 5% level
**   significant at 1% level
n.i.   not included in the model

3 The NHS: new prescriptions needed?

Ken Judge, Jo-Ann Mulligan and Bill New [*]

Health policy occupied a larger part of Conservative thinking after 1979 than is commonly supposed and in many ways the National Health Service was strengthened as a result of the reforms and investment that took place during their period in government. For example, public expenditure on the National Health Service, in real volume terms, rose by more than one third under the Thatcher and Major governments. Alongside these real achievements, however, there was also always a somewhat ambivalent approach to the welfare state in general and to the National Health Service in particular. The Conservatives' underlying scepticism, if not hostility, to high social spending was not only at the heart of its strategy throughout the period, but also at the forefront of its public image.

Background

During the first Thatcher government (from 1979 to 1983) there was little evidence of the radicalism that came to be associated with Conservatism (or Thatcherism) in the later 1980s. Even so, there were strands within Conservative thinking in the early days that saw the 1979 election victory as an opportunity to promote private health insurance and so limit the voracious appetite of a comprehensive and tax-financed NHS for ever larger injections of public spending. But the report of the Merrison Royal Commission (Royal

[*] Ken Judge is Professor of Social Policy, University of Kent, Jo-Ann Mulligan is a Research Officer at the King's Fund Policy Institute and Bill New is a Senior Research Officer at the King's Fund Policy Institute.

Commission on the National Health Service, 1979) soon poured scorn on such radical ideas and dampened the enthusiasm of Ministers for social experimentation in such a sensitive area as health care. In the event, the most noteworthy aspect of Conservative health policy during Mrs Thatcher's first term was the organisational restructuring during 1982. Also of significance was the then Secretary of State for Health and Social Services Patrick Jenkins' forthright dismissal of the Black report's review of health inequalities on the grounds that:

> ... additional expenditure on the scale which could result from the report's recommendations is quite unrealistic in present or any foreseeable economic circumstances. (Townsend and Davidson, 1992: 39)

Despite this rejection of a report commissioned by the previous Labour government, health policy during the first Conservative term of office was relatively bipartisan. Once the consequences of the "winter of discontent" had been overcome during 1980, the average level of annual increase in the volume of resources made available to the NHS in the three years before the 1983 election was a relatively generous 3.1 per cent. Yet the seeds of future policy change and political turbulence were clearly being sewn. There was a growing recognition within government that this rate of increase was inconsistent with broader policy goals.

Encouraged by the resounding success of the post-Falklands election victory in 1983, the second Thatcher government was much more determined to apply the spending brakes to the NHS. So, for the remainder of the 1980s, with the single exception of 1987/88, increases in annual spending on the NHS were much more modest. The watchword for the mid-1980s was "efficiency gains", and new styles of management were introduced to achieve them, replacing the old culture of "administration". In his influential report Sir Roy Griffiths (then Managing Director of Sainsburys) put it memorably:

> ... if Florence Nightingale were carrying her lamp through the corridors of the NHS today, she would almost certainly be searching for the people in charge. (Griffiths, 1983: 22)

As a result of his recommendations a new breed of general manager was introduced into the NHS, soon to be followed by a policy agenda that was seen to be dominated by considerations of value for money almost to the exclusion of anything else. It did not take long, however, for a sort of backlash to develop as select committees, think tanks, and professional organisations almost vied with one another to point out the size and extent of the funding crisis that was now facing the NHS. Eventually, after her third election victory in 1987, and in response to intense pressure from medical leaders in particular, Mrs Thatcher announced a major review of the NHS,

which resulted in the white paper, *Working for Patients* (1989) that presaged the introduction of the so-called 'internal market' in 1991.

These reforms largely ignored many of the issues to do with overall levels of finance for the NHS, concentrating instead on promoting competition between providers, and later purchasers, in order to improve efficiency within the health care system. Although Mrs Thatcher's administration was the architect of these reforms, it fell to Mr Major's administration to implement them. His more inclusive rhetoric about social policy, together with the proximity of a general election and the need to sell the new reforms to a hostile medical profession, all combined, perhaps, to help bring about substantial annual increases in spending on the NHS, averaging around 4 per cent per year, in the three years between 1990 and 1993. Subsequently, after the 1992 election victory, and once the health care professions had acquiesced to, if not embraced, the new reforms, spending levels once again fell somewhat, most of all surprisingly in the financial year immediately prior to the 1997 election. By then tight spending limits for health authorities were already in place and some of the anxieties about levels of spending - so evident during the mid-1980s - had begun to resurface. Prominent among these was a warning from Sir Duncan Nicol, a former chief executive of the NHS, that a tax-financed and comprehensive health service was no longer viable.

While the 18 years of Conservative government saw many changes in health policy and practice which are likely to have influenced public attitudes to the NHS and to spending levels in particular, it is certainly the case that public interest in the financing of the NHS during these years was fuelled by the growing amount of media attention paid to this topic. During the highly contentious political debate about the introduction of an internal market for the NHS proposed by *Working for Patients*, the amount of media attention paid to the financing and expenditure of the NHS increased significantly from the levels of media coverage earlier in the 1980s (as illustrated by the table in the appendix to this chapter). In the early 1990s the number of stories reduced somewhat while remaining at a much higher level than had been the case in the 1980s. Then, as spending levels fell after the 1992 election victory, the number of references in the media started to rise significantly once again, reaching almost their 1990 peak. The amount of media attention linking falling spending on the NHS to falling standards is certainly likely to have registered itself in the public's mind. For instance, using data from the *Eurobarometer* survey covering 15 European countries, Mossialos (1997) found that citizens' dissatisfaction with health services were strongly linked with their country's per capita expenditure on the health service.

So, before reviewing some of the trends in social attitudes to health care since 1983, it is worth recording precisely what the changing economic fortunes of the NHS have actually been since 1979. The next figure charts annual increases in spending on the NHS between 1979/80 and 1996/97.[1]

NHS Funding, 1979-1997

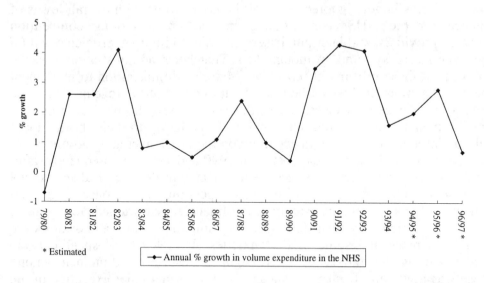

* Estimated

——— Annual % growth in volume expenditure in the NHS

Source: Dixon and Harrison, 1997

There is clear evidence of a political business cycle at work, with spending peaks associated with the general elections of 1983, 1987 and 1992. The average spending increase in these three election years of 3.5 per cent was almost twice the overall rate. The higher than average level of spending associated with the introduction of the *Working for Patients* reforms also stands out. In contrast, the low levels of spending between 1983 and 1989 - with the exception of the short-lived election boost in 1987 - are clearly illustrated. The average increase in spending in the six non-election years after 1983 was only 0.8 per cent per annum. One of the most interesting aspects of this graph is the extent to which the Major government in 1997 was prepared to enter the general election after such a meagre financial allocation for the NHS in the run up to it. The miserly increase of 0.7 per cent in spending in 1996/97 was less than one-half of the average for the period as a whole and only one-fifth of the amount immediately prior to the three previous general elections.

Public spending and the NHS

The *British Social Attitudes* series has tracked public attitudes to the NHS since 1983. Each year, respondents are asked to give their first and second priorities between each of ten possible areas of extra government spending. In each year health care has been, without exception, the most popular public priority for extra spending.

The level of demand for more health spending does, however, appear to be associated partly with the pattern of funding. For instance, it was less likely to be seen as a priority directly after the injection of funds leading to the 1992 general election. However, since 1993, the proportion naming health as a first priority out of the ten areas of government spending has risen a full ten percentage points. In the latest reading a near record eight out of ten people thought that health care should be the first or second spending priority.

First or second priority for extra spending[2]	1983	1986	1990	1991	1993	1995	1996
	%	%	%	%	%	%	%
Health	63	75	81	74	70	77	80
Education	50	57	60	62	57	66	66
Housing	20	21	20	21	22	14	12
Police and prisons	8	7	7	6	10	10	11
Help for industry	29	16	6	10	14	9	9
Social security benefits	12	11	13	11	13	11	8
Base	1761	3100	2797	2918	2945	1234	3620

Changes in public satisfaction

Another way of looking at trends in public opinion on the NHS is to look at changes in levels of expressed satisfaction or dissatisfaction both with the NHS as a whole and with its particular components. Each year respondents are asked:

All in all, how satisfied or dissatisfied would you say you are with the way in which the National Health Service runs nowadays?

	1983	1986	1990	1991	1993	1996
	%	%	%	%	%	%
Satisfied	55	40	37	40	44	36
Neither satisfied nor dissatisfied	20	19	15	19	18	14
Dissatisfied	25	40	47	41	38	50
Base	1761	3100	2797	2918	2945	3620

Reassuringly, perhaps, levels of public dissatisfaction do seem to be associated with the priority people attach to health spending. Thus they rose substantially during the 1980s, culminating in 1990. Then, following the publication of *Working for Patients*, the early 1990s saw some abatement of

dissatisfaction from a high of 47 per cent in 1990 to a low of 38 per cent in 1993 (though still a large 10 points higher than the benchmark level a decade earlier). So, when we last visited this subject in *The 11th Report*, the author concluded that the Conservative health reforms were "beginning to reduce the level of political conflict surrounding the NHS" (Bosanquet, 1994: 53). It looked then as if either the NHS reforms were beginning to be seen to be working, or at any rate that the unusually large injection of cash for three years in succession from 1990 had helped to allay fears that the service was being starved of resources. This increased level of funding also enabled high profile innovations such as the Waiting List initiative and the Patient's Charter to get off to a flying start.

But it now seems to have been a false dawn. The trend has clearly reversed again, with the proportion expressing dissatisfaction with the NHS in 1996, at 50 per cent, the highest ever.[3]

In any event, while these questions on overall satisfaction may be valuable for monitoring the public mood, they can conceal sharp differences in attitudes towards particular aspects of the health service. It is to these more specific components of the NHS to which we now turn.

Primary health care

For most people the first and only contact with the NHS about a particular episode of illness is an appointment with their GP or dentist. It is therefore reasonable to suppose that evaluations of these primary health care services might be particularly important in influencing the public view about the health service in general. We asked:

> *From your experience, or from what you have heard, please say how satisfied or dissatisfied you are with the way in which each of these parts of the National Health Service runs nowadays.*

As the next table shows, however, public satisfaction with local GPs proves to be much higher and much more consistent than with the NHS as a whole. As it turns out, it is also higher than with any other part of the health service we asked about either. Similarly, dissatisfaction with dentists was rather low to begin with, but it rose sharply during the nineties, possibly reflecting the fact that a growing proportion of new patients (up to 50 per cent, according to Harrison, 1996) find it difficult these days to get NHS treatment at all as an increasing proportion of dentists withdraw from the NHS. A similar rise in dissatisfaction might therefore follow any other service that was to change from being 'free at source' to 'pay as you go'.

Satisfaction with local doctors and NHS dentists

	1983	1986	1989	1991	1993	1994	1995	1996
	%	%	%	%	%	%	%	%
Local doctors								
Satisfied	80	77	80	83	83	80	79	77
Neither satisfied nor dissatisfied	7	8	8	8	7	9	10	9
Dissatisfied	13	14	12	9	10	11	11	13
NHS dentists								
Satisfied	73	74	70	68	58	57	55	52
Neither satisfied nor dissatisfied	15	14	16	16	19	17	17	16
Dissatisfied	10	10	11	12	20	22	23	25
Base	*1761*	*3100*	*3029*	*2918*	*2945*	*3469*	*3683*	*3620*

Among the various aspects of GP services we asked about in more detail, it turned out to be the GPs' appointment system rather than the quality of medical service from the GP that came in for most criticism.[4] Over 40 per cent of respondents consistently rate their GP's appointment system as in need of "a lot" or "some" improvement, and this has been true since the question was first introduced in 1987.

The hospital service

As for hospital services, however, here the pattern is closer to that for the NHS as a whole. As the next table shows, when this survey series began in 1983 an impressive three in four people expressed satisfaction with inpatient care and around three in five with outpatient care. By 1990, the levels had dropped sharply. Then, following extra public spending on the NHS and much-publicised innovations, the trendline steadied but only to fall again in the period from 1993 to 1996. On the other hand, we also found in 1996 (table not shown here) that people with recent experience of using both inpatient and outpatient care are much more impressed (by around 14 points in each case) than those without recent experience. Nevertheless, in terms of overall public impact on levels of public satisfaction, the Conservative reforms appear not to have done the trick.

Satisfaction with inpatient and outpatient services

	1983	1986	1990	1991	1993	1996
	%	%	%	%	%	%
Inpatient care						
Satisfied	74	67	63	64	64	53
Neither satisfied nor dissatisfied	17	15	19	16	18	17
Dissatisfied	7	13	15	13	14	22
Outpatient care						
Satisfied	61	55	51	52	57	52
Neither satisfied nor dissatisfied	16	14	18	16	17	18
Dissatisfied	21	29	28	27	23	25
Base	*1761*	*3100*	*2797*	*2918*	*2945*	*3620*

As with GP services, the survey also asks a number of questions about which particular aspects of hospital services are thought to be most in need of treatment. As the next table shows, people turn out to be much more critical of the components than of the whole. Indeed, the majority of respondents think that all but three aspects of the hospital service are in need of some improvement.

While the quality of medical and nursing care in NHS hospitals does not come in for much criticism, waiting times for treatment (whether inpatient or outpatient) gets almost universal criticism. Over three-quarters of people feel they are in need of improvement. On the other hand, the trend since 1987 has in fact been downwards, suggesting perhaps that the Government's targeting of waiting lists has indeed achieved a modest impact.

% saying needs "a lot" or "some" improvement

	1987	1990	1996
	%	%	%
Waiting time before getting appointments with hospital consultants	83	82	79
Hospital waiting lists for non-emergency operations	87	83	77
Time spent waiting in accident and emergency departments	n/a	n/a	73
Staffing levels of nurses in hospitals	75	72	71
Staffing levels of doctors in hospitals	70	68	70
Time spent waiting in outpatient departments	n/a	n/a	68
Waiting areas in accident and emergency departments in hospitals	n/a	57	56
General conditions of hospital buildings	53	54	50
Waiting areas for outpatients in hospitals	n/a	53	49
Time spent waiting for an ambulance after a 999 call	n/a	n/a	36
Quality of medical treatment in hospitals	30	31	32
Quality of nursing care in hospitals	21	24	27
Base	*1281*	*2430*	*3085*

n/a = not asked

Who are the most and the least satisfied?

A key question about people's perceptions of the NHS is the extent to which they reflect, for instance, their local experiences, their socio-demographic backgrounds or their political allegiances. Previous research (Judge and Solomon, 1993) has shown that socio-demographic characteristics, areas of residence and recent experience of using health services are indeed all associated with people's attitudes. But little is known about the extent to which such views may also be influenced by people's values and political opinions.

Using the *British Social Attitudes* data collected in 1996 we have used the technique of logistic regression to explore these questions further.[5] Regression models identify the association between each of a number of characteristics with, say, the level of dissatisfaction, while controlling for all of the other characteristics included in the model. So the particular impact of each characteristic is *independently* tested. We have used it here to explore associations between various background characteristics and levels of dissatisfaction with the running of the NHS in general, the care provided by GPs and dentists, and both inpatient and outpatient services in hospitals.[6]

A number of distinct patterns emerge, such as that Londoners are more likely than others to be dissatisfied with all aspects of health care. We cannot tell whether this reflects the turbulence in the capital's health care system following the report by Tomlinson (1992) or other aspects of metropolitan life, but this finding is certainly consistent with other studies (Judge and Soloman, 1993; Mulligan and Judge, 1997).

Those with higher social status and incomes also tend to be more dissatisfied, just as those with low incomes and education, together with the unemployed and retired, tend to be more satisfied. Of course, these results may well reflect differences in expectations between different social groups. Meanwhile, people employed within the NHS have a particularly high tendency to be dissatisfied with the way the NHS is run in general and with hospital inpatient services in particular. This dissatisfaction could derive either from their own experience of working within a service felt by many to be under extreme pressure, or it could, of course, be merely a form of special pleading.

But most interesting, perhaps, is the strong association between views about the NHS and people's wider ideological perspective. To investigate this, two of the *British Social Attitudes* scales were used. The first is a scale measuring people's views towards welfare provision as a whole. Surprisingly, perhaps, we find that people who are the most supportive of the welfare state in general turn out to be more critical of the present standard of the health service in particular. A second scale is one that measures people's 'left-right' leanings, in particular to do with income and wealth inequalities. Once again we find that those on the left of the political spectrum are more likely to be critical.

A cautionary note

We know from many sources that methodological considerations can influence answers to questions in surveys. This is true not only of the precise wording of questions, but also of the context and order in which questions are asked. The table below compares responses to identical questions about satisfaction with the NHS and its component parts asked in two different probability-based national surveys carried out at much the same time (the *British Social Attitudes* survey and the government's Office of National Statistics *Omnibus Survey*. In all cases the extent of dissatisfaction recorded in the BSA surveys is greater and often much greater than that obtained by the government figures. The differences in relation to the running of the NHS are particularly striking.

Comparison between ONS Omnibus and British Social Attitudes survey data

	ONS Omnibus		BSA	
	1991/2	**1996/7**	**1991**	**1996**
% dissatisfied	%	%	%	%
Running of the NHS	18	29	41	50
Local doctors/GPs	8	9	9	13
Hospital inpatient services	9	14	13	22
Hospital outpatient services	18	18	27	25

As Judge & Solomon suggest, "the most likely explanation ... is that this variation arises from the different contexts in which the same question was asked in the different surveys" (1993, pp. 307-8). While the ONS Omnibus asks about satisfaction with the NHS as the first in a series of questions about health services, SCPR's *British Social Attitudes* questions are always preceded by a range of questions about priorities for government spending in general. Could it also be that dissatisfaction with the running of the NHS may be more difficult for people to express in a government survey than in an independent one? In any event, it is at least reassuring that the *trends* are largely consistent between the two different survey findings, both showing marked increases in dissatisfaction over the period with both the running of the NHS and with hospital inpatient services, and a contrasting degree of stability in relation to outpatient services. In this respect, it is only the trends about GPs that are obviously discordant. The point to note is that, as with all survey data of this kind, it is the *gradient* of a trendline that matters rather than the often spurious precision of the proportion expressing a particular viewpoint - another reason for preferring rigorous trend measures for divining public attitudes to one-off opinion polls.

From patients to customers?

The Conservatives' hope for a reformed NHS with an internal market was that it would transform the role of the patient from a passive recipient of care to that of a consumer who would have more say in shaping their own treatment. Indeed, the Department of Health's own Annual Report for 1995 set out two objectives for the NHS:

> ... to promote user involvement in their own care, as active partners with professionals; and to enable them to become informed about their treatment and care and to make informed decisions and choices if they wish. (Department of Health, 1995)

To what extent does the public believe this has occurred? Although not all questions were included in the 1996 survey, the *British Social Attitudes* series has asked a range of questions over the past five years on what might be referred to as Patient Charter issues. They cover, for instance, the extent to which people feel they have the chance to communicate properly with their doctors, their degree of choice over where they receive hospital treatment, and whether they could change their GP if they wished to do so.

An impressive majority of respondents (around two-thirds) believe that hospital doctors would not only "give them all the information they required" but also "take seriously" their views on preferred treatment. Even bigger majorities (77 per cent and 84 per cent respectively) felt that doctors and nurses respectively would "take seriously any complaints they might have". (Only 56 per cent, however, thought they would be able to press on with a formal complaint "without fuss or bother", probably reflecting the perceived difference between dealing with health professionals and dealing with the 'system'). More disturbing, however, is the growing proportion of people (up from 32 per cent in 1991 to 45 per cent in 1995), who believed that they "definitely" or "probably" might be discharged from hospital before they were "really well enough to leave". This suggests that recent initiatives to increase the efficiency of NHS hospitals, to shorten waiting lists and to reduce average lengths of stay have left the public with an impression of a service in danger of concentrating too much on 'process' rather than treatment.

So, despite the government's insistence that patient choice would prevail *throughout* the new NHS, most people feel they have far more choice in respect of primary health care than of secondary health care. Over two thirds (69 per cent) in the 1996 survey believed they would be able to change their GP without much difficulty. But only half that proportion (34 per cent) felt they could have a say in choosing which hospital they were sent to. These proportions are lower in London, supporting the evidence from, for instance, Boyle and Hamblin (1997) that Londoners have relatively poor primary health care services.

The future of the NHS

We have shown that the public seems to be increasingly worried about the government's ability to fund and run the NHS. While GPs and other health professionals continue to enjoy public confidence, there are signs that specific aspects of both the hospital service and the primary care sector are under increasingly visible strain. That being so, prioritising the NHS for extra spending remains high on the public's agenda.

Increasingly of late, concerns are being expressed as to whether the NHS can be sustained under its current funding regime, especially given the extra demands upon it from demographic changes and the growth of public expectations. Some voices, such as that of Healthcare 2000 - a group financed by the pharmaceutical industry - question the future viability of a comprehensive and universal service free at the point of use, arguing forcefully that policy makers need to consider "raising the proportion of healthcare funding provided by individuals through options such as user chargers and/or patient co-payments"(Healthcare 2000, 1995: 9). Meanwhile the new Secretary of State for Health has announced a 'no holds barred' review of health provision in the NHS.

What evidence can we glean from successive *British Social Attitudes* surveys about public opinion on these sorts of fundamental issues to do with the future of the NHS? For some years now the survey has asked searching questions about the extent to which 'free' health care might be more selectively given, leaving some to fend for themselves through private medical insurance.

A two-tier service?

To gauge the level of public commitment to the principle of a universal health service, we ask:

> *It has been suggested that the National Health Service should be available only to those with lower incomes. This would mean that contributions and taxes could be lower and most people would take out medical insurance or pay for health care. Do you support or oppose this idea?*

In 1996 we added a similar question on dental services:

> *Many dentists now provide NHS treatment only to those with lower incomes. This means that other people have to pay the full amount for their dental treatment, or take out private insurance to cover their treatment. Do you support or oppose this happening?*

As the next table shows, opposition to both a selective NHS and selective NHS dentistry is high. In fact the proportion who favour a selective NHS has *fallen* since we first asked this question in 1983. Then, almost 30 per cent of respondents supported the idea of a selective service, compared with the 20 per cent who do so now.

	NHS	NHS dentistry
	%	%
Support	21	20
Oppose	77	77
Base	*3620*	*3620*

So, while concern about the performance of the NHS may have increased, an alternative system of provision is not at all popular. Over three quarters of the population want to retain a universal 'free at source' health service. More surprisingly, perhaps, given the actual changes to dentistry over the last few years, public feelings seem just as strong about the need for universal free dentistry.

On the other hand, although the majority of people feel that universal free care should be available, should those who can afford it have an absolute right to buy better medical care for themselves? We asked:

Do you think that health care should be the same for everyone, or should people who can afford it be able to pay for better health care?

	%
Same for everyone	60
Able to pay for better health care	39
Base	*1221*

Even more surprisingly, perhaps, a growing proportion of people, now six in ten, would ideally deny the choice to others to buy themselves out of the system. This above all suggests the extent to which the NHS is still seen by the British public as a resource to be protected and cherished. On the other hand, nearly one-third of those who oppose a two-tier NHS *also* believe that people *should* have the choice to pay for private health care. Being opposed to restricted access to the NHS does not in itself lead people to deny others the right to opt out of the system. As always, the pattern of public opinion is complex. People's views are related to their support for the welfare system in general and inevitably to their political views too. There are elements of self-interest too. People who work in the NHS, for instance, are particularly opposed to any move which might weaken it, such as restricting its access to the poor. Similarly, there are variations in response according to age, such as the comparative indifference among those under 30 towards a decline in

'free' dentistry. This might of course have something to do with the fact that this group has grown into adulthood with an increasing expectation of paying for dental care.

Rationing: old questions in new forms?

Rationing has always existed in the NHS as an inevitable consequence of wants and needs exceeding resources. The process is not, of course, confined to highly publicised cases of individuals being denied treatment, still less to whole services being threatened or withdrawn. It is far more pervasive and mundane, as the continual presence of waiting lists throughout the life of the NHS amply testifies.

It is more difficult to explain the recent explosion of interest in the subject. One possible explanation is that the size of the gap between available resources and technological potential is growing. That being so, the medical profession and the public alike are increasingly aware that what could be done in an ideal world and what can be done are growing further and further apart. Another explanation is that the 1991 NHS reforms encouraged health authorities to focus on specific strategies for rationing, rather than letting the allocation of resources 'emerge' from the interplay of a large number of independent factors. Moreover, in focusing on their resident populations, each health authority and GP fundholder is now able to specify which services should (and should not) be available for those living in their area.

Increasingly, too, the mass media have been giving a more prominent place to aspects of the rationing debate. The NHS reforms precipitated a flood of media scrutiny which has barely eased off since. This might well have contributed to a loss in public confidence.

Background to the debate

The issues involved in rationing are far too complex to be encompassed within one section of one survey. For instance, there are linked questions about who should make rationing decisions and at which level in a health care system they should be made. Such choices depend in part on bureaucratic considerations and on issues of trust and confidence. Should rationing decisions be left to clinicians who deal with individual cases and who seem to enjoy public trust, or should managers at the health authority level have a significant role, or should central government impose rules (Lenaghan, 1996)? Some, such as Mechanic (1995) argue for clinicians continuing to make the bulk of rationing decisions, but such a disaggregated system of decision-making is thought by others to lead to unacceptable variations in outcome. They prefer a national body to advise on priority setting to provide a framework within which clinicians can work (Turnberg et al., 1996).

Then there is the vexed issue of how to choose between individual candidates for treatment. Should smokers, for instance, get lower priority for certain interventions on the grounds that their likely lifespan is more limited than that of non-smokers? And, by the same token, should people get a lower priority for certain interventions as they get older? (See Underwood *et al.*, 1993; Williams, 1997; Grimley Evans, 1997.) This principle could be extended to obese people, and so on.

Lying behind support or rejection of such criteria are different understandings of what constitutes justifiable need. Some argue that the mere existence of ill-health is sufficient reason for intervention and that other factors should be irrelevant (Harris, 1997). Indeed, it is sometimes argued that, say, the elderly or an overweight person is in greater need simply because their prospect of long term benefit from treatment is less good than that of younger and slimmer people. Others who interpret need more strictly as the ability to benefit, measured by concepts such as 'quality adjusted life-years', would regard the claims of smokers, the elderly and the overweight as less pressing. They view the NHS as essentially about maximising the health gain of the whole community, not only about treatment of the individual in ill health.

Others argue that smoking and weight are characteristics which, to some extent, depend on choice and lifestyle preferences. And although it is still rare for commentators to advocate openly that these lifestyle factors should lead to a lower priority for treatment, it has been suggested that smokers, for instance, should contribute relatively more to the *finance* of health care - through a tax on tobacco products (Le Grand, 1991).

What do people think about health rationing?

In view of our somewhat sparse knowledge of public opinion on health rationing (see Kneeshaw, 1997), the 1996 *British Social Attitudes* survey introduced several new questions on the topic. First, respondents were asked to consider three scenarios, each of which concerned two men on a hospital waiting list. Both men had a heart condition and both would benefit from an operation. In each scenario, the men differed on only one point:

> *Scenario 1   One man was a heavy smoker, the other a non-smoker;*
> *Scenario 2   One man was aged 40, the other aged 60;*
> *Scenario 3   One man was overweight and ate unhealthily, the other*
> *was of average weight and ate healthily.*

People were asked first whether they thought each difference between the two men *would* currently be used to prioritise one over the other for the operation.

Currently, who *would* get priority, or are decisions not made on this basis?

Smoking	%	Age	%	Weight	%
- non-smoker	53	- younger man	35	- average weight	42
- heavy smoker	3	- older man	6	- overweight	4
- no difference	33	- no difference	48	- no difference	41
- can't choose	10	- can't choose	11	- can't choose	12

Base 3085

In each case, a significant proportion of people believe that rationing on the basis of these criteria does occur in the NHS and that those following a 'healthy lifestyle' or who are younger will be given priority. This applies most to non-smokers: more than one half believe their claim to a heart operation would get precedence over those of a heavy smoker. As the table shows, smaller but still rather high proportions believe that weight-related and age-related rationing exists too.

Having established what people think actually happens, we asked what they think should happen in each case.

Who *should* get priority, or should decisions not be made on this basis?

Smoking	%	Age	%	Weight	%
- non-smoker	39	- younger man	20	- average weight	29
- heavy smoker	2	- older man	5	- overweight	3
- no difference	49	- no difference	65	- no difference	55
- can't choose	9	- can't choose	9	- can't choose	12

Base 3085

As the table shows, the proportions of people who support health rationing by lifestyle or age are considerably lower than the proportions who believe it happens under the present system. There is most support (four in ten respondents) for discriminating in favour of non-smokers and least support (two in ten) for discriminating by age.

This does not, of course, imply that the majority reject the idea of rationing in principle. It is quite possible that they simply reject the three criteria for rationing implied by our questions. Other criteria, such as the degree of need, whether the treatment is likely to work, or whether the candidate has a dependent family, might be more popular.

Who supports health care rationing?

As before, we used regression models to investigate which socio-demographic factors or attitudes are associated with people's beliefs about rationing.[7] In the first place, people with pro-welfare views in general are

much less likely than others to favour health care rationing on the basis of either lifestyle or age - perhaps because it is felt to constitute a challenge to the principles of equality of treatment implied by universal welfare. There are also predictable elements of self-interest in people's views on rationing. Non-smokers, for instance, are significantly more likely than smokers to favour discrimination in favour of the non-smoker. But, with respect to discrimination on grounds of age, the story is more complex. Not only those under 30 (predictably) but also those over 75 turn out to be more accepting than others of rationing by age. This may be a function of a more accepting attitude generally among older people, coupled perhaps with long experience and wisdom about the realities of life and a degree of humility about what an individual ought to expect from the state. Moreover, many of them - old enough to remember the period before the NHS - might be less likely to hold the idealistic view that the NHS is capable of doing everything.

Women are less likely than men to favour rationing, reflecting, perhaps, the widely-held stereotype that women are more 'caring' at the individual level. As for class differences, the higher one's social class and education level, the more pro-rationing one is, all other factors being equal. This could, of course, be a function of their likely greater interest in public affairs and therefore a greater familiarity with the debates. Or it could be that they are simply more likely to accept an apparent weakening of the concepts of universality and comprehensiveness in welfare provision.

Who should make the rationing decisions?

We asked all respondents:

> *If decisions like this had to be made, who would you most trust to decide whether non-smokers or smokers should get the operation first?*

As the next table shows, choosing from a given list, most people wanted doctors to take rationing decisions, with little support for any of the other candidates.[8]

Where should responsibility for rationing reside?

	%
The government	2
Managers working for health authorities	2
Managers in hospitals	4
Hospital doctors	75
Can't choose	16
Base	*3085*

This represents an overwhelming vote of confidence in doctors as opposed to politicians or bureaucrats of one kind or another. It suggests too that people favour decisions based at least partly on individual circumstances rather than ones made at a political level and then implemented according to a prescribed set of 'rules'.

Conclusion

The financing and organisational structure of the National Health Service has risen in political prominence during the 1980s and 1990s, gaining in the process a high and sustained media interest. Partly deriving from this, public interest has been high too.

Levels of dissatisfaction with health care provision fluctuated somewhat between 1983 and 1996, but they rose inexorably over the period and ended higher than ever. It would not be surprising if this turned out to be one of the factors contributing to the defeat of the Conservatives at the 1997 general election. Certainly a strong association exists between actual levels of government spending on the NHS, people's public spending priorities and their dissatisfaction with the NHS. As the chart below shows, public support for higher spending and their levels of dissatisfaction with the NHS increased in tandem in the second half of the 1980s while funding increases were relatively small, then fell back somewhat in the early 1990s in the wake of the spending increases prior to the 1992 election, only to reassert themselves when spending levels faltered once again almost to a standstill in the period prior to the 1997 election.

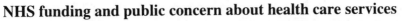

NHS funding and public concern about health care services

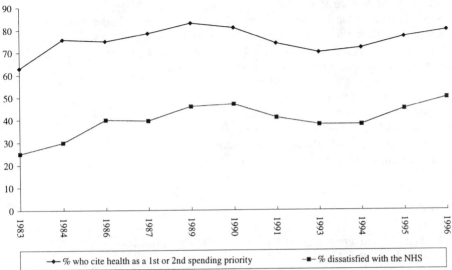

—◆— % who cite health as a 1st or 2nd spending priority   —■— % dissatisfied with the NHS

It has been argued that cuts in health spending can precipitate increases in private insurance which would lead to a reduction in demand for increased spending on the NHS (Besley *et al.*, 1996). But our findings offer little support for this conclusion, with only a two percentage point rise since 1991 in the number of people covered by private health insurance. On the contrary, it seems that despite growing dissatisfaction with the NHS, only a very small proportion of the public either wish to, or can afford to, abandon it in favour of private health provision.

So what of the future of the NHS? On the basis of public opinion alone, there appears to be little support for major changes in the traditional mechanism of financing the NHS through the tax system. Radical moves in the direction of promoting private health insurance or of restricting access to health care to certain social groups would risk offending public opinion at large and Labour supporters in particular. Less risky, it seems, would be to contemplate new and more explicit forms of health care rationing. But the public's willingness to embrace change in the NHS should not be overestimated. Caution will need to be the watchword in any future policy.

Notes

1. The increases shown are in volume terms; they have been adjusted to take account of general inflation in the economy as a whole and the higher than average level of costs of providing labour intensive services such as health care. This indicator is the best possible guide to the real volume of service inputs available to the NHS but it understates the real costs to the taxpayer because it takes account of the relative price effect.
2. The table shows the top six priorities (from a list of ten) for government spending.

3. Mulligan and Judge (1997) have also shown a rise in dissatisfaction with the overall running of the NHS since 1991.

4. The same is true of the hospital service, where organisational issues, such as waiting times, are more often criticised than the service from doctors and nurses.

5. The variables used in the models included: *sex, age, ethnicity, tenure, economic activity, occupation, education, social class, income, the 'welfarism' scale, the 'left-right' scale, experience of hospital services, and region.* For details of the welfare and left-right scales, see Appendix I to this Report.

6. The models can be found in the Appendix to this chapter. For a fuller description of regression models, see Appendix I to this Report.

7. The models can be found in the Appendix to this chapter.

8. These results are consistent with other surveys (e.g. Kneeshaw, 1997).

References

Besley, T., Hall, J. and Preston, I. (1996), *Private Health Insurance and the State of the NHS,* London: Institute for Fiscal Studies.

Bosanquet, N. (1994), 'Improving health' in *British Social Attitudes, 11th Report,* Jowell, R., Curtice, J., Brook, L. and Ahrendt, D. (eds.), Aldershot: Dartmouth.

Department of Health (1989), *Working for Patients,* London: HMSO.

Department of Health (1995), *The Government's expenditure plans 1995/6 to 1997/98,* London: HMSO.

Dixon, J. and Harrison, A. (1997), 'A little local difficulty?', *British Medical Journal,* **314**.

Griffiths, R. (1983), *NHS Management Inquiry: the Griffiths report,* London: DHSS.

Grimley Evans, J. (1997), 'Rationing healthcare by age: the case against', *British Medical Journal,* **314**.

Harris, J. (1997), 'Maximising the health of the whole community: the case against', *British Medical Journal,* **314**.

Harrison, A. and New, B. (1996), *Health Care 1995/96: An Annual Review of Health Care Policy,* London: King's Fund.

Healthcare 2000. (1995), *UK Health and Healthcare Services. Challenges and Policy Options,* London: Healthcare 2000.

Judge, K. and Soloman, M. (1993), 'Public opinion and the National Health Service: patterns and perspectives in consumer satisfaction', *Journal Social Policy,* **22**.

Kneeshaw, J. (1997), forthcoming, 'What does the public think about rationing? A review of the evidence' in New, B. (ed.) *Rationing: Talk and Action in Health Care,* London: King's Fund/British Medical Journal.

Le Grand, J. (1991), *Equity and Choice: An Essay in Economics and Applied Philosophy,* London: Harper Collins.

Lenaghan, J. (1996), *Rationing and Rights in Health Care,* London: Institute for Public Policy Research.

Mechanic, D. (1995), 'Dilemmas in rationing health care services: the case for implicit rationing', *British Medical Journal,* **310**.

Mossialos, E. (1997), 'Citizens' views on health care systems in the 15 member states of the European Union', *Health Economics,* **6**.

Mulligan, J. and Judge, K. (1997, forthcoming), 'Public opinion and the NHS' in Harrison, A. and New, B. (eds.), *Health Care UK 1996/97: An Annual Review of Health Care Policy,* London: King's Fund.

Royal Commission on the National Health Service (1979), CMND 7615, *Report* (Chairman: Sir Alec Merrison), London: HMSO.

Tomlinson, B. (1992), *Report of the Inquiry into London's Health Service, Medical Education and Research,* London: HMSO.

Townsend, P. and Davidson, N. (1992), *Inequalities in Health: The Black Report*, London: Penguin.

Turnberg, L., Lessof, M. and Watkins, P. (1996), 'Physicians clarify their proposal for a National Council for Health Care Priorities', *British Medical Journal*, **312.**

Underwood, M. *et al.* (1993), 'Should smokers be offered coronary bypass surgery?', *British Medical Journal*, **306**.

Williams, A. (1997), 'Rationing healthcare by age: the case for', *British Medical Journal*, **314**.

Acknowledgements

SCPR is grateful to the Department of Health whose financial support for the *British Social Attitudes* survey since 1990 has enabled us to continue to ask questions about health care. The authors would like to thank Lucy Johnson, Research Librarian at the King's Fund, for compiling data on NHS media stories.

Appendix

Media coverage of National Health Service issues

This table shows the number of stories about health or the NHS which mentioned one or more of the terms 'finance', 'expenditure' or 'spending' and which appeared in the main daily broadsheet newspapers in England between 1983 and 1997.

Number of media stories on health

	1983	1985	1987	1989	1990	1991	1992	1993	1994	1995	1996
Telegraph	82	110	157	408	349	269	240	222	206	246	295
Times	97	170	181	77	318	202	230	216	209	214	268
Guardian	111	153	153	35	331	296	273	287	280	353	362
Independent	0	0	0	300	358	318	270	284	256	299	331
Total (excludes *Independent*)	290	433	491	520	998	767	743	725	695	813	925
Total (includes *Independent*)	290	433	491	820	1356	1085	1013	1009	951	1112	1256

Multivariate analysis

The logistic regression models referred to in the chapter follow. Logistic regression is explained in more detail in Appendix I to this Report.

The models report the *coefficients* (or parameter estimates) for each of the characteristics specified on the left side of the table. Each coefficient shows whether that particular characteristic differs significantly from its 'comparison group' in its association with the 'dependent variable', the variable we are investigating. The association between the dependent variable and each of the variables included in the model is significant at a 95% level. The same variables were not included in all models. Only those where the coefficient is shown were included in the relevant model. In each case, the comparison group will be all those not included in the model (for example, in looking at Model B, all those aged 18-29 or 30-44 are compared to all those aged 45 and over; in Model C, as only the 18-29 year olds are included in the model, they are compared to all those aged 30 and over).

The derivation and meaning of most variables in the models is clear. Those requiring further explanation are defined below:

Lower income:	household income less than £10,000 per annum.
Higher income:	household income greater than £32,000 per annum.
Higher social class:	social class I or II.
Pro-welfare:	scored 0 to 2.5 on the welfare scale.
Anti-welfare:	scored 3.5 to 5 on the welfare scale.
Left:	scored 0 to 2 on the left-right scale.
Right:	scored 3 to 5 on the left-right scale.

Models A to E: Dissatisfaction with health services

	Model A NHS	Model B GPs	Model C NHS dentists	Model D Inpatient care	Model E Outpatient
Works in NHS	0.90**		0.51**		
Female		-0.30*			
Age					
18-29		0.81**	-0.32**		
30-44		0.48**			0.30**
Non-white		0.74**		0.52*	
Highest qualification					
None				-0.36**	
Degree					
Income level					
Lower income	-0.34**	-0.32*	-0.58**		
Higher income					0.40**
Social class					
Higher class			0.37**		
Economic status					
Retired	-0.65**			-0.80**	-0.63**
At home	-0.56**				
Unemployed					-0.56*
Welfare scale					
Pro-welfare	0.52**		0.25*	0.36**	
Anti-welfare					
Left-right scale					
Left	0.57**	0.55**	0.24*		0.35**
Right	-0.50**		-0.38**		
Lives in London	0.38**	0.38*	0.30*	0.71**	0.55**

*   = significant at 0.05
** = significant at 0.01

Models F to K: Should rationing decisions be made according to lifestyle or age?

	Smoking	
	Model F **Priority for non-smoker**	*Model G* **No difference**
Female	-0.23**	
Age		
18-29	0.21*	-0.27*
Qualifications		
Degree	0.30**	
Income level		
Lower income		-0.23*
Welfare scale		
Pro-welfare	-0.27**	0.50**
Anti-welfare	0.43**	
Non-smoker	1.71**	-1.51**

	Age	
	Model H **Priority for young**	*Model I* **No difference**
Female	-0.39**	0.28**
Age		
18-29		-0.61**
75+		-0.85**
Higher social class	0.26**	
Welfare scale		
Pro-welfare		0.19*
Anti-welfare	0.40**	-0.29**

	Weight and diet	
	Model J **Priority for average weight**	*Model K* **No difference**
Age		
75+	0.49**	-0.68**
Qualifications		
None	-0.33**	
Retired	0.24**	-0.21*
Higher social class	0.33**	
Welfare scale		
Pro-welfare	-0.38**	0.36**

* = significant at 0.05
** = significant at 0.01

4 Benefit claimants: villains or victims?

Caroline Bryson[*]

Both the late Conservative and current Labour governments have been committed to cutting spending on social security. Extra spending in this area is certainly not at the top of the public agenda.[1] Yet government spending on social security has never been higher than over the past decade. Historically high unemployment levels, increased economic inactivity among men, the growth of lone parenthood, increased reliance on in-work benefits and an ageing population mean that over a quarter of families are now reliant on means-tested benefits (Piachaud, 1997).

Successive governments have sought to make paid work more attractive, and state benefits less so, by keeping increases in benefit levels below those of average earnings, by introducing more stringent benefit eligibility requirements[2] and by improving in-work benefits. On the Conservative side, this approach has been motivated by the belief that social security claimants often *choose* to rely on benefits. If pushed, the argument goes, they could find work or other means of support (Lilley, 1993; Conservative Party, 1997). True, the new Labour government shares the Conservative view that benefit fraud is a widespread problem, but their 'welfare to work' rhetoric takes as its starting point the belief that it is the benefit system, and not claimants, which is at fault. The system is seen to 'trap' claimants on benefits: Labour's aim is to reform it to become a 'springboard' into work and self-sufficiency (Labour Party, 1997).

This chapter begins by examining public attitudes towards welfare in general, focusing on how these may have changed over time. We then

[*] Caroline Bryson is a Senior Researcher at SCPR and a Co-director of the *British Social Attitudes* survey series.

examine attitudes towards benefits and benefit recipients (concentrating largely upon unemployment benefits and recipients). We start by assessing public support for the two broad views of benefit recipients previously outlined. Do, in other words, people see benefit claimants as 'villains' engaged in 'working the system', or in some way as being its 'victims'? Further, how do the public perceive life on benefits to be? Are claimants seen to be living in poverty, or in relative comfort? Finally, we examine the attitudes of the unemployed themselves, in order to assess that most common of stereotypes - that of the 'work-shy' claimant.

Data and definitions

The *British Social Attitudes* survey has included questions on social security since the mid-1980s, enabling us to examine changes in attitudes over time. However, during the last fifteen years many other changes have taken place, which can make it difficult to interpret findings. The economy has moved up and down in line with the business cycle. And the socio-demographic composition of the population has changed. Throughout this chapter we will refer to regression models which test the impact of these sorts of changes on attitudes towards social security. In particular, they enable us to evaluate whether any changes we find reflect the movements of the business cycle, changes in the composition of the population as a whole or, conversely, a more fundamental shift in attitudes.[3]

The growth or decline of welfarism?

Attitudes towards welfare can be seen as lying along a continuum. At one end are those most in favour of welfare provision and its role in redistributing income from rich to poor; at the other, those who take a more 'individualist' approach and would rather minimise the government's involvement in this area. To assess this, we ask a number of questions which have been developed over time to measure what we call 'welfarism'. Using responses to these questions we can construct a 'scale', which gives people a score of between one and five. The lower a person's score on the scale, the more 'pro-welfare' or 'welfarist' they are.[4]

Over the last decade public support for welfare has fluctuated. As the next table shows, attitudes became more 'pro-welfare' between 1987 and 1993 (that is, the average 'score' on our scale went down) and more 'anti-welfare' from 1994 onwards. Thus, during the mid-1990s people have increasingly tended to feel that welfare provision is making people less willing to take responsibility for themselves and that many of those dependent on benefits are in some way 'undeserving'.

Mean score on welfare scale

	1987	1989	1991	1993	1994	1995	1996
	2.91	2.88	2.85	2.82	2.94	3.05	3.02
Base	*1281*	*1307*	*2481*	*2567*	*2929*	*3135*	*3119*

These scores relate closely to the economic climate of the time. In times of high unemployment, such as 1987 and 1993, 'welfarism' is relatively high, subsequently falling again as the economic climate improves. Scores also vary substantially between different groups. The highly educated (those with degrees or higher level qualifications) are, for instance, more pro-welfare than those with no qualifications, and the unemployed more pro-welfare than those in work. People in Scotland or the north of England are more pro-welfare than those in southern England. Age also matters, with the over-60s being the most anti-welfare in their outlook. So before we can assess whether attitudes towards welfare have really changed over time, we need to disentangle these other relationships. Otherwise we will be unable to see whether there has been a long term shift in attitudes or whether this change reflects other changes, either in the socio-demographic make-up of Britain or in external factors such as the unemployment rate. In order to do this we use a form of analysis known as regression, a statistical modelling technique which establishes the importance of relationships between various factors (a more detailed description of regression techniques can be found in Appendix I to this Report). Our model clearly shows that although some of the movements in attitudes reflect the state of the economy - with people being more pro-welfare when unemployment is high - this alone does not fully account for a shift towards a more favourable view of welfare during the early 1990s and a less favourable view since then. This movement is apparent even when socio-demographic characteristics and changes over time are taken into account (see model A in the appendix to this chapter).

Benefit claimants: villains or victims?

Our findings show that over the last three years attitudes to welfare have shifted slightly towards a more anti-welfare position. How then do people view the most visible recipients of welfare - those on welfare benefits (and, in particular, those on unemployment benefits)? In this section we explore public support for two common political views of benefit recipients: one which 'blames' the individual more than the system; and the other which takes the system to be more at fault than individual claimants.

Firstly, are claimants 'unworthy' of the help they receive? The majority view is quite clearly 'no'. We asked people whether they thought many people getting social security didn't actually "deserve any help". Although a substantial minority (28 per cent) agreed, the majority did not. We also asked more specifically about the unemployed - whether they were 'work-shy' and

could find a job if they really wanted one, and whether most of those on unemployment benefits were 'fiddling' the system. Here the picture is more mixed. On each of these two subjects as many people agree as disagree with the statement. Still, on none of the propositions is the negative view of benefit recipients the majority view.

Attitudes towards benefit recipients (1996)

		Agree	Neither agree nor disagree	Disagree
Many people who get social security benefit don't really deserve any help	%	28	28	42
Around here, most unemployed people could find a job if they really wanted one	%	39	22	37
Most people on the dole are fiddling in one way or another	%	35	32	31

Base 3119

Perhaps not surprisingly, attitudes towards benefit recipients, and the unemployed in particular, harden when the unemployment rate is low, and soften in recession. As the next table shows, during the 'Lawson' boom of the late 1980s people may have felt that opportunities existed for *everyone* to work, and that anyone who remained unemployed was simply not trying hard enough. Then, in 1989, 52 per cent thought most unemployed people in their area could find a job 'if they really wanted one'. But during the worst of the recession in the early 1990s, people's views softened, with the proportion taking this view falling to 27 per cent by 1993, and then rising slightly as the economy began to recover. Despite this, criticism of the unemployed has never again reached its 1989 levels.

Attitudes towards benefit fraud do not follow the same trend. Here there has been very little change at all over the last decade. Throughout the period around a third of people take the view that many of the unemployed are 'fiddling the system', with two-thirds not sharing this view. The late Conservative government's focus upon fraud and benefit dependency appears neither to have been based upon the concerns of a clear public majority, nor to have been particularly successful in changing public attitudes over time.

Attitudes towards benefit recipients

	1987	1989	1991	1993	1994	1995	1996
% agree							
Many people who get social security benefit don't really deserve any help	31	29	26	24	26	30	28
Around here, most unemployed people could find a job if they really wanted one	41	52	38	27	32	38	39
Most people on the dole are fiddling in one way or another	32	33	28	31	34	33	35
Base	*1281*	*1307*	*2481*	*2567*	*2929*	*3135*	*3119*

Regression analysis confirms that people are more likely to perceive claimants as undeserving and the unemployed as work-shy when unemployment levels are low, and that attitudes towards benefit fraud are indeed unrelated to unemployment levels (see model B in the Appendix to this chapter). However, even when we take into account changes in the unemployment rate, attitudes have still changed over time. For instance, people nowadays are more likely than they were in the late 1980s to think that social security claimants are undeserving of help, but are less likely to think the unemployed are work-shy. Given the slight move towards a more 'anti-welfare' culture since the late 1980s, we can only speculate as to the reasons behind such increased sympathy for the unemployed. It is possible that attitudes have lagged some way behind economic recovery, or that the recession, perhaps by touching some of those previously immune to such insecurity (such as professionals or those living in the south of England) has had a more than cyclical impact. Now, perhaps, people are slightly less inclined to blame the unemployed and are more likely to feel some degree of sympathy for their plight. Or it may simply be that other groups of claimants - lone parents, for instance - have replaced the unemployed as the public's *bête noir* when it comes to social security issues.

What, however, of the alternative view - that the system is in some way to blame for the predicament of benefit recipients? Perhaps, rather than being 'villains' within the system, many of those on benefits are its 'victims', unable to escape from a situation which has sapped their self-sufficiency? Certainly, there is some support for the general view that the welfare state has made people "less willing to look after themselves". Over four in ten people (44 per cent) take this view, and three in ten disagree. But when it comes to the more specific view that benefits actually prevent people standing on their own feet, only a third agree, with 42 per cent disagreeing.

Attitudes towards the welfare system (1996)

		Agree	Neither agree nor disagree	Disagree
The welfare state makes people nowadays less willing to look after themselves	%	44	24	30
If welfare benefits weren't so generous people would learn to stand on their own two feet	%	33	24	42

Base 3119

As the next table shows, concern about the system fell in the early 1990s and rose again in the middle of the decade. In the case of whether or not the welfare state prevents people 'standing on their own feet', statistical models show that this movement is partly a reflection of the business cycle (see model C in the Appendix to this chapter). But changes in the business cycle do not fully account for the shift in attitudes over the decade. Together with the remainder of our findings so far, it seems that we can indeed conclude that the climate for welfare has become somewhat less favourable in recent years.

Attitudes towards the welfare system

	1987	1989	1991	1993	1994	1995	1996
% agree							
The welfare state makes people nowadays less willing to look after themselves	52	39	33	41	44	47	44
If welfare benefits weren't so generous people would learn to stand on their own two feet	33	32	26	25	27	33	33
Base	*1281*	*1307*	*2481*	*2567*	*2929*	*3135*	*3119*

These findings suggest that attitudes towards welfare recipients conform neither to a 'villain' nor a 'victim' model. These two views should not be seen as mutually exclusive alternatives. Many of those who agree with the notion that benefit recipients are in some way to blame for their plight are also critical of the system as well. The next table focuses on those people who expressed a negative view of the benefit system, and shows whether they also have a negative view of benefit recipients. As many as 45 per cent of those who have a negative view of the system also have a negative view of welfare recipients, compared with only 28 per cent among the population in general. Rather than either blaming benefit recipients *or* blaming the welfare system, many people blame both - but the majority blame neither.[5]

Blaming recipients versus blaming the system (1996) [6]

	All	All who agree with negative system view
	%	%
Negative view of recipient		
Agree	28	45
Neither agree nor disagree	28	29
Disagree	42	26
Base	*3119*	*1378*

Living on benefit: poverty or relative comfort?

How can we interpret the concern that exists about welfare? Is it based upon a clear perception of the issues at stake and the way in which the system operates? Or, rather, is it the product of social myths and stereotypes about benefit claimants and, in particular, the unemployed. We turn now to examine this question, concentrating upon the knowledge people have about unemployment benefits and the extent to which they allow an adequate daily existence. To examine this, we ask people to consider two scenarios. In the first we refer simply to 'unemployment benefits', whereas in the second we specify the exact amount of money that these benefits would entail:

> *Thinking of a married couple without children living only on unemployment benefits. Would you say that they are really poor, hard up, have enough to live on or have more than enough to live on?*

> *Now thinking of a married couple without children living on £78 per week.[7] Would you say that they are really poor, hard up, have enough to live on or have more than enough to live on?*

If public perceptions of the unemployed are based upon a clear understanding of the value of the benefits to which they are entitled, we would expect people to respond to both these questions in a similar way. Instead, we find that many people obviously grossly overestimate how much benefit people are paid. For instance, a sixth consider a couple "living only on unemployment benefits" to be "really poor". But when the actual *amount* this couple live on is specified, the proportion who think they are "really poor" more than doubles - to over a third.[8]

How well-off are the unemployed ... (1996)

		... really poor	... hard up	... enough to live on	... more than than enough
Married couple on unemployment benefits	%	15	50	24	2
Married couple on £78 per week	%	37	50	11	1

Base 614

As the next table shows, this gap between what we might call people's 'superficial' perceptions about the financial position of unemployed and their views once more 'informed' has always existed. And while superficial perceptions have fluctuated slightly over time, with sympathy seeming to peak during times of high unemployment, attitudes towards the more informed scenario have remained relatively constant over the last decade. Many public reactions to welfare recipients and the benefits they receive thus seem more to reflect the economic climate and general attitudes towards welfare than a clear understanding of the financial situation that the unemployed find themselves within.

How well-off are the unemployed?

% saying couple are "really poor"	1986	1989	1991	1993	1996
Married couple on unemployment benefits	12	12	17	18	15
Married couple on £78* per week	39	42	41	40	37
Base	*1548*	*1516*	*1473*	*1461*	*614*

* £78 per week was the amount cited in 1996. This amount has risen over the years to reflect actual benefit levels at the time.

The 'work-shy' unemployed?

We have seen that public attitudes towards welfare recipients, particularly the unemployed, have fluctuated over time. What of the views of claimants themselves? Here we focus on the unemployed, traditionally the group most likely to come under fire from policy makers and the public as being undeserving.

Views of the benefit system

It is not surprising that we find that the unemployed are more 'pro-welfare' on our 'welfarism' scale than those in paid work. As the next table shows, they are also much less likely than workers to feel that benefit claimants are undeserving of help, are 'working the system' or are work-shy. For instance,

15 per cent of the unemployed agree that "many people who get social security don't really deserve any help", compared with 28 per cent of workers. And these differences remain even when we take account of key differences between the unemployed and workers in characteristics such as qualification levels (see models A, B and C in the appendix to this chapter). Of course, the remaining differences probably stem largely from the varying self-interests of these two groups (Taylor-Gooby, 1995). After all, workers are the least likely, and the unemployed the most likely, to rely on current help from the benefit system.

Attitudes towards claimants (1996)

	In paid work	Unemployed
% agree		
Many people who get social security benefit don't really deserve any help	28	15
Around here, most unemployed people could find a job if they really wanted one	43	31
Most people on the dole are fiddling in one way or another	35	24
Base	*1597*	*159*

Similarly, the unemployed are substantially less likely than workers to have negative views of the benefit system itself. A third of workers agree with the view that the generosity of welfare benefits prevents people standing 'on their own two feet', double the proportion of the unemployed who feel this way. Once again, this holds true even when we take into account other differences between workers and the unemployed.

	In paid work	Unemployed
% agree		
The welfare state makes people nowadays less willing to look after themselves	43	29
If welfare benefits weren't so generous people would learn to stand on their own two feet	32	15
Base	*1597*	*159*

Attitudes of the unemployed to work

That the unemployed are more supportive than average of welfare is hardly perhaps surprising. Their views, just as those of workers, will be strongly coloured by their own interests. But does this self-interest stem from

something deeper than a simple unwillingness to attack a system they depend on? Might it, perhaps, partly reflect a lack of interest in, or commitment to, the world of work? Does this merely support the stereotype of the 'work-shy' unemployed?

Since 1985, we have asked those in work and the unemployed about the meaning they attach to work:

> *To some people their job is simply something they do in order to earn a living. For others it is much more than that...*
> Workers: *On balance, is your present job just a means of earning a living, or does it mean much more to you than that?*
> Unemployed: *In general, do you think of work as just a means of earning a living, or does it mean much more to you than that?*

Now, as in previous years, nearly two thirds of the unemployed (64 per cent) say that work means more to them than being "just a means of earning a living". A similar proportion of those in work give this response. Of course, we should compare these figures cautiously. For workers, the question relates specifically to their current job - whereas for the unemployed it refers more widely to work 'in general'. However, it is very clear that the unemployed certainly value work in much the same way as many of those in paid work.

Commitment to work (1996)

	In work	Unemployed
	%	%
Work...		
... is just a means of earning a living	31	35
... means much more than that	68	64
Base	*1597*	*159*

A number of different factors are related to attitudes towards work. Having a stronger 'work ethic' or more positive attitude towards work is more common among those with higher level qualifications and who work in non-manual occupations (Hedges, 1994). As these are precisely the groups which are under-represented among the unemployed, it is likely that we have actually underestimated the extent to which work means more to this group than simply "earning a living". Statistical modelling which 'controls' for the characteristics of the unemployed and those in work bears this out (see model D in the appendix to this chapter). In fact, once these characteristics are taken into account, the unemployed actually have a *higher* level of work commitment than workers (although we still need to bear in mind the need for caution when comparing the responses of these two groups). Clearly, however, an overwhelming majority of the unemployed feel work should

fulfil more than just material needs alone. This certainly does not sit easily with notions of the 'job-shy' unemployed.

Conclusion

During the late 1970s, the state's role in redistributing income from tax-paying workers to non-workers through the social security system (and the welfare state in general) was considerably challenged (Joseph, 1975). Many of these debates subsequently informed policy formation for almost two decades. Concerns existed that social security claimants, particularly the unemployed, had become 'dependent' on welfare and were 'scroungers' wilfully avoiding work (Murray, 1984).

The fervour and ferocity of many of these debates makes it all the more surprising that a majority of the public do not appear to have had the same concerns. True, in the mid-1990s there has been a slight movement towards a more 'anti-welfare' perspective, but even now only a minority agree, for instance, that claimants are generally undeserving or that the unemployed are' 'fiddling' the system. The Conservative government's crusade certainly does not seem to have significantly increased public concern. In the future, reformers would be wise to bear this in mind. Furthermore, the concern that does exist about welfare benefits shows that it does not divide neatly into two exclusive camps: those of 'blame the victim' versus 'blame the system'. Rather, these concerns are highly related to one another. Any attempt to focus on one to the exclusion of the other will probably obtain lower public support than a more integrated approach.

Finally, what of the unemployed themselves? There certainly seems little evidence that many of the unemployed lack the motivation to work, or that they fail to value work in the same way as those already in employment. Consequently, removing disincentives to work and improving the supply of work available might well receive the desired response from the unemployed - without, perhaps, requiring some of the penalties mooted at times by a public gallery keen to see the responsibilities of claimants vigorously enforced.

Notes

1. Since 1983, *British Social Attitudes* has included a question on government spending priorities. When asked what should be the government's first priority for extra spending, people have consistently chosen health care and education (54 per cent and 28 per cent respectively in 1996). Never more than seven per cent of people have thought that the first spending priority should be social security benefits (three per cent in 1996).
2. This preoccupation has guided reform to unemployment benefits and incapacity benefits (Lilley, 1993). Here, and throughout the chapter, the figures for the years 1983 to 1995 are taken from Bryson, 1996.

3. The models we report on include the following characteristics and are reported on in detail in the Appendix to this chapter:
   Socio-demographic characteristics: age; sex; presence of children in the household; housing tenure; qualifications; economic activity (work, unemployment etc.); economic activity of partner; region or country; social class.
   External factors: year; unemployment rate (according to the *International Labour Organisation* - or ILO - definition).
4. More details of the 'welfarism' scale are shown in Appendix I to this report.
5. Statistical models, not shown here, back up these findings.
6. The question used to illustrate the 'blame the system' view is 'the welfare state makes people less willing to look after themselves'. The question used for 'blame the recipient' view is 'many people who get social security don't really deserve any help'.
7. £78 per week was the amount cited in 1996 (the benefit level for a couple on unemployment benefits in 1996). This amount cited has risen over the years to reflect actual benefit levels at the time.
8. This gap may partially be explained by confusion over whether "£78 per week" includes or excludes housing costs (it excludes them).

References

Bryson, C. (1996), *Trends in Attitudes to Health Care 1983 to 1995*, London: SCPR.

Conservative Party (1997), *The Choice of Two Futures: the Conservative Party Manifesto*, London: The Conservative Party.

Hedges, B. (1994), 'Work in a changing climate', in Jowell, R., Curtice, J., Brook, L. and Ahrendt, D. (eds.), *British Social Attitudes: the 11th Report*, Aldershot: Dartmouth.

Joseph, K. (1975), 'Reversing the trend: a critical reappraisal of Conservative economic and social policies', Seven speeches by the Right Honourable Keith Joseph, Barry Rose.

Labour Party (1997), 'Getting welfare to work: a new vision for social security', *The Road to the Manifesto*, London: The Labour Party.

Lilley, P. (1993), 'Benefits and costs: securing the future of social security', Mais Lecture.

Murray, C. (1984), *Losing ground*, New York: Basic Books.

Piachaud, D. (1997), 'The growth of means testing' in Walker, A. and Walker, C. (eds.), *Britain Divided: the Growth of Social Exclusion in the 1980s and 1990s*, London: CPAG.

Taylor-Gooby, P. (1995), 'Comfortable, marginal and excluded: who should pay higher taxes for a better welfare state?', in Jowell, R., Curtice, J., Park, A., Brook, L. and Ahrendt, D. (eds.), *British Social Attitudes: the 12th Report*, Aldershot: Dartmouth.

Acknowledgement to the Department for Social Security

SCPR is grateful to the Department for Social Security whose financial support for the survey since 1991 has enabled us to continue to ask questions about welfare and social security.

Appendix

Multivariate analysis

Models referred to in the chapter follow. Two multivariate techniques were used: multiple regression (Model A) and logistic regression (Models B to D). These are explained in more detail in Appendix I to this Report.

Each model is based upon all respondents who answered the relevant question. This means that certain survey years are excluded because the question was not asked that year. The models report the *coefficients* (or parameter estimates) for each of the characteristics specified on the left side of the table. Each coefficient shows whether that particular characteristic differs significantly from its 'comparison group' in its association with the 'dependent variable', the variable we are investigating (in Model A below, for instance, the dependent variable is the 'welfarism' scale). Details of the comparison group are supplied in brackets. Two asterisks indicate that the coefficient is statistically significant at a 99% level, and one asterisk that it is significant at a 95% level.

Not all models are shown in this appendix. Full details are available from the author.

Model A: The 'Welfarism' scale

Here a negative coefficient indicates that those with the characteristic have a more welfarist view than the comparison group; a positive coefficient that they have a less welfarist view.

Characteristic (comparison group in brackets)	Coefficient
Year (1987-1989)	
1991-1993	- 0.06**
1994-1996	0.31**
High unemployment rate (low)	- 0.10**
Age (60 plus)	
18-29	- 0.16**
30-44	- 0.28**
45-59	- 0.18**
Male (female)	- 0.05**
Having children in the household (none)	- 0.05**
Owner occupier (not owner occupier)	0.16**
Highest qualification (no qualifications)	
Degree	- 0.41**
Higher education	- 0.13**
A level	- 0.11**
O level	- 0.06**
CSE	0.01
Economic status (in paid work)	
Unemployed	- 0.40**
Retired	- 0.01
At home	- 0.16**
Other	- 0.32**
Status of partner (not in work)	
Partner working	0.12**
No partner	0.06**
Region (South of England)	
Scotland	- 0.21**
North of England	- 0.12**
Midlands	- 0.00
Wales	- 0.00

Social Class was included in the model, but was insignificant

Models B and C: Benefit claimants: villains or victims?

Here a positive coefficient indicates that those with the characteristic are more likely than the comparison group to agree with the statement; a negative coefficient that they are less likely to agree.

Characteristic (comparison group in brackets)	**Model B:** *Many people on social security don't deserve any help* Coefficient	**Model C:** *The welfare state makes people less willing to look after themselves* Coefficient
Year (1987-1989)		
1991-1993	- 0.01	- 0.16*
1994-1996	0.14**	0.31**
High unemployment rate (low)	- 0.15**	0.00
Age (60 plus)		
18-29	- 0.70**	- 0.73**
30-44	- 0.68**	- 0.69**
45-59	- 0.42**	- 0.44**
Male (female)	0.06	0.10*
Having children in the household (none)	- 0.11*	- 0.16**
Owner occupier (not owner occupier)	0.07	0.28**
Highest qualification (no qualifications)		
Degree	- 1.07**	- 0.42**
Higher education	- 0.43**	- 0.01
A level	- 0.39**	- 0.03
O level	- 0.24**	- 0.01
CSE	- 0.12	- 0.05
Economic status (in paid work)		
Unemployed	- 0.67**	- 0.45**
Retired	- 0.19*	0.04
At home	- 0.30**	0.01
Other	- 0.49**	- 0.37**
Status of partner (not in work)		
Partner working	0.09	0.07
No partner	- 0.11*	- 0.08
Region (South of England)		
Scotland	- 0.36**	- 0.18**
North of England	- 0.27*	- 0.18**
Midlands	- 0.15**	0.05
Wales	- 0.06	- 0.04
Social Class (I)		
II	0.17*	- 0.03
III non-manual	0.16	- 0.07
III manual	0.17	- 0.23**
IV	0.07	- 0.21**
V	- 0.01	- 0.33**

Model D: The work commitment of workers and the unemployed

A positive coefficient indicates that those with the characteristic have higher levels of work commitment than the comparison group; a negative coefficient that they have lower levels of work commitment.

Characteristic (comparison group in brackets)	Coefficient
Year (1987-1989)	
1991-1993	- 0.19**
1994-1996	- 0.32**
High unemployment rate (low)	- 0.09*
Age (45 plus)	
18-29	- 0.39**
30-44	- 0.09
Male (female)	- 0.33**
Highest qualification (no qualifications)	
Degree	0.96**
Higher education	0.60**
A level	0.45**
O level	0.20**
CSE	0.14
Economic status (in paid work)	
Unemployed	0.18**
Region (South of England)	
Scotland	- 0.15
North of England	- 0.24**
Midlands	- 0.06
Wales	- 0.09
Social Class (I)	
II	0.26*
III non-manual	- 0.74**
III manual	- 0.90**
IV	- 1.00**
V	- 1.23**

Presence of children, tenure and partner status were included in the model but were insignificant

5 Trust in the political system

John Curtice and Roger Jowell [*]

The final years of the last Conservative government were marked by a widespread sense of falling confidence not only in the government itself but also perhaps in the political system at large. Many of the concerns arose from allegations of sexual and financial 'sleaze' - mostly but not always relating to Conservative politicians. Some were accused of taking money to ask questions in the House of Commons, others of marital infidelity. In any event, Conservative MPs (and perhaps all MPs?) were increasingly having to fight off charges of hypocrisy: while advocating 'family values' for others, too many of them were palpably succumbing to financial or sexual temptation themselves.

We reported two years ago (Curtice and Jowell, 1995) that public trust in politicians and the political system was already in decline. But we wondered whether this was necessarily such a bad thing for democracy. A 'sceptical electorate' might well be preferable to a too deferential one. Moreover, our findings did not suggest that people with little trust in the system were less likely than others to vote in elections. On the contrary, far from rejecting the system and withdrawing from it along the lines of the so-called discontented minority in the US (Galbraith, 1992), they seemed particularly keen on improving democracy through reforms to the constitution such as those advocated by Charter '88.

---

[*] John Curtice is Reader in Politics and Director of the Social Statistics Laboratory, University of Strathclyde. Roger Jowell is Director of SCPR and a Visiting Professor at the LSE. John Curtice is also Deputy Director and Roger Jowell Co-Director of the ESRC Centre for Research into Elections and Social Trends (CREST), based at SCPR and Nuffield College, Oxford.

In this chapter we update and develop the picture we drew two years ago. First we examine the trend in public confidence in the political system during the dying days of the last government. Then, bearing in mind that the new Labour government is committed to a wide ranging package of constitutional changes, we examine how much public support there is for some of its proposed reforms, how strong and consistent that support is, and among whom. In short, we examine whether the new government has anything approaching a mandate to introduce radical constitutional change.

A crisis of confidence?

In an attempt to obtain a shorthand general indication of public confidence in the political system *per se*, a number of surveys conducted over the last twenty years or so have included the following question:

> *Which of these statements best describes your opinion on the system of governing Britain?*
>
> *It works extremely well and could not be improved*
> *It could be improved in small ways but it mainly works well*
> *It could be improved quite a lot*
> *It needs a great deal of improvement*

As the next table shows, a far higher proportion now believe that the system could be improved than was the case when the Kilbrandon Commission first asked this question a quarter century ago in 1973. On the other hand, the latest reading suggests that any long-term downward decline in confidence had abated and possibly been reversed by 1996, a year or so before the general election. Indeed, the 1996 figures are virtually identical to those obtained in 1977, some twenty years earlier. If the allegations of sleaze during the last parliament did indeed undermine confidence in the system as a whole, then on this evidence we might conclude that such damage was temporary: it could well be the 1994, and particularly the 1995, figures rather than the latest reading that are outliers. In any event, while the figures in the table hardly represent an unqualified public endorsement of the system, with nearly two in three still believing that the way we are governed could be substantially improved, they certainly do not represent any new crisis of confidence either.

Evaluations of the system of governing Britain

	1973	1977	1991	1994	1995	1996
The system of governing Britain ...	%	%	%	%	%	%
... "could not be improved" or "could be improved in small ways"	48	34	33	29	22	35
... could be improved "quite a lot" or "a great deal"	49	62	63	69	76	63

Sources: 1973: Royal Commission on the Constitution, *Memorandum of Dissent*, 1973; 1977: Opinion Research Centre Survey; 1991, 1995: MORI/Rowntree Trust State of the Nation Survey; 1994, 1996: SCPR's *British Social Attitudes* survey series.
Base (1996): 1180

One reason for believing that things are in need of improvement might be a lack of confidence in the people who run the system. If politicians and others are seen routinely to place their own interests above the wider public interest, then the public's confidence in the system itself is bound to suffer. On this subject we also have figures dating back more than twenty years, based on the following question:

*How much do you trust British governments of **any** party to place the needs of the nation above the interests of their own political party?*

	1974	1986	1987	1991	1994	1996
"Just about always" or "most of the time"	39	38	37	33	24	22
"Only some of the time" or "almost never"	57	57	60	63	73	75

Source: 1974: Political Action Study; 1986-1996: SCPR's *British Social Attitudes* survey series.
Base (1996): 1180

Here the answers confirm the strong downward trend in trust that we reported two years ago. Less than one in four people now trust governments to put the interests of the nation above that of party, a decline of some 15 percentage points in less than ten years; in contrast, the proportion had been more or less constant in the thirteen years prior to 1987. True, the British electorate have never been particularly trusting of their politicians, but events since 1987 seem to have made a big dent in whatever confidence there had been.

Naturally, aggregate answers to questions such as these - however carefully framed - are likely to be influenced by the popularity or otherwise of the current government. Yet, even among Conservative identifiers in our sample, only 32 per cent in 1996 said they now trusted the government to place the public interest over their party's interests either most of the time or always. Moreover, compared with two years earlier, party allegiance appears to have declined as a factor in determining respondents' views, for while Conservative identifiers have become less trusting, Labour identifiers (in the

year before the election) had perversely become a little more so - perhaps in anticipation of a new government.

Answers to similar questions about trust in other major institutions of government confirm this general pattern. As the next table shows, levels of trust in a variety of other public bodies are still substantially the same as they were two years ago. But it is even more the case now than it was ten years ago that those involved in central or local government - whether as local councillors, civil servants or (particularly) MPs - are viewed in a much worse light than, for instance, those who enforce the law, such as the police or the judiciary.

Trust in other institutions

	1987	1991	1994	1996
% saying following can be trusted "just about always" or "most of the time"				
British police not to bend the rules in trying to get a conviction	52	49	47	51
Judges to stand up to a government which wishes them to reach a particular verdict	n/a	n/a	n/a	48
Local councillors of any party to place the needs of their area above the interests of their party	31	25	31	28
Top civil servants to stand firm against a minister who wants to provide false information to parliament	46	n/a	27	28
Politicians of any party in Britain to tell the truth when they are in a tight corner	n/a	n/a	9	9

Base (1996): 1180
Source: 1987 for civil servants: British Election Study
n/a = not asked

Another possible reason for a widespread sense that the system of government is in need of improvement is that it is seen to be unresponsive to the demands and grievances of the public. This phenomenon is usually referred to as low *system efficacy*. Our findings suggest no abatement of the increased public frustration with the system of government that we first recorded in 1994. Over a quarter of the population now *strongly* agree that political parties and MPs alike are out of touch with the needs of the electorate, an increase of ten or more percentage points in the last ten years. Once again, recent years seem to have taken their toll.

System efficacy

% "strongly agree"	1974	1986	1987	1991	1994	1996
Parties are only interested in people's votes, not in their opinions	19	19	15	16	25	28
Generally speaking those we elect as MPs lose touch with people pretty quickly	19	16	16	16	25	26
It doesn't really matter which party is in power. In the end things go on much the same	n/a	n/a	n/a	11	16	16

Base (1996): 1180
Source: 1974: Political Action Study (Marsh). In that study respondents were given a four point scale ranging from "strongly agree" to "strongly disagree". In the subsequent *British Social Attitudes* studies answers were given on a five-point scale with a mid-point labelled "neither agree nor disagree".
n/a = not asked

Another rather different measure of efficacy is *personal efficacy* - the extent to which people feel they are themselves able to participate effectively in politics. Two years ago we reported that people were increasingly likely to feel frustrated in this respect too. But this trend now seems to have levelled off and possibly even to have reversed itself. In fact, on two of the three measures of personal efficacy included in the next table, the proportion *strongly* agreeing with pejorative statements is now no higher than it was more than twenty years ago. True, on the third item, the proportion strongly believing that they have no say in what the government does is still a lot higher than it was in 1974, but even so it is no higher than in 1986. So, while our regard for the British political system seems to have taken a tumble, our confidence in our own ability to participate effectively within the political arena does not seem to have been undermined in the process.

Personal efficacy

% "strongly agree"	1974	1986	1987	1991	1994	1996
People like me have no say in what the government does	14	23	20	16	28	24
Voting is the only way people like me can have any say about how the government runs things	15	n/a	n/a	12	19	15
Sometimes politics and government seem so complicated that a person like me cannot really understand what is going on	21	17	n/a	16	22	22

Base (1996): 1180
Source: 1974: Political Action Study (Marsh). See also note to previous table.
n/a = not asked

Protest potential

This mixture of declining public trust in politicians (low system efficacy) combined with relatively high levels of self-confidence in ability to participate effectively in politics (high personal efficacy) represents the classic conditions (see Marsh, 1977) for unconventional political behaviour. After all, if politicians cannot be trusted to do the right thing *and* ordinary people can be relied on to make an impact on events, then - so the argument goes - protest action of one sort or another becomes much more likely. When we investigated this issue two years ago, we found no evidence at all of an increase in people's propensity to take unconventional political actions, but we did find evidence of a growing tolerance of unconventional political action by others.

As the next table shows, this continues to be true (perhaps even more so). While in 1986, over half would have supported a ban on a nationwide strike against the government, now only just over a third would take that view. Similarly, the proportion who would outlaw the occupation of a government office has dropped by 14 percentage points to below one half of the population. These are large shifts, suggesting not only a sense of declining sympathy and deference for government *per se*, but also a growing sympathy for those who are brave enough to take it on.

Tolerance of undemocratic protest

	1985	1986	1990	1994	1996
% saying the following "should definitely not" be allowed					
Seriously damaging government buildings	91	91	91	83	83
Occupying a government office and stopping work there for several days	61	61	58	50	47
Organising a nationwide strike of all workers against the government	52	54	43	39	35

Base (1996): 989

This trend is confirmed by another similar finding. Two years ago we reported that public endorsement for the automatic precedence of the law over individual conscience had also sharply declined. Only two in five then felt that the law should be obeyed regardless, having fallen 12 percentage points since 1983. There has been no recovery since in support for law above conscience.

Attitudes towards the law

	1983	1984	1986	1989	1991	1994	1996
	%	%	%	%	%	%	%
People should obey the law without exception	53	57	55	50	52	41	41
On exceptional occasions people should follow their consciences even if it means breaking the law	46	42	43	48	47	56	55

Base (1996): 1180

None of these findings suggest, of course, that the existing political system is *actually* more likely to be challenged by unconventional or illegal means than it was before. They do suggest, however, that groups who choose to challenge the system by protest actions of one sort or another might well find it somewhat easier to secure public sympathy for their actions than they previously could have done. In this respect at least, the decline in political trust over the years has surely exacted its toll.

Changing expectations?

There are at least two ready explanations as to why confidence in our political system appears to have declined. The first, which comes to mind whenever another politician is 'disgraced' by a sexual or (particularly) a financial scandal, is that those in office have failed to match the ethical or performance standards that were apparently expected of their predecessors. A second, alternative explanation, however, is that while the political system is in fact working as effectively as it has ever done, our expectations of what governments and politicians should be able to do have gone up (Huntington, 1981; Dalton and Kuechler, 1990).

In order to test this alternative explanation, we repeated two sets of questions about MPs and governments that we had previously asked in the earliest years of the *British Social Attitudes* series. As far as MPs were concerned, we asked people to rate a number of qualities that it might be thought desirable for them to possess. If expectations of MPs have indeed increased since 1983, we should be able to see such a trend from the next table.

Qualities MPs should have

% saying following "important"	1983	1994	1996
To be well educated	50	55	61
To have been brought up in the area s/he represents	48	60	62
To be loyal to party s/he represents	42	42	45
To be independent minded	37	48	52
To know what being poor means	27	41	47
To have business experience	22	30	34
To have trade union experience	14	13	15
Other qualities	3	13	8

Base (1996): 1180

On this indicator our expectations of MPs certainly do appear to have risen. There has been a rise in every item in the list and in most cases a substantial one. Interestingly too, the balance of desirable qualities appears to have changed. Although party loyalty might now be regarded as perhaps a shade more important than it was in 1983, independence of mind in contrast is now much more highly prized, as is an understanding of poverty and close personal links with their own constituency.

The fact that none of these items refers to ethical standards in either the financial or moral sphere reveals the fact that they were designed in 1983 and merely repeated in the 1990s. This in itself might be construed as a clear indicator of change! Still, even though these items cannot tell us anything about the relative importance people attach to probity as opposed to other qualities, they certainly suggest that public expectations of what we expect of our politicians have risen rather than fallen.

So higher public expectations seem on the face of it to be a prime suspect for the decline in confidence in the political system. As the public comes to expect more of the system, so the system (without necessarily changing itself) might merely be seen to be less effective in meeting those expectations. On the other hand, if this were so, we should surely anticipate that public expectations of the role of government should have grown in tandem over the period. But, as the next table shows, we have actually come to expect less rather than more from government over the last decade.

We gave our respondents a list of tasks or goals that the government might be expected to perform or achieve. In each case the proportion saying it should definitely be the government's responsibility is lower now than it was a decade ago. This trend was apparently already under way in the second half of the 1980s. As can be seen, the *relative* importance that people attach to the various tasks and goals has not changed. Thus, providing health care for the sick is still the task which has the highest level of support and providing a job for everyone still has the least. So it looks as though it is our attitude towards the role of government that has changed rather than our attitude to the tasks themselves.

Expectations of government

% saying following should "definitely" be government's responsibility	1985	1986	1990	1996
Provide health care for the sick	85	84	84	81
Provide a decent standard of living for the old	77	80	77	70
Keep prices under control	59	52	47	40
Provide industry with help to grow	52	40	41	38
Give financial help to university students from low-income families	n/a	n/a	48	35
Provide decent housing for those who can't afford it	n/a	n/a	45	34
Reduce differences between the rich and the poor	45	46	40	32
Provide a decent standard of living for the unemployed	42	38	30	27
Provide jobs for everyone who want one	36	30	23	26

Base (1996): 989

One of the striking features of British politics over the last decade has been a reduction in expectations of the state by both the Conservative and the Labour parties. Both parties argue much less than they did in the early 1980s (even in the those early years of Thatcherism) for government involvement in social and economic affairs. And accordingly the state has reduced the scope of what it does. These changes may well have helped to lower public expectations of what government can or should do, but if so that makes the decline of confidence in our political system all the more noteworthy.

The Conservative legacy

The British have always been reluctant to place too much trust in their politicians. They have also always been rather sceptical about the extent to which their political system is capable of delivering the goods. Even so, such confidence as they did have appears to have drained away in the final years of the Conservative government. Despite attempts to restore public confidence by, for instance, establishing the Nolan Committee and then adopting its recommendations, trust in government continued to decline.

What then are the likely consequences of these developments? It has often been assumed that a decline in confidence in our political system is bound to lead to a more alienated electorate who will increasingly withdraw from participation in or interest in politics. In contrast, we argued two years ago (Curtice and Jowell, 1995) that those who had lost confidence in the system seemed to be responding by wanting to change the political system rather than withdraw from it. Their participation levels were no different from those of people with more confidence; they simply seemed to be more interested in treating rather than ignoring the patient. How far does our new evidence

from our latest survey substantiate these conclusions? And how far is the new Labour government, committed as it is to a wide-ranging package of constitutional change, likely to enjoy solid public support for this programme?

Trust, efficacy and participation

Most people do not, of course, regularly participate in politics. For the majority, perhaps, the only overtly political act in which they ever engage is voting in elections - and in general elections at that!

Yet recently even this willingness to participate in general elections has come into question, since a growing proportion of those eligible to vote fail to register to do so on the electoral registers (Boundary Commission for England, 1995; Smith, 1993). Meanwhile, at 71.5 per cent, the turnout in the 1997 general election was lower than in any previous post-war election. Are then the predictions coming true that declining confidence in our political system will lead to fewer people contributing formally to our political life?

To substantiate this claim, we would have to show that those who fail to register to vote or who do not turn out in elections are broadly the same sort of people as those with least confidence in the political system. But, according to our evidence, this is patently not the case.

First, in our latest survey we asked people whether they were registered to vote, either at their current address or at a previous address. The vast majority claimed that they were. Indeed, just three per cent thought they were definitely not on the register - a rather lower figure than that suggested by previous detailed research (Smith, 1993). But even if some respondents who thought they were on the register may in fact not have been, our question should at least have identified those who had knowingly removed themselves from the register.[1] If they had done so as a result of their lack of trust in the political system or a weak sense of political efficacy, then we should find a higher level of non-registration amongst those who are most distrustful or sceptical.

But in fact the opposite is the case. So, for example, among those who trust governments to put the needs of the nation first (all or most of the time), around five per cent claimed not to be on the electoral register, compared to only two per cent among those who are less trusting. Similarly, among those who believe that parties are only interested in votes, only two per cent are not on the register, compared with four per cent of those who are less sceptical. And this pattern persists with our other measures of political efficacy. On this evidence, then, confidence in our political system may well lead more to complacency rather than to participation and engagement.

We are also able to examine more directly whether declining confidence might have been responsible for the low participation at the 1997 general election. For although our survey was conducted in the spring of 1996, as many as possible of our respondents were reinterviewed on three subsequent

occasions before and after the 1997 general election (as part of the 1997 British Election Campaign Panel, one of a suite of studies we are undertaking as part of the 1997 British Election Study). So we are able to discover whether those who in 1996 were most distrustful of, or sceptical about, the system were also less likely to participate in it by voting in a general election twelve months later.[2]

  Once again, there is little to suggest this was so.[3] Amongst those who said they trusted the government "only some of the time" or "almost never", 84 per cent claimed to have voted in the 1997 election, only slightly lower than the figure of 87 per cent amongst those who trusted the government "just about always" or "most of the time". Meanwhile 85 per cent of those who agreed that parties were only interested in votes claimed to have made the journey to the polling station, slightly higher than amongst the 82 per cent who did not agree. So, whatever the reason for the low turnout at the 1997 election, it cannot plausibly be blamed on declining confidence in the political system.

Support for constitutional change

We asked a number of questions designed to tap public attitudes towards most of the constitutional changes in which the Labour party (and the Liberal Democrats) have expressed an interest. As we had included many of the same questions in a previous round of the *British Social Attitudes* series, we can now examine whether the decline in confidence is in any way associated with growing public support for constitutional change.

  It is certainly the case that substantial, and in many cases growing, public support exists for much of the government's proposals for constitutional change. For instance, a majority now favours reform of the House of Lords, devolution for Scotland, and allowing the courts to 'overrule parliament on any law which denies people their basic rights' (which is likely to be the way in which a Bill of Rights would be enforced). There is also substantial support for the principle of freedom of information. But there is less support for changing the electoral system towards a form of proportional representation, and no discernible trend over time in its favour.

  The strongest trend is in favour of House of Lords reform. While in 1983, a comfortable majority of 57 per cent wanted to keep the House of Lords as it is, now only half that proportion (29 per cent) take that view. As the next Table shows, support for the *status quo* appears to have fallen sharply even over the last two years. And this change has occurred alongside a similar drop (from around two-thirds to one-third) in the proportion who believe in keeping the monarchy as it now is. So it may well be the case that the hereditary principle itself is losing legitimacy in the eyes of the public.

Attitudes towards the House of Lords

House of Lords should ...	1983	1994	1996
	%	%	%
... remain as it is	57	36	29
... change needed	33	50	57

Base (1996): 1180

Meanwhile, no less than three people in five agree that "British courts should be allowed to overrule parliament on any law which denies people their basic rights" while only just over one in five are opposed.[4] But the most popular potential change of all would appear to be making government more open. We asked three questions which effectively pitted a government's right to secrecy in different circumstances against the public's right to know. Even in the case of defence plans, there is quite a bit of ambivalence as to whether or not the government should have a right to conceal things. But when it comes to economic plans, or plans for new laws, a derisory proportion of less than one in ten believe in the government's right to conceal them from the electorate, a 'right' that would normally often be invoked under present constitutional practice.

Freedom of information (1996)

	Government have right to keep secret	Public have right to know
% agree		
Defence plans	52	45
Economic plans	9	88
Plans for new laws	6	92

Base = 989

There are two other features of the pattern of support for many of these items that are important to register. First, it remains generally true (as we reported two years ago) that those who have less trust in the political system are more likely to favour constitutional change. But, as the next table shows, the increase in support for constitutional change over the last two years has in fact been greatest among those with the *highest* level of trust.[5] So it appears that demand for constitutional change is only weakly tied to levels of trust in the political system. We certainly cannot assume that any increase in the level of political trust (or indeed a growth in perceived system efficacy) would necessarily result in a weakening of support for constitutional change.

Constitutional reform and political trust (1996)

Level of political trust

% agreeing	High	Base	Medium	Base	Low	Base
Independence or devolution for Scotland	75 (+19)	332	65 (+1)	543	66 (-3)	229
Courts should be allowed to overrule parliament	56 (n/a)	303	60 (n/a)	479	66 (n/a)	206
Change needed to House of Lords	51 (+13)	346	58 (+5)	579	64 (-1)	247
Public has right to know defence plans	38 (n/a)	346	45 (n/a)	579	53 (n/a)	247

Figures in brackets show change since 1994.
n/a = not asked in 1994

Second, although it also remains true that Conservative identifiers are less likely to favour constitutional change than are Labour or the Liberal Democrat identifiers, the Conservative party's opposition to constitutional change is only partly shared by its own supporters. For instance, a clear majority of Conservative identifiers supported some kind of constitutional change for Scotland, and over half endorsed the idea that courts should be able to overturn laws made by parliament. Nearly half also believe that the House of Lords should be changed. Moreover, the trend over the last two years towards increased support for constitutional change has been at least as substantial amongst Conservative identifiers as among those of other parties. To date at least, Conservative opposition to demands for constitutional change does not seem to have struck a chord with the party's own supporters.

Constitutional reform and party identification (1996)

Party identification

% agreeing	Conservative	Base	Labour	Base	Liberal Democrat	Base
Independence or devolution for Scotland	66 (+8)	322	73 (+9)	556	75 (+9)	121
Courts should be allowed to overrule parliament	52 (n/a)	285	67 (n/a)	418	63 (n/a)	112
Change needed to House of Lords	46 (+10)	331	68 (+8)	501	54 (-1)	126
Public has right to know defence plans	28 (n/a)	331	56 (n/a)	501	47 (n/a)	126

Figures in brackets show change since 1994.
n/a = not asked in 1994

There appears therefore to be a favourable public climate for constitutional change, a climate that is not simply the product of low levels of political trust. But when it comes to the possibility of changing the electoral system, a rather different picture emerges. Here we asked respondents more than one question, but for the moment let us consider the answers to the following question which we have asked on a number of occasions since 1983:

> *Some people say that we should change the voting system to allow smaller political parties to get a fairer share of MPs. Others say we should keep the voting system as it is, to produce effective government. Which view comes closest to your own: that we should change the voting system, or, keep it as it is.*

As the next table shows, we have never found more than one-third supporting changes in the voting system, and over one-half has always been in favour of keeping the existing system. Moreover, there is no apparent trend towards increasing support; opinion hardly appears to have shifted at all during the last parliament.[6]

Attitudes towards electoral reform

	1983	1986	1987	1987b	1990	1991	1992	1994	1995	1996
We should	%	%	%	%	%	%	%	%	%	%
Change the voting system	39	32	30	36	34	37	33	34	37	33
Keep it as it is	54	60	64	58	59	58	60	60	58	59

Source: 1983, 1987b, 1992: British Election Study
Base: 1180

Answers to a different question on the same subject did, however, produce a rather different distribution of answers (see also Dunleavy and Margetts, 1997). We also asked:

> *How much do you agree or disagree with this statement: Britain should introduce proportional representation so that the number of MPs each party gets matches more closely the number of votes each party gets?*

In response to this statement, no less than 45 per cent agreed and only 16 per cent disagreed. This may suggest that support for electoral reform may in fact be much higher than we have implied so far, although even on this question there is no sign that sympathy for proportional representation has increased in recent years. This divergence between the answers to the two questions has been found on a number of different surveys (see also Curtice and Jowell, 1995; Curtice 1993). Of course, the two questions address the issue of electoral reform in different terms, but the fact that this seems to make such a

significant difference to responses suggests an absence of any very fixed views about electoral reform among the public. With the government committed to holding a referendum on the subject, the outcome could well be determined by whichever set of arguments were the more effective during the campaign, or, perhaps to whichever side the various political parties end up supporting.

The public's apparent ambivalence towards electoral reform is further underlined when we look at attitudes towards the desirability of one of its likely consequences - coalition governments. The proportion who say they prefer single party government is, at 47 per cent almost identical to the proportion (48 per cent), who say they think that Britain would be better off if two or more parties were to get together to form a government. These figures are virtually identical to those we obtained when we first asked the question in 1983. Not only is the public split on the issue, but the sort of people who most favour coalition government are in fact different from those who most favour electoral reform. In particular, people with high educational qualifications are more likely to favour electoral reform, but less likely to favour coalition government. We find a similar divergence when we look at our liberal-authoritarian scale. (The construction of the libertarian-authoritarian scale is described in more detail in Appendix I to this Report). Those at the libertarian end of the spectrum are also more likely to favour electoral reform, but less likely to favour coalition government.

It seems then that although organisations such as Charter 88 have campaigned in favour of the whole package of constitutional reforms considered here, they do not necessarily form a similar package in the public's mind. In particular, support for electoral reform appears to be more fragile than for many of the other items on the constitutional reformers' agendas.

We have already noted that on most items of constitutional change support is lower among Conservative identifiers. And we also noted that although many of these measures have been long-standing features of Liberal Democrat policy, support for them nowadays is much the same, or even higher, among Labour identifiers as among Liberal Democrat identifiers.

But, as the next table shows, a rather different picture emerges if we look at the distribution of attitudes towards electoral reform. While support for change is again lowest amongst Conservative identifiers, here it is Liberal Democrats rather than Labour identifiers who are keenest. Of course, although the Labour party is committed to holding a referendum on the electoral system, it is not committed to supporting any change. Evidently the party's supporters remain at least equally sceptical of change.

Electoral reform and party identification (1996)

Party identification

% agreeing	Conservative		Labour		Liberal Democrat	
		Base		*Base*		*Base*
Should change voting system	20	*331*	36	*501*	59	*126*
Coalition government would be better for Britain	38	*331*	50	*501*	62	*126*
Should introduce PR so MPs match votes	33	*285*	52	*418*	66	*112*

A factor analysis carried out of the various constitutional items we have been considering here, confirms that attitudes towards electoral reform constitute a separate dimension from the other items of constitutional change (with the possible exception of the item on a Bill of Rights). Certainly, attitudes towards Scotland, the House of Lords and the monarchy form a separate and largely unified dimension. Interestingly too, those who favour devolution or independence for Scotland also tend to believe that Northern Ireland's long-term future lies outside the United Kingdom, but attitudes towards the European Union do not form part of the same dimension.[7]

Attitudes towards referendums

While there may be some doubts about the merits of changing our electoral system, referendums do seem to be popular. We asked our respondents how decisions should be made about three important areas of public policy. Two of the subjects, the introduction of a single European currency and changing the voting system, were issues of constitutional significance where the government is already committed to holding a referendum before any change is made. The third, the introduction of the death penalty, is commonly cited as an instance where the decisions of the House of Commons are persistently at variance with public opinion.

Previous surveys have commonly found high levels of support for referendums (see, for example, Worcester, 1995). However, these findings have been based on questions which tend to ask respondents merely whether they are in favour of or against referendums, and it may not be surprising that most people say they want a vote for themselves. The constitutional argument about referendums, in contrast, is about the relative merits of direct *versus* representative democracy. We therefore posed respondents a question which invited them to make that comparison. We asked:

> *Here are some decisions that could be made **either** by the MPs we elect to parliament **or** by everyone having a say in a special vote or referendum.*

Despite this wording, our respondents were also firmly in favour of holding referendums in respect of the issues we asked about. Over three in four say that a referendum should be held about a single currency, seven in ten say the same about the death penalty, and just under two-thirds say a referendum is the best way of making a decision about proportional representation. Britain may well experience more referendums in the next few years than in the whole of its previous democratic history, and this development would not, it appears, be unwelcome. Perhaps the low level of political trust we have discovered has undermined whatever commitment there ever was among the general public to the principles of representative, as opposed to direct, democracy (see also Fuchs and Klingemann, 1995).

Measures against 'sleaze'

Although the public may not believe that MPs can be trusted to make many important decisions, they evidently do believe that being an MP should be a full-time job. We asked respondents which of these two statements came closest to their view:

> *It is a bad thing for MPs to have another paid job because being an MP is a full-time job in itself.*
> *or*
> *It is a good thing for MPs to have another paid job because it keeps them in touch with the outside world.*

Nearly two-thirds say that it is a bad thing for an MP to have another paid job, rejecting outright the common argument that such outside employment helps MPs to keep in touch with the outside world. It was, of course, concerns about the propriety of the relationship between some MPs and their sources of external income that were at the heart of some of the allegations of sleaze during the last parliament. As our data and other surveys have shown (Dunleavy *et al.*, 1995), there is in fact little support for MPs engaging in any such activities in the first place.

On the other hand there appears to be relatively little public support for tightening of the rules regulating the financing of political parties, another area of recent debate. It has been suggested, for instance, that political parties should be required to publish the names of those who give them significant amounts of money, and that there should be a limit on the amount of money that any one individual can give to a party. Yet nearly half of *British Social Attitudes* respondents agree that "any individual who gives money to a political party should be allowed to keep their gift private if they wish", compared with only just over a quarter who disagree. As to the imposition of a limit on how much money any individual can give to a party, around a third agree and another third disagree that "there should be a limit on how much money a single individual can give to a political party", with the remaining

third being undecided. Meanwhile, only one in three support the idea that "political parties need to be funded by the government to do their job properly" - a measure that might free parties from their reliance on individual donors. So while the public may be concerned about aspects of 'sleaze' in politics, they do not seem to endorse with any enthusiasm many of the measures that have been proposed to deal with the issue at one of its possible sources.

The impact of the 1997 general election

We have seen then that the amount of trust we have in our political system and in the degree of efficacy that it exhibits are still at a low ebb. We have also found increasing levels of support for at least some of the proposed constitutional changes. But since our initial survey work took place well before the 1997 election perhaps the change of government has produced a change of mood.

Our reinterviews with our respondents at the time of the 1997 general election do provide some support for this hypothesis. In these reinterviews we repeated the three items on system efficacy, both during the election campaign itself and then after polling day when the election result was known.

The impact of the 1997 election on system efficacy

	1996	1997	
		before polling day	after polling day
% "strongly agree"			
Parties are only interested in people's votes, not in their opinions	25	20	14
Generally speaking those we elect as MPs lose touch with people pretty quickly	26	23	18
It doesn't really matter which party is in power, in the end things go on much the same	12	17	11

Source: 1997 British Election Campaign Panel. Based on 536 respondents interviewed in all three waves.

As the table shows, on two of the three items at least we found a significant improvement in the level of efficacy compared with our initial reading, and especially so once the election result was known. Some commentators have suggested that modern elections with their emphasis on so-called 'negative campaigning' alienate voters from the political system (Franklin, 1994; Paterson 1993). There is clearly no support for that proposition in these data. Equally, however, we should not too readily assume that the 1997 election has resulted in a long-term restoration of confidence in our political system.

As might be expected, efficacy increased much more among Labour identifiers than among Conservatives, suggesting that much of the changed response to these questions merely reflects partisan rejoicing in the immediate wake of the election result. We will need to see what the public says later in the life of this parliament before making any judgement about the medium- or long-term impact of the 1997 election on public confidence in government per se.[8]

Moreover, we should not assume that any restoration of public confidence will necessarily translate itself into a reduction in support for constitutional change. As we have seen, support between 1994 and 1996 for some forms of constitutional change increased despite little or no change in overall levels of public confidence. The two phenomena are simply not that closely linked.

Conclusion

Britain still appears to have low levels of confidence in both its political system and its politicians. But we should be wary of drawing hasty conclusions about the implications of this (see also Dalton, 1996). It certainly does not appear to be true that lack of confidence in the system makes people less willing to turn out and vote at election time. Similarly, while support for constitutional change is related to people's confidence or otherwise in the political system, it is far from being a straightforward response to it.

Rather, there appears to be a substantial and growing demand for certain constitutional changes which appears likely to persist despite the slight restoration of public confidence in the system in the wake of the 1997 general election. The case for reform of the House of Lords, Scottish devolution and freedom of information appears to have been won in the minds of the public. But when it comes to what many constitutional reformers regard as the most important change of all, reform of the electoral system, the public still speaks in an uncertain voice.

There is clearly public support for constitutional change in Britain. But it is neither as extensive as some might have hoped, nor as negligible as others might have wished.

Notes

1. We are in fact attempting to verify our respondents' answers by looking for their names on the electoral register, and aim to report the results of this in future work. It should also be borne in mind of course that those who refuse to participate in surveys such as ours or who could not be contacted were more likely not to appear on the electoral register. Our check of the electoral registers therefore includes non-respondents in order to enable us to estimate the degree of any such bias.
2. We are reliant here also on respondents' reports as to whether or not they voted in the general election. These are in the course of being verified against the marked-up registers

giving details of those to whom a ballot paper was issued on polling day, and we aim to be able to use these also in future research. Previous research suggests that patterns of association with turnout are similar whether we look at respondent's reported turnout or the official record (Swaddle and Heath, 1989).

3. The figures in this paragraph are based on the results of 704 persons who were asked questions about political trust in 1996 and who were successfully recontacted after the general election campaign. They include those who were 17 in 1996 but had come of age by the time of the general election; these persons are excluded in our reports of the 1996 survey alone. The data have not been weighted for the possible effects of differential attrition.

4. Note that this result is rather different from what we found when we asked a differently worded question in 1994 which simply asked whether the courts should have the power to overturn laws made by the parliament without specifying the grounds on which they might be allowed to do so. We then found only 43 per cent in favour of allowing the courts to overturn laws. We suspect that few people take any principled view on the issue of whether parliament should always be sovereign or whether its actions should be subject to judicial review. Rights in contrast are always popular.

5. The level of trust in this table has been created as follows. Respondents were given a score of 1 for each item on which they said they trusted the organisation or group 'just about always' or 'most of the time', 2 if they said 'only some of the time' and 3 if they said 'almost never'. Respondents who said they 'did not know' were also given a score of 1 for that item. The item on trust in judges was excluded in order to maintain comparability with 1994 when it was not asked. This produced a scale with values ranging from 5 to 15. Those with a score of 8 or less were then classified as having high trust, those with a score of 9 to 11, medium trust, and those with a score of 12 or more, low trust.

6. Note also that when we reinterviewed these respondents after the 1997 election as part of the British Election Campaign Panel, there was even a small swing away from support for electoral reform. Amongst 536 respondents who were successfully recontacted before and after polling day, support for changing the system remained steady at 36 per cent in 1966 and 37 per cent before polling day, but fell to 30 per cent thereafter. For evidence that opinion also swung against proportional representation during the 1992 general election see Curtice (1993).

7. The analysis identified four dimensions where the principal factor loadings on each dimension (ignoring signs) were as follows:-

Factor 1: Agree PR fairer 0.77; Change electoral system 0.73; Coalition government 0.66; Courts overrule parliament 0.42 (eigenvalue 2.59).

Factor 2: Monarchy 0.68; Scottish Parliament 0.60; House of Lords 0.54; Future of N. Ireland 0.54; Right to know Defence Plans 0.48 (eigenvalue 1.58).

Factor 3: Long-term policy to EU 0.85; European currency 0.82 (eigenvalue 1.34).

Factor 4: Right to Know plans for new laws 0.81; Right to know Economic Plans 0.80; Right to know Defence Plans 0.34 (eigenvalue 1.05).

The solution accounted for just over 50 per cent of the variance.

The existence of the fourth factor clearly reflects the virtually unanimous level of support for the public's right to know the government's plans for new laws and the economy. This unanimity explains why we have largely excluded these two items from much of the analysis in this section.

8. Our results however do clearly raise doubts about the argument that the decline in the level of political trust has been caused by social changes, such as a change in support for postmaterialist values (Dalton 1996; Inglehart, 1997; Nie *et al.*, 1997) rather than occasioned by political events such as 'sleaze' (Listhaug, 1995).

References

Boundary Commission for England (1995), *Fourth Periodical Report*, London, HMSO.

Curtice, J. (1993), 'Popular support for electoral reform: the lessons of the 1992 election', *Scottish Affairs*, **4**, 23-32.

Curtice, J. and Jowell, R. (1995), 'The sceptical electorate', in Jowell, R., Curtice, J., Park, A., Brook, L. and Ahrendt, D., *British Social Attitudes; the 12th. report*, Aldershot: Dartmouth.

Dalton, R. (1996), *Citizen Politics*, Chatham, NJ: Chatham House.

Dalton, R. and Kuechler, M. (1990) (eds.), *Challenging the Political Order: New Social and Political Movements in Western Democracies*, Oxford: Oxford University Press.

Dunleavy, P. and Margetts, H. (1997), 'The Electoral System', *Parliamentary Affairs*, **50**, 733-49.

Dunleavy, P., Weir, S., and Subrahmanyam, G. (1995), 'Public Response and Constitutional Significance', *Parliamentary Affairs*, **48**, 602-16.

Franklin, B. (1994), *Packaging Politics*, London: Edward Arnold.

Fuchs, D. and Klingemann, H.D. (1995), 'Citizens and the State: A Relationship Transformed', in Klingemann, H.D. and Fuchs, D. (eds.), *Citizens and the State*, Oxford: Oxford University Press.

Galbraith, J. (1992), *The culture of contentment*, Harmondsworth: Penguin.

Huntington, S. (1981), *American Politics: The Promise of Disharmony*, Cambridge, Mass.: Harvard University Press.

Inglehart, R. (1997), *Modernization and Post-Modernization: Cultural, Economic and Political Change in 43 Societies*, Princeton, NJ: Princeton University Press.

Listhaug, O., (1995), 'The Dynamics of Trust in Politicians', in Klingemann, H.D. and Fuchs, D. (eds.), *Citizens and the State*, Oxford: Oxford University Press.

Marsh, A. (1977), *Protest and Political Conciousness*, Beverley Hills: Sage.

Nye, J., Zelikow, P. and King, D. (1997), *Why Americans Mistrust Government*, Cambridge: Harvard University Press.

Paterson, T. (1993), *Out of Order*, New York: Knopf.

Smith, S. (1993), *Electoral Registration in 1991*, London: HMSO.

Swaddle, K. and Heath, A. (1989), 'Official and Reported Turnout in the British General Election of 1987', *British Journal of Political Science*, **19**, 537-51.

Worcester, R. (1995), 'The People and the Party System', *Political Quarterly*, **66**, 335-41.

Acknowledgements

The authors would like to thank the Leverhulme Trust for funding to support the modules of questions on trust in the political process asked in both 1994 and 1996. We are also grateful to the Economic and Social Research Council for the funding of the re-interviews undertaken during the 1997 election campaign in pursuance of the British Election Campaign Panel (BECP). The BECP was undertaken in conjunction with our colleagues in the Centre for Research into Elections and Social Trends, Anthony Heath and Pippa Norris, from whose intellectual input we have benefited. We also wish to thank Ann Mair of the Social Statistics Laboratory, University of Strathclyde for invaluable computing assistance.

6 Green in word ...

Bridget Taylor [*]

Over the past fifteen years or so, awareness of, and concern about, many environmental problems has risen substantially. Environmental issues now command wide media attention and environmental priorities are slowly being absorbed into the policy-making process, at both central and local level. The need to reduce environmental impacts is now widely recognised in most sectors of society, and politicians now recognise that they must be green not just in word but in deed. Yet moves towards implementing measures at a collective level or towards modifying individual behaviours have been, as yet, limited. The recent review of the goals aspired to by the 1991 Rio de Janiero Accord have exposed their slow progress.

In this chapter we examine the extent to which attitudes towards green issues have changed over the last fifteen years or so, ask which environmental concerns are the most prominent in the 1990s and see if we can identify any policy initiatives that may prove acceptable (if not necessarily popular). What levels of support do various policies attract? Does an abstract concern with environmental issues translate into support for policies designed to protect the environment? And how does concern about green issues relate to people's actual behaviour - the decisions that they make in their daily lives? We end by considering some of the characteristics associated with people who *are* particularly green in their behaviour, and with those who are not.

Since its inception in 1983, the *British Social Attitudes* survey series has regularly included questions on environmental issues. In addition, there has also been consistent coverage of a range of 'countryside' issues. This chapter

[*] Bridget Taylor is Research Officer in the ESRC Centre for Research into Elections and Social Trends (CREST) based at SCPR and Nuffield College Oxford.

draws from both these sources, sometimes using attitudes towards countryside issues as surrogates for attitudes to the environment more broadly. There is, however, evidence to justify the validity of this approach. Earlier analyses of the data have shown that attitudes towards these two subjects are closely related. We also draw upon a series of questions about transport issues that has been regularly included since 1993.

Of course, we must remember that attitudes to the environment are likely to be subject to a 'social acceptability' bias - perhaps increasingly so as public concern and media attention rise. Expressions of opinion are cost-free. Similarly, reports of green behaviour are also likely to be subject to bias in a 'green-ward' direction. Furthermore, what may appear to be green attitudes or behaviour may be motivated by other considerations, such as concerns about health, household economy, social conformity or simple convenience. Thus we must guard against over-interpreting the strength of green attitudes and practices.

Environmental concern: change over time

We start by looking at public concern about the environment generally, and how this has changed over the last decade or so. Has concern about the environment risen? What issues have come to the fore or receded?

The environment as a spending priority

We begin by looking at a set of questions which present eight major areas of public spending and ask, for each, whether the respondent "would like to see more or less government spending". The question carries a warning - "if you say 'much more', it might require a tax increase to pay for it".

As the next table shows, support for more public spending on the environment rose substantially between 1985 and 1991. The environment moved from sixth to fourth position as a spending priority, overtaking police and law enforcement and unemployment benefits, peaking around 1990/91 at around 60 per cent. However, it is clear that extra spending on health, pensions, education and, more recently, 'law and order' is much more popular than spending on the environment.

Areas of government spending

	1985	1990	1991	1993	1994	1996
% **saying "spend** **more" or "much more"**						
Health	87	89	89	87	87	90
Old age pensions	73	80	76	79	74	76
Education	72	78	82	80	73	82
Unemployment benefits	40	36	39	50	36	33
Police and law enforcement	38	50	54	68	72	70
Environment	34	61	60	56	48	41
Military and defence	17	8	14	22	19	17
Culture and arts	9	12	15	9	12	6
Base	*1530*	*1197*	*1224*	*1268*	*970*	*989*

Since 1990/91 support for more public spending on the environment has fallen successively each year. Moreover, its popularity has continued to decline, despite the subsequent economic recovery, though not so far as to reach its mid-1980s levels. So, while concern about the environment generally appears to have reached high levels in the early 1990s, this seems to have been dented considerably by changes in people's priorities during the recession. It seems, then, that concern about the environment is vulnerable to experiences of individual and collective economic hardship.

These findings are supported by changes in levels of concern about the countryside. Since 1985, we asked:

> *Are you personally concerned about things that may happen in the countryside, or does it not concern you particularly?*

Concern about the countryside generally has become both more widespread and more intense. The proportion saying that they are "very concerned" has increased - rising from 31 per cent in 1985 to 43 per cent in 1996, an increase of 12 points. Just one person in five (22 per cent in 1996) says that the countryside "does not concern me particularly". Again we see the possible impact of the recession, with concern about the countryside declining from a peak in 1993. Other long-standing measures which pit protection of the countryside *versus* economic imperatives such as job creation and keeping down prices, also show the impact of the recession. In all cases, the substantial and growing majorities giving priority to countryside protection fell back in the early 1990s. However, unlike the popularity of the environment as a spending priority, attitudes to the countryside have more or less returned to their pre-recession levels.

Our findings suggest that concern for the environment is, to some extent, seen as an 'extra' - affordable in a time of plenty, but disposable when hard times come. Then other issues, such as law enforcement, unemployment benefits, job creation and inflation, take over as priorities. By contrast, major spending

programmes, like health and education, prove remarkably robust to changes in the economic climate.

Change over time in attitudes towards particular environmental issues

Have public perceptions as to what constitute particular 'threats' to the environment changed over the last decade or so? We begin by looking at a set of questions asking people how they feel about different types of development in the countryside. As the next table shows, the biggest increase over time has been in opposition to the provision of new roads in the countryside, followed by an increase in opposition to building new homes. Both are opposed by large majorities, along with putting the needs of farmers above the protection of wildlife. In contrast, just one in five oppose increasing the number of picnic and camping sites in the countryside, a figure that has barely changed over the last ten years.

	1986	1990	1996
% saying should be "stopped altogether" or "discouraged"			
Putting the needs of farmers before protection of wildlife	69	75	70
Building new housing in country areas	64	70	70
Providing more roads in country areas	50	66	68
Increasing the amount of countryside being farmed	53	37	32
Increasing the number of picnic areas and camping sites in the countryside	17	20	20
Base	*1321*	*1197*	*1058*

A more detailed picture of public concern is found by looking at responses to a question asking respondents to choose, from a list of seven potential hazards, the "greatest (and next greatest) threat to the countryside". As the next table shows, in 1985 industrial pollution and use of chemicals were the dominant concerns, with almost half the sample citing each of these as a threat to the countryside. This pattern persisted until 1994, when the proportions naming each fell back sharply (although industrial pollution remained the dominant concern). In contrast "motorways and road-building", which had crept up by ten points over the previous eight years, shot up by 12 points between 1993 and 1994. This is now the second most commonly cited threat, with a dramatic rise from its sixth place ranking in 1985. As we shall see later in the chapter, this concern with road-building and traffic is one of the most prominent features of recent years.[1]

Threats to the countryside[2]

% naming each as the "greatest" and "next greatest" threats	1985	1987	1990	1993	1994
Industrial pollution	47	53	57	57	46
Use of chemicals and pesticides	43	44	42	38	27
Litter	26	21	21	18	32
Urban growth and housing development	25	28	29	29	29
Removal by farmers of traditional land-scapes such as hedgerows/woodlands	25	23	19	18	14
Motorways and road-building	21	22	25	33	43
Tourism and visitors	3	3	3	3	3
Base	*1804*	*1410*	*1397*	*1452*	*1165*

It is evident that hardly anyone identifies tourism as a threat to the countryside, even though some of the more commonly perceived threats (such as litter and road-building) can result from it. Possibly "tourism", with its connotations of freedom, recreation and opportunity, has a positive resonance that far outweighs any negative aspects such as traffic generation or litter.

More recent data confirm these findings. In 1995 and 1996 we asked respondents to choose, this time from a list of nine potential "threats", which they saw as the "greatest (and next greatest) threat to the countryside". The main menaces nowadays are seen to be "land and air pollution, or discharges into rivers and lakes", named by 50 per cent as a threat. And "building new roads and motorways" moved from being the fourth most commonly perceived threat in 1995, to the second most in 1996 (from 29 per cent to 33 per cent). While two measures 12 months apart hardly represent a trend, the direction is clearly consistent with our earlier findings. Once again, "the number of tourists and visitors in the countryside" (perhaps because they are most of us) continues to generate negligible concern, with just four per cent of people citing this in 1996 as the greatest or next greatest threat to the countryside. Clearly the major threats to the countryside are seen to be pollution and roads, with worries about the latter apparently rising.

While land and air pollution is still perceived to be the main threat to the countryside, the greatest change in recent years - especially in just the last three years - has been the rapid increase in concern about roads and traffic. This is attributable partly to the real and continuing increase in traffic levels in both the countryside and urban areas, the greater attention being given to transport issues by the media and perhaps also to the rather belated attention now being given to these problems by politicians. Yet tourism and recreational use of the countryside are hardly seen as threats at all, despite their environmental impacts. This suggests, perhaps, that many people do not make a connection between broad 'lifestyle' choices, such as leisure activities, and environmental problems, such as traffic generation, that might result from these.

Perceived environmental dangers in the 1990s

So what are the major environmental concerns of the 1990s? We look first at a number of different problems and assess how *dangerous* these are perceived to be, first "for the environment" and, secondly, "for you and your family". As the next table shows, all of the issues mentioned were associated with high levels of perceived danger. Four of the six "problems" were thought by majorities to be "extremely dangerous" or "very dangerous" to the environment. Little more than one in ten respondents (and in most cases fewer) thought that each problem was "not very dangerous" or "not dangerous at all".

Water pollution is the most widely perceived danger, perhaps due in part to widespread media attention to water quality at the time these questions were asked in 1993. Next comes air pollution caused by industry, closely followed by pollution caused by cars. Indeed air pollution from cars was thought a greater danger to the environment than nuclear power stations, a position which would have surely been astonishing even five years earlier.[3] The perceived danger to the environment from pollution and road traffic is consistent with findings regarding threats to the countryside.

**Danger of different 'problems' for the environment
and for the respondent and his or her family (1993)**

% saying "extremely" or "very" dangerous	... dangerous for environment	... dangerous for family
Pollution of Britain's rivers, lakes and streams	61	47
Air pollution caused by industry	54	45
Air pollution caused by cars	48	40
A rise in the world's temperature caused by the 'greenhouse effect'	51	44
Nuclear power stations	44	38
Pesticides and chemicals used in farming	37	32

Base 1268

Curiously, as the table shows, the perceived level of danger each of these problems posed to respondents and their families was significantly lower than the level of danger each was seen as posing to the environment in general. A possible interpretation is that, while these problems are widely perceived as *general* threats, they continue to be seen by many people as being removed from their own experience - as being long-term and diffuse in nature, rather than immediate, specific and personal. This is consistent with the relatively low levels of perceived danger seen to be posed by pesticides and chemicals used in farming, although some would argue that these present a substantial risk to individuals' health, as well as to the environment. It seems that, although most have taken on board that there are long-term dangers posed to the environment, fewer appear to see these as current and immediate problems in their own daily lives.

Other questions also reveal high levels of concern across a range of environmental problems. For instance, a set of questions asked in 1993 (some of which were repeated in 1995) shows the widespread seriousness with which waste disposal ("finding official sites to dump or burn household waste") is regarded. In 1993, 74 per cent thought that it would "definitely" or "probably" be a serious problem in 20 years time, more serious than the greenhouse effect (61 per cent) or oil and gas depletion (59 per cent). Another question in the same set reveals that an overwhelming majority (86 per cent in 1995) sees traffic congestion as being one of the most serious problems facing Britain, and approaching two-thirds (63 per cent in 1995) say the same of traffic noise.

Finally, in this section, we turn to transport and traffic. We asked, for a range of transport and traffic problems, how serious each was perceived to be. As the next table shows, the major problem identified is exhaust fumes in urban areas. Nearly two-thirds think this is a "very serious" problem, an increase of 13 points over a one year period. This is followed by urban traffic congestion (also up on the previous year), then congestion on motorways (up by a massive 20 points over a two-year period). While seen as less serious than urban and motorway traffic problems, concerns about traffic levels in the countryside have been rising.

Seriousness of traffic problems

	1993	1994	1995
% saying a "very serious" problem			
Congestion on motorways	22	44	42
Traffic congestion at popular places in the countryside	16	18	22
Increased traffic on country roads and lanes	11	18	21
Exhaust fumes from traffic in towns and cities	n/a	50	63
Traffic congestion in towns and cities	n/a	44	50
Noise from traffic in towns and cities	n/a	27	32
Base	*1452*	*1165*	*1172*

n/a = not asked

How do these concerns with specific transport and traffic problems relate to one another? Factor analysis of the previous six transport and traffic issues suggests that worries about congestion and traffic levels in urban areas, on motorways or in the countryside, are related - in other words, that people who are very concerned about one of these issues tend also to be concerned about the others (factor analysis is discussed in more detail in Appendix I to this Report). Those with worries about congestion tend not, however, to be those concerned about exhaust fumes and traffic noise. Concern with *traffic levels* cannot, therefore, be taken as an indicator of concern about the *environment* itself (see also Stokes and Taylor, 1994). Such concern is, it seems, more

likely to be motivated by resentment of the personal inconvenience caused by traffic congestion than by any green sentiments.

Support for policies aimed at protecting the environment

We can see that many people express high levels of concern about a broad range of environmental issues. In fact, very few seem to think that the environment and countryside are *not* under threat. But these sorts of attitudes alone do nothing to protect the environment. For long-term protection measures to have any chance of success, there need to be changes in people's behaviour, either at the individual and domestic level, or at a collective level - or at both. In this section we discuss a variety of possible green policies, starting with what can be termed 'collective' measures, and then considering those aimed more specifically at the individual.

At the collective level, there could be a range of measures arising from central or local government initiatives, actions, directives or enforcement, possibly (but not necessarily) requiring legislation. These would aim to limit particular activities or actions that cause environmental damage, and perhaps encourage less damaging alternatives. Such measures may entail some restrictions on choices or impose costs, as well as providing benefits at a collective and/or an individual level. Furthermore, the costs of such policies may be more immediate or tangible than the actual benefits. How do expressions of concern stand up to these sorts of tests? To what extent do people support various policies which aim at ameliorating threats to the environment?

Of course, expressions of support for policies are virtually cost-free. In the context of rising public concern, there are also increasing social pressures to make the right noises about environmental issues. So we need not believe that *everyone* who voices support for a particular policy during the survey interview would actually welcome its implementation with open arms. Nonetheless, we can examine the extent to which expressions of concern about the environment translate into expressions of support for measures to protect it, and compare levels of support for different types of measures.

General policy priorities

We start by looking at the priority given to environmental protection in general when pitted against purely economic considerations. We ask people whether they agree or disagree with a number of statements, the first of which reads:

> *Government should do more to protect the environment, even if it leads to higher taxes*

This is followed by two similar statements, the first asking about action taken by industry, the second action taken by "ordinary people". In 1996, as in almost all earlier years, majorities put the environment first, suggesting that most people both recognise a need to make sacrifices for the sake of environmental protection, and are willing to pay in some form. People are particularly keen on *industry* taking action, since its consequences for them (described as "lower profits and fewer jobs") are less direct than the consequences of action taken by government ("higher taxes"). Perhaps not surprisingly, higher taxes have always been the least popular penalty, most probably because most people see them as a greater, or more immediate, or more certain threat to their own standard of living.[4]

Sacrifices for the sake of environmental protection

	1990	1991	1993	1994	1995	1996
% strongly agreeing/agreeing						
Government should do more to protect the environment, even if it leads to higher taxes	66	60	43	58	61	57
Industry should do more to protect the environment, even if it leads to lower profits and fewer jobs	75	64	51	65	61	67
Ordinary people should do more to protect the environment, even if it means paying higher prices	75	68	50	72	67	60
Base	*1197*	*1224*	*1268*	*975*	*1023*	*1058*

So a substantial majority appears willing, in principle at least, to make sacrifices for the sake of the environment. How does this support stand up when we ask about more specific trade-offs and measures?

Government intervention versus laissez-faire

Is government intervention or legislation necessary, or can people - individually or collectively - be trusted to look after the environment? Here we consider environmental protection laws *versus* the 'rights' of individuals and businesses to decide what to do for the best. Evidently the need for legislation is widely recognised, but there is a distinction between individuals and businesses, the latter being trusted by only a handful to 'do the right thing'. This is consistent with evidence from other BSA surveys. People believe that businesses have a responsibility not to damage the environment, that those that do so should be penalised, and that they are not generally trusted to act responsibly. In contrast, just under half (48 per cent) would place environmental protection before individual rights, down from 56 per cent in 1993, with one-quarter putting the rights of the individual before environmental protection. A further quarter were unable to make a choice.

Government intervention *versus laissez-faire*

	1993	1996
	%	%
Government should let ordinary people decide for themselves how to protect the environment, even if it means they don't always do the right thing	24	24
Government should pass laws to make ordinary people protect the environment, even if it interferes with people's rights to make their own decisions	57	48
Can't choose	18	27
	%	%
Government should let businesses decide for themselves how to protect the environment, even if it means they don't always do the right thing	6	4
Government should pass laws to make businesses protect the environment, even if it interferes with business' rights to make their own decisions	84	83
Can't choose	9	11
Base	*1268*	*1058*

Whereas, clearly, businesses are widely distrusted when it comes to environmental protection, attitudes towards farmers as custodians of the countryside are more ambivalent. During the late 1980s, there was quite a steep drop in the proportions willing to leave environmental decisions up to the farmer and, since 1989, on balance respondents have favoured more government intervention.

	1985	1986	1987	1989	1994	Change '85-'94
Government authorities should have more control over what's done and built on farms	34	34	38	46	44	+10
There are enough controls and farmers should be left to decide what's done on farms	51	47	44	37	39	-12
Bases	*1530*	*1321*	*1212*	*1297*	*975*	

Protecting the countryside

We have already seen that huge majorities put protection of the countryside above lower prices and the creation of jobs. Substantial majorities put protecting wildlife before the needs of farmers, and oppose building new housing and more roads in country areas. But to what extent are attitudes to these different sorts of policy issues related? Are there distinct themes underlying these attitudes?

In 1994 respondents were asked about a wide range of countryside policy issues. A factor analysis of 15 of these issues[5] suggests that there are four separate *dimensions* to concern about the countryside. One is to do with priority for environmental protection generally; a second, a concern with excessive use of the countryside; a third, a concern with planning controls; and a fourth, a concern with the role of farmers and farming. The analysis suggests that, in respect of countryside policy issues at least, the public tends to associate environmental protection with planning, and - to a lesser extent - with how the land is farmed. However, people do not see unrestricted use of the countryside for tourism and leisure as related to the issue of environmental protection.[6]

Our data suggest that there is strong (and, it seems, still growing) support for enforcing planning laws to protect the countryside, and for preserving green belts. Most think that new housing should be built in cities, not in the countryside. All this suggests that even fairly draconian planning controls, if they help protect the countryside, might gain widespread public support. The role of farmers in the countryside continues to be viewed fairly favourably, though they have lost some support over recent years. There are also signs of a realisation of the impact of intensive farming, and of a shift from priority for low food prices towards greater protection for the countryside.

Opinion change seems to lag, however, when it comes to that other major and rapidly growing rural industry, tourism and leisure. Only a quarter of respondents agree with the statement "the beauty of the countryside depends on stopping too many people from visiting it", although more people agree now than did in the past (24 per cent in 1994 compared with 14 per cent in 1987). True, in 1994 just over half (54 per cent) agreed that "some parts of the countryside are now so popular that it is no longer a pleasure to visit them" - but this does not necessarily indicate *concern* for the countryside. It may simply reflect a recognition of the personal inconvenience that such popularity can cause and an annoyance that one's own pleasure is being spoiled.

Who should pay to protect the countryside and how?

In 1996, for the first time, respondents were asked who, out of five different groups, should "have the most (and the next most) responsibility for footing the bill" for "looking after the countryside". Interestingly, over half believe that the general public should be responsible, paying through taxation, rather than specific groups such as visitors to (or residents of) the countryside - or indeed farmers. It appears then that many people recognise that the countryside is in some senses of benefit to us all, and take on board that we need to pay to look after this resource. However, people are almost as keen to pin the responsibility on (non-farming) businesses and industries in the countryside, and make them pay through their profits. We might speculate whether this is felt to be justified because people believe that these industries

are responsible for much of the damage to the countryside. Or is it simply an eagerness for others to pick up the tab, rather than members of the public?

There is moderate support for the view that visitors to the countryside have a responsibility for paying for its maintenance. Interestingly, farmers are the least likely to be held responsible for paying - confirming the public's generally favourable view of the farming industry, as distinct from other rural industries.

Paying for the protection of the countryside

% saying should have most or next most
responsibility for "footing the bill"

The general public, through income tax and VAT	59
Other (i.e. non-farming) businesses and industries in the countryside, through their profits	57
Visitors and holidaymakers, through fees and charges	29
Everyone who lives in the countryside, through their council tax	22
The farming community, through its profits	18
Base	*1219*

There is other evidence too of at least an expressed willingness to pay for protection of the countryside. When we asked respondents to give their views on a number of measures that could be taken to limit visitors to the most "popular places in the countryside", the most favoured approach, supported by around half in 1995, was "making visitors pay and using the extra money to help protect" these popular spots. Nearly half (46 per cent) also supported "advertising and promoting other popular places in the countryside instead" - clearly a short-term rather than a long-term solution.[7]

To sum up, again we find a shortfall between expressed concern about the countryside and willingness to support those policies which could be the most effective in protecting it. Alongside expressions of willingness to pay for countryside protection, with a role for *everyone* as well as for those who actually use it, there is clearly an enthusiasm to let businesses pay or to find some other apparently painless way round the problem.

What sort of environmental protection measures?

In 1993 we asked respondents how much they favoured or opposed various measures that governments might use to try to get people to change their behaviour "for the sake of the environment". Four types of behavioural change were covered: to use less energy; to cut back on driving; to produce less household waste; and to do less harm to the environment. For each one a number of possible policies were described, and respondents asked to what extent they were in favour of each.

Attitudes towards environmental protection measures, 1993

% "strongly" or "somewhat" in favour

To "get people to use less energy" the government should ...
... spend public money on grants to help all households put in
    better home insulation   79
... spend public money on campaigns to persuade people   56
... put up energy taxes each year for the next 10 years   18
... restrict or ration the amount of energy that each household
    is allowed   17

To "get people to cut back on driving" the government should ...
... spend public money on campaigns to persuade people   39
... put a special environment tax on private cars and use the
    money to improve public transport   30
... put up taxes on petrol each year for the next 10 years   17
... restrict or ration the amount of petrol or diesel that people
    are allowed to buy   13

To "get people to produce less household waste" the government should...
... control the amount and type of packaging on products, even if
    it leads to higher prices or less convenience for the customer   50
... spend public money on campaigns to persuade people   48
... make each household pay for its rubbish collection according to the
    amount of rubbish it leaves out   21

To "get people to do less harm to the environment" the government should ...
... pass strict environmental laws   69
... spend public money on campaigns to persuade people   54
... put up taxes on things which harm the environment each year for the
    next 10 years   38

Base   *1268*

Overall, support was highest for the measures aimed at reducing harm to the environment - the least specific of the four changes in behaviour. Support was lowest for the most specific measures: those aimed at reducing driving - a familiar story.

Even though the protection measures we asked about were varied, there are some consistent patterns in the responses. Not surprisingly, the approach gaining the greatest support is one where there is a direct personal benefit - publicly-funded grants to improve home insulation. There was also substantial support for the introduction of strict laws to stop people harming the environment (possibly because these are seen fair in that they would compel *everyone* to conform). However, this measure has no price-tag attached (such as increases in costs or restrictions on choices), which might considerably reduce its popularity. Support is lower, but still substantial, for government controls on packaging even if this led to higher prices.

Publicly-funded campaigns aimed at persuading people to behave in a more environmentally-friendly way consistently attract the support of around half the sample. That support is not higher is perhaps because many might question

their effectiveness. An "environmental tax" on private cars is less popular (especially among drivers). Even though it was stated that this tax would be used to improve public transport, fewer than one-third are in favour. The least popular approaches are those which restrict or ration energy resources, perhaps because people see it as an attack on individual freedom of choice. Higher taxes on fuel are also unpopular, supported by fewer than one in five respondents.

Earlier in this chapter, we saw that majorities (often very substantial ones) express high levels of concern about a variety of environmental problems. Now we see that support for measures aimed at redressing such problems is rather patchy, and far from overwhelming even for the most anodyne of proposals. Enthusiasm is greatest for those measures which are seen to have a direct personal benefit to the respondent, and lowest where increases in costs and restrictions on choice (or both) are most evident. Clearly there is a shortfall between expressed concern for the environment and countryside, and support for measures aimed at protecting them.

Support for transport policies

Priorities for government spending on transport

We have seen that there are widespread worries about road traffic, especially about its contribution to pollution and ill health, and its threat to the countryside. Concern has tended to increase over the last decade, and in recent years its acceleration has been remarkable. But what, if anything, do people think should be done about traffic? What sorts of policy objectives, and what sort of specific measures, gain public support, and which do not?

We look first at views on general transport policy priorities. We asked, for four areas of transport spending, whether the respondent "would like to see more or less government spending". The question carries a warning - "if you say 'much more', it might require a tax increase to pay for it".

As the next table shows, a substantial majority supports more spending on provision for cyclists and pedestrians (politically correct and comparatively cheap), and around half supports more spending on improvements to local and long-distance rail services and local bus services. All of these are more popular than increased spending on roads. We suspect that just a few years before the reverse would have been the case. Approaching two in five support more spending on improving existing roads, but only one in five higher spending on building *more* roads.

Support for government spending on transport (1995)

% saying spend "much more" or "more"

Improving facilities for cyclists and pedestrians	63
Improving local rail services	55
Improving local bus services	51
Improving long distance rail services	46
Improving and widen existing roads	37
Building more roads	20
Base	*1023*

There is plenty of evidence elsewhere of support for improvements to public transport, even at the expense of roads and car users. In 1996 we asked:

> *If over the next few years the government had to choose, to which should it give greater priority - the needs of motorists or the needs of public transport users?*

Nearly three-quarters (73 per cent) said that the needs of public transport users should take priority, with only 15 per cent putting the needs of motorists first. And, when we asked about road improvements *versus* improving public transport, around 70 per cent opted for improvements to public transport over improvements to roads (this was true for both urban and rural areas).

To a green campaigner, such widespread enthusiasm for government support for public transport looks rather promising. But does it indicate a willingness on behalf of members of the public to forego car use and actually *use* public transport? There is plenty more evidence to suggest that this is not the case.

Attitudes of the public to transport issues seem to be encapsulated in responses to two questions we asked in 1996. While as many as 68 per cent think it "very important" to improve public transport in Britain, only 28 per cent think it "very important" to cut down the number of cars on the roads - despite the concerns we have seen. Who then, we might wonder, do people think will use the improved public transport? Alongside support for public transport and an increasing realisation that car traffic must be reduced, there is an enormous reluctance to accept the corollary of reducing car use, at the price of reduced convenience and choice, or increased costs - or both.

Measures to ameliorate transport problems

The next table shows the public's views on a range of transport policy options.

Support for a range of possible transport policies (1995)

Many more streets in cities and towns reserved for pedestrians only	68
Cyclists and pedestrians should be given more priority in towns and cities even if this makes things more difficult for other road users	64
Buses should be given more priority in towns and cities even if this makes things more difficult for car drivers	61
Britain should do more to improve its public transport system even if its road system suffers	58
Only vehicles with permits for essential business allowed in city centres in working hours	49
Banning company cars except where they are essential for employees in their work	49
Motorists charged for driving in city centres in working hours	25
Drivers charged tolls on all motorways	22
Shops and offices encouraged to move out of town and city centres	21
Much higher parking charges in town and city centres	17
Local rail services that do not pay for themselves should be closed down	13
Local bus services that do not pay for themselves should be closed down	12
Base	*1032*

The most popular measures, supported by around two-thirds of people, are pedestrianisation of town and city centres, giving cyclists greater priority, and public transport improvements. There is middling support for vehicle permits and for banning non-essential company cars, though the latter probably has little to do with the environment or even transport policy. The least popular options are closing rail and bus services that fail to pay for themselves. Nearly as unpopular are higher parking charges, motorway tolls and urban road pricing - supported by only around one in five. Similarly, when we asked, in 1996, whether "for the sake of the environment, car users should pay higher taxes", only one in five supported this policy.

The picture could hardly be clearer: 'carrot' measures are widely acceptable, perhaps because people hope that these will encourage other car users to adopt alternative means of transport. In contrast, 'stick' measures, which restrict or increase the cost of car use, gain little support.

Factor analysis of these policy options confirms that there is a distinction between general and popular 'pro-alternative transport' policies (such as promoting public transport, walking and cycling), and specific and unpopular policies which aim to restrict car use (even when these are directly designed to benefit public transport).[8] This is consistent with earlier analyses of BSA data (Taylor and Stokes, 1994). The findings also suggest that the issue of the location of shops and offices is not (yet) widely seen as being integral to transport policy (see also Taylor and Brook, 1997).

What changes have there been over time in attitudes to sustainable transport policies? Change in this area has been quite startling, even over a fairly short period, but patchy. For instance, support for building more motorways "to ease congestion" fell from 39 per cent in 1991 to 25 per cent in 1996; and agreement with the view that "building more roads just encourages more

traffic" rose from 47 per cent in 1993 to 57 per cent in 1996. Evidently some messages of the 'new realism' that is entering into the transport policy debate (Goodwin, 1994) have been getting through. Furthermore, disagreement with the proposition that "people should be allowed to use their cars as much as they like, even if it causes damage to the environment" rose seven percentage points (from 43 to 50 per cent) between 1991 and 1995. Fewer people than before are plumping for the neutral ("neither agree nor disagree") option.

On the other hand, when it comes to what seems to be the major sticking point - restricting car use - there has been much less change over time. For example, the proportion disagreeing that "for the sake of the environment, car users should pay higher taxes" was the same in 1996 as it had been in 1990 (53 per cent). While road traffic problems are widely recognised, many of the more demanding policy options, aimed at ameliorating these problems, gain only limited support. Clearly there is a deep-seated reluctance to reduce car use.

Funding public transport

Our findings suggest that most people support government spending on improvements in public transport. However, when we ask people how far they support or oppose a number of different ways of raising money specifically to improve public transport, we find that their enthusiasm wanes. As the next table shows, none of the six options presented gains the support of much more than a third of respondents. Support barely outweighs opposition even when it comes to cutting spending on new roads. Fewer than one-third favour road pricing on motorways and urban roads, though these solutions are less unpopular than doubling fuel prices or increasing VAT across the board. Perhaps not surprisingly, the least popular option of all is cutting spending on maintenance of existing roads.

Ways of raising money to improve public transport (1996)

	Support	Oppose
Cutting in half spending on new roads	36	34
Charging all motorists £2 each time they enter city/town centres at peak times	30	51
Charging £1 for each 50 miles motorists drive on motorways	30	48
Gradually doubling the cost of petrol over the next 10 years	16	61
Increasing taxes like VAT that we all pay on goods and services	12	68
Cutting in half spending on maintenance on roads we have already	6	72

Base 1058

Here again, we see a shortfall between expressed support for improvements to public transport in principle, and a distinct lack of enthusiasm for any of the specific measures to generate funds for such improvements.

Green behaviour

Three general patterns have emerged so far. First, levels of *support* for more sustainable policy measures are generally lower than expressed levels of concern about environmental problems. Secondly, people are keener on 'carrot' measures (which encourage), than on 'stick' measures (which restrict or charge). And, thirdly, the more specific the discussion of policy options become, the faster support seems to fall away.

What, however, of people's *behaviour*? We turn now to this, focusing particularly on that behaviour which reflects environmental awareness (rather than behaviour which, though appearing green, actually reflects other concerns - such as health or economy). After all, an individual's behaviour - what people themselves do (or profess to do) - is a stronger test of commitment to environmental causes than are expressions of support for particular policy measures. Of course, reports of behaviour are subject to the same kinds of biases - acquiescence, social acceptability and political correctness - as are expressions of concern and support for environmental policies. So levels of green behaviour are very likely to be overstated. Nonetheless, it is useful to compare professed green actions both with levels of concern and with support for different policy options (see Witherspoon and Mohler, 1995; Witherspoon, 1996). To do this we can examine two different types of behaviour: that of 'the public' in general (and consumers in particular) and that of drivers.

Environmental consumer behaviour

Respondents to the 1993 survey were asked how often they did each of the actions described in the next table, all of which can be regarded in some way as being green. Clearly we might expect some over-statement of green behaviours - nonetheless the comparisons *between* types of actions are informative.

Green consumer behaviour (1993)

% who do the following "always" or "often"

Switch off lights in rooms you leave for a short time	75
In mid-winter, lower or turn off heating in your home when you are out for, say, more than four hours	70
Make a special effort to sort glass or tins or plastic or newspapers and so on for recycling	42
Pay attention to environmental labelling	29
Pay attention to the amount of wrapping or packaging used on a product before you decide to buy something	28
Make a special effort to buy fruits and vegetables grown without pesticides or chemicals	20
Not buy something because it had too much wrapping	15
Refuse to eat meat for moral or environmental reasons	10
Cut back on driving a car for environmental reasons	9

Base 1268

The two most common green actions - switching off lights and turning down heating - are both ones which also have a financial motive. For many people this could well be more important than any environmental consideration - indeed, it may be the *only* motivation. Factor analysis confirms that these two actions form a separate 'dimension' which is only slightly correlated with other actions asked about (which are all related).

Nonetheless, as many as two in five people claim to recycle materials often, behaviour which has no financial reward and which requires some effort. Fewer people pay attention to environmental labelling or to packaging, and fewer still buy organic products (many perhaps because of their cost). Least prevalent is vegetarianism (whether for moral or environmental reasons) and cutting back on driving. Overall, almost 20 per cent of respondents did *none* of these things often. A further 20 per cent or so did only one or two, and a mere six per cent did six or more.

We also ask about four examples of actions for the sake of the environment. The most common action we asked about was "signing a petition about an environmental issue". In 1994, nearly half the sample (48 per cent) claimed to have done this at some point in the previous five years, an increase on 1993 (36 per cent). Even so, this proportion remains far lower than that expressing concern about environmental problems. In 1994 a quarter of people had "given money to an environmental group", eight per cent belonged to an environmental group and four per cent had taken part in a "protest or demonstration about an environmental issue".

In order to find out how the population groups in terms of these behaviours, we carried out cluster analysis of these 'actions' alongside the domestic behaviour items discussed earlier. This suggests that there are three behavioural groups. The first (the majority at around 55 per cent) is one that does nothing or relatively little - perhaps turning off lights, turning down their heating, or doing a little recycling. These we shall call 'non-greens'. A second group (21 per cent of the population) signs petitions and gives money

to environmental groups, as well as limiting its use of lighting and heating. We might call these 'indirect' greens. The third group (the remaining 24 per cent) also signs petitions, donates money and limits energy use, but is characterised by relatively high levels of recycling, attention to wrapping and labelling. People in this group are also the most likely to buy organic vegetables and to be vegetarian and, to the extent that *anyone* goes on demonstrations, people in this third group are the most likely to. These we can call 'direct' greens.

We have seen some evidence that green action may have increased over time. To examine environmental activism in more detail we turn now to a question which asks people whether they have ever done any of a number of things "to help protect the countryside". As already noted, there is evidence to suggest that findings about the wider environment are likely to be similar. In 1986 a quarter of people had taken at least one of the actions listed in the next table. By 1994, almost half of respondents had. So people clearly are reporting doing more - although by far the most common action was "signing a petition", and the next most common was "giving money to a campaign", the two easiest actions to take.

Trends in environmental activism

	1986	1994
% who have "ever done" the following		
Signed a petition	18	41
Given money to a campaign	7	15
Contacted an MP or councillor	4	8
Contacted a government or planning department	4	7
Joined a conservation group	3	5
Volunteered to work for a campaign	2	4
Gone on a protest march or demonstration	1	3
Contacted radio, TV or a newspaper	1	2
Base	*1548*	*1165*

We can also use these data to examine environmental activism in more detail. Cluster analysis shows that people appear to fall into one of three basic groups. The majority (79 per cent of the respondents interviewed in 1994) has done very little or nothing at all. A further 14 per cent were distinguished by relatively 'indirect' activity, mainly signing petitions and giving money, and to a lesser extent joining a conservation group. 'Direct' actions had been undertaken by an even smaller group (eight per cent). These environmental activists are clearly very much a minority.

It appears then that the gap between concern for the environment and willingness to do anything about it is even greater than that between concern and policy support; and it is greatest when it comes to green activism - rarer even than professed environmentally-friendly domestic and consumer behaviour. Even those who say they are willing to support policies which would restrict freedom of choice, or lead to increased costs (or both) do not

behave in a consistent manner in their home life, and are even less likely to take an active role in protecting the environment.

Green travel behaviour

In 1993 we asked car drivers about any changes they might have made, over the previous two or three years, in their car use, "for the sake of the environment". These are their responses:

Changes in car use "for the sake of the environment" (1993)

% doing each "a bit" or "a lot" more often
nowadays compared with two or three years ago

Cutting down on your driving speed to save petrol	44
Walking rather than driving to local shops and services	40
Giving people lifts, or taking lifts, to cut down on using cars	38
Making fewer car trips to out-of-town shopping centres to save petrol	33
Using public transport instead of a car	19
Parking your car on the outskirts of towns and using public transport to get to the centre	17
Base	*838*

The two changes *least* likely to have happened both involve using public transport and both, perhaps, entail the greatest personal effort. Each of the others have financial (and perhaps other) motivations, in addition to any environmental considerations. Even so, the majority had not changed their behaviour recently in any of these ways.[9] As for car drivers, just seven per cent said they had made five or six changes; around two-thirds had made two or fewer changes; and more than one in five said that they had made *none* of these changes at all.

Cluster analysis of these measures of change in travel behaviour suggests that people fall into three basic groups: a majority (52 per cent) who have not made any changes to their behaviour; a group (20 per cent) who report reducing their speed, making fewer out-of-town shopping car trips, giving or taking more lifts, and to a lesser extent walking more, using park-and-ride and, less still, using public transport; and a third group (28 per cent) characterised by reportedly walking more, but also by more switching to public transport.

On the whole then, car drivers appear to be fairly reluctant to travel by alternative means, especially by switching to public transport. These findings are consistent with other investigations of the likely effect of measures designed to reduce car use (Taylor and Brook, 1997). On this further evidence, none of the measures we asked about appears likely to make any big differences to car use. In addition to a 'carrot' in the form of improved -

and probably cheaper - public transport (if indeed this is possible), some firm sticks will be needed as well.

Who are the real environmentalists?

It is clear that, although substantial majorities express concern about various environmental problems, and more modest proportions support various policy options, most fail to pass the test when it comes to putting words into action. However, some do. Our last task is to identify this small minority. For this we use multivariate analysis. We carried out logistic regressions of the membership of the groups identified by the cluster analyses in the previous sections. This allows us to see which characteristics are significant predictors of green behaviour, net of other associated characteristics.

We first consider domestic and consumer behaviour, where we identified three basic groups: a majority who does little beyond perhaps limiting domestic fuel and electricity use; and two smaller groups, one which takes 'indirect' actions (such as signing petitions) and another which is engaged in more 'direct' and committed actions (such as purchasing organic products and regularly recycling waste). We start by looking at what distinguishes *either* of these two latter groups from the majority who does very little. We find that they are likely to be middle-aged or younger, to use *both* public transport and the car as a means of travelling (as opposed to other modes of transport) and to be Liberal Democrat identifiers (as opposed to identifiers with other political parties). They are also more likely than not to have educational qualifications, especially 'A' levels or above. However, the most powerful single predictor of green behaviour is degree-level education. Neither gender, nor income, nor the type of area people lived in, had a significant effect.

When we look at the difference between those engaged in 'direct' and 'indirect' green behaviour we find that the main distinguishing characteristic is age. Younger people are more likely to engage in 'direct' green behaviour than older people. Education to 'A' level or above, Liberal Democrat identification and regular use of public transport also had significant effects.

Turning to environmental activism, we examine the two small groups identified earlier - 'indirect' and 'direct' activists. What distinguishes these from the inactive majority is social class and educational levels. Those in the professional and managerial class and those with 'O' level (or equivalent) qualifications or above, are much more likely than the working class people or those with lower qualifications to have engaged in some form of activism. Again, this is especially true of those with degrees. Other characteristics, such as age, gender or party identification, had no significant effect. However, when it comes to distinguishing 'direct' and 'indirect' activists we find that young people are *less* likely than older ones to undertake direct actions, which is somewhat surprising.[10] We also found that *not* identifying with a particular political party is associated with higher levels of direct

environmental activity.   This seems entirely plausible: disillusion with conventional politics may well dispose people to be more active in other ways.

We now turn to car drivers. Here we found that what most distinguishes those who report making changes from those who have not is where one lives. People living in villages and the countryside report *less* change than those in towns and cities (even after the key differences between these groups are taken into account). Of course, country-dwellers (with limited or no public transport and longer distances to travel) have less choice in how they get around, so what we are measuring may be lack of *opportunity* to change rather than *reluctance* to do so. However, it is plausible that there may be attitudinal or value differences associated with living in the countryside which also dispose people to stick to their cars.

Of course, regression modelling tells us nothing about cause and effect. It only shows us if there is a statistically significant association between certain characteristics and behaviour patterns. We can only speculate as to the *direction* of any relationship. It may be, for example, that higher levels of education (and all that entails) dispose people to behave in environmentally appropriate ways. Or that those who are disposed towards green behaviour may (for instance) adapt their travel behaviour by walking or cycling or using public transport in addition to driving. It is certainly likely that people's underlying values play a part, but this remains to be explored. Certainly the significance of education is a familiar story. It may be that experience of higher levels of education engenders a broader world view, encompassing greater consideration of our physical environment.   Or possibly the possession of particular values disposes people both to remain in education for longer and to be more active politically.   It would be particularly interesting to explore further the role of social and political values and personal efficacy in environmental behaviour and activism.

We have seen that the characteristics associated with green consumer behaviour and activism are rather different from those associated with travel behaviour. Here some practical factors - where people live and their current travel behaviour - weigh in (though we suspect that values have a role as well). This finding is consistent with other studies of attitudes to transport policies, where current travel behaviour and car ownership, in addition to social characteristics and values, play a significant role (Taylor and Stokes, 1996). Travel and transport seem to be areas where practical considerations weigh heavily, perhaps more so than over other environment-related issues. This perhaps contributes to, and partly explains, most people's reluctance to change their travel behaviour.   If the government is to succeed in its expressed aim of reducing car use, the case for tough policies (as well as dangling carrots) looks all the stronger.

Conclusions

Majorities, often very large ones, express concern about a wide range of environmental, countryside and transport problems. Some of this concern, we suspect, is attributable to social pressure to be 'politically correct'. Nonetheless, whatever *levels* of concern may be, there is no doubting the direction of the *trends* over time. There has been a significant increase in concern over the last ten years or so, during which time environmental issues have gained prominence in the media and more recently on the political agenda. In particular, the growth in road traffic as a serious environmental problem has shot up the agenda.

But despite this rise in environmental awareness and concern, there is clear evidence to suggest that many people still see environmental degradation as a somewhat distant problem. While now attuned to some of the global environmental threats, most people are slower to realise more immediate threats to themselves and their families.

When we examine attitudes towards policies aimed at environmental protection, we find generally lower levels of support than people's expressions of concern might lead us to expect. Support tends to be highest at the level of general policy aims, and to fall away as the policy becomes specific. Not surprisingly, people are generally more willing to be wooed by 'carrots' than threatened by 'sticks'. But the evidence suggests that, particularly when it comes to car use, 'carrots' are pretty ineffective, and that some substantial 'sticks' will be needed to bring about the changes in behaviour that will be required to limit some of the worst consequences of global environmental degradation.

Notes

1. In addition, the 1994 survey included an 'open' question (that is, one to which respondents were invited to reply in their own words) which asked about threats to the countryside. Up to five answers were coded for each respondent. The problem most frequently mentioned was roads and motorways (35 per cent), then litter (33 per cent), pollution (23 per cent) and new non-residential building (22 per cent). Note that tourism and leisure were mentioned by only 5 per cent of respondents.
2. In 1994 two of the options in this question were reworded. "Litter" was rephrased to "rubbish-tipping and litter", and "tourism and visitors" was rephrased to "too many people visiting the countryside".
3. We should note, however, that 28 per cent of respondents said that nuclear power stations are "*extremely*" dangerous, compared with 22 per cent who said the same about air pollution from cars.
4. In 1993 we asked some additional questions about willingness to pay for environmental protection. Forty-six per cent of people said they would be willing "to pay much higher prices in order to protect the environment" (with 23 per cent being unwilling); 37 per cent were willing "to pay much higher taxes in order to protect the environment" (with 33 per cent being unwilling); and just 30 per cent were willing "to accept cuts in [their] standard of living in order to protect the environment" (with 45 per cent being unwilling).
5. The variable names of the 15 items asked in 1994 and included in the factor analysis are:

Damage, CtryJobs, GovEnvir, IndEnvir, PplEnvir, HousBuil, KeepBelt, PlanLaws, FarmrSay, LessVist, CntrPeo, CntrPop, Country1, Country2 and Country4. Country3 ("*Farmers do a good job in looking after the countryside*") was excluded, since it is not a policy.

6. The correlation between the first factor (environmental protection) and the third (planning) is moderate at .42; with the fourth (farmers), it is low at .26. The other dimensions are unrelated to each other.

7. The other measures asked about ("stopping anyone at all from visiting at particular times each year", "issuing free permits in advance so people will have to plan their visits", "cutting down or closing car parks near the site", and "cutting down on advertising and promoting it") were each less popular, but even so were supported by just over two in five respondents. Factor analyses of the responses to these questions in 1994 and 1995 suggest that no distinct factors emerge from these sets of questions.

8. Factor analysis of the 1995 items resulted in a four-factor solution. The first factor includes improving public transport, giving priority to pedestrians and cyclists, pedestrianisation, agreeing with the statement that "car drivers are still given too easy a time in Britain's towns and cities", opposition to unrestricted car use, and banning company cars. The second factor includes closure of unprofitable rail and bus services; the third, motorway tolls, urban road pricing, increased parking charges and urban vehicle permits - all charges of one kind or another; and the fourth, alone, that shops and offices should move to out-of-town sites. The correlation of the third factor (charges) with the second (favouring alternatives to cars and roads) is moderate (at .39), but correlations between the other factors are low.

9. Factor analysis of these six items results in two factors. The first consisted of "walking instead of driving to local shops and services", "using public transport instead of a car" and "park-and-ride"; the second, "cutting down your driving speed to save petrol" and "making fewer car trips to out-of-town shopping centres to save petrol". The item about giving or accepting lifts loads about equally on the two factors.

10. This may in part be explained by methodological factors: survey response rates are lower for the more mobile under 30s than for most other age groups, and the sample of young people may be rather unrepresentative, lacking some of the more politically active who (almost by definition) are harder for the interviewer to track down.

References

Goodwin, P. (1994), *Traffic Growth and the Dynamics of Sustainable Transport Policies*, Linacre Lecture 1994-5, given on 13th October 1994, Oxford: Transport Studies Unit.

Stokes, G. and Taylor, B. (1994), 'Where next for Transport Policy?', in Jowell, R., Curtice, J., Brook, L. and Ahrendt, D. (eds.), *British Social Attitudes: the 11th Report*, Aldershot: Dartmouth.

Taylor, B. and Brook, L. (1997 forthcoming), 'Public Attitudes to Transport Issues: Findings from the *British Social Attitudes* Surveys', in Banister, D. (ed.), *Transport and the Environment*, London: Chapman and Hall.

Taylor, B and Stokes, G. (1996), *Public Attitudes towards Sustainable Transport Policies'* CREST Working Paper, no.43, Oxford and London: CREST.

Witherspoon, S. (1994), 'The Greening of Britain: romance and rationality', in Jowell, R., Curtice, J., Brook, L. and Ahrendt, D. (eds.), *British Social Attitudes: the 11th Report*, Aldershot: Dartmouth.

Witherspoon, S. (1996), 'Democracy, the environment and public opinion in Western Europe', in Lafferty, W. and Meadowcroft, J. (eds.), *Democracy and the Environment*, Cheltenham: Edward Elgar.

Witherspoon, S. and Martin, J. (1992), 'What do we mean by Green?', in Jowell, R., Brook, L., Prior, G. and Taylor, B. (eds.), *British Social Attitudes: the 9th Report*, Aldershot: Dartmouth.

Witherspoon, S. and Mohler, P. (1995), Report on Research into Environmental Attitudes
    and Perceptions (REAP), prepared for the European Commission on behalf of the European
    Consortium for Comparative Social Surveys, Mannheim: ZUMA.
Young, K. (1991), 'Shades of Green', in Jowell, R., Brook, L. and Taylor, B. (eds.), *British
    Social Attitudes: the 8th Report*, Aldershot: Dartmouth.

Acknowledgements

Financial support for the questionnaire modules reported on in this chapter
has come from the Countryside Commission (since 1985), with extra funding
since 1994 to continue to ask questions on transport issues; from the
European Union (in 1993); from the ESRC (again in 1993) in the form of an
award under its Transport and the Environment Programme (No. L 119 251
021) and under a three year grant between 1994 and 1996 (Award No. R 000
221 282); and from the Department of Transport (in 1996). We are grateful
to them all.

7 The housing divide

Alan Murie[*]

At the beginning of the twentieth century, Britain was a nation of private tenants. Now, at the end of that same century, it is a nation of home-owners. In the intervening period council housing has grown and then diminished in importance.

As the various sectors have changed in size, so too has their character. Over the last twenty years council housing has changed from a sector characterised by high quality housing accommodating a relatively wide social mix of people, to one providing for a narrower social group. Meanwhile, home-ownership has changed from being the preserve of an exclusive minority to a mass housing tenure catering for a wide range of income and social groups (Saunders, 1990; Malpass and Murie, 1994; Forrest, Murie and Williams, 1990).

Housing was one of the flagship policies of the last Conservative government. It deliberately sought to encourage the growth of home-ownership and diminish the role of council housing. It provided incentives for council tenants to buy their own homes and hailed home-ownership as a natural aspiration for all, an upward escalator to material prosperity. Ownership would help create a 'property-owning democracy' in which all would have a material stake in the success of the nation. It would enable people to accumulate wealth which they could pass on their children. Indeed, during the house price boom of the 1980s, the returns from owning a home could outstrip those to be gained through employment. Some commentators viewed such rising house prices and public support for home-ownership as

[*] Alan Murie is Professor and Director of the Centre for Urban and Regional Studies, University of Birmingham.

being inherent features of the housing system. As a result, they argued, housing tenure was a key social division - more important indeed than social class. Saunders, for instance, stated that "social and economic divisions arising out of ownership of key means of consumption such as housing are now coming to represent a new major fault line in British society" (Saunders, 1984: 203).

In 1989 the bubble burst. Interest rates rose and economic recession set in. People who had borrowed at unprecedented levels against the promise of rising prices found it difficult enough to maintain their mortgage payments while they were in work, let alone when they lost their job. House prices started to tumble. The home-ownership dream of the 1980s turned into a nightmare of mortgage arrears, repossessions and negative equity. Families were trapped in properties which they could neither sell nor afford to live in. Moreover, this recession in the housing market then proceeded to last longer than had ever been the case before.

By the time of our latest survey, there were signs of an upturn in the housing market, with borrowers benefiting from record low interest rates. We can therefore now begin to assess whether the experience of the housing recession has had any long-term impact on attitudes towards housing. Five years ago, we found that confidence in home-ownership had declined (Cairncross, 1992). Was that decline in confidence a temporary response to the economic cycle? Or did it have a more permanent impact? Were Saunders and others correct in believing that most people would always aspire towards home-ownership? Or might that desire have been attenuated by the experience that an Englishman's home could be his prison as well as his castle?

The first task of this chapter is to address these questions. Has recent history left households with less confidence in the housing sector, damaging the British love affair with home-ownership? Or was the Conservative government's instinct about our attitudes towards housing correct? The chapter then proceeds to look at some of the possible *consequences* of the growth of owner-occupation and the decline of council housing that were encouraged by the last government. Has a significant new social and political divide been opened up between owners and renters? Or has the spread of owner-occupation, and the increasing 'variegation' of home-owners, meant that we can no longer consider (if, indeed, we ever could) owner-occupiers as a single cohesive social group with common interests and attitudes?

To achieve its first task the chapter examines the attitudes of the general population between 1986 and 1996, using data from the *British Social Attitudes* survey series. To undertake its second task it looks both at differences in the social attitudes of those in owner-occupied and council housing, and at differences between those in owner-occupied housing according to the *value* of their housing. It argues that not only have attitudes to home-ownership been changed by the experience of the recession but that the home-ownership sector is now so diverse that it is increasingly inappropriate to talk of home-owners as if they were a single social group.

We begin however by looking a little more closely at how housing has changed in Britain over recent years.

Changing tenures

Since the introduction in 1980 of 'Right to Buy' legislation by the Conservative government some two million council homes have been sold in Great Britain. Consequently, the proportion of households living in council houses has fallen, from 32 per cent in 1979 to 19 per cent in 1995. Owner-occupation has grown rapidly over the same period, rising from 55 per cent of households in 1979 to 67 per cent in 1995 (Department of the Environment *et al.*, 1996). The private rented sector has been little changed (at 11 per cent in 1979 and 10 per cent in 1995).

The market conditions for owner-occupied housing have moved from boom to bust over the last decade. The following table summarises the changes in house prices in recent years.

UK house prices (1985-1995)

	Average price (£)	Real change year on year
1985	34,900	2.9
1986	39,800	10.1
1987	46,400	11.9
1988	58,200	19.7
1989	70,400	12.2
1990	69,500	- 9.8
1991	68,600	- 6.9
1992	66,000	- 7.2
1993	64,300	- 4.0
1994	66,300	0.6
1995	66,700	- 2.6

Figures are for 'mix adjusted' house prices at mortgage completion stage amongst all houses
Source: *Council for Mortgage Lenders*, 1996

Alongside these changes in market conditions have been changes in the kind of people who live in owner-occupied and council housing. Most dramatic have been the changes in the composition of those living in council housing. Those who exercised their 'Right to Buy' were largely those from more affluent households living in the most desirable properties. Exacerbated by this and other recent changes, council housing has increasingly come to be dominated by the poor, the long-term sick and unemployed, the disabled and lone-parent households (Lee and Murie, 1997). For instance, the proportion of households living in council housing which contain someone in employment has declined, and the proportion receiving benefits increased. In our 1984 survey, 34 per cent of those living in council houses belonged to households whose incomes were substantially below average; by 1996 the

figure had reached some 57 per cent.[1] However, as owner-occupation has grown it has extended its reach to poorer households. For instance, this sector now includes a substantial population of low income elderly households who were certainly not owner-occupiers during the early years of the housing market boom (Forrest, Murie and Williams, 1990). Our 1996 survey found that 43 per cent of those in households with substantially below average incomes were in owner-occupied housing, compared with 34 per cent only twelve years before in 1984.

Attitudes to home-ownership

Have attitudes towards owning a home changed? What long-term impact, if any, did the recession have? Our first indicator comes from a question we have asked on a number of occasions over the last ten years:

> *Supposing a newly married couple, both with steady jobs, asked your advice whether to buy or rent a home. If they had the choice, what would you advise them to do?*
>
> *To buy a home as soon as possible*
>
> *To wait a bit, then try to buy a home*
>
> *Not to plan to buy a home at all*

In 1986, the middle of the housing boom, as many as 74 per cent said that they would advise a couple to buy a home as soon as possible. In 1991, by which time the housing market had gone into reverse, only 60 per cent took this view. And, far from recovering, the figure in our latest survey has fallen still further to just 54 per cent. So, while a majority still believe that owner-occupation is best achieved sooner rather than later (with only three per cent saying that the couple should not plan to buy a home at all), on this measure attitudes towards owner-occupation have become distinctly more cautious in the wake of the recession.

Why is this so? We asked our respondents, "still thinking of what you might say to this young couple", whether they agreed or disagreed with a series of statements about the advantages and disadvantages of home-ownership. Let us look first at the possible disadvantages.

Disadvantages of home-ownership

% agreeing	1986	1991	1996
Owning a home is too much of a risk for couples without secure jobs	59	68	68
Owning a home is a big financial burden to repair and maintain	50	57	55
Owning your own home can be a risky investment	25	43	50
Owning a home ties up money you may need urgently for other things	35	35	33
Owning a home is just too much of a responsibility	12	10	12
Base	*1387*	*1207*	*3087*

On some items the recession has clearly had little impact. For instance, just one in eight believes that owning a home is "just too much of a responsibility", the same proportion as did so ten years earlier. But in two key respects there has been a clear change. Whereas in 1986 only a quarter thought that owning your home could be a "risky investment", now no less than half take this view. And, far from diminishing since the early days of the recession in 1991, this sentiment has become even more widespread since then. Meanwhile, 68 per cent now agree that owning a home can be "too much of a risk" for those without secure jobs, up from 59 per cent in 1986.

So, not surprisingly, the experience of the recession has apparently had an impact on attitudes towards owner-occupation. Nowadays people appear to be much more aware of the financial risks associated with owner-occupation than they were in the middle of the boom years of the 1980s. This interpretation is bolstered by the fact that in our latest survey those who are pessimistic about the prospects for the housing market in their area are more likely to say that owning a home can be a risky investment than those who are optimistic. No less than two-thirds of those who expect house prices in their area to fall over the next year agree that owning your home can be a risk, compared with less than half of those who expect house prices to rise. And those who expect house prices in their area to fall are also more likely to say that the young couple should "wait a bit" before buying.

What about the advantages of home-ownership? Here also there is some evidence of a decline in confidence. True, there is still an overwhelming belief in the merits of owner-occupation as a relatively inexpensive form of housing which both gives people freedom to do what they want to their home and which can be passed on to one's family after death. But the proportion agreeing with the latter two of these advantages has fallen somewhat. So far as one's home being "something to leave to your family" is concerned, this decline has only occurred since 1991, suggesting that it may not so much reflect the impact of the recession as the growing publicity given in recent years to the need for some elderly people to sell their homes in order to pay for care. And, although confidence in the economics of owner-occupation declined a little in the immediate wake of the recession, it appears subsequently to have been restored by the fall in interest rates after 1992.

Advantages of home-ownership

% agreeing	1986	1991	1996
Over time, buying a home works out less expensive then paying rent	82	76	82
Your own home will be something to leave your family	80	83	76
Owning a home gives you the freedom to do what you want to it	82	77	71
Base	*1387*	*1207*	*3087*

What judgement can we pass on the Conservative legacy of home-ownership promotion? It appears to be more ownership - but less confidence. The damage that was done to people's confidence in the early years of the recession has still not been fully restored. While most people still want to be owner-occupiers there is now a wider appreciation of the disadvantages that home-ownership can incur, as well as the advantages.

Tenure polarisation

It has long been argued that there are major attitudinal differences between owner-occupiers and council tenants. But has this divide widened as owner-occupation has expanded? There are two possible reasons as to why this might have happened. The first is that any differences simply reflect the changing social composition of the two tenures. Thus, as council housing increasingly becomes the preserve of the poor, so we can anticipate that those living in council houses should become more distinctive in their attitudes. A second reason why attitudes might have diverged is concerned with the increasing dominance of owner-occupation as a form of tenure. Consequently, those living in council housing are more likely to feel socially excluded (and perhaps those in owner-occupation may also feel less compassion towards those less fortunate than themselves). So this second account sees the changes that have occurred within the housing market as themselves influencing attitudes (unlike our first account which simply sees any changes in attitudes as reflecting the increasing social differences between those who are council tenants and those who are owner-occupiers).

We shall look here at two sets of attitudes which we might expect to show differences between owner-occupiers and council tenants. The first concerns people's attitudes towards their neighbourhoods (and, in particular, the incidence of crime). The *British Crime Survey* shows that crime, and fear of crime, is much higher than average in council neighbourhoods (Hope and Hough, 1988). In British cities, both offenders and victims are more likely to live in council neighbourhoods than in other areas (Foster and Hope, 1993). If council housing has come to be seen as the sector into which those with social problems are marginalised, we might anticipate that these characteristics of council housing may have become more pronounced.

The second set of differences we shall look at is attitudes towards politics. If council housing is increasingly used only to house the socially excluded, we might anticipate that these people feel politically excluded as well and feel more alienated from the political system. They may believe that more should be done to reduce social inequality and, if this is the case, may be distinctive in terms of their support for different political parties.

We begin by looking at our respondents' attitudes towards the neighbourhoods within which they live. Firstly, we examine their reports of the frequency of a variety of social nuisances that stop short of criminal offences. This shows that in every case those living in council houses are more likely than those in owner-occupied housing to say that the particular nuisance was "very" or "fairly" common in their neighbourhood. The differences are narrowest in respect of "drunks or tramps on the streets" (where indeed those living in private rental accommodation report a higher figure than do council tenants) and on "teenagers hanging around on the streets", an experience reported as common by nearly half of all our respondents. But on each of the other four items the differences between council tenants and owner-occupiers are substantial. For instance, over a quarter of council tenants say that graffiti is common in their area, double the equivalent proportion among owner-occupiers (12 per cent).

Yet it is far from clear that there is anything markedly new in these findings. We previously asked the same set of questions in 1990 and the next table shows, in brackets, the change between then and 1996. True, many of the changes in the council housing sector had already taken place and so our data will not capture fully any process of polarisation. But it is clear that for the most part any particular nuisance has increased or diminished by approximately the same amount amongst council tenants as it has amongst owner-occupiers. Moreover, in those cases where this has not occurred, this is sometimes because the gap between the two groups has *narrowed* rather than because it has widened. For instance, while the reported incidence of rubbish and litter lying around the streets has increased among council tenants but declined slightly amongst owner-occupiers, reports of teenagers hanging around the streets have increased *more* amongst owner-occupiers than they have amongst council tenants.

Neighbourhood nuisances (1996)*

% saying "very" or "fairly" common in their area	All	Council tenants	Private tenants	Owner-occupiers
Teenagers hanging around on the streets	47 (+11)	50 (+4)	43 (+9)	43 (+10)
Rubbish and litter lying about	41 (+1)	53 (+5)	48 (+2)	36 (-2)
Graffiti on walls or buildings	16 (+2)	26 (+1)	20 (+7)	12 (+1)
Homes and gardens in bad condition	16 (-1)	28 (-4)	27 (-2)	11 (0)
Noisy neighbours or loud parties	13 (-1)	22 (-1)	19 (-1)	9 (0)
Drunks or tramps on the streets	10 (+2)	18 (+4)	20 (+3)	10 (+4)
Bases	*3087*	*590*	*304*	*2193*

* Each figure in brackets shows the percentage point change between 1990 and 1996

When we look at actual criminal offences, as in the next table, the gap between council tenants and owner-occupiers is, with the singular exception of vandalism, mostly small. The perceived incidence of car theft and burglary amongst council tenants is little higher than it is amongst owner-occupiers. And on the two items where, again, we can compare our latest results with our 1990 survey, the gap between the two groups appears to have narrowed rather than increased.

Neighbourhood crime (1996)*

% saying "very" or "fairly" common in their area	All	Council tenants	Private tenants	Owner-occupiers
Cars broken into or stolen	43 (n/a)	47 (n/a)	38 (n/a)	42 (n/a)
Homes broken into	38 (-7)	41 (-12)	33 (-7)	38 (-5)
Vandalism and deliberate damage to property	27 (+8)	40 (+5)	25 (+2)	23 (+8)
People attacked in the streets	9 (n/a)	15 (n/a)	13 (n/a)	6 (n/a)
Base	*3087*	*590*	*304*	*2193*

* Each figure in brackets shows the percentage point change between 1990 and 1996
   n/a = not asked in 1990

While these data do generally show a higher incidence of nuisance and crime amongst council tenants, it is important to register the consistently high proportion of tenants in this sector who report that a particular nuisance or crime is uncommon. Despite all the changes of the last twenty years, clearly not all those living in council houses are on 'problem estates'.

There is, however, one marked difference between council tenants and owner-occupiers in their feelings about their neighbourhood and crime. We asked:

Do you think you live in the sort of area where people who thought a
house was being broken into would do something about it or just turn
a blind eye?

Among owner-occupiers nearly three-quarters thought that people in their
area would "do something about it", compared with only just over a half of
council tenants. And when we asked whether they thought burglaries in their
area were "mostly done by people from other areas or mostly done by people
around here", over a quarter of council tenants said "people around here",
compared with just 15 per cent of owner-occupiers. So, whatever the actual
differences between the two tenures in the incidence of crime, those living in
council houses are less inclined than owner-occupiers to trust in their
neighbours, perhaps increasing their sense of vulnerability.

We turn now to the political views of these two groups. Is there any
evidence that council tenants are increasingly likely to feel excluded from the
political system? Are they distinctive in their political views, either in terms
of their attitudes towards issues concerned with economic inequality, or in
terms of the parties they support?

In the following table we look at the responses given to a number of
statements designed to measure what is called 'system efficacy' - the extent
to which people feel that the political system is capable of responding to the
demands that are made of it (for further details see the chapter by Curtice and
Jowell in this volume). Two patterns immediately stand out. First, those
living in council houses are markedly more likely to agree with these
statements, suggesting a low sense of system efficacy. Second, on both the
statements where we can compare our latest results with our 1986 survey
data, the proportion of council tenants who agree has risen more rapidly than
has been the case among owner-occupiers. Here, at least, we do appear to
have some evidence of polarisation among the different housing tenures.

Housing tenure and system efficacy (1996)*

	Council tenants	Private tenants	Owner-occupiers
% **"strongly agree"**			
Generally speaking, those we elect as MPs lose touch with people pretty quickly	43 (+21)	19 (+1)	23 (+9)
Parties are only interested in people's votes, not in their opinions	42 (+15)	23 (+7)	26 (+10)
MPs don't care much about what people like me think	26 (n/a)	8 (n/a)	13 (n/a)
It doesn't really matter which party is in power, in the end things go on much the same	24 (n/a)	11 (n/a)	14 (n/a)
Bases	*215*	*82*	*821*

* Each figure in brackets shows the percentage point change between 1986 and 1996
n/a = not asked in 1986.

However, when it comes to attitudes towards economic inequality or towards the political parties, there is little evidence of such polarisation. To measure attitudes towards inequality we use the 'left-right' scale (described in detail in Appendix I to this report). In essence, the lower a person's score on this scale, the more 'left-wing' (and thus in favour of equality) this person is. The next table shows the average score of respondents in each housing tenure over the course of the last eleven years. From this it is clear that council tenants are undoubtedly more left-wing than owner-occupiers. In every year since we first administered this scale in 1985, council tenants have had a lower score on our scale than have owner-occupiers. But there is no evidence that the *gap* between them is consistently widening. In 1985, the average score of owner-occupiers was 0.3 greater than that of council tenants, exactly the same as in our most recent survey.

Average score on the 'left-right' scale by housing tenure

	1985	Base	1986	Base	1989	Base	1991	Base	1994	Base	1996	Base
Council tenants	2.4	416	2.1	269	2.0	523	2.2	581	2.0	257	2.1	596
Private tenants	2.8	98	2.6	111	2.3	134	2.3	189	2.6	107	2.4	272
Owner-occupiers	2.7	942	2.7	902	2.6	1856	2.6	1781	2.5	861	2.4	2047

Similarly, council tenants are more likely to identify with the Labour party than are owner-occupiers. As many as 57 per cent of council tenants identified with the Labour party in our most recent survey, compared with just 38 per cent of owner-occupiers. But this gap is, if anything, *smaller* than that recorded in most *British Social Attitudes* surveys. There is certainly no evidence to support the view that housing tenure has become more strongly associated with people's political sympathies.

So, with the possible exception that council tenants appear to have become more alienated from the political system since 1990, we have found little evidence of a growing social and attitudinal polarisation between council tenants and owner-occupiers. Council tenants certainly do differ from owner-occupiers in their social experience and political experience, but much of this difference has always been present. We have certainly not uncovered a growing divide.

Different home-owners

What of the owner-occupied sector itself? Now that they comprise two-thirds of the population, do owner-occupiers still have enough in common with one another to be considered as a cohesive social group? Or are there differences between categories of owner-occupiers as stark as those between owner-occupiers and council tenants?

There are a number of ways in which we might break down owner-occupiers into different groups. Some, for instance, own their homes outright; others are buying them on a mortgage. For the former, higher interest rates will mean better returns on their savings; for the latter it will mean higher monthly mortgage payments. However, those buying on a mortgage will eventually expect to own their homes outright, and have just as much interest as those who own their homes outright in the state of the housing market as a whole.

We have therefore taken a different approach and classified owner-occupiers according to the value of their homes (as measured by the council tax band of the property was reported by the respondent). These bands are, of course, determined by the estimated value of the property at the beginning of the decade. Our reason for classifying owner-occupiers in this way is that property values will reflect a number of features of housing that might engender a particular outlook amongst their occupants. For example, those living in higher valued properties will tend also to live in more desirable areas that have access to good public services, schools and shops. Further, they are more likely than other owner-occupiers to profit from rising house prices and clearly have a bigger stake than most in the success of the housing market. On one level we might expect that calls for greater social equality or more government spending on public services have less appeal to this group than to others.

We start, however, by examining whether those living in higher valued properties actually find their neighbourhoods more desirable places to live than do other groups. In the following table we examine the same measures of 'nuisance' as we considered in the previous section. We divide owner-occupiers into three groups: those in properties banded A or B (the lowest values); those in C or D; and, finally, those in any band between E and H. For comparison purposes we show once again the comparable figures for those who live in council housing.

Home-owners and neighbourhood nuisance (1996)

	Owner-occupiers (Council Tax band)			Council tenants
	E-H	C-D	A-B	
% saying "very" or "fairly" common in their area				
Teenagers hanging around on the streets	32	45	51	59
Rubbish and litter lying about	26	35	48	53
Graffiti on walls	7	11	17	26
Homes and gardens in bad condition	3	11	20	28
Noisy neighbours or loud parties	6	8	15	22
Drunks or tramps on the street	8	9	12	18
Bases	*558*	*920*	*598*	*590*

There are clearly some substantial differences among owner-occupiers in their reported experience of nuisance. On all of the items, those living in the lowest valued properties are more likely to say that the nuisance is common in their area than are those living in the highest valued properties. Moreover on many of the items the *gap* between those in the highest and lowest valued properties is as large as (or, indeed, even larger than) that between owner-occupiers in general and council tenants. For example, there is a 22 point gap between those in the highest and lowest valued properties when it comes to "rubbish and litter lying about" being common, compared with a 17 point gap between all owner-occupiers and council tenants. True, on all of the items, the reported incidence among those in the lowest valued owner-occupied properties is still lower than that reported by council tenants. But, even so, on most measures the experience of owner-occupiers in the lowest valued property is more similar to that of council tenants than it is to that of those living in the highest valued properties.

When we considered the incidence of crime earlier we found that many of the differences between owner-occupiers and council tenants were smaller than they were when we looked at 'nuisances'. This narrowed gap is also true when we examine those in high and low valued owner-occupied homes. But, when it comes to vandalism, where there was a 17 point gap between owner-occupiers and council tenants, so too is there a large (16 point) gap between those in high and low valued properties. And so far as car crime is concerned, those living in low valued properties are slightly more likely to say it is common in their area than are council tenants.

Home-owners and crime (1996)

	Owner-occupiers (Council Tax band)			Council tenants
% saying "very" or "fairly" common in their area	E-H	C-D	A-B	
Cars broken into or stolen	38	39	50	47
Homes broken into	40	34	43	41
Vandalism and deliberate damage to property	16	22	32	40
People attacked in the streets	4	5	8	15
Bases	*558*	*920*	*598*	*590*

This picture of substantial heterogeneity amongst owner-occupiers is repeated when we look at their political views. For example, it is not just council tenants who are more likely to have a low sense of 'system efficacy'; so too are those in low valued owner-occupied properties. Indeed they are almost as likely to agree that it "it doesn't really matter which party is in power" as are council tenants. In this respect, their views are certainly very different to those of owner-occupiers in more highly valued properties.

Home-owners and system efficacy (1996)

	Owner-occupiers (Council Tax band)			Council tenants
% "strongly agree"	E-H	C-D	A-B	
Generally speaking, those we elect as MPs lose touch with people pretty quickly	19	21	32	43
Parties are only interested in people's votes, not in their opinions	22	22	35	42
MPs don't care much about what people like me think	7	13	18	26
It doesn't really matter which party is in power, in the end things go on much the same	8	12	23	24
Bases	*170*	*358*	*256*	*215*

When it comes to party identification, those living in the lowest-valued properties are very similar to council tenants in their sympathies, and are consequently very different from other owner-occupiers. No less than 55 per cent of those in A or B banded properties identify with the Labour party, only just below the 57 per cent of council tenants who do so. In contrast, just 35 per cent of those in C or D banded properties identify with the Labour party, and only 24 per cent of those with properties in bands E-H. So, the political 'fault-line' in partisan sympathies appears *not* to lie between all owner-occupiers and council tenants, but rather between those who own high and middle value owner-occupied homes and those who own low value homes or rent housing from the council. Owner-occupation *per se* is not automatically associated with Conservative party sympathies, as was widely assumed in the 1980s.

This is reinforced when we look again at our 'left-right' scale. The average score of those in low valued properties is, at 2.2, only a little higher than that of council tenants (who score 2.1). But, in contrast, those in high-valued properties are much more likely to take a right-wing, non-egalitarian view, with an average score of 2.7.

Conclusion

The picture of housing and social attitudes painted by this chapter is very different to what many would have anticipated a decade ago. The crisis in the home-ownership sector between 1989 and 1996 has had a measurable impact upon people's attitudes towards, and expectations of, owner-occupation. Even if most people evidently would still prefer to own their home, they now appear much more aware of the risks associated with owner-occupation. Meanwhile, we have uncovered little evidence of a growing polarisation

between owner-occupiers and council tenants, either in terms of their attitudes towards the neighbourhoods within which they live or in their political attitudes.

At the same time, we have discovered how varied owner-occupation and owner-occupiers themselves now are. Different households in different parts of the market have quite different views of their interests and of the circumstances in which they live. Clearly we can no longer regard home-owners as a single group with common interests, attitudes and political responses that easily distinguish them from council tenants. Rather, the key divide in housing appears not to be between home-owners and council tenants, but rather between, on the one hand, council tenants and home-owners at the lower end of the market and, on the other, home-owners at the more affluent end of the housing market. Britain may indeed be a 'nation of home-owners'; but it is a nation where an expensive home entails something quite different to its owners than a cheaper one.

Note

1. Households are defined as having a 'substantially below average income' if their income lies in the bottom quintile of the household income distribution.

References

Cairncross, F. (1992), 'The influence of the recession', in Jowell, R., Brook, L, Prior, G. and Taylor, B. (eds.), *British Social Attitudes: the 9th Report*, Aldershot: Dartmouth.

Council for Mortgage Lenders (1996), *Housing Finance*, **30**, May 1996, Council for Mortgage Lenders: London.

Department of the Environment, the Scottish Office and the Welsh Office (1996), *Housing and Construction Statistics*, London: HMSO.

Forrest. R., Murie, A. and Williams, P. (1990), *Home-ownership: Differentiation and Fragmentation*, London: Unwin Hyman.

Foster, J. and Hope, T. (1993), *Housing, Community and Crime: the Impact of the Priority Estate Project,* Home Office Research Study, **131**, HMSO: London.

Heath, A., Jowell, R. and Curtice, J. (1985), *How Britain Votes,* Oxford: Pergamon Press.

Hope, T and Hough, M. (1988), 'Area, crime and incivilities: a profile from the British Crime Survey' in Hope, T. and Shaw, M. (eds.), *Communities and Crime Reduction,* Home Office Research and Planning Unit: London.

Johnston, R.J. (1987), 'A note on housing tenure and voting in Britain 1983', *Housing Studies*, **2**: 2.

Lee, P. and Murie, A. (1997), *Poverty, Housing Tenure and Social Exclusion*, Bristol: Policy Press.

Malpass, P. and Murie, A. (1994), *Housing Policy and Practice,* Basingstoke: Macmillan.

Saunders, P. (1984), 'Beyond housing classes: the sociological significance of private property rights in means of consumption', *International Journal of Urban and Region Research,* **8**.

Saunders, P. (1990), *A Nation of Home-owners*, London: Unwin Hyman.

8 Politics and the news media: mobilisation or videomalaise?

Kenneth Newton[*]

The impact of the mass media on modern government and politics is hotly disputed by politicians, journalists, and social scientists. Some argue that the media have little direct effect; they can only reflect or reinforce political patterns, rather than create or change them. Others say that the modern mass media permeate so much of life that their influence is profound, with far reaching effects on government and politics. But many of those who believe in media effects are divided between two diametrically opposed camps which we can call the *mobilisation school* and the *videomalaise school*.

  The *mobilisation school* argues that the modern media help to sustain democracy, even improve its quality. It claims that a combination of higher levels of education and the spread of the mass media have produced citizens who are better informed, more understanding, and more sophisticated about political affairs. Never before have so many people found so much information so easily available at such a low cost. For the best educated strata, the media provide a constant flow of information and comment which keeps them abreast of the news and helps them form their own opinions. For the less well educated, the media perform the invaluable service of simplifying and analysing complex issues, and by introducing politicians into everybody's living room, television enables ordinary citizens to see for themselves and make up their own minds. As evidence for their claims the mobilisation school points to rising levels of political knowledge and understanding, to higher levels of ideological sophistication and to more interest and involvement in politics in many countries in the western world

[*] Kenneth Newton is Professor of Government at the University of Essex and Executive Director of the European Consortium for Political Research.

(Dalton, 1996; Topf, 1995; Holtz-Bacha, 1990). A recent British study finds that people who watch the television news regularly are better informed, have higher levels of political efficacy, and are more likely to participate in politics (Norris, 1996a).

In opposition to this, the *videomalaise* school argues that the modern news media, especially television, tend to undermine democracy. It claims that the news media often oversimplify, trivialise, and sensationalise events. Complex issues are reduced to two simple, usually opposing camps. Other opinions are excluded, while subtleties and complexities are ignored. The news is usually about conflict and disagreement, and if there is no conflict the media will seek it out or exaggerate it. Elections are not presented as a contest between parties with different programmes and policies, but as a horse race between two party leaders. The media take less interest in the policies and political beliefs of political leaders than in their dress, appearance, and accent. Instead of serious news or discussion we are presented with sound-bites and photo-opportunities. At the same time, the news changes in a fast and furious manner, with one event replacing another other in rapid but incomprehensible succession - 'one damn thing after another'. This, it is said, induces political fatigue and confusion, rather than informing and mobilising. Worst of all, a great deal of the news is 'bad news' about disasters, corruption, crime, wars, lies, violence, incompetence, scandals, and sleaze.

At best, this sort of news wearies or worries people; at worst, it alienates them and creates political cynicism, fear, and disillusionment. The modern media give ordinary citizens the feeling that they neither understand nor control politics, and that politicians are corrupt or incompetent, or both. Thus, the modern media generate videomalaise (see, for example, Robinson 1976; Ansolabehere, *et al.*, 1995; Schudson 1995; Postman 1987).

In recent years social scientists have used the videomalaise literature to explain what they see as an alarming loss of 'social capital' in the western world, especially in the USA (Putnam 1995). By social capital they mean the attitudes and values of civil society and its social networks and voluntary associations, which encourage citizens to trust each other and to co-operate in order to solve social, economic, political problems. Trust and reciprocity are particularly important as a basis for civic engagement and political co-operation. The media, especially television, are singled out as the prime factor in the erosion of social capital. The rapid expansion of television in the last few decades has overturned age-old social patterns of civic engagement in which people spend time with one another in community associations and voluntary organisations. It has, the argument goes, isolated and privatised individuals in their own living rooms, and at the same time promoted a sense of distrust and suspicion, especially of politics and politicians.

This chapter is about the impact of the news media on political attitudes. Its main question is: what effect, if any, do the modern news media have on political attitudes and behaviour in Britain? Do they inform and mobilise the

population politically, or do they, on the contrary, cause political alienation and videomalaise? The focus will be on newspapers and television because these are at once the main sources of news for the majority of people and the main focus of the mobilisation and videomalaise debate.

Different media, different people, different uses

One of the problems with both mobilisation and videomalaise theories is that they tend to generalise broadly about 'the impact of the media', as if there were only one kind of effect. Yet among the print media there is a world of difference between the tabloid newspaper and a broadsheet in their news reporting, and television differs from both. A strong contrast also exists in television between news and current affairs programmes on the one hand, and chat-shows, soap-operas and movies, on the other. So, generalisations about the political effects of the media are likely to be misleading. Instead, it seems reasonable to work on the assumption that different kinds of people use different kinds of media for different kinds of purposes.

The data from the *British Social Attitudes* survey series can be used to show how different groups use the news media. In the case of newspapers we can distinguish between three groups: those whose usual newspaper is a tabloid, those whose usual newspaper is a broadsheet and those who do not regularly read a newspaper. (Regularly is defined here as "at least three times a week"). It should be noted, of course, that the tabloids dominate newspaper readership: almost one half of the population take a tabloid as their regular newspaper, compared with only one in ten who take a broadsheet. (The remaining two-fifths take no regular newspaper).

As shown by the next table, there is a predictably big difference between broadsheet and tabloid readers. The former have higher incomes, socio-economic status, and education, are more economically active and more likely to be male and Conservative. They watch less television in general, but about the same amount of television *news* as tabloid readers. There is less difference between tabloid readers and those who do not regularly read a paper, except that those who do not read a paper regularly are more likely to be women and to watch both less television in general and less television news.

An interesting finding is thus that those who do not read a newspaper regularly are also less likely than other groups to watch the television news, or to watch television in general. So it seems there is a group of people who make less than average use of *all* the news media, and this group includes a higher proportion of women. They differ from tabloid readers who watch a lot of television in general, including television news, and from broadsheet readers, who watch comparatively little television other than television news.

Social characteristics of different types of newspaper readers

	No regular paper	Regular tabloid	Regular broadsheet
Age (average)	43	48	48
Annual household income (£s - approx average)	17,500	15,000	28,000
Age completed full-time education (average)	16.8	15.9	19.1
Socio-economic group (average) (scored from 1 to 6)	3.8	3.5	4.9
% economically *in*active	39	45	34
% women	60	53	40
% Conservative Party identifiers	29	35	44
TV hours (per week)	23.4	27.5	15.0
TV news (days per week)	4.8	5.3	5.3
Base	*1539*	*1573*	*381*

Similarly, we can divide the population into groups according to their use of television. Here there are two distinct dimensions: whether a person watches a lot of television in general and whether he or she watches a lot of television news in particular. We could show the continuum in each case from watching nothing to watching a great deal, but so as to cut down on the sheer weight of figures, we show only the extreme groups in the next table; that is, those who watch the least and the most television in general, and those who watch the least and the most television news. In any case, the figures for the categories in between broadly fit the overall pattern.

It should be noted first that television dominates the lives of many people. Although nearly one in ten people watch it for less than a hour a day on average, around the same proportion watch it for more than seven hours a day; and on average the British watch television for twenty one hours a week. The dominance extends to television news too, with more than half (56 per cent) watching it every day of the week. Tabloid readers and those who do not read a newspaper regularly watch the television news on average four to five times a week.

As can be seen from the next table, the characteristics of heavy television viewers are similar to those of tabloid readers: they tend to be older, to have have lower incomes and less education. A very high proportion are economically inactive, including pensioners. They are more likely to be tabloid than broadsheet newspaper readers. Moreover, those who watch a lot of television in general are *also* likely to watch a lot of television news, perhaps just because the television set happens to be turned on at the time.

Social characteristics of different types of TV viewers

	General TV		TV News	
	1 hour or less per weekday	**5 hours or more per weekday**	**Not at all**	**7 days a week**
Age (average)	43	51	40	52
Annual household income (£s - approx average)	21,000	11,000	17,500	15,500
Age completed full-time education (average)	17.8	15.5	16.5	16.4
Socio-economic group (average) (scored from 1 to 6)	4.4	3.2	3.5	3.8
% economically *inactive*	29	66	32	51
% women	53	60	53	53
% Conservative Party identifiers	35	28	29	33
TV hours (per week)	-	-	18.3	27.0
TV news (days per week)	3.7	5.7	-	-
Newspaper consumption	%	%	%	%
No regular paper	48	39	52	39
Regularly take tabloid	27	60	39	50
Regularly take broadsheet	25	1	9	11
Base	*193*	*283*	*349*	*2045*

It is no surprise that education is a strong determinant of news media use in general. As the next table confirms, those with the highest educational qualifications are much more likely than those with lower or no qualifications to read a broadsheet newspaper (yet it must be stressed that even among the best educated tabloid newspapers are somewhat more popular than broadsheets), and are more likely to pay attention to economic and political news in their newspaper. Those educated to the highest level also tend to watch less television in general but to pay more attention to its economic and political news.

Meanwhile, the least well educated watch *a lot* of television - one half watch four or more hours per day on an ordinary weekday. And, as we have noted, they take in a lot of television news coverage *en route*, more so in fact than the best educated do: 59 per cent (compared with 50 per cent of those with the highest qualifications) watch television news seven days a week.

Use of the news media, by educational qualifications

	O-level/ GCSE or less	A-level	Higher education or degree
Newspaper use	%	%	%
Regular tabloids readers	54	41	31
Regular broadsheet readers	4	13	27
% paid attention to economic report in their newpaper yesterday	24	26	38
% paid attention to political report in their newspaper yesterday	31	47	57
TV use			
% who watch TV more than 4 hours a day on weekdays	50	35	19
% who watch TV news 7 days a week	59	44	50
% who paid attention to economic report on TV news yesterday	48	48	55
% who paid attention to political report on TV news yesterday	51	52	60
Base	*2244*	*431*	*911*

Use of other forms of television and film (satellite, cable, video, and cinema) do not vary much according to educational qualifications, and are unlikely, therefore, to account for much variation in any media induced effects we may find. They will not therefore be considered in this chapter.

According to the videomalaise school, it is the 'inadvertent viewers', those who simply fall into the news because the television happens to be on, who are especially prone to videomalaise. The explanation given is that they tend to lack the background to make sense of the ceaseless, rapid, and confusing flow of bad news. In contrast, those with a good education who tend to talk more about politics with friends and colleagues and who read broadsheet newspapers, are supposed to be better-equipped to make sense of the news, to sift and appraise it, and thus to protect themselves from the ravages of videomalaise. We now consider that thesis in more detail.

Measures of political mobilisation and videomalaise

The key issue is whether different patterns of media use actually affect people in different ways. In particular, do they influence political knowledge, interest and understanding, thus helping or hindering mobilisation? And do they influence people's sense of efficacy and trust in the political system, thus promoting or inhibiting videomalaise?

The *British Social Attitudes* survey contains a great many questions covering such subjects as political knowledge, political understanding, political interest, trust in politicians and public officials, beliefs about democratic politics, the effectiveness of elections, citizen influence and government responsiveness. In fact, such is the wealth of material available that it is necessary to simplify and reduce its weight by grouping questions into distinct dimensions and by producing indices for each dimension which provide an overall score for each respondent for each index. Pooling responses to groups of related questions in this way also enables us to smooth out difficulties with any one question, making the index score a more reliable indicator of underlying attitudes than is the answer to any one question. Twenty questions were chosen and grouped into six dimensions. The groupings not only seemed to make intuitive sense, but factor analysis confirmed that they made statistical sense too (see the appendix to this chapter).

The six dimensions are:

- **Political knowledge:** four factual questions about party policies
- **Political interest and understanding:** four questions in which respondents rate themselves on their understanding and interest in political matters
- **Internal (or personal) efficacy:** two questions about how much influence (or efficacy) people feel they have on politics or the political system
- **Trust in officials:** six questions about trust in public officials and the political system
- **External efficacy:** three questions about how respondents rate the the workings of the political system and its effectiveness
- **Democracy:** one general question on how well democracy works in Britain

The full question texts and details of the indices are given in the appendix to this chapter.

Testing the competing theories

These six indices will help to show the links, if any, between media use and political mobilisation and/or malaise. First we show in the next table the average index scores for each group of newspaper users.

Looking at political knowledge, if the media do have an impact on levels of political knowledge - as the mobilisation and videomalaise theories both suggest - we would expect the knowledge index to vary according to whether or not people read a newspaper regularly, and according to whether they read a tabloid or a broadsheet. And indeed there is a clear pattern: broadsheet readers are far better informed about politics than tabloid readers. On

average they get 3.3 out of four of political quiz questions correct, compared with the tabloid readers' average of 2.2.

The same pattern is repeated for the other relevant indices. For instance, broadsheet readers express higher levels of interest in politics, feel better able to understand them, have stronger feelings of internal efficacy, trust public officials more, and express higher levels of confidence in the British system of democracy. In short, the figures suggest that reading a quality newspaper is indeed associated with mobilisation and with comparatively low levels of political malaise.

In order to test whether reading a tabloid actually has a *negative* impact on political trust and belief in the political system - as the videomalaise school suggests - we can compare regular tabloid readers with those who do not regularly read a newspaper at all. But here we find no link. Those who do not read a newspaper regularly are in fact almost indistinguishable from those who do: they get the same (low) average number of correct answers to the quiz and the same pattern for the other indices. So, as the table below shows, while reading a tabloid newspaper does not seem to contribute much to one's political knowledge or political trust, neither does it, in itself, seem to induce political malaise.

Measures of political mobilisation and malaise by newspaper readership

	No regular newspaper	Regular tabloid readers	Regular broadsheet readers	All
Knowledge	2.2	2.2	3.3	2.2
Political understanding and interest	11.0	10.8	14.0	10.8
Internal efficacy	4.8	4.6	5.4	4.1
Trust in officials	6.8	6.6	8.2	7.1
System efficacy	3.8	3.3	5.1	3.9
How well British democracy works	3.7	3.7	3.9	3.7
Base	*408*	*440*	*103*	*951*

The next table presents the average index scores according to both general television use and news programme consumption. It shows that those who watch a lot of television in general are less well-informed (2.0) than those who watch little or no television (2.7). They seem to know this too, since their self-rated political understanding and interest are lower. Watching a lot of television in general also seems to be associated with greater political malaise: compared with less heavy viewers, they tend to express lower levels of internal efficacy, less political trust, and they evaluate the workings of the political system less positively. So heavy viewers resemble tabloid readers in their responses - not surprisingly, perhaps, as the two groups overlap a good deal.

Watching the television *news* a lot, however, has the opposite effect. Heavy news consumers tend to know more about politics than those who watch less often and they also have higher self-rated political understanding and interest. The group which tunes into television news every day of the week get an average of 2.7 of the quiz answers correct, while those who never watch television news average only 1.8 answers correct.

Notably, however, consumption of television news does not seem to be linked to political malaise. There is little consistent difference between those who watch the news every day and those who never watch it in terms of people's degree of trust in the system or their sense of political efficacy.

Measures of political mobilisation and malaise by TV use

	General TV		*TV News*	
	1 hour or less per weekday	**5 hours or more per weekday**	**Not at all**	**7 days a week**
Knowledge	2.7	2.0	1.8	2.5
Political understanding and interest	12.3	10.5	9.7	11.7
Internal efficacy	5.3	4.4	4.9	4.7
Trust in officials	7.1	6.9	6.1	6.7
System efficacy	4.6	3.0	3.4	3.5
How well British democracy works	3.8	3.6	3.5	3.8
Base	*131*	*226*	*91*	*542*

This finding that television news is associated with relatively high levels of political knowledge, interest and understanding, but not with political malaise, is important. After all, as we saw earlier, a high proportion of those who read no newspaper regularly (or who are tabloid readers) make heavy use of the television and, in doing so, 'fall' into watching a lot of television news too. Thus, the information they do not acquire from a newspaper seems to be supplied, in part, by the television news. Even though as we saw earlier the less well-educated tend to pay less attention to economic and political news reports, the more important thing seems to be that they watch the news at all. Television news viewing *per se* appears to be positive in its effect on knowledge, interest and understanding and to have no independent negative effect on levels of malaise - a sort of antidote, perhaps, to the absence of a broadsheet newspaper and even to a constant diet of general television. Although this antidote does not appear to be as strong as reading a broadsheet newspaper would be, it does involve a much larger proportion of the population.

The effect of education, class and party identification

The figures presented so far suggest that most of the indicators of mobilisation and of malaise are associated with media use. To put it at its simplest, the general pattern is one in which those who read a tabloid regularly, and who watch a lot of television in general, are most likely to show signs of political malaise. In comparison, those who watch a lot of television news, and particularly those who read a broadsheet, show stronger signs of political mobilisation and fewer signs of malaise.

However, these generalisations do not take account of other underlying factors which might explain both patterns of media use *and* patterns of political knowledge and attitudes. For example, we have already seen how education is closely associated with media use, and it is reasonable to expect the well educated are also more interested and better informed about politics. Perhaps education is a powerful intervening variable which explains both media use and political attitudes?

For that matter, social class might explain a great deal. The socio-economic status of broadsheet readers might in itself be associated with greater satisfaction with the system of government and less political alienation. Similarly, support for or opposition to the government of the day might be important. Those whose party were in power (the Conservatives at the time of the fieldwork) may be less likely than others to feel disaffected with government and politics in general.

In other words, we simply cannot take the figures presented so far at their face value. We must control for the possibly strong effects of education, class, and party identification. By using the statistical technique of multiple regression analysis we can estimate how closely attitudes and media use are associated, while controlling for the possible impact of other intervening variables.

The results of this analysis are shown in detail in the appendix to this chapter. In summary, the models showed the following factors to have a statistically significant link to each of the indices, in order of importance (according to the size of the standardised regression coefficients).

Political knowledge	Interest and understanding	Internal efficacy
Broadsheet readership	Broadsheet readership	Level of education
Level of education	TV news consumption	Conservative identifier
TV news consumption	Socio-economic group	
Socio-economic group	Level of education	

Trust in officials	System efficacy	How well democracy works
Conservative identifier	Level of education	Conservative identifier
Broadsheet readership	Conservative identifier	Low general TV viewing
	Broadsheet readership	
	Low general TV viewing	

Thus, education is certainly a powerful factor in its own right. Other factors being equal, the higher their education level the more people tend to know about politics, take an interest in it, understand it, and feel a sense both of personal efficacy and trust in the system.

Identification with the party of government is also important. It is not associated with political knowledge or understanding (there is no reason it should be), but is closely related to the other indices. So, other things being equal, those who identify with the governing party feel better about how the political system works, while those who identify with opposition parties are more critical. Surprisingly, perhaps, socio-economic group is a weaker factor in its own right. It is certainly associated independently with levels of political knowledge and understanding (regardless of education), but not with the malaise-related indices.

But what is particularly important for this chapter is the pattern of association that media use shows with knowledge and malaise, even once these other factors have been taken into account. Now we can see that heavy general television viewing has no independent relationship with political knowledge or understanding, but that it is associated very weakly with two of the four indicators of political malaise. So the supposed association of general television with political alienation turns out to be patchy and not at all strong.

Watching a lot of television *news*, however, has the opposite pattern. It is has a close independent association with levels of knowledge and understanding, but not with any indicators of political malaise. Once again it should be noted that this is true once education has been controlled for: thus, for *any* given level of education, watching television news tends to improve one's political knowledge but not to affect one's sense of efficacy or trust in the system.

In contrast, those who read a broadsheet newspaper (again after controlling for education and other factors) are not only significantly better informed than tabloid readers, with higher levels of political understanding and interest, but

also significantly more trustful and more positive in their evaluations of the political system.

But what of the tabloid readers? The videomalaise school suggests that tabloid reading may be actively harmful. Yet our analyses indicate that such differences as there were between tabloid readers and irregular paper readers do not suggest that the tabloids are responsible for political malaise. Rather, the broadsheets do seem to promote a degree of political mobilisation.

Overall then, the evidence offers scant support for videomalaise theory and stronger support for mobilisation theory. So, while watching a lot of television in general does not lead to greater political knowledge or understanding, neither does it lead to greater alienation and political malaise. Conversely, while watching a lot of television *news* is strongly associated with more political knowledge and understanding, it does not prevent malaise. Similarly, while reading a broadsheet newspaper is strongly associated with higher levels of knowledge and understanding, and with a more favourable view of the political system, tabloid readers are no worse off (as some would have it) than those who do not read a newspaper regularly at all.

Conclusion

Mobilisation theory argues that improving levels of education combined with the greater penetration of the news media into everyday life helps to mobilise people - to inform them and to sustain their interest in and understanding of politics. Videomalaise theory argues in contradiction that the modern media, especially television and tabloid newspapers, tend to alienate and encourage a sense of political cynicism and distrust. The two theories are, of course, causal theories - they argue that the media are responsible for these good or bad effects. We cannot of course prove or disprove causes and effects, but merely observe patterns of association between media use and political attitudes and knowledge. Establishing causal relations would require much more complex survey designs and subsequent statistical analyses. Nevertheless, it has been possible to test some of the claims and counterclaims of the two theories.

By and large, of course, better educated people and those in the higher socio-economic groups are more likely to read a broadsheet to keep up with political and other news (although many do read a tabloid). They also tend to watch less television than the less well-educated, but overall around the same amount of television news. People with less education tend to read tabloids for their news or not to read any newspaper regularly. They tend to watch a lot of television, and their reading and watching is primarily for entertainment. Although these patterns are very weakly associated with some measures of political malaise, the effects are very much smaller than those who adhere to the theory would have wished. Despite the demonisation of

television, it turns out to be the print media that have the bigger effects on our indices.

But even as far as newspapers are concerned, the data do not really support the videomalaise theory. It is true that reading a broadsheet newspaper (even after allowing for the fact that it is the better educated and the middle classes who tend to read one) is associated with being better informed - objectively and subjectively - and with viewing the process of government and politics more favourably. On the other hand, tabloid newspapers, while admittedly adding very little to their readers' political knowledge or understanding (in comparison with non-readers), do not seem to be actively *harmful*. Their readers display neither more ignorance nor a greater sense of political malaise than those who do not regularly read a paper at all.

Moreover, our findings about television *news* watching tends to lend support to the mobilisation theory. Those who watch a lot of television news are substantially better informed - both objectively and subjectively - even after taking educational attainment into account. And there is no evidence that television news is associated with any of the measures of political malaise. In this respect British and West German findings (Holtz-Bacha, 1990) are similar, although our study finds even less support for the videomalaise theory than the German one did.

So, whereas broadsheet newspaper reading is clearly and strongly associated with political mobilisation, the television viewing pattern is more mixed and generally weaker. This is surely because television seems to pull in different directions. Watching a lot of television in general is not associated with levels of political information and only weakly associated with measures of political malaise, giving some (but precious little) solace to the videomalaise theory. But watching a lot of television *news* is strongly associated with higher levels of political information and understanding and with none of our indicators of political malaise - hence lending further support to the mobilisation theory. In this respect British and recent American findings are very similar (see Norris, 1996b).

What makes this an interesting and important finding is that many of the people who read a tabloid and also watch a lot of general television, habits associated with low levels of information and (perhaps) with mild malaise, are also people who watch a lot of television *news*, a habit associated with mobilisation. Yet over half of the population watches television more than three hours a day or more, and a similar proportion watches television news as much as seven days a week. 'Falling into the news' in this way turns out thus to be associated with information and mobilisation rather than malaise. So, as long as reading the tabloid press and watching entertainment television remain largely unconnected to a sense of political malaise, and as long as reading a broadsheet and watching television news remain strongly connected to mobilisation, the mobilisation theory will hold sway over the videomalaise theory.

References

Ansolabehere, S. Iyengar, and Simon, A. (1995), 'Evolving perspectives on the effects of campaign communication' in P. C. Wasburn, ed., *Research in Political Sociology*, Volume 7: Mass Media and Politics. Greenwich, Conn.: Jai Press.

Dalton, R. (1996), *Citizen Politics: Public Opinion and Political Parties in Advanced Western Democracies*. Chatham, N.J. : Chatham House.

Holtz-Bacha, C. (1990), 'Videomalaise revisited: media exposure and political alienation in West Germany.' *European Journal of Communication*, **5**, 78-85.

Norris, P. (1996a), 'Political communication in election campaigns: reconsidering media effects, in D. Denver and C. Rallings, (eds.), *British Elections and Parties Yearbook*, London: Frank Cass.

Norris, P. (1996b), Does TV erode social capital? A reply to Putnam. PS: *Political Science and Politics*, September, 1996: 1-7.

Postman, N. (1987), *Amusing Ourselves to Death*. London: Methuen.

Putnam, R. D. (1995), 'Tuning in, tuning out: the strange disappearance of social capital in America', PS, XXVIII, No. **4**: 664-83.

Robinson, M.J. (1976), 'Public affairs television and the growth of political malaise: the case of 'Selling the Pentagon', *American Political Science Review*, LXX, June, No. **2**: 409-32.

Schudson, M. (1995), *The Power of the News*, Cambridge: Harvard University Press.

Topf, R. (1995), 'Beyond electoral participation', in H-D. Klingemann and D. Fuchs, (eds.), *Citizens and the State*, Oxford: Oxford University Press.

Acknowledgements

I would like to thank the President and members of the Wissenschaftszentrum Berlin für Sozialforschung where I spent a sabbatical year during which this chapter was written. In particular I would like to thank Andreas Dams for his excellent computing work, and Christiane Eilders, Max Kaase, Barbara Pfetsch, and Katrin Volmar for the helpful comments on an early draft of the chapter.

SCPR also wishes to thank The Leverhulme Trust for funding to support the module of questions on trust in the political system; the Economic and Social Research Council for funding the module of questions which included the political knowledge quiz and the television news consumption and attention items (grant number H552255003); and the British Board of Film Classification, the Broadcasting Standards Commission, the Independent Television Commission and the British Broadcasting Corporation for funding the module that included the questions on general media consumption.

Appendix

Indices of political mobilisation and malaise

Political knowledge

- *Which party would you say is most in favour of changing the voting system to a form of proportional representation?* (Correct answer: Liberal Democratic).
- *And which party would you say is most in favour of reducing government spending in order to cut taxes?* (Correct Answer: Conservative).
- *And which party would you say is most in favour of letting private industry run the railways?* (Correct answer; Conservative).
- *And which party would you say is most in favour of setting a minimum wage level, below which no-one can be paid?* (Correct answer: Labour).

Index scores range from 0 to 4.

Political understanding and interest

- *I feel that I have a pretty good understanding of the important issues facing our country. (strongly agree/agree/neither agree nor disagree/disagree/strongly disagree).*
- *Sometimes politics and government seem so complicated that a person like me cannot really understand what is going on. (strongly agree/agree/neither agree nor disagree/disagree/strongly disagree).*
- *I think that most people are better informed about politics and government than I am. (strongly agree/agree/neither agree nor disagree/disagree/strongly disagree).*
- *How interested would you say you personally are in politics? (very/fairly/somewhat/not very/ not at all interested).*

Index scores range from 4 to 20.

Internal (or personal) efficacy

- *People like me don't have any say about what the government does. (strongly agree/agree/neither agree nor disagree/disagree/strongly disagree).*
- *Voting is the only way people like me can have any say about how the government runs things. (agree strongly/agree/neither agree nor disagree/disagree/disagree strongly).*

Index scores range from 2 to 10.

Political trust

- *How much do you trust British governments of any party to place the needs of the nation above the interests of their own political party? (just about always/most of the time/only some of the time/almost never).*
- *How much do you trust politicians of any party in Britain to tell the truth when they are in a tight corner? (just about always/most of the time/only some of the time/almost never).*
- *And how much do you trust councillors of any party to put the needs of their area above the interests of their own party? (just about always/most of the time/only some of the time/almost never).*
- *And how much do you trust British police not to bend the rules in trying to get a conviction? (just about always/most of the time/only some of the time/almost never).*

- *And how much do you trust top civil servants to stand firm against a minister who wants to provide false information to parliament? (just about always/most of the time/only some of the time/almost never).*
- *And how much do you trust high court judges to stand up to a government which wishes them to reach a particular verdict? (just about always/most of the time/only some of the time/almost never).*

Index scores range from 6 to 24.

External (or system) efficacy

- *Generally speaking those we elect as MPs lose touch with people pretty quickly. (agree strongly/agree/ neither agree nor disagree/disagree/ disagree strongly).*
- *Parties are only interested in people's votes, not in their opinions. (agree strongly/agree/ neither agree nor disagree/disagree/ disagree strongly).*
- *It doesn't really matter which party is in power, in the end things go much the same. (agree strongly/agree/ neither agree nor disagree/disagree/ disagree strongly).*

Index scores range from 3 to 15.

British democracy

- *All in all, how well or badly do you think the system of democracy in Britain works these days. (works well and needs no changes/works well but needs some changes/does not work well and needs a lot of changes/ does not work well and needs to be completely changed).*

Index scores range from 1 to 4.

Principle Component Analysis of responses to questions about political knowledge and attitudes component

	1	2	3	4	5	6
Political knowledge						
Proportional Representation	.46					
Tax and spending cuts	.63					
Privatise Rail	.75					
Minimum Wage	.74					
Political interest and understanding						
Self-rated political interest		.79				
Self-rated information		.71				
Self-rated understanding of gov.		.80				
Gov. too complex to understand		-.57				
Internal (or personal) efficacy						
People like me have no say			-.62			
Voting only influence on gov.			-.60			
Political trust						
Trust gov. to put country before party				.71		
Trust MPs to tell truth				.55		
Trust civil servants				.68		
Trust councillors				.73		
Trust police				.58		
Trust judges				.78		
External (or system) efficacy						
MPs lose touch					.71	
Parties only interest in votes					.66	
Doesn't matter which party in power					.47	
British democracy (one question)						.41

Note: Principal Component Analysis, varimax with Kaiser normalisation.

Multiple regression model

Multiple regressions of media use, education, social class, and party identification on political knowledge and attitudes (entries are standardised regression coefficients, t-ratios in brackets)

Only statistically significant coefficients are shown in the table.

	Know-ledge	Under-standing	Internal efficacy	System efficacy	Trust	British democracy
TV General				-.092 * (2.16)		-.110 * (2.42)
TV News	.166 *** (4.50)	.215 *** (5.29)				
Paper (Broadsheet)	.189 *** (4.56)	.279 *** (6.13)		.150 *** (3.47)	.192 *** (3.97)	
Education	.183 *** (4.30)	.123 ** (2.63)	.190 *** (4.18)	.186 *** (4.18)		
SEG	.160 *** (3.83)	.156 *** (3.40)				
Identify with government party			.176 *** (4.59)	.175 *** (4.67)	.202 *** (4.81)	.223 *** (5.03)
R^2	.22	.26	.12	.16	.09	.08
F ratio	28.72 ***	27.82 ***	14.19 ***	19.37 ***	8.91 ***	7.38 ***

*** = significant at .001
** = significant at .01
* = significant at .05
Variables are entered simultaneously in the regression equations.

TV General: General TV watching is scored from an average of one hour or less per week day, to five hours or more on a scale of 1 to 5.
TV News per week is scored from 0 to 3 (none, 1-3 times a week, 4-6, and 7 days a week).
Paper: Regular tabloid readers are scored 1, broadsheet readers 2.
Education is scored from 1 to 4 (no qualifications, O-level or GCSE, A-level, or a degree or further educational qualification).
Socio-economic group is scored from 1 (unskilled manual) to 6 (professionals/ employers/managers).
Identification with government party is scored 2 for Conservatives and 1 for supporters of opposition parties.

9 How we view violence

Steven Barnett and Katarina Thomson [*]

In last year's *British Social Attitudes* Report we showed that many people want restrictions on the portrayal of sex in the media - particularly on the regular television channels - but that their views are heavily influenced by the context in which the sex is shown (Barnett and Thomson, 1996). This year, we report on a similar module of questions asked on the 1996 *British Social Attitudes* survey about the portrayal of violence in the media.

Over the 18 years of Conservative government, the media environment has changed beyond recognition. In 1979, there were just three television channels, three-quarters of homes had just one television set, fewer than three per cent had video recorders, satellite television was non-existent and film-going was in decline (Gunter and Svennevig, 1988). Those 18 years have seen a massive increase in the number of media outlets, and, therefore, the sheer volume of material available.

Inevitably, as new channels have struggled to fill this burgeoning air-time, the amount of violent material being shown has increased in absolute terms - although whether it has increased in *proportional* terms during that time is difficult to assess. There does appear to be a *perception* that violent content has increased, although longitudinal research by the Independent Television Commission and the Independent Broadcasting Authority suggests that the number of viewers offended by violence on the two main channels over the last 18 years has risen only slightly.

---

[*] Steven Barnett is Senior Lecturer at the Centre for Communication and Information Studies, University of Westminster. Katarina Thomson is a Research Director at SCPR and a Co-Director of the *British Social Attitudes* survey series.

We aim in this chapter to address a number of questions. Is the public more or less concerned about violence than about sex in the media? Do people make a distinction between the different media - that is, is violence more acceptable in less accessible media such as cinema, video, and cable and satellite television than on regular television? What distinctions do people make between different types of violence? How important is the context in which the violence is shown? What social factors are linked to attitudes towards showing violence and are they the same as those linked to attitudes towards showing sex?

In last year's chapter, we started by examining the philosophical dilemma which underpins policy decisions in this area: individual freedom of creative expression *versus* the need, in J.S. Mill's words, to "prevent harm to others". While the roots of this dilemma are similar when considering arguments about the portrayal of violence, the notion of 'harm' has somewhat different connotations. Accordingly, although 'sex and violence' are often lumped together as posing identical questions of taste and decency, the moral arguments, regulatory frameworks and public concerns are in practice somewhat different.

In particular, most people see acts of violence as inherently wrong (except, say, in self defence), in contrast to sex where many (though not all) people see a variety of behaviour as acceptable. Those who defend the portrayal of violence in films or on television therefore have a rather harder job to argue their case. Their defence is usually one of three related types. The first is based on the desirability of creative freedom and realism: as elements of violence have always been part of the human condition, excluding them from drama would mean that "Montagues and Capulets would not brawl nor Mercutio die on a televised stage" (Broadcasting Research Unit, 1989:23). The second defence is that in a healthy democracy, citizens are entitled to accurate, uncensored factual information in order to be properly informed (Murdock, 1997). And the third defence - an elaboration of the first two - is that by not conveying the horror and brutality of some of the violence that occurs in real life, society will become less well-equipped to understand the world or to influence governments. This has been a particularly pertinent argument in the coverage of war reporting (e.g. Bell, 1996).

Objections to the portrayal of violence also tend to be different from those levelled against the portrayal of sex. While scenes of explicit sex tend to provoke concern largely because they may offend or disgust some sections of the population, objections to the portrayal of violence tend to be more 'effects' based - that is, they are based on the assumption that watching violence may well have adverse behavioural consequences. These behavioural consequences are of four broad types.

The most commonly cited is imitation, a charge that tends to attract popular support after major tragedies involving violence (particularly against children). There is frequently speculation in these cases about whether the perpetrators have been exposed to violent films, videos or television programmes. This 'copycat' theory has in fact been the subject of much

psychological experimentation, particularly in the United States, but there is as yet no clear scientific evidence to support it (Cumberbatch and Howitt, 1989).

A second concern expressed by campaigners for greater restrictions on violent content is 'desensitisation': that frequent exposure to violent images is likely to lead to progressively less revulsion to either the images themselves or, worse still, to real-life violence. It is this concern, among other factors, that gives rise to the analysis of television content with a view to quantifying the volume of violence on different channels (e.g. BBC *et al.*, 1996).

A third issue is the extent to which portrayals of violence, and in particular violent crime, leads to unwarranted fear in the community. Research has repeatedly shown that feelings of vulnerability to violent crime are poorly correlated with actual statistical risk: the elderly in particular have an exaggerated sense of their own vulnerability. Some research attributes this partially to television and in particular to the crime reconstruction programmes which have recently proliferated across all channels (Home Office, 1989).

Finally, there is the more inchoate (and ultimately unmeasurable) accusation that exposure to violent images can create psychological damage to individuals, particularly those who might anyway be vulnerable to influence from external sources. Children, in particular, are perceived as more likely to be disturbed or suffer some psychological trauma after watching scenes of violence, whether fictionalised or as part of real-life television such as news bulletins or current affairs programmes.

Public opinion about restricting the levels of violence shown is therefore likely to be based at least partly on assumptions about these behavioural effects and not purely on a sense of 'mere' moral outrage. This may well contrast with public opinion about restricting sex on television and in films. These considerations may also have a material influence on the prevalent regulatory regimes in film and television.

The regulatory regimes

There are four main sources of regulation: for films and videos, the British Board of Film Classification; and for television, the Independent Television Commission (which regulates all non-BBC output on television), the BBC itself, and the Broadcasting Standards Commission which has responsibility for monitoring 'taste and decency' issues in all broadcasting.

The British Board of Film Classification (BBFC) has never had a written Code of Practice. In its own words, "classification policy has developed on the common law model, adapting and evolving in response to changes in public taste, attitudes and concerns" (BBFC, 1995:3). Precedent is therefore an important element of its thinking, but the context of particular films is also crucial: "sadistic cruelty.... is not always unacceptable. It can be found in

children's fairy tales, in James Bond movies, even in Shakespeare" (*ibid*:5). The same principles of precedent and context are applied by the BBFC in classifying videos, although an amendment to the Video Recordings Act placed this responsibility on a statutory footing. Context, in both film and video, will include not just the on-screen context but also the likely viewing context and the possibility of under-age viewing.

The Independent Television Commission (ITC) makes a distinction between violence in fiction and violence in the real world, arguing that both can be justifiable in different circumstances. In the former case, "conflict is the essence of drama, and conflict often leads to violence". In both fiction and fact, "when television seeks to reflect the world.... it would be unrealistic and untrue to ignore its violent aspects" (ITC, 1995:7). The ITC Code places special emphasis on scheduling and the need to be sensitive to the young, and prohibits the portrayal of 'gratuitous' acts of violence. It attempts to balance the need to protect creative freedom with the need to acknowledge a possibly traumatic effect on some individuals: "imagination, creativity or realism on television cannot be constrained to such an extent that the legitimate service of the majority is always subordinated to the limitations of a minority" (*ibid*:8).

The BBC's producers' guidelines - supplemented by more detailed rules specifically covering the portrayal of violence on television - also emphasise that violence must be 'justifiable': "most audiences expect any violent scenes to serve a moral or social point" (BBC, 1996:62; BBC, 1993). There are separate codes for real-life and fictional violence, drawing attention in news stories to the need to balance a full understanding of the facts with the risk of desensitisation. In fiction, the guidelines state that context should determine "the degree and type of violence, and the detail that can be shown" and draw attention in particular to the risk of imitation in portrayals which feature "easily accessible weapons" (*ibid*:65-6).

The Broadcasting Standards Council (BSC) (which became the Broadcasting Standards Commission in April 1997) has a comprehensive Code of Practice, which also makes a clear distinction between real-life and entertainment programmes. It provides the clearest statement of the obligation on broadcasters not to deceive audiences by removing violence from their news and documentary programmes: "any shrinking from the retelling of savage and bitter truths about the world does the audience a substantial disservice and, with it, a disservice to democracy" (BSC, 1994:17). As well as making similar points on scheduling and context as the BBC and ITC Codes do, the BSC emphasises the need to look at surrounding programmes in order to avoid a sequence of programmes with violent content.

Where are we now?

It is possible to distil from these approaches to regulation, as indeed from most of the public debates about restrictions on the portrayal of violence, four particular themes that guide programme makers and regulators. The first is scheduling or classification: what sort of material is appropriate for what ages and at what times? The second issue is the scope or degree of violence itself: how important is the nature of the act and the detail with which it is depicted? Third is the question of context, and whether the violence is an integral part of the plot. And fourth is the distinction between violence in fiction and in factual programmes, and whether different levels of tolerance apply to the reporting of real-life acts of violence. Our aim was to examine each of these issues, as well as identifying differences in attitude towards different media.

Previous British research has attempted to address some of these questions, although almost exclusively in the context of television. The Independent Television Commission, in its annual survey of attitudes, assesses what proportion of viewers have been offended by material on each of the four main channels, and the most recent figures have followed a similar pattern to previous years: in 1996 between 8 and 16 per cent said they had been offended by violence on one of the channels in the previous year. Nearly a third (32 per cent) said they had turned the television off or over to another channel because of the amount of violence (ITC, 1997).

In a wide-ranging report on attitudes to violence in factual television, the Broadcasting Standards Council concluded that "violence in factual television was more acceptable because it was real", although it pinpointed a natural dilemma for viewers who might - for that very reason - find it more upsetting (Millwood Hargrave, 1993:26). The same research found substantial support for the notion that 'closeness' was an issue, with 82 per cent saying they would be more upset if the victim of portrayed violence was "someone like your own friend and neighbour". It also found that the victim's status was important, with 87 per cent saying they would be more upset if the victim was "particularly weak and vulnerable". This compared to the 47 per cent who said they would be less upset if the victim "deserves to be punished" (*ibid*:19-21).

The same piece of research found widespread support for the various behavioural 'effects' models of televised violence, with 58 per cent agreeing with a version of the desensitisation argument and 56 per cent agreeing with the argument that it might provoke fear (*ibid*:11)[1]. This confirmed previous research by the Independent Broadcasting Authority which found that nearly two thirds (64 per cent) thought that children would imitate the violence they see on television (Gunter and Wober, 1988).

Our starting point

Previous research has not tended to explore reactions to specific scenarios of violence, thereby leaving the term itself open to many different interpretations by respondents (and researchers). Our aim was to test the themes and issues outlined above not just across different media but with more precise explanations of what we meant by violence. We had anticipated, in particular, that attitudes might be framed to some extent by how explicitly the violence was portrayed. Our first scenario was therefore posed as follows:

> *I am now going to ask what you think should be allowed or not allowed to be shown on television or at the cinema. Thinking first about a film which contains a scene, filmed in close-up, of someone **being repeatedly stabbed and cut**. I have in mind a scene where you can see a lot of blood.*

Respondents were then asked what age limits should be placed on such a film at the cinema, at what time of the evening it could be shown on regular television and on a paid satellite or cable channel, and what age limits should be placed on the sale or rental of such a video. In line with our reasoning in last year's Report, we have operated on the assumption that a ten o'clock time limit may be considered roughly equivalent to an 18 age limit, nine o'clock to a 15 age limit, and eight o'clock to a 12 age limit.[2]   These are the equivalences applied by the Independent Television Commission in their Programme Code (ITC, 1995: 6).

Three further scenarios of different kinds of violence were then tested to see, first, whether attitudes changed if scenes were implicitly just as violent but were portrayed at a more discreet distance; second, whether attitudes were tempered if the violence was part of an unambiguous fantasy; and third, whether it made any difference if the violence did not involve the use of a weapon but was therefore perhaps more likely to be open to imitative behaviour. The three scenarios were as follows:

> *Now how about a film with the scene of someone being stabbed or cut, but this time filmed **from a distance** so that you could not see any blood.*

> *Now think again of a film with a scene of someone being repeatedly stabbed or cut, filmed **in close-up**, but this time the stabbing is done, not by another human being, but by a **fantasy monster**.*

> *Now think of a film where there was a realistic scene of someone being severely beaten or kicked by another person.*

Three further questions were designed first to test the importance of context and how attitudes differed to gratuitous *versus* relevant scenes of violence;

and second how attitudes changed if the violence was part of a television news bulletin rather than fictional.

Are we more restrictive towards portrayals of sex or of violence?

The effects-based nature of people's concerns about violence probably accounts for the fact that the portrayal of violence is seen overwhelmingly as a greater problem than the portrayal of sex. We asked people directly which they were more worried about on television:

	%
We should worry more about violence on TV than about sex on TV	63
We should worry more about sex on TV than about violence on TV	4
Can't choose	31

Base: 989

In the abstract then, those who are more worried about violence on television outnumber those who are more worried about sex by around 15 to one. But this does not necessarily translate itself into active support for censorship in particular cases. Only around half of the people questioned would actually ban our hypothetical close-up scene of a gory stabbing, and only around a quarter would ban the distant, less gory scene of a stabbing.

As it turns out, these distributions of answers correspond closely to the distribution of answers about explicit homosexual and heterosexual sex respectively which we reported last year (Barnett & Thomson, 1996).

However, when looking at the media other than regular television, a substantial difference emerges between attitudes to films containing sex and those containing violence. In the case of sex, the option of special film clubs, special video shops and special satellite/cable channels is quite popular, attracting 17 to 27 per cent of the respondents. But the idea of special cinemas showing violent films, special shops selling violent videos or special satellite/cable channels showing violent material is, not surprisingly, much less acceptable - attracting only five to 13 per cent of responses. This partly reflects the fact that special channels or cinemas dedicated to showing violent material do not exist. But it may also reflect concern about the possibility of cultivating a taste for violence which might then have behavioural implications.

Differences between the media

We found last year that attitudes to the portrayal of sex varied according to the medium on which the material was shown. People were least restrictive about media which had limited access, such as the cinema, and most

restrictive about widely accessible media such as the regular television channels and radio. However, the differences were rather small - for example, the proportion wanting to ban a heterosexual sex scene varied from 19 per cent in the case of a film at the cinema to 27 per cent in the case of a film on regular television.

Do these differences between the media hold in the case of violent material? We find that the picture is rather more complex. Looking first at the most violent scenario, the stabbing filmed in close-up, we find a rather similar picture to last year's. The most restrictive views are held about regular television (where half would ban the scene altogether and only around a third think that a ten o'clock or earlier threshold is adequate). The least restrictive views are held about cinema and videos (where over two fifths think an age threshold of 18 or lower would suffice). Satellite and cable television fall somewhere between the two.[3]

Scene showing stabbing, filmed close up

	Regular TV	Satellite/ Cable	Video for sale or rent	Cinema
Should be	%	%	%	%
Not allowed at all	51	42	46	43
After midnight/special channel or shop or cinema	15	23	10	8
After 10pm/age 18+	25	24	40	43
After 9pm/age 15+	6	6	2	3
After 8pm/age 12+/anytime/anyone	2	3	1	2

Base 1180

However, the differences between the media are less clear when we turn to the three 'milder' scenarios - the stabbing filmed at a distance, the stabbing by a fantasy monster and the beating and kicking scene.

Scene showing stabbing, filmed at a distance

	Regular TV	Satellite/ Cable	Video for sale or rent	Cinema
Should be	%	%	%	%
Not allowed at all	27	26	27	23
After midnight/special channel or shop or cinema	16	19	9	5
After 10pm/age 18+	36	34	45	51
After 9pm/age 15+	15	13	14	14
After 8pm/age 12+/anytime/anyone	5	6	4	5

Base 1180

In the case of all three of the 'milder' scenarios, the proportion wanting a total ban is fairly uniform across the media. For example, it ranges from 23 to 27 per cent for the stabbing at a distance and from 35 to 39 per cent for the fantasy monster stabbing despite the fact that such scenes are shown on British television without any evidence of widespread revulsion or complaints on this scale. As we shall see, this apparent paradox is probably caused by the context in which the respondent is imagining that the scene in the question will be shown.

As with last year's findings on the portrayal of sex, the tendency is for attitudes to be more restrictive the more open the medium. The proportion who think that 18 (or below) is an appropriate age threshold for the fantasy monster stabbing is 56 per cent for cinema, compared with 47 per cent who think that ten o'clock is an appropriate watershed for regular television. This is mainly a result of the larger proportion (13 per cent) who chose the "only after midnight" option for television compared with the "only at special film clubs" option for cinema (six per cent).

Scene showing stabbing by a fantasy monster

Should be	Regular TV	Satellite/ cable	Video for sale or rent	Cinema	Computer game
	%	%	%	%	%
Not allowed at all	39	36	35	36	41
After midnight/special channel or shop or cinema	13	20	8	6	10
After 10pm/age 18+	30	26	39	40	25
After 9pm/age 15+	12	11	13	12	14
After 8pm/age 12+/ anytime/anyone	5	5	3	4	8

Base 1180

In the case of the fantasy monster we also asked about computer games with a similar scene and, interestingly, people were rather restrictive about these. Here 41 per cent wanted a ban while 47 per cent thought that an 18 (or lower) age threshold was appropriate, so attitudes seem to be rather similar to those towards regular television.

Scene showing beating and kicking

Should be	Regular TV	Satellite/ Cable	Video for sale or rent	Cinema
	%	%	%	%
Not allowed at all	38	34	37	38
After midnight/special channel or shop or cinema	14	19	7	4
After 10pm/age 18+	31	30	42	45
After 9pm/age 15+	12	11	9	8
After 8pm/age 12+/anytime/anyone	3	4	3	3

Base 1180

We argued last year that the differences between the media suggest that accessibility matters and that the introduction of barriers to access which require a positive act of personal selection, such as smartcards, would prevent certain age groups from having access to this sort of material, and therefore would probably allay many fears. The material on violence supports these conclusions, but it should be noted that this principle does not extend to the concept of, for example, certain film clubs or satellite channels showing violent material. Again, this is partly explained by the absence of such outlets in practice. What seems to be happening is that people who opt for

"after midnight" on regular television and satellite/cable, prefer to go for the 18 age limit rather than an outright ban on the cinema. One interpretation is that the public is simply less censorious (and less fearful) of hypothetical individuals who seek a strong diet of sexual material than of those who seek a strong diet of violent material.

Different types of violence and the impact of context

The purpose of asking about four different violent scenarios was to look at the extent to which the sort of violence shown has an effect on attitudes. There is no doubt that there is a difference: the stabbing filmed in close-up was consistently seen as requiring the most restrictive policies, while the stabbing filmed at a distance consistently attracted the least censorious attitudes. For example, while 43 per cent would ban the *close-up stabbing* altogether from the cinema, the proportion wanting the same treatment of a *distant stabbing* fell to 23 per cent. Conversely, 48 per cent wanted a close-up stabbing to be subject to an 18 (or lower) age threshold, but this rose to 71 per cent for a distant stabbing.

We had expected that the level of realism of the scene would also be an important consideration. We had therefore anticipated that the realistic stabbing by a human in close-up would attract more restrictive attitudes than the stabbing by a fantasy monster in close-up, and also that the beating and kicking scene would attract more restrictive attitudes than the fantasy monster scene. The first of these two hypotheses was borne out - attitudes to the fantasy monster scene fell somewhere in between the two stabbing scenarios. But the second hypothesis was not: attitudes towards the fantasy monster and the beating and kicking scenes were, in fact, very similar. Some 36 per cent wanted to ban the fantasy monster scene at the cinema and 38 per cent the beating and kicking scene, and the proportion who thought that an 18 (or lower) age threshold was sufficient was 56 per cent in both cases.

We showed last year the importance of context in influencing attitudes towards the portrayal of sex. In the case of a film containing a 'gratuitous' sex scene, the proportion who thought it acceptable for 15 year olds was around one in four. This rose to almost one half if the same scene was justified by the plot, and to almost three-quarters if it was in an educational video. We asked a similar series of questions this year about violence:

We have been talking about films and videos containing violence, but there are, of course, different ways of handling violence within a film. Some films contain violent scenes which are part of a developing story. Others show violent scenes which don't seem to be essential to the plot.
*Think first of a film containing a scene of someone being repeatedly stabbed and cut, filmed in close-up, that does **not** seem to be essential to the plot. Should it **ever**, in your view, be ...*
... allowed to be seen by 12 year olds?
...allowed to be seen by 15 year olds?
...allowed to be seen by 18 year olds?
...allowed to be seen by anyone at all?

We then asked:

*And how about a film containing a scene of someone being repeatedly stabbed, filmed in close-up, that **is** a **central** part of the plot.*

In the same way as for the portrayal of sex, the context made a very substantial difference:

The impact of context

	Gratuitous	Plot-based
	%	%
Not allowed at all	42	26
Not allowed at age 18+ except certain circumstances	4	4
Allowed for age 18+	43	50
Allowed for age 15+	8	14
Allowed for age 12+	1	4

Base 1180

The proportion who favours banning the violent scene altogether falls from 42 per cent for the gratuitous scene to 26 per cent for the plot-based scene, and the proportion who think that it is acceptable for those aged 18 or below rises from 53 to 68 per cent.

A comparison between the answers to these gratuitous *versus* plot-based questions and the previous scenario questions, which omitted any reference to context, clearly demonstrates what we also found last year - that when people are answering these sorts of questions in the absence of any reference to context they seem to assume that the violence (or sex) being referred to *is* gratuitous. We conclude this because their responses as to how they feel about 'gratuitous' and plot-based scenes are almost identical to the ones they

initially gave about close-up and distant stabbing scenes at the cinema (respectively) in which context was unspecified.

All this underlines how difficult it is to gauge public opinion on this subject and how cautiously we need to frame questions and interpret answers if we are not to exaggerate the strength or otherwise of people's views.

We asked a further question designed to elicit opinions about the reporting and portrayal of 'real life' or factual violence. At the end of the beating and kicking scenario, we asked:

> *What if the scene of someone being severely beaten or kicked was not a fictional film, but was **documentary film footage** being shown in a **television news broadcast**?*

Again, we can confirm that context matters: people are much less likely to disapprove of the portrayal of 'real life' violence, partly perhaps for the reasons explored by the regulatory codes of the various broadcasting bodies, and partly perhaps because the nature of the portrayal in this case is much less likely to be 'gratuitous'. The proportion wanting a total ban falls from 38 to 21 per cent and the proportion thinking it acceptable at nine o'clock or earlier rises from 16 to 37 per cent.

Beating and kicking: fictional versus real life portrayal

	Regular TV	Documentary footage
Should be	%	%
Not allowed at all	38	21
After midnight	14	6
After 10pm/age 18+	31	34
After 9pm/age 15+	12	22
After 8pm/age 12+/anytime/anyone	3	15

Base 1180

Variations across the population

In last year's chapter we developed indices for attitudes to the heterosexual sex scene, the homosexual sex scene and the film full of swearwords and used these indices to show how attitudes to the portrayal of sex are linked to a number of socio-demographic and attitudinal factors. In particular, age makes a large difference, as does a person's underlying moral framework including their attitudes to pre-marital, extra-marital and homosexual sex. Moreover, it was the importance of age rather than the life cycle situation (such as whether or not a person had the responsibilities of parenthood) that led us to believe that we were witnessing primarily a cohort effect (see Heath

and Martin, 1996 for a discussion of cohort and life-cycle effects). In any event, the findings imply that the younger, less censorious age groups will retain their relatively more permissive attitudes towards sex in the media as they grow older. Thus, the long-term outlook is towards a decline in disapproval.

We are now in a position to compare the findings on violence with those on sex. Given the very real differences in the nature of public concerns about sex and violence, we had every reason to believe that the factors associated with attitudes to violence might well be different.

To investigate this we combined responses to seventeen questions in order to construct an index of attitudes towards the portrayal of violence (see the appendix to this chapter for further details). Scores on the index range from one to six, where a score of one indicates that the respondent wanted to ban outright all four scenes in all the media and a score of six that the respondent would allow all the scenes to be shown to all ages in the cinema or on video or at any time on any television channel. It is, of course, a somewhat crude measure but is nonetheless robust enough to show variations among individuals and subgroups in their overall attitudes to violence in films and on television and, in particular, to compare these attitudes with our findings last year on attitudes towards the portrayal of sex in the media. We first show below the overall scores which indicate a distinct skew towards outright censoriousness rather than outright permissiveness in allowing violence free rein.

Tolerance of screen and TV violence:
overall index scores

	%
1 - 1.99	38
2 - 2.99	31
3 - 3.99	26
4 - 4.99	3
5 - 6	1

Base: 1110

Socio-demographic factors

As noted, age was comfortably the most important socio-demographic factor related to attitudes to the portrayal of sex. And, not surprisingly perhaps, this turns out to be the case for violence too. On average, the younger one is (our sample were, of course, all 18+), the less restrictive one is towards the portrayal of violence in the media.

However, in the case of violence gender is rather more important than it was for sex. Men are less restrictive than women in every age group, although the

difference is at its greatest among the youngest age group. Thus, although the number of cases in the youngest and the oldest age group are too small when split by gender to draw firm conclusions, it certainly appears that young men (particularly men under 25 but also men under 45) are by far the most tolerant towards the portrayal of violence in the media.

These findings contrast with tolerance towards the portrayal of sex, where young women appeared to be the most permissive, but again the numbers were rather too small to be certain. Further research with a larger sample would be needed to investigate these findings. If supported, they would confirm what many regulators suspect - that young men are not only the largest watchers of violent material but also the least critical of it.

Tolerance index scores by age and sex
(low scores = restrictive attitudes; high scores = permissive attitudes)

	Male		**Female**		**All**	
		Base		*Base*		*Base*
All	2.50	*459*	2.23	*648*	2.34	*1110*
Age						
18-24	3.29	*33*	2.81	*40*	3.03	*73*
25-44	2.94	*192*	2.51	*279*	2.68	*471*
45-64	2.14	*141*	1.98	*174*	2.06	*315*
65+	1.77	*93*	1.69	*155*	1.72	*248*

As with attitudes to the portrayal of sex, a person's religiosity - as measured by frequency of church (or similar) attendance - shows a relationship with their attitudes to the portrayal of violence. Those with no religion are markedly less restrictive than those who attend a place of worship once a week or more. On the other hand, since church attendance is itself related to age, the strength of this relationship could be partly attributable to the fact that older people are less tolerant. As our multivariate analyses show later, however, even when we account for the link between age and church attendance, religiosity remains a strong predictor of attitudes.

Tolerance index scores by religious attendance
(low scores = restrictive attitudes; high scores = permissive attitudes)

		Base
All	2.34	*1110*
Once a week	1.92	*121*
Once a month	2.21	*81*
Less often	2.36	*810*
No religion	2.91	*96*

In contrast, a person's class or socio-economic group and their educational attainment - both of which were related to attitudes to the portrayal of sex - do *not* bear any consistent relationships to attitudes to the portrayal of violence.[4] As for whether or not one has parental responsibility, a factor which, as noted, did not influence attitudes to the portrayal of sex as much as we had expected it would, the same is true of tolerance towards the portrayal of violence. At first sight it did seem to be associated, in that parents (and parents with children aged 11-19 in particular) appeared to be particularly restrictive, but the relationship did not turn out to be statistically significant once other socio-demographic factors and attitudinal had been taken into account.[5]

Tolerance index scores by parental responsibility
(low scores = restrictive attitudes; high scores = permissive attitudes)

		Base
All	2.34	*1110*
Has child under 5	2.64	*109*
Has child 5 -10	2.58	*150*
Has child 11-15	2.39	*113*
Has child 16-19	2.28	*69*
Has no children:		
Respondent under 45	2.86	*305*
Respondent 45+	1.88	*505*

Media exposure

Our initial expectation was that people's tolerance towards the portrayal of both sex and violence would be influenced heavily by the extent of their exposure to them. Thus, we anticipated that those who watched more television, had cable or satellite, watched video films more often, or went to the cinema more often would take both sexual and violent images more in their stride. In the event, we were rather surprised last year to find that, after discounting for age effects, only cinema attendance bore a significant relationship to permissiveness. Now, once again, we find a substantially similar pattern. Television viewing habits bear no significant relationship to levels of tolerance of violence on screen. While satellite/cable access, frequency of watching videos and frequency of going to the cinema do all seem to bear a weak relationship to attitudes in isolation, once we discount the effect of age, only a person's frequency of watching videos retains its significance.[6] Thus, the most frequent viewers of video films are indeed the most tolerant of on-screen violence and the least frequent (in particular, those who have no video) are indeed the least tolerant, even after discounting for age.

Tolerance index scores by frequency of watching video films
(low scores = restrictive attitudes; high scores = permissive attitudes)

		Base
All	2.34	*1110*
Once a week or more	2.63	*112*
Once a month	2.61	*185*
Once a year	2.55	*297*
Less often	2.07	*341*
No video recorder	1.97	*175*

The role of underlying beliefs and value systems

Following age, the most important factor associated with one's attitudes to the portrayal of sex in the media was one's broader belief and value system. The measures we used in last year's chapter were the person's score on the *British Social Attitudes* libertarian-authoritarian scale (see Appendix I to this Report for further details), and their attitudes towards pre-marital, extra-marital and homosexual sex. We have no equivalent to these last three questions in respect of violence, since there are no ready-made measures which tap people's general attitudes to violence. So we have to confine ourselves to the standard and well-tested libertarian-authoritarian scale on its own.

The relationship certainly holds in the expected direction: those with the most libertarian values tend to be the most tolerant towards allowing the portrayal of violence in the media, and those with the most authoritarian values tend to be the most restrictive. This may, of course, be measuring no more than that libertarian values tend to be inconsistent with being pro-censorship.

Violence index scores by libertarian-authoritarian scale scores
(low scores = restrictive attitudes; high scores = permissive attitudes)

		Base
All	2.34	*1110*
Most libertarian quintile	2.80	*169*
2nd quintile	2.51	*173*
3rd quintile	2.34	*211*
4th quintile	2.16	*180*
Most authoritarian quintile	2.00	*194*

A combined model

In order to isolate the relative importance of each factor we have mentioned in the overall scheme of things, we need to hold all others constant - which we do by multivariate statistical analysis (for details see the appendix to this chapter). As a result, we can itemise all the factors that turn out to be significantly related to the respondents' scores on the tolerance index, in order of importance. We show this in the first column below and compare the factors with those we derived last year in respect of three indices to do with the frank sex scenes and swearwords.[7]

Violence	Heterosexual sex scene	Homosexual sex scene	Swearwords sex scene
Age	Age	Age	Age
Libertarian-authoritarian	Libertarian-authoritarian	Libertarian-authoritarian	Libertarian-authoritarian
Religiosity	Religiosity	Education	Religiosity
Gender	Gender	Socio-economic group	Gender
Frequency video films	Parental responsibility	Religiosity	Socio-economic group
	Cinema attendance	Gender	

We can now confirm that a person's age outweighs all other factors in their tolerance of both sex and violence in the media, followed by their underlying beliefs and values. In the case of violence, the next most important factors are religiosity and gender, both of which figure with slightly different degrees of strength in attitudes towards sex in the media. The last factor associated with tolerance of the portrayal of violence in the media is one's frequency of watching video films, a factor that is not associated significantly with one's attitudes to the portrayal of sex or to swearwords (although frequency of cinema attendance is associated with tolerance towards the heterosexual sex scene). As noted, factors such as parental responsibility, socio-economic group and education, all of which had modest but different roles to play in attitudes to the portrayal of sex and to swearwords, make no appearance whatever among the factors significantly related to tolerance of on-screen violence.

The overall picture is therefore that the factors associated with attitudes towards the portrayal of violence are, perhaps surprisingly, rather similar to those associated with attitudes towards the portrayal of sex. There are some differences but not as many as we might have anticipated. (However, the overall statistical model here has rather less predictive power for violence than the ones we developed last year did for sex and swearwords. It explains just over a quarter of the variance in people's attitudes while the ones for sex explain just over a third of the variance).

Once again, the overwhelming importance of age relative to life-cycle effects (such as parental responsibility), suggests that this is a cohort effect in changes in attitudes over time. In other words, those who are young today are not likely to become more restrictive as a result of specific events in their

lives (like having children).   Instead they are likely to carry their more
tolerant attitudes with them as they get older so that, as time goes by, the
overall attitudes of the population will become more tolerant than now.

Conclusion

In many respects, our findings are similar to those we discovered last year on
attitudes to the portrayal of sex. Over half the population would ban scenes
of graphic and bloody violence from regular television altogether, and over
four in ten would censor such scenes from even the more restricted media of
satellite and cable television, video and the cinema but we can deduce that
this is when they assume the scenes to be gratuitous and not plot-related.
Attitudes are a little less restrictive towards similar scenes involving either a
fantasy monster inflicting the violence or scenes which, though not gory, still
involve serious violence. But even in these cases, over a third would ban
them completely from any outlet. Only for more distantly filmed scenes of
violence does the level of support for absolute censorship fall to those we
found last year in response to frank heterosexual sex scenes. So tolerance
towards the portrayal of violence in the media seems to be at a somewhat
lower level than tolerance towards the portrayal of sex, although less so
among young men.
   At first sight it appears that it might be the fact of violence itself rather than
the story line or the level of goriness which dictates reactions. But more
detailed questions on context reveal very similar patterns to those uncovered
last year. Attitudes become much less restrictive towards violent scenes that
are relevant to the plot or to those which are part of a television news bulletin.
As last year, our questions which did not specify the context seemed
automatically to be interpreted as referring to gratuitous violence. So
responses to 'taste and decency' questions in general should be viewed in that
light. But the conclusion of our two modules of questions is that the general
thrust of regulatory guidelines - which emphasise the centrality of 'relevance'
and the distinction between fictional and real-life portrayal - are in line with
majority opinion.
   Perhaps the most interesting differences and similarities with last year are in
the socio-demographic breakdown of attitudes. As with attitudes to sex
scenes, age was the great discriminator and attitudes to violence became
progressively more intolerant with age. This time, however, it was young
men rather than young women who tended to be the most tolerant group.
Given that this happens to be the group most likely to commit acts of
violence, there may be a temptation to surmise a causative link. But
behavioural research in this area has been contradictory and we know that
young male offenders, in fact, watch similar television and video material to
non-offenders (Hagell and Newburn, 1994). The fact that young men are
least likely to want violence banned from the media is probably more a

reflection of their taste for 'action' films than for any particular thirst for real life violence.

Equally interesting is the similarity in those factors which appear to explain differences in people's attitudes to showing sex and violence. After age, it is people's underlying value systems and religiosity which are the most highly linked to attitudes to the portrayal of violence, and - rather contrary to our expectations - neither their level of education nor their parental responsibility. This suggests that people's attitudes towards censorship in each case are not dissimilar and are rooted more in the spirit of their generation and their basic beliefs than in the stage of their life-cycle.

We need to do further research to confirm whether individuals with more tolerant attitudes towards portraying violence in the media are the same as those with more tolerant attitudes towards portraying sex, but the clear implication is that they are, except possibly among the youngest age group. If so, then it seems likely that aggregate national attitudes will become more permissive towards both sex and violence. However, in view of the effects-based concerns about showing violence and continuing fears about growing levels of violence in society, this trend is likely to present regulators with some very awkward decisions. They will certainly need to pay close attention to questions of relevance, context and factual reporting.

Notes

1. Respondents in a national survey were invited to respond to the statements "Violence in factual TV makes people *more* ready to accept violence in real life" and "Violence on TV has made people *unnecessarily* afraid". Fifty-eight per cent strongly agreed or tended to agree with the former, while 56 per cent strongly agreed or tended to agree with the latter.
2. All the questions had answer options of "should not be shown at all" and "to anyone"/ "at any time". The cinema questions had an answer option of "only at special film clubs", the video questions "only in special shops", and the regular television questions "only after midnight". The satellite/cable television questions had answer options both of "only after midnight" and of "only on special channels". In the analysis of the satellite/cable questions, these two options have been combined .
3. There was an error in the show card initially issued for the questions about satellite and cable television. These questions should have had the following options:
   - Should not be shown at all
   - Only on special channels
   - On any satellite or cable channel but only after midnight
   - On any satellite or cable channel but only after 10 o'clock in the evening
   - On any satellite or cable channel but only after 9 o'clock in the evening
   - On any satellite or cable channel but only after 8 o'clock in the evening
   - On any satellite or cable channel at any time

   On the show cards initially issued, the third option ("On any channel but only after midnight") was missing. Fieldwork started on 16 April, and researchers were alerted to the mistake on 3 May. Interviewers were informed of the problem as soon as possible, and from 7 May onwards new show cards were used.

   The impact of the error on the data is reduced by two factors:
   - The satellite and cable television show card was one of a sequence of show cards for different media and the card immediately preceding it (for regular television) had the

"only after midnight" option correctly printed on it. Some respondents therefore gave the "only after midnight" reply even before the correct show cards were issued. (The questionnaire was correct, so their answer could be recorded if they did).

- As explained in note 2 above, the categories of "only on special channels" and "only after midnight" have been combined in analysis of the satellite and cable answers (in order to produce a six point answer scale comparable with the other media).

The effect of using the whole sample rather than the 7 May onwards sample is as follows (positive values show that the whole sample estimate is higher than the 7 May onwards sample, negative values that the whole sample estimate is lower):

	Stabbing close-up	Stabbing at a distance	Fantasy monster	Beating and kicking
Not allowed at all	0.0	-0.9	+0.2	-1.2
Special channel/after midnight	-1.1	-0.5	0.0	-0.3
After 10pm	+1.0	+2.0	+0.4	+1.6
After 9pm	-0.6	-0.4	-0.4	-0.1
After 8pm	-0.2	-0.8	-0.6	-0.3
Anytime	+0.3	+0.4	+0.2	0.0
Don't know	+0.7	+0.4	+0.3	+0.5
Refusal	-0.1	-0.1	-0.1	-0.1

Base: whole sample: *1180*
*   7 May sample onwards:*   *881*

Some of these differences will, of course, be due to sampling variation and in this respect the whole sample, being bigger, is more reliable than the 7 May onwards sample. Sampling error apart, there seems to be a reasonably consistent tendency for the whole sample to underestimate the "special channel/after midnight" category and overestimate the "after 10 o'clock" category. No consistent pattern emerged with the 'outright ban' category. However, none of the differences reported above are statistically significant at the 5 per cent level.

There are two main reasons for not wanting to limit the analysis to the 7 May onwards sample:

- The sample size would be reduced by a quarter (from 1,180 to 881), which would increase variance of estimates.
- No special measures are taken to ensure random subsamples across various parts of the fieldwork period. In fact, there is every reason to suppose that respondents interviewed early in the fieldwork period are those who are most accessible, and this is likely *not* to be a random subsample. Limiting the sample to those interviewed from 7 May onwards could therefore introduce other biases into the analysis.

In view of the fact that the differences in estimates reported above are not statistically significant, it was decided to use the whole sample and simply to note that this may involve a very slight underestimate of the "special channel/after midnight" category and a slight overestimate of the "after ten o'clock category" for the medium of satellite and cable television.

4. Although the relationship between socio-economic group and the violence index and between highest educational qualification and the violence index are statistically significant in a bivariate analysis, they are not monotonic - i.e. permissiveness does not rise consistently with rising socio-economic group or education - and are therefore difficult to interpet. Neither relationship is statistically significant once other socio-demographic factors are taken into account. However, if the violence index is unpacked

into the constituent scenarios, socio-economic group is significantly related to attitudes to the stabbing close-up scene and education to the stabbing at a distance scene even after other socio-demographic and attitudinal factors have been taken into account (see appendix to this chapter).

5. Parental responsibility is, however, significantly related to attitudes to the fantasy monster scene even after other socio-demographic and attitudinal factors have been taken into account (see appendix to this chapter).

6. Cinema attendance is, however, significantly related to the stabbing at a distance scene even after other socio-demographic and attitudinal factors have been taken into account (see appendix to this chapter).

7. The models for heterosexual sex scene, homosexual sex scene and swearwords indices have been slightly re-specified compared with those presented in last year's chapter, in order to make them comparable to the violence index. In particular, the questions on pre-marital, extra-marital and homosexual sex have been excluded as there is no equivalent questions about violence. Full details of the models are given in the appendix to this chapter.

References

Andrews, F., Morgan, J. and Sonquist, J. (1967), *Multiple Classification Analysis: a report of a computer program for multiple regression using categorical predictors*, Ann Arbor, Michigan: Survey Research Centre, Institute for Social Research.

Barnett, S. and Thomson, K. (1996), 'Portraying sex: the limits of tolerance' in Jowell, R., Curtice, J., Park, A., Brook, L. and Thomson, K. (eds.) *British Social Attitudes: the 13th Report*, Aldershot: Dartmouth.

Bell, M. (1996), *In Harm's Way*, London: Penguin.

British Board of Film Classification (1995), *Annual Report 1994/5*, London, BBFC.

BBC (1993), *Guidelines for the portrayal of violence on BBC television*, London: BBC.

BBC *et al.* (1996), *Violence on Television in Britain: a content analysis*, London: Independent Television Commission.

Broadcasting Research Unit (1989), *Quality in Television*, London: John Libbey.

Broadcasting Standards Council (1994), *A Code of Practice* (2nd edition), London: BSC.

Cumberbatch, G. and Howitt, D. (1989), *A Measure of Uncertainty*, London: John Libbey.

Gunter, B. and Wober, M. (1988), *Violence on Television: what the viewers think*, London: John Libbey.

Gunter, B. and Svennevig, M. (1988), *Attitudes to broadcasting over the years*, London: John Libbey.

Hagell, A. and Newburn, T. (1994), *Young offenders and the media*, London: Policy Studies Institute.

Heath, A. and Martin, J. (1996), 'Changing attitudes towards abortion: life-cycle, period and cohort effects' in Taylor, B. and Thomson, K. (eds.) (1996), *Understanding change in social attitudes*, Aldershot: Dartmouth.

Home Office (1989), *Report of the Working Group on the Fear of Crime*, London: Home Office Standing Conference on Crime Prevention.

Independent Television Commission (1995), *The ITC Programme Code*, London: ITC.

Independent Television Commission (1997), *Television: The Public's View 1996*, London: ITC.

Millwood Hargrave, A. (1993), *Violence in Factual Television*, London: John Libbey.

Murdock, G. (1997), "Reservoirs of dogma: an archaeology of popular anxieties" in Barker, M. and Petley, J. (eds.), *Ill Effects: the media/violence debate*, London: Routledge.

Acknowledgements

SCPR is grateful to the British Board of Film Classification, the Broadcasting Standards Commission, the British Broadcasting Corporation, and the Independent Television Commission for their financial support which enabled us to ask the questions reported in this chapter. We are also grateful to these bodies, and particularly to James Ferman of the BBFC who convened the group, for their ideas and guidance in devising and designing the questions.

Appendix

Permissiveness index

To construct the violence index, the answers to the four questions (regular television, satellite/cable television, video and cinema) for each of the four scenarios plus the fantasy monster computer game question (but not the beating and kicking documentary footage question) were averaged. The categories of "only on special adult channels" and "only after midnight" were combined for the satellite and cable questions, giving all the questions the same number of answer categories (i.e. six). Cases with missing data were excluded.

Similar indices were also created for each of the four scenarios separately, to ensure that there were no major differences between the scenarios.

Cronbach's alpha for the indices are:

Violence (combined) index	(17 questions)	0.97
Stabbing close-up index	(4 questions)	0.90
Stabbing at a distance index	(4 questions)	0.95
Fantasy monster index	(5 questions)	0.95
Beating and kicking index	(4 questions)	0.96

Multivariate modelling

The multivariate modelling was done using Multivariate Classification Analysis (MCA). MCA is a technique for examining the interrelationships between several independent (explanatory) variables and an interval level (or above) dependent variable (here, the indices scores). The independent variables need be no more than nominal level measures. MCA shows the effect of each independent variable after taking into account the effects of all other independent variables that are entered into the model (Andrews et al, 1967).

MCA produces a partial beta for each independent variable roughly equivalent to a standardised partial regression coefficient. This is a measure of the ability of the variable to explain variation in the dependent variable after adjusting for the effects of all other independent variables. For the model as a whole, MCA produces a multiple correlation coefficient, which when squared (R^2) indicates the proportion of the variance in the dependent variable explained by all the independent variables together (after adjusting for degrees of freedom).

A major limitation of this technique, however, is that it requires a large amount of computer power. The number of independent variables, and the number of levels within each variable, entered into the model therefore needs to be kept strictly limited. Some summarising of variables was therefore necessary before carrying out the modelling and variables which did not attain significance in the earlier models have been excluded from the combined model.

The models presented here are main effects models. In the larger models it was impossible to compute interaction effects owing to empty cells. The smaller models have therefore also been presented as main effects models in the interest of comparability. It is known that there is an interaction effect between age and sex (as reported in the text of the chapter). However, exploratory analysis suggests that the inclusion of this interaction in the models does not substantially alter the picture presented here (the order and significance level of variables in the combined model is unaffected).

Respondents for whom the relevant index score or key independent variables are unobtainable (due to "Don't know" answers, refusal or missing data) are excluded from the analysis for that scale.

Model 1 - Socio-demographic characteristics

Independent variables:

RAGECAT - respondent's age
1   18-24
2   25-44
3   45-64
4   65+

RSEX - respondent's gender
1   male
2   female

CHATTEND - religious attendance
1   Once a week or more
2   Less often but at least once a month
3   Less often than that
4   No religion

RSEGGRP2 - socio-economic group
1   Professional/employer
2   Intermediate non-manual
3   Junior non-manual
4   Supervisor/ skilled manual
5   Semi-skilled manual/personal services
6   Unskilled manual/ Armed forces

HEDQUAL - highest educational qualification
1   Degree
2   Higher education below degree
3   A-level or equivalent
4   O-level or equivalent
5   CSE or equivalent
6   None/ Foreign qualification

CHILDRE1 - children of the respondent in the household
0   No children
1   Child under 12, no child 12-19
2   Child under 12 and child 12-19
3   Child 12-19, no child under 12

	Stabbing close-up	Stabbing at distance	Fantasy monster	Kicking & beating	Violence (combined)
	Beta	Beta	Beta	Beta	Beta
RAGECAT	0.32 **	0.36 **	0.38 **	0.40 **	0.41 **
RSEX	0.09 **	0.14 **	0.13 **	0.10 **	0.13 **
CHATTEND	0.11 **	0.12 **	0.13 **	0.08	0.13 **
RSEGGRP2	0.13 **	0.06	0.06	0.06	0.08
HEDQUAL	0.06	0.12 **	0.05	0.09	0.07
CHILDRE1	0.04	0.08	0.09 *	0.07	0.07
R^2	0.164	0.218	0.192	0.204	0.231

Base: 1062

**	Significant at 1% level
*	Significant at 5% level

Model 2 - Media exposure plus age

Independent variables not previously described:

TOTALTV - hours watched per week
1   0 - 14 hours
2   15 - 20 hours
3   21 - 30 hours
4   31+ hours

SATELLI2 - whether has access to satellite/cable TV
1   Has satellite/cable TV
2   Does not have satellite/cable TV

VIDFILM - how often watches video films
1   once a week or more
2   less often than once a week, but at least once a month
3   less often than once a month, but at least once a year
4   less often than once a year
5   no video

CINEOFT - how often goes to the cinema
1   once a week or more
2   less often than once a week, but at least once a month
3   less often than once a month, but at least once a year
4   less often than once a year

	Stabbing close-up	Stabbing at distance	Fantasy monster	Kicking & beating	Violence (combined)
	Beta	Beta	Beta	Beta	Beta
RAGECAT	0.31 **	0.36 **	0.33 **	0.38 **	0.38 **
TOTALTV	0.08	0.06	0.07	0.06	0.07
SATELLI2	0.03	0.02	0.04	0.02	0.03
VIDFILM	0.10 *	0.10 *	0.11 *	0.07	0.10 *
CINEOFT	0.05	0.09 *	0.06	0.05	0.07
R^2	0.142	0.195	0.165	0.188	0.210

Base: 1105

**	Significant at 1% level
*	Significant at 5% level

Model 3 - Underlying beliefs and values plus age

Independent variables not previously described:

LEFTRIGQ - left-right scale in quintiles
1   Leftmost quintile
5   Rightmost quintile

LIBAUTHQ - libertarian-authoritarian scale in quintiles
1   Most libertarian quintile
5   Most authoritarian quintile

WELFAREQ - welfare scale in quintiles
1   Most welfarist quintile
5   Least welfarist quintile

	Stabbing close-up	Stabbing at distance	Fantasy monster	Kicking & beating	Violence (combined)
	Beta	Beta	Beta	Beta	Beta
RAGECAT	0.31 **	0.36 **	0.33 **	0.37 **	0.38 **
LEFTRIGQ	0.05	0.03	0.07	0.07	0.05
LIBAUTHQ	0.15 **	0.20 **	0.16 **	0.16 **	0.19 **
WELFAREQ	0.06	0.02	0.09	0.04	0.05
R^2	0.145	0.205	0.162	0.192	0.211

Base: 925

**	Significant at 1% level
*	Significant at 5% level

Model 4 - Combined model - violence

	Stabbing close-up	Stabbing at distance	Fantasy monster	Kicking & beating	Violence (combined)
	Beta	Beta	Beta	Beta	Beta
RAGECAT	0.24 **	0.26 **	0.27 **	0.32 **	0.30 **
RSEX	0.07	0.11 **	0.11 **	0.10 **	0.11 **
CHATTEND	0.15 **	0.13 **	0.16 **	0.11 *	0.15 **
RSEGGRP2	0.13 **	0.07	0.08	0.07	0.09
HEDQUAL	0.06	0.09	0.07	0.07	0.06
CHILDRE1	0.04	0.07	0.08	0.06	0.06
VIDFILM	0.10 *	0.09	0.12 *	0.09	0.11 *
CINEOFT	0.04	0.05	0.06	0.03	0.05
LIBAUTHQ	0.17 **	0.20 **	0.16 **	0.16 **	0.19 **
R^2	0.203	0.259	0.229	0.230	0.272

Base: 893

**	Significant at 1% level
*	Significant at 5% level

Model 5 - Combined model - sex

Note: these models have been respecified compared to those presented in last year's Report in order to make them comparable with the models for attitudes to violence. In particular, the sexual morality questions - which have no parallel in the violence module - have been excluded. There has also been some changes to the details of the independent variables. All independent variables in model 5 are identical to variables of the same name in model 4.

Independent variable not previously described:

CHILDRE2 - children of the respondent in the household
0   No children
1   Child under 5 no child 5-19
2   Child under 5 and child 5-19
3   Child 5-19, no child under 5

	Heterosexual sex scene	Homosexual sex scene	Swearwords
	Beta	Beta	Beta
RAGECAT	0.36 **	0.28 **	0.39 **
RSEX	0.13 **	0.10 **	0.13 **
CHATTEND	0.15 **	0.13 **	0.18 **
RSEGGRP2	0.10	0.14 **	0.11 *
HEDQUAL	0.10	0.18 **	0.07
CHILDRE2	0.11 **	0.08	0.05
VIDFILM	0.03	0.02	0.08
CINEOFT	0.11 *	0.07	0.07
LIBAUTHQ	0.19 **	0.23 **	0.20 **
R^2	0.349	0.335	0.389

Base: 772

10 Crime and punishment

Roger Tarling and Lizanne Dowds[*]

Although crime has always apparently ranked high among issues of public concern, there was until 1983 little systematic research that tapped people's experience of crime and the effects it had on their lives. Still less was known about people's attitudes towards crime policy and practice, the police and the courts. Both these problems began to be rectified in the early 1980s with the more or less simultaneous start of two durable survey series. One of them is, of course, the annual *British Social Attitudes* survey. The other, funded by the Home Office after a great deal of internal and external debate, is the now biennial *British Crime Survey*. Designed jointly by the Home Office and SCPR, its primary contribution among others was for the first time to complement police statistics of recorded crime with a series of direct measures of people's own experiences as victims of crime, many of which, as expected, were never reported to the police. Successive surveys in both series have greatly increased our understanding of a wide range of criminological issues.

Between the mid-1950s and 1993 there had been an inexorable rise of around five per cent per year in reported crime figures (according to police records).[1] Yet, despite this rise, until 1979 a broad consensus continued to exist among the major political parties on questions of law and order - even with respect to latterly controversial issues such as capital punishment and the rehabilitation of offenders. Party differences, such as they were, tended to be ones of detail rather than substance. As a result, only rare references to crime

[*] Roger Tarling is Professor of Social Research at the Institute of Social Research, University of Surrey; Lizanne Dowds is Research Affiliate at the Centre for Social Research, Queen's University, Belfast.

were made prior to 1979, either in political speeches or in party manifestos. All this was, however, to change dramatically from then on. A content analysis of more recent manifestos confirms this (Downes and Morgan, 1994).

While recorded crime continued to rise at much the same pace during the 1980s as before, major differences began to surface between the parties over what to do about it. A crucial aspect of this new divide was a sharp difference between the Conservative and Labour parties over the causes of crime - the Conservatives emphasising individual responsibility and Labour stressing social and economic factors, such as increasing inequalities and the growth in unemployment. This debate was to crystallise in the two 1980s' general elections into fierce arguments over the relationship, if any, between unemployment and crime. Labour blamed the economic policies of the Conservative government for the rise in crime among the young in particular, while the Conservatives in turn attributed the problem to what they saw as diminished individual responsibility, brought about by Labour's liberalising reforms during the 1960s and 1970s. As Prime Minister Thatcher put it: "We need to establish that the main person responsible for crime is the criminal." (Speech to the Annual Conference of Conservative Officers, March, 1988)

As data from the *British Social Attitudes* series show, the public's view on the causes of crime, while somewhat ambivalent, seemed to accord rather more with the Conservative than with the Labour position. Approaching two-thirds believe that firmer discipline in the family and in schools would be "very effective" in alleviating the problem, compared with around four in ten who feel that tackling poverty would help. And this broad balance of opinion is to be found even among Labour identifiers.

Even so, despite the change in political rhetoric between the parties that had begun in 1979, the policies themselves were not all that different. True, one or two 'tough' measures were introduced by the government in response largely to calls from party activists, such as the introduction of the 'short, sharp shock' approach to young offenders. But the major legislation of the period, the Criminal Justice Acts of 1982 and 1988, the Police and Criminal Evidence Act, 1984 and the Prosecution of Offenders Act, 1985 might well have been implemented by any of the three major political parties. In effect, greater attention was being paid to crime prevention and to addressing the needs of victims. As for sentencing policies, the late 1980s saw the government beginning to restrict the use of imprisonment to all but the most serious and dangerous offenders and punishing property offenders with a growing range of community penalties. These policies were incorporated into the 1991 Criminal Justice Act.

In any event, returning to the rhetoric as opposed to the substance, the Conservatives during the 1980s were at pains to distinguish themselves as the true and only party of law and order. In the latter years of the Thatcher administration, Douglas Hurd was the Home Secretary and adopted as one of his primary tasks the reduction of overcrowding in Britain's prisons. Soon to become Home Secretary in John Major's administration in the early 1990s

was Michael Howard who, in contrast, adopted as one of his primary tasks the introduction of new measures that would - as he saw it - remove obstacles in the way of bringing criminals to justice. The effect was a sharp change in the political agenda and a flurry of legislative activity. The 1993 Criminal Justice Act, for instance, amended the 1991 Act. The Bail (Amendment) Act was also passed that year. Then in 1994, the Criminal Justice and Public Order Act was to come into force, followed by the Drug Trafficking Act and the Police and Magistrates' Courts Act. Finally, borrowing from initiatives in the United States, the Home Secretary in 1995 set out proposals to increase sentences for repeat offenders, in particular mandatory life sentences for recidivists convicted of serious violent and sexual crimes and mandatory minimum sentences for recidivist burglars. This became law in the 1997 Crime (Sentences) Act. The proposals also called for 'truth' in sentencing, that is for the time actually served by convicted criminals to approximate much more closely to the sentence the court had imposed.

The impact of all this legislation was a major shift in both policy and practice. Police powers were greatly strengthened as were the powers of the court over 'uncooperative' witnesses. Up to then, in the then Home Secretary's words, the criminal justice system had "been tilted too far in favour of the criminal and against the protection of the public" (1993 Conservative Party Conference). Following these changes in legislation, Britain's prison population was to rise dramatically from around 46,000 in the period between 1991 and 1993 to over 56,000 by 1996.

In this chapter, we examine first how public attitudes to crime and punishment have changed during the same period and then ask whether the last Conservative government's recent shifts in policy during the 1990s have reflected or flown in the face of the public mood.

Breaking the law

One indication of people's respect for the rule of law is the extent to which they feel it should invariably be obeyed, even when conscience strongly argues otherwise (see also the chapter by Heath and Park in this volume). We ask:

> In general, would you say that people should obey the law without
> exception, or are there exceptional occasions on which people should
> follow their conscience, even if it means breaking the law?

In fact only a minority of the public gives automatic precedence to the claims of the law over individual conscience. In three iterations of the question spanning six years since 1990, increasing proportions of 52 per cent, 57 per cent and 59 per cent respectively give precedence (on exceptional occasions) to the claims of conscience over those of law. But being tolerant of others breaking the law is one thing. Being prepared to do so oneself, even in

response to a "law to which [they] were very strongly opposed" is quite another. On each occasion that we have asked this question over the same period, fewer than one in three people said they would *themselves* contemplate breaking the law in such circumstances. The large sub-group differences we uncovered on this issue also persisted during the six years. In particular, people of different ages and levels of education vary sharply in how they view the primacy of law over conscience. As might be expected, the claims of conscience are endorsed more strongly by the younger and the more educated. In contrast, party differences are not nearly so great, with as many as one-quarter or more of Conservative party identifiers themselves conceding that they might at least seriously contemplate breaking a law they considered to be wrong.

Other forms of protest

Protest actions come in very different forms, from the relatively bland, to the inconvenient, to the unlawful. In 1996 respondents were asked whether or not people should be entitled to engage in six very different forms of protest action "against a government action they strongly oppose". The next table shows the distribution of answers - from near-unanimous support for some rights to near-unanimous opposition to others.

The right to protest

% saying it should "definitely" or "probably" be allowed	%
Public protest meetings	84
Protest pamphlets	77
Marches and demonstrations	68
Nationwide political strike	30
Occupying government buildings and stopping work there for several days	8
Serious damage to government buildings	2
Base	*989*

So, while almost nobody advocates the right to commit illegal damage to property or, for that matter, the right to take over buildings and bring government business to a standstill, all the other actions get some support. Even a nationwide political strike is thought permissible by around one person in three, while marches and demonstrations are endorsed by more than two in three. Given that these questions were asked during the fifteenth year of a Conservative administration, it is hardly surprising that Labour identifiers (though still a small minority of them) were rather more tolerant than others of stopping work in government buildings. On the other hand, Liberal Democrat identifiers were almost indistinguishable from the Conservatives on this issue. When it comes to more 'conventional' protest

actions, however, differences along party political lines tend to recede. To the extent that sub-group differences exist at all, graduates are the most supportive of the right to engage in conventional protest, while older and retired people are the least enthusiastic.

Though we show only data for 1996 in the above table, the questions have in fact been asked episodically since 1985. But there has been no discernible trend in the answers apart from a slight 'dip' in support for demonstrations and other forms of protest in 1986 - perhaps in response to the sporadic violence during the miners' strike or even to the passage of the 1986 Public Order Act. In general, however, attitudes towards the right to protest - including the sorts of peaceful protests that might nonetheless fall foul of the 1994 Criminal Justice Act - are fairly positive and stable.

So much for other people's abstract right to engage in protest actions of one sort or another. But what about the respondents themselves? Have they protested or might they protest or demonstrate against, say, a law being considered by parliament which they considered to be "really unjust or harmful"? As expected, the number who have done so is rather small, although it has risen over the last decade or so. The number who feel they *might* do so is only slightly larger, having doubled since 1983, from eight per cent to 16 per cent.

Those who would be most prepared - in theory, anyway - to go on a protest are graduates and people in social classes I and II. The propensity to do so declines in tandem with educational attainment. As always the young are more willing to engage than the old. But the patterns also vary according to party preference, with - as might be expected - only 11 per cent of Conservative identifiers in 1996 willing to contemplate protest action compared with 21 per cent of Labour and 22 per cent of Liberal Democrat identifiers respectively.

As noted, the police powers implicit in the 1994 Criminal Justice and Public Order Act could in theory put pay to many forms of protest that most people do not currently regard as untoward 'trouble-making'. These powers may, of course, never be invoked to the full. If they were, it would inevitably lead to a sharp reduction in the availability of protest action as a means of exerting pressure on governments - whether in relation to cuts in education spending, veal calf transportation, the siting of roads or airports or any other controversial policies.

Police powers and the rights of suspects

Should the police be given additional powers to enforce the law? If so, should these powers be wider when the police are dealing with a known criminal than when they are not? The surveys contained two parallel sets of questions on these complicated issues, one about a hypothetical "man without a criminal record" and one about "a man with a long criminal record":

*Suppose the police get an anonymous tip that a man **without a criminal record** is planning to break into a warehouse. Do you think the police should be allowed, without a court order...*

	1985	1994
% saying police should "definitely" or "probably" be allowed		
...to keep the man under surveillance?	72	79
...to detain the man overnight for questioning?	33	37
...to tap his telephone?	14	21
...to open his mail?	8	14
Base	*1530*	*970*

*Suppose the police get an anonymous tip that a man **with a long criminal record** is planning to break into a warehouse. Do you think the police should be allowed, without a court order...*

	1985	1990	1994
% saying police should "definitely" or "probably" be allowed			
...to keep the man under surveillance?	90	90	95
...to detain the man overnight for questioning?	63	64	67
...to tap his telephone?	38	37	46
...to open his mail?	24	23	34
Base	*1530*	*1197*	*970*

In general then, there is strong public support for police powers to keep a suspect under surveillance *without* a court order, regardless of whether or not he has a criminal record. Around two people in three also regard it as legitimate for the police to detain a suspected 'known criminal' overnight, and around one in three would allow the same treatment of a suspect without a criminal record. There was markedly less enthusiasm for powers to tap telephones and intercept mail, though in both cases people with a criminal record are seen to have much less claim to civil liberties than those who are not 'known to the police'. Still, quite large majorities of the public would deny the police power to tap telephones or intercept mail at all in these circumstances, perhaps because of publicity given in earlier years to inadequate regulation of these matters (Brook and Cape, 1991).

On the other hand, what is most notable about these results is the increase since 1990 in public support for many of these powers. In answer to another question, for instance, the proportion of people agreeing that "on duty police officers should always carry guns" doubled in four years (from 14 per cent to 28 per cent in 1994). In April 1995 the police themselves, in a ballot of Police Federation members, rejected the idea by a margin of around four to one. In surveys of officers (see Sargent *et al.*, 1994) police support for the

idea of 'routine arming' halved between 1991 and 1994, from 50 per cent to 25 per cent. The only similar item in the survey on which there has been no upward movement since 1990 is the rather extreme one of whether police should be given the power "to question suspects for up to a week without letting them see a solicitor". In 1990 only one in ten agreed with this proposition, with over 80 per cent disagreeing. Four years later that balance was substantially unchanged.

Only a minority regard other similar measures with equanimity. So, around three in four people are against the use in evidence of uncorroborated confessions which are later withdrawn. Again graduates and those in social classes I and II are the most strongly against the use of such evidence, but on this issue younger and older respondents have similar views.

The suspect's 'right to silence' was abolished in the Criminal Justice and Public Order Act of 1994, against the recommendation of the Royal Commission on Criminal Justice. The public's view on this issue is somewhat ambivalent. In 1990, around one in three (31 per cent) supported the government's view that "if someone remains silent under police questioning, it should count against them in court". By 1994, however, after a great deal more publicity had been given to the issue during parliamentary debates and elsewhere, the proportion of people in favour had risen to 42 per cent, outnumbering those who were opposed (a substantial one quarter or so remained undecided on this issue). So, it appears that the last government's reforms - tilting the balance away from suspects - have a fairly large measure of public support.

But whatever safeguards for the innocent the public is prepared to give up in the interests of convicting the guilty, the right to a jury trial is not one of them. The question in 1990 that dealt with this issue deliberately encouraged respondents to give a non-normative answer by offering two alternatives, the second suggesting that jurors may sometimes be in danger. Nonetheless, by a fairly comfortable margin of 49 to 38 per cent, the public came down in favour of the proposition that "people charged with serious crimes should *always* have the right to a jury trial", rather than the alternative that "there should not always be a right to a jury trial - for instance when the jury might be in danger". There was a large measure of consensus on this issue across sub-groups, although support for jury trials is related to education, social class and party in the now familiar way.

Moving slightly further away from the strict domain of police powers and the rights of suspects, the *British Social Attitudes* survey has now carried a question on three occasions over the past six years on the peculiarly British concern about the possible introduction of identity cards, whether voluntary or mandatory. Expert views differ as to their practicality, their potential success for helping to control crime and their likely impact on personal freedom and liberty. But in 1995 the government published a Green Paper advocating their adoption. The survey invited respondents to agree or disagree with the following statement:

Every adult in Britain should have to carry an identity card

	1990	1994	1996
Agree	37	53	57
Neither	22	21	21
Disagree	40	26	20
Base	*1197*	*970*	*2047*

Not only in aggregate but in every sub-group too there has been a big rise over the four years in public support for the compulsory introduction of identity cards in Britain. The change in mood is strongest among Conservative identifiers (up from 42 per cent in 1990 to 72 per cent in 1996). Meanwhile, support among Labour identifiers went up from 31 to 50 per cent, but among Liberal Democrat identifiers the rise was smaller, up from 48 to 55 per cent. Young people and graduates are still the least willing to accept the idea, just as the elderly and retired are the keenest. Moreover, these age and education gaps have widened. So a majority of the population, before and after the publication of the Green Paper, now appears to be more relaxed about the notion of identify cards than are its many outspoken critics.[2]

Confidence in the police and the courts

Public attitudes towards, and satisfaction with, the police service have been monitored since its inception by the *British Crime Survey,* and from time to time in the *British Social Attitudes* survey series. The *British Crime Survey* asks how good a job the police do in the respondent's local area, and the responses reveal a consistent decline in confidence with the police throughout the 1980s and early 1990s. But this is only half the story. This fall is from an astonishingly high base in 1982 of 92 per cent who felt that the police did a "very" or "fairly" good job to a still impressive 82 per cent in 1992. Slightly more worrying, however, is the sharper decline in the proportion who considered that the police were doing a *very* good job, from 43 to 24 per cent. Since 1992, however, the level of satisfaction seems to have stabilised. The *British Social Attitudes* survey results confirm this trend and show a similar decline (eight per cent) during the 1980s.

Overall, women tend to rate the police more highly than do men, and older people more highly than do younger ones. People living outside inner cities and those living in the southern part of the country also tend to have more favourable views, as do the better-off. The views of Asians and Afro-Caribbeans are less favourable, but for no sub-group did satisfaction levels fall below 73 per cent (Mirrlees-Black and Budd, 1997).

Surprisingly, perhaps, people's satisfaction with the police does not depend on whether or not they have had any recent contact with the police. It seems that public opinion about the police is shaped more by general perceptions

and, perhaps, other people's reports. As Brook and Cape (1991) note: "... it is apparently not what people experience in their encounters with the police that reduces their confidence; rather it is what they read or hear about the institution that seems to cause concern."

On the other hand those who themselves had initiated contact with the police (mostly as victims) did appear to be increasingly disappointed with the police response. In 1983, 50 per cent of these people regarded the police as "very helpful", but by 1990 this proportion too had fallen to 41 per cent (where it seems more or less to have stabilised). In contrast, where contacts had been initiated by the police, such as when the respondent was stopped and questioned, no worsening of relations seems to have taken place.

Distrust of the police

It is important to any democracy that the police and criminal justice system are seen to operate fairly and without fear or favour. In particular, public confidence in the police inevitably depends on a belief that they themselves follow the rules imposed on them by the law that they are appointed to enforce. Yet, according to our evidence, the public's image of the British police on these criteria gives cause for concern. For instance, can the police be trusted "not to bend the rules to get a conviction"? As the next table shows, *British Social Attitudes* respondents have been asked that question on four occasions between 1987 and 1996 and remain stably ambivalent.

Trust police "not to bend the rules"

	1987	1991	1994	1996
	%	%	%	%
"Just about always" or "most of the time"	51	49	47	51
"Only some of the time"	33	36	38	35
"Almost never"	11	11	15	10
Base	*1410*	*1445*	*1137*	*1180*

Only around one-half of the public believes that the police can mostly be trusted not to bend the rules. Unexpectedly, Conservative identifiers are the most trusting but even so only about 60 per cent of them trust the police ("just about always" or "most of the time"), while those in social classes IV and V and those with no educational qualifications are the least trusting (around 40 per cent in both groups say the same).

There is always a certain ambiguity in responses to questions like these. Some people who believe that the police bend the rules also believe that they should do so, in the interests of securing convictions of those they are convinced are guilty. But it is unlikely that many respondents answer in this way since, as the next table shows, there is also strong and consistent public

support for setting up an *independent* body to investigate complaints against the police.

> *Serious complaints against the police should be investigated by an independent body, not by the police themselves*

	1990	1994	1996
	%	%	%
"Agree strongly"	38	40	44
"Agree"	55	52	45
"Neither agree nor disagree"	4	4	5
"Disagree" or "disagree strongly"	3	4	3
Base	*1197*	*970*	*989*

Such near-universal support for a new independent body is unusual and does suggest a degree of public concern, arising (almost certainly) from several recent high-profile cases in which evidence turns out to have been fabricated.

The fairness of the courts

Brook and Cape (1991) drew attention to widespread public scepticism about the fairness of the judicial system, based on the answers to two related questions in particular. The first posited a case in which two people - one black and one white - were appearing in court charged with a crime they did *not* commit. Which one, if either, had the greater chance of being found guilty? The second question asked about the two innocent people, one rich and the other poor. The next table shows the extent to which the courts are not thought to be even-handed.

	Even-handedness of the courts	
	1990	1994
% saying	%	%
White person is more likely to be found guilty	3	4
Black person is more likely to be found guilty	42	44
Both have the same chance	49	49
Rich person is more likely to be found guilty	2	2
Poor person is more likely to be found guilty	56	66
Both have same chance	38	30
Base	*1400*	*1137*

The question is not, of course, about the probability of miscarriages of justice, but about the relative chances of different sorts of people being in danger of

wrongful conviction. Not surprisingly, almost nobody thinks that either the white person or the rich person is more at risk than their opposite numbers. But it is something of an indictment of the criminal justice system that approaching one-half of the population feel that black people are more likely than whites to suffer miscarriages of justice and that around two-thirds feel that poor people are more vulnerable in this respect than the rich.

There is once again some divergence on this issue between different subgroups, with Conservative identifiers most likely to believe in the impartiality of the courts. Even so, theirs is hardly a vote of confidence: one-third believe that the black defendant is more likely to be found guilty, and half that the poor defendant is the more vulnerable. Graduates are once again the most likely to be sceptical about the impartiality of the courts, with as many as two-thirds nominating the black defendant as the more vulnerable and about three-quarters believing that the poor person would come off badly. A particular source of concern must be the increase of 10 percentage points in just four years in the public's perception of a poor person's chances of being treated equally by the courts.

What might account for this large rise? Two kinds of high-profile legal battles in the early 1990s may have helped to sway public opinion. One was typified by the outcome of the Guinness/Distillers take-over trial, and the resultant public disquiet over what was widely regarded as the leniency of the sentences handed down to the 'super-rich' defendants. The other was typified by the release from many years in prison of people (such as the 'Birmingham Six') at the opposite end of the social spectrum, their incarceration resulting from what turned out to be wrongful convictions.

But it is a moot point as to how much all this is of central concern to most of the public. On five occasions between 1985 and 1996, we asked the following question:

All systems of justice make mistakes, but which do you think is worse ...

	1985	1986	1990	1994	1996
	%	%	%	%	%
... to convict an innocent person	67	58	62	58	56
or to let a guilty person go free?	20	26	19	24	27
Can't choose	12	16	19	18	16
Base	*1530*	*1321*	*1197*	*970*	*989*

True, most people feel it is worse to convict an innocent person, but the trend - though somewhat wobbly - is in the opposite direction - another indication of fairly widespread public support for the 1990s' legislative changes that tilted the balance of the criminal justice system against those suspected of having broken the law.

Spending on the criminal justice system

Whatever concerns people may have about crime, they do not translate themselves into any great push for higher public spending on the criminal justice system. In every survey round, respondents are asked to select from a list of ten items of government spending their highest and second highest priorities for *extra* spending. Since the start of the survey series in 1983, health and education have, not surprisingly, dominated respondents' choices. But despite the inexorable rise in crime we noted earlier, extra spending on the police has never in any of the last thirteen years been the highest priority of more than five per cent of the population.

True, pitted against such popular programmes as extra health and education spending, it may come as no surprise that extra spending on the police is a relatively low priority. In response to another set of questions asking about similar areas of public spending, but this time without requiring respondents to choose between them, the call for "much more" spending on "police and law enforcement" has risen steeply from eight per cent in 1985 to 25 per cent nine years later. So rising crime is increasingly seen to be in need of attention. Yet, with public spending nowadays essentially a matter of priorities rather than preferences, responses to the first set of questions may be considered to be the more realistic of the two.

Stiffer sentences?

Investigations of public attitudes towards sentencing are always bedevilled by the fact that people tend to think that sentences are actually much more lenient than they really are. Partly this may be accounted for by regular press 'outrage' at seemingly light sentences for serious cases. Partly, it is explained by the fact that most people are simply not exposed to the everyday reality of the criminal justice system at work. Reassuringly, perhaps, in studies where representative samples are put in the place of judges and asked to arrive at a sentence on the basis of 'all the relevant facts', they tend to impose penalties reasonably close to those awarded in similar cases by the courts (Hough and Moxon, 1985; Hough, 1996). This general problem is hardly new to attitude research, in which people are asked about issues of which, however strong their opinions, they may know little. It is one of the reasons why almost all questions in the *British Social Attitudes* surveys include a "neither/nor", "don't know" or "can't choose" answer category. This option is one that interviewers are briefed to accept readily and, reassuringly, a large minority of respondents often eagerly pick this option. We also know from this and other studies that attitudes often change when people are provided with more information about a subject, as in 'deliberative polls' where opinions are measured from representative samples before and after they are given detailed information about a subject (see Fishkin, 1995).

So we must be somewhat cautious in interpreting the rhetoric of 'tough' opinions on law and order. They are usually based much less on well-considered critiques of judges' and magistrates' sentencing practices than on expressions of frustration that 'something must be done' about crime and criminality. It is almost certainly no coincidence that punitive public attitudes peaked in the 1993 survey, fieldwork for which was carried out shortly after the James Bulger murder. As the next table shows, about one-third of the population are strongly in favour of stiffer sentences in the abstract, a proportion that has not in the end changed much, but has fluctuated widely, over the decade. The fluctuations suggest that answers to this question are more a function of the temporary salience of the issue itself than with people's underlying values. Too much can, perhaps, be read into these fluctuations. Nonetheless, we might note that the proportion favouring stiffer sentences fell in 1990 and 1991 following the government's attempts to reduce the prison population, but rose again in 1993 - the year of the murder of James Bulger. Then it fell sharply and has stayed at much the same level ever since (at around the 1986 level). And this was despite the then government's highly publicised legislative programme designed to combat crime, partly by getting more convictions and partly by imposing stiffer sentences.

People who break the law should be given stiffer sentences

	1986	1989	1990	1991	1993	1994	1995	1996
	%	%	%	%	%	%	%	%
Agree strongly	31	33	27	20	41	28	33	28
Agree	41	44	44	47	43	49	46	43
Neither agree nor disagree	20	15	21	17	12	16	14	20
Disagree	6	6	7	13	3	5	5	7
Disagree strongly	1	1	1	2	1	*	1	1
Base	*1321*	*2604*	*2430*	*1257*	*1327*	*2929*	*3135*	*3085*

The rise between 1990 and 1993 in support for stiffer sentences is reflected in the rise in punitive attitudes in response to another question which also employs popular rhetoric. Between 1990 and 1994, the proportion who agreed (strongly or slightly) with the view that "too many convicted criminals are let off lightly by the courts" rose from an already high 79 per cent to 86 per cent.

Significantly, however, when rhetorical terms such as 'stiffer sentences' and 'let off lightly' are replaced by more sober or prosaic wording, the calls for greater punitiveness become, in contrast, rather muted. In response to the bald statement that "courts should give longer sentences to criminals", only 61 per cent agreed, some 25 points below the proportion who, as noted above, agreed with much the same view expressed differently that "too many convicted criminals are let off lightly". This is, of course, still a sizeable

majority, but may perhaps be a more 'realistic' measure of *underlying* attitudes towards sentencing.

Moving on from sentencing in general to particular classes of criminal, the next table shows responses to two further questions first introduced into the series in 1994 and repeated two years later.

Punishment of offenders

% agree	1994	1996
Only hardened criminals should be sent to prison	31	31
Life sentences should mean life	87	87
Prisons contain too many people who ought to be given a lighter punishment	48	28
Prisoners who behave well should usually be released before the end of their sentence	36	35
Base	*1945*	*2047*

These responses provide evidence of a very high level of support across nearly all groups for being 'tough on crime'. The view that prisons are too overcrowded already does not seem to hold sway among a public clearly more worried by the rise in crime. Graduates were the only sub-group we identified who, for instance, displayed anything but overwhelming support for the oversimplified but popular slogan that "life sentences should mean life". Here then is even stronger evidence than before that the last government's conversion to a more 'fundamentalist' approach to crime and criminals brought them into closer accord with the public's own *instincts*, though not necessarily with their more considered views (Hough, 1996; Fishkin, 1995).

These more considered views are, perhaps, revealed in responses to a series of questions on community penalties and other penalties, included for the first time in 1994. In sharp contrast they suggest that these sorts of punishment command widespread support as a way of dealing with less serious offenders who are "not a big threat".

Punishment of less serious offenders (1994)

% agreeing "more offenders who are not a big threat should be ..."	
...made to spend a certain amount of time helping people in the community	73
...made to get training and counselling	64
...made to do military service for a period of time	62
...made to report regularly to probation officers	60
Base	*1945*

Among these options, community service was the penalty with most appeal, but the other options all commanded much the same fairly widespread support. The most surprising thing about this finding, perhaps, is that training and counselling was not singled out as the 'soft option' in this list.

Respondents were not, of course, asked to give priorities between these and other options, so it might be that training and counselling is seen not so much as an alternative in its own right: more, perhaps, as in conjunction with one of the other penalties.

Electronic tagging, and parental responsibility for fines incurred by their defaulting children, are relatively new proposals. We covered both in the 1990 survey for the first time and found that both were fairly popular, each supported by around 60 per cent of the population. Attitudes to parental responsibility for their child's fines (we asked about a '16-year old') did, however, vary (predictably) by class, but perhaps not as sharply as might have been anticipated: 70 per cent of people in social classes I and II support parental responsibility for fines, compared with only 54 per cent of those in social classes IV and V. It is, of course, people in these latter groups who would be the most likely to be penalised by this sort of legislation.

Conclusions

In the *12th Report,* Brook and Cape (1995) concluded that:

> *"There is consistent evidence that Britain has become less libertarian during the 1990s, especially in respect of public attitudes towards crime and punishment ... When we look at changes in attitudes over the four years, we can find no single sub-group ... which has been conspicuously swimming against the tide ."*

Recent developments and more recent *British Social Attitudes* data appear to confirm this general conclusion - at least in part. Public instincts are certainly on the side of conceding more powers to the police in order to catch criminals, even to the extent of monitoring the movements and activities of suspects (especially ones with a record). Public support has also diminished for other rights: for instance, a suspect's absolute "right to silence" and protection from surveillance *via* telephone tapping or opening mail.

Yet for most people, it is still worse in principle for our system of justice to convict the innocent than to let a guilty person go free, and the right to a trial by jury is still widely cherished. And there is increased public support for an independent body to investigate complaints against the police, support based, in part at least we suspect, on growing scepticism about the trustworthiness of the police and the fairness of the courts. We recall that half of the population believes that the police cannot be trusted with any confidence not "to bend the rules" in order to secure a conviction, while a majority believes that the courts are not even-handed between either rich and poor or white people and black people. And in general, the shifts that have occurred on all these measures have not been confined to any particular sub-groups in the population. All but graduates, perhaps, are swimming with the tide.

So are we to conclude, then, that as crime and concern about crime increase, so the public is more and more prepared (or resigned) to see certain freedoms relinquished as an acceptable sacrifice towards a more important goal? Our findings certainly do not imply that the public would be prepared to see the agencies of the criminal justice system given unfettered powers. On the contrary, its scepticism about the fairness of the police and courts is growing. This is translated into support for impartial investigation of complaints against the police.

We suspect that some of the attitudes uncovered here derive more from a frustrated reaction against trends in crime, some manifestations of which will have touched our respondents (some in petty, but others in traumatic, ways) in the year before we interviewed them. These sorts of experiences do (understandably) matter. Yet there is still rather sparse evidence of any underlying value change - rather that something must be done to cut crime.

Between 1979 and 1993, recorded crime rose from 2.5 million to 5.6 million cases a year. Although it has since fallen back, the figure is still double what it was at the end of the 1970s. Earlier suggestions that the trend in recorded crime did not in fact reflect a 'true' rise in crime, merely a greater propensity among victims to report it or more efficient recording of it by the police, has been shown by the *British Crime Survey* to be largely without foundation. During the period of the survey, for those crimes we can compare by looking at both sources, the number recorded by the police rose by 91 per cent and those recorded by the survey by 83 per cent (Mirrlees-Black *et al.*, 1996). Moreover, evidence from the *British Social Attitudes* survey shows that the public remains highly concerned about many types of crime (Dowds and Ahrendt, 1995).

On the face of it, the public is more and more punitive towards convicted criminals. But, of course, questions in the *British Social Attitudes* surveys tend to be framed *relative* to current practice - whether sentences be 'longer' or 'tougher', and so on. So people's answers inevitably reflect their perception of how long or tough sentences currently are. What we find therefore is somewhat trendless fluctuation in answers, reflecting perhaps the mood of the moment in response to recent cases, rather than any robust change in overall punitiveness.

And what of the dramatic shift in emphasis which characterised Home Office policy in the last three years of Conservative government? Our findings suggest that it was popular. But a change in public attitudes is by no means the only possible explanation for the shift in policy. It probably has more to do with party politics. As poll evidence for the period shows, by the early 1990s the Labour Party had effectively begun to challenge the Conservative Party's position as *the* party of law and order. Perhaps stimulated by the results of the *British Crime Survey*, and other data showing that those most at risk of crime were people living in traditional Labour strongholds such as inner-city estates, the Labour Party began to develop policies encapsulated in its slogan 'tough on crime and tough on the causes of crime'. In response, perhaps, the last Conservative government may have felt

compelled to get tougher. What will continue to be fascinating is how, under a Labour government, public attitudes and crime policy respond to one another and, in particular, which - in the long run - carries the most clout.

Notes

1. It is not sufficiently well-recognised that crime has in fact been rising, on average, 5 per cent per year since the end of the First World War. The only break to this remarkably consistent trend occurred during the Second World War and the decade immediately after, that is 1939-55. Taking a longer historical perspective casts doubt on explanations that either take too short a view of crime trends in general, or which pinpoint causes to one comparatively short period.
2. Brook and Cape (1995) reported the rise in support for identity cards between 1990 and 1994 but felt that this may be an artefact due to the inclusion in 1994 of a prior question about whether *benefit claimants* should carry an identity card. The rise in 1996 when the benefit claimant question was not asked suggests that the rise between 1990 and 1994 was a real increase.

References

Brook, L. and Cape, E. (1991), 'Interim report: civil liberties' in Jowell, R., Brook, L. and Taylor, B. (eds.), *British Social Attitudes: the 8th Report*, Aldershot: Dartmouth.

Brook, L. and Cape, E. (1995), 'Libertarianism in retreat?' in Jowell, R., Curtice, J., Park, A., Brook, L. and Ahrendt, D. (eds.), *British Social Attitudes: the 12th Report*, Aldershot: Dartmouth.

Dowds, L. and Ahrendt, D. (1995), 'Fear of crime' in Jowell, R., Curtice, J., Park, A., Brook, L. and Ahrendt, D. (eds.), *British Social Attitudes: the 12th Report*, Aldershot: Dartmouth.

Downes, D. and Morgan, R. (1994), 'Hostages to fortune?', in Maguire, M., Morgan, R. and Reiner, R., *The Oxford Handbook of Criminology*, Oxford: Clarendon Press.

Fishkin, J. (1995), *The Voice of the People: Public Opinion and Democracy*, New Haven: Yale University Press.

Hough, M. (1996), 'People talking about punishment', *The Howard Journal, 35 (3)*, 191-214.

Hough, M. and Moxon, D. (1985), 'Dealing with offenders: public opinion and the views of victims', *The Howard Journal, 24 (3)*, 160-175.

Mirrlees-Black, C. and Budd, T. (1997), *Policing and the Police: Findings from the 1996 British Crime Survey*, Research Findings No 60, London: Home Office.

Mirrlees-Black, C., Mayhew, P. and Percy, A. (1996), *The 1996 British Crime Survey*, Home Office Statistical Bulletin 19/96. London: Home Office.

Sargent, S., Brown, J. and Gourlay, R. (1994), *Policing*, **10**, 4, 242-252.

Acknowledgements

For many years the Home Office has provided financial support for the BSA survey enabling many of the questions analysed here to be repeated and trends in attitudes to be measured. SCPR is extremely grateful for their continuing support.

We are also grateful to the Nuffield Foundation which funded two fieldwork rounds (in 1990 and 1994) in which we asked questions about civil libertarian

concerns. We also thank the ESRC for its grant to CREST (No.M 543 285 001) in support of the ISSP 1990 and 1996 modules on the "role of government". Some of the findings from both these modules are quoted here.

Appendix I
Technical details of the surveys

British Social Attitudes

As in 1995, three versions of the 1996 *British Social Attitudes* questionnaire were fielded. Each 'module' of questions is asked either of the full sample (around 3,600 respondents) or of a random two-thirds or one-third of the sample. The structure of the questionnaire (versions A, B and C) is shown at the beginning of Appendix III.

Sample design

The *British Social Attitudes* survey is designed to yield a representative sample of adults aged 18 or over. Since 1993, the sampling frame for the survey has been the Postcode Address File (PAF), a list of addresses (or postal delivery points) compiled by the Post Office.[1]

For practical reasons, the sample is confined to those living in private households. People living in institutions (though not in private households at such institutions) are excluded, as are households whose addresses were not on the Postcode Address File.

The 1996 BSA survey also acted as a baseline for the *British Election Study* (BES) Campaign Panel survey, one of a number of studies carried out as part of the long-running BES series.[*] Respondents interviewed in the spring and

---

[*] The BES studies have been carried out by the Centre for Research into Elections and Social Trends (CREST), an ESRC Research Centre linking SCPR and Nuffield College Oxford.

early summer of 1996 were contacted again three more times (by telephone), during and after the 1997 general election campaign and, when possible, interviewed.

Two steps were taken to ensure that the PAF sample drawn could be turned into a sample of *electors*. First, the sample was extended to include 17 year olds (most of whom would become eligible to vote by the date of the 1997 general election). Secondly, the names of all those interviewed were checked against the then-current Electoral Register and the information as to whether or not they were registered to vote was added to the dataset.

In effect, then, there are *two* BSA 1996 datasets, one including the 17 year olds and the other excluding them. For those exploring the BSA survey series data to look at trends over time, it is of course the dataset excluding 17 year olds that should be used. All chapters in this book exclude 17 year olds, as do the annotated questionnaires in Appendix III.

The sampling method involved a multi-stage design, with three separate stages of selection.

Selection of sectors

At the first stage, postcode sectors were selected systematically from a list of all postal sectors in Great Britain. Before selection, any sectors with fewer than 500 addresses were identified and grouped together with an adjacent sector; in Scotland all sectors north of the Caledonian Canal were excluded (because of the prohibitive costs of interviewing there). Sectors were then stratified on the basis of:

- Standard Statistical Region
- Population density (persons per hectare) with variable banding used according to region, in order to create three equal-sized strata per region
- Ranking by percentage of homes that were owner-occupied, from the 1991 Census figures.

Two hundred postcode sectors were selected, with probability proportional to the number of addresses in each sector.

Selection of addresses

Thirty addresses were selected in each of the 200 sectors. The sample was therefore 200 x 30 = 6,000 addresses, selected by starting from a random point on the list of addresses for each sector, and choosing each address at a fixed interval. The fixed interval was calculated for each sector in order to generate the correct number of addresses.

The Multiple-Output Indicator (MOI) available through PAF was used when selecting addresses. MOI shows the number of accommodation spaces sharing one address. Thus, if the MOI indicates more than one accommodation space at a given address, the chances of the given address being selected from the list of addresses would increase so that it matched the total number of accommodation spaces. As would be expected, the vast majority (98 per cent) of MOIs had a value of one. The remainder, which ranged between two and 12, were incorporated into the weighting procedures (described below).

Selection of individuals

Interviewers called at each address selected from PAF and listed all those eligible for inclusion in the sample - that is, all persons currently aged 17 or over and resident at the selected address. The interviewer then selected one respondent using a computer-generated random selection procedure. Where there were two or more households or 'dwelling units' at the selected address, interviewers first had to select one household or dwelling unit using the same random procedure. They then followed the same procedure to select a person for interview.

Weighting

Data were weighted to take account of the fact that not all the units covered in the survey had the same probability of selection. The weighting reflected the relative selection probabilities of the individual at the three main stages of selection: address, household and individual.

First, because addresses were selected using the Multiple Output Indicator (MOI), weights had to be applied to compensate for the greater probability of an address with an MOI of more than one being selected, compared to an address with an MOI of one. Secondly, data were weighted to compensate for the fact that dwelling units at an address which contained a large number of dwelling units were less likely to be selected for inclusion in the survey than ones which did not share an address. (We use this procedure because in most cases these two stages will cancel each other out, resulting in more efficient weights). Thirdly, data were weighted to compensate for the lower selection probabilities of adults living in large households compared with those living in small households.

The distribution of weights used is shown below:

Weight	No.	%	Scaled weight
0.00	42	1.1	0.0000*
0.09	1	0.0	0.0879
0.13	1	0.0	0.1319
0.18	1	0.0	0.1759
0.20	1	0.0	0.1978
0.26	5	0.1	0.2638
0.32	1	0.0	0.3165
0.35	3	0.1	0.3517
0.40	1	0.0	0.3957
0.44	2	0.1	0.4396
0.46	1	0.0	0.4616
0.53	1146	31.3	0.5276
0.63	2	0.1	0.6631
0.79	1	0.0	0.7913
0.88	1	0.0	0.8793
0.99	1	0.0	0.9892
1.06	1904	52.0	1.0551
1.32	1	0.0	1.3189
1.58	380	10.4	1.5827
2.11	132	3.6	2.1102
2.64	18	0.5	2.6378
2.81	1	0.0	2.8136
3.17	9	0.2	3.1654
4.22	2	0.1	4.2205
5.80	5	0.1	5.8031

* The 42 respondents aged 17 were given a weight of zero.

All weights of those aged 18 or above fell within a range between 0.09 and 5.80. The average weight applied was 1.3. The weighted sample was scaled down to make the number of weighted productive cases exactly equal to the number of unweighted productive cases (n = 3,620 if the 17 year olds are excluded).

All the percentages presented in this Report are based on weighted data.

Questionnaire versions

Each address in each sector (sampling point) was allocated to either the A, B or C third of the sample. The first address in the sampling point was allocated the A version, the second the B version, the third the C version and so on. Each version was thus assigned to 2,000 addresses.

Fieldwork

Interviewing was mainly carried out during May, June and July 1996, with a small number of interviews taking place in August.

Fieldwork was conducted by interviewers drawn from SCPR's regular panel and conducted using face-to-face computer-assisted interviewing.[2] Interviewers attended a one-day briefing conference to familiarise them with the selection procedures and questionnaires.

The average interview length was 69 minutes for version A of the questionnaire, 67 minutes for version B and 70 minutes for version C. Interviewers achieved an overall response rate of 68 per cent (including 17 year olds). Details are shown below:

	No.	%
Addresses issued	6,000	
Vacant, derelict and other out of scope	626	
In scope	5,374	100.0
Interview achieved	3,662	68.1
Interview not achieved	1,712	31.8
Refused [1]	1,278	23.8
Non-contacted [2]	125	2.3
Other non-response	182	3.4

1   'Refusals' comprise refusals before selection of an individual at the address, refusals to the office, refusal by the selected person, 'proxy' refusals (on behalf of the selected respondent) and broken appointments after which the selected person could not be recontacted.

2   'Non-contacts' comprise households where no one was contacted and those where the selected person could not be contacted.

As in earlier rounds of the series, the respondent was asked to fill in a self-completion questionnaire which, whenever possible, was collected by the interviewer. Otherwise, the respondent was asked to post it to SCPR. If necessary, up to three postal reminders were sent to obtain the self-completion supplement.

A total of 517 respondents (14 per cent of those interviewed) did not return their self-completion questionnaire. Version A of the self-completion questionnaire was returned by 85 per cent of respondents to the face-to-face interview, version B by 87 per cent and version C by 85 per cent. As in previous rounds, we judged that it was not necessary to apply additional weights to correct for non-response.

Advance letter

Letters describing the purpose of the survey and the coverage of the questionnaire were posted to sampled addresses approximately one week before the start of fieldwork on the 1996 survey.[3]

Analysis variables

A number of standard analyses have been used in the tables that appear in this report. The analysis groups requiring further definition are set out below. For further details, see Lilley *et al.* (1997).

Region

The ten Standard Statistical Regions have been used, except that we generally distinguish between Greater London and the remainder of the South-East. Sometimes these have been grouped into what we have termed 'compressed region': 'Northern' includes the North, North-West, Yorkshire and Humberside. East Anglia is included in the 'South', as is the South-West.

Standard Occupational Classification

Respondents are classified according to their own occupation, not that of the 'head of household'. Their spouses or partners are similarly classified. The main Social Class variables used in the analyses in this report are Registrar General's Social Class, Socio-economic Group (SEG) and the Goldthorpe schema.

  Since 1991, the OPCS *Standard Occupational Classification* (SOC) has been used for the occupation coding on the BSA survey series.[4] SOC has a hierarchical structure, consisting of 371 Unit Groups which can be aggregated into 77 Minor Groups, 22 Sub-major Groups and nine Major Groups.

Registrar General's Social Class

Each respondent's Social Class is based on his or her current or last occupation. Thus, all respondents in paid work at the time of the interview, waiting to take up a paid job already offered, retired, seeking work, or looking after the home, have their occupation (present, past or future, as appropriate) classified into Occupational Unit Groups according to SOC. The combination of occupational classification with employment status generates the following six Social Classes:

I	Professional, etc. occupations	
II	Managerial and technical occupations	'Non-manual'
III (Non-manual)	Skilled occupations	
III (Manual)	Skilled occupations	
IV	Partly skilled occupations	'Manual'
V	Unskilled occupations	

They are usually collapsed into four groups: I & II, III Non-manual, III Manual, and IV & V.

The remaining respondents are grouped as "never had a job" or "not classifiable". For some analyses, it may be more appropriate to classify respondents according to their current social class, which takes into account only their present economic position. In this case, in addition to the six social classes listed above, the remaining respondents not currently in paid work fall into one of the following categories: "not classifiable", "retired", "looking after the home", "unemployed" or "others not in paid occupations".

Socio-economic Group

As with Social Class, each respondent's Socio-economic Group (SEG) is based on his or her current or last occupation. SEG aims to bring together people with jobs of similar social and economic status, and is derived from a combination of employment status and occupation. The full SEG classification identifies 18 categories, but these are usually condensed into six groups:

- Professionals, employers and managers
- Intermediate non-manual workers
- Junior non-manual workers
- Skilled manual workers
- Semi-skilled manual workers
- Unskilled manual workers

As with Social Class, the remaining respondents are grouped as "never had a job" or "not classifiable".

Goldthorpe schema

The Goldthorpe schema classifies occupations by their 'general comparability', considering such factors as sources and levels of income, economic security, promotion prospects, and level of job autonomy and authority. The Goldthorpe schema was derived from the SOC unit groups combined with employment status. Two versions of the schema are coded: the full schema has 11 categories; the 'compressed schema' combines these into the five classes shown below.

- Salariat (professional and managerial)
- Routine non-manual workers (office and sales)
- Petty bourgeoisie (the self-employed, including farmers, with and without employees)
- Manual foremen and supervisors
- Working class (skilled, semi-skilled and unskilled manual workers, personal service and agricultural workers)

There is a residual category comprising those who have never had a job or who gave insufficient information for classification purposes.

Industry

All respondents whose occupation could be coded were allocated a Standard Industrial Classification (SIC 1992). For comparison with previous years, the 1996 *British Social Attitudes* data has also been coded to the older SIC 1980 classification. Two-digit class codes are used. As with Social Class, SIC may be generated on the basis of the respondent's current occupation only, or on his or her most recently-classifiable occupation.

Party identification

Respondents can be classified as identifying with a particular political party on one of three counts: if they consider themselves supporters of that party, as closer to it than to others, or as more likely to support it in the event of a general election (responses are derived from Qs. 113-118). The three groups are generally described respectively as *partisans, sympathisers* and *residual identifiers*. In combination, the three groups are referred to as 'identifiers'.

Attitude scales

Since 1986, the *British Social Attitudes* surveys have included two attitude scales which aim to measure where respondents stand on certain underlying value dimensions - left-right and libertarian-authoritarian. Since 1987 (except 1990), a similar scale on 'welfarism' has been asked.[5]

A useful way of summarising the information from a number of questions of this sort is to construct an additive index (DeVellis, 1991; Spector, 1992). This approach rests on the assumption that there is an underlying - 'latent' - attitudinal dimension which characterises the answers to all the questions within each scale. If so, scores on the index are likely to be a more reliable indication of the underlying attitude than the answers to any one question.

Each of these scales consists of a number of statements to which the respondent is invited to "agree strongly", "agree", "neither agree nor disagree", "disagree", or "disagree strongly".
The items are:

Left-right scale

The government should redistribute income from the better-off to those who are less well off. *[Redistrb]*

Big business benefits owners at the expense of workers. *[BigBusnN]*

Ordinary people do not get their fair share of the nation's wealth. *[Wealth]* [6]

There is one law for the rich and one for the poor. *[RichLaw]*

Management will always try to get the better of employees if it gets the chance. *[Indust4]*

Libertarian-authoritarian scale

Young people today don't have enough respect for traditional British values. *[TradVals]*

People who break the law should be given stiffer sentences. *[StifSent]*

For some crimes, the death penalty is the most appropriate sentence. *[DeathApp]*

Schools should teach children to obey authority. *[Obey]*

The law should always be obeyed, even if a particular law is wrong. *[WrongLaw]*

Censorship of films and magazines is necessary to uphold moral standards. *[Censor]*

Welfarism scale

The welfare state makes people nowadays less willing to look after themselves. *[WelfResp]*

People receiving social security are made to feel like second class citizens. *[WelfStig]*

The welfare state encourages people to stop helping each other. *[WelfHelp]*

The government should spend more money on welfare benefits for the poor, even if it leads to higher taxes. *[MoreWelf]*

Around here, most unemployed people could find a job if they really wanted one. *[UnempJob]*

Many people who get social security don't really deserve any help. *[SocHelp]*

> Most people on the dole are fiddling in one way or another. *[DoleFidl]*

> If welfare benefits weren't so generous, people would learn to stand on their own two feet. *[WelfFeet]*

The indices for the three scales are formed by scoring the leftmost, most libertarian or most pro-welfare position as 1 and the rightmost, most authoritarian or most anti-welfarist position as 5. The "neither agree nor disagree" option is scored as 3. The scores to all the questions in each scale are added and then divided by the number of items in the scale giving indices ranging from 1 (leftmost, most libertarian, or most pro-welfare) to 5 (rightmost, most authoritarian, most anti-welfare). The scores on the three indices have been placed on the dataset.[7]

The scales have been tested for reliability (as measured by Cronbach's alpha). The Cronbach's alpha for the scales in 1996 are 0.81 for the left-right scale, 0.84 for the 'welfarism' scale and 0.77 for the libertarian-authoritarian scale. This level of reliability can be considered "respectable" for the libertarian-authoritarian scale and "very good" for the other two scales (DeVellis, 1991: 85).

Other analysis variables

These are taken directly from the questionnaire and to that extent are self-explanatory. The principal ones are:

Sex (Q.28)

Age (Q.88)

Household income (Q.933)

Economic position (Q.240)

Religion (Q.802)

Highest educational qualification obtained (Q.829-855)

Marital status (Q.91)

Benefits received (Q.926-7)

Sampling errors

No sample precisely reflects the characteristics of the population it represents because of both sampling and non-sampling errors. If a sample were designed as a random sample (if every adult had an equal and independent chance of inclusion in the sample) then we could calculate the sampling error of any percentage, *p*, using the formula:

$$s.e. (p) = \sqrt{\frac{p(100-p)}{n}}$$

where *n* is the number of respondents on which the percentage is based. Once the sampling error had been calculated, it would be a straightforward exercise to calculate a confidence interval for the true population percentage.

For example, a 95 per cent confidence interval would be given by the formula:

$$p \pm 1.96 \times s.e.(p)$$

Clearly, for a simple random sample (srs), the sampling error depends only on the values of p and n. However, simple random sampling is almost never used in practice because of its inefficiency in terms of time and cost.

As noted above, the *British Social Attitudes* sample, like that drawn for most large-scale surveys, was clustered according to a stratified multi-stage design into 200 postcode sectors (or combinations of sectors). With a complex design like this, the sampling error of a percentage giving a particular response is not simply a function of the number of respondents in the sample and the size of the percentage; it also depends on how that percentage response is spread within and between sample points. The complex design may be assessed relative to simple random sampling by calculating a range of design factors (DEFTs) associated with it, where

$$DEFT = \sqrt{\frac{\text{Variance of estimator with complex design, sample size } n}{\text{Variance of estimator with srs design, sample size } n}}$$

and represents the multiplying factor to be applied to the simple random sampling error to produce its complex equivalent. A design factor of one means that the complex sample has achieved the same precision as a simple random sample of the same size. A design factor greater than one means the complex sample is less precise than its simple random sample equivalent. If the DEFT for a particular characteristic is known, a 95 per cent confidence interval for a percentage may be calculated using the formula:

$$p \pm 1.96 \times complex\ sampling\ error\ (p)$$

$$= p \pm 1.96 \times DEFT \times \sqrt{\frac{p(100-p)}{n}}$$

Calculations of sampling errors and design effects were made using the World Fertility Survey 'Clusters' programme.

The following table gives examples of the confidence intervals and DEFTs calculated for a range of different questions, some fielded on all three versions of the questionnaire and some on one only; some asked on the interview questionnaire and some on the self-completion supplement. It shows that most of the questions asked of all sample members have a confidence interval of around plus or minus two to three per cent of the survey proportion. This means that we can be 95 per cent certain that the true population proportion is within two to three per cent (in either direction) of the proportion we report. The confidence intervals calculated for questions asked of only a third of the sample tend to be greater than those calculated for questions asked of the entire sample.

It should be noted that the design effects for certain variables (notably those most associated with the area a person lives in) are greater than those for other variables. This is particularly the case for party identification and housing tenure. For instance, Labour identifiers and local authority tenants tend to be concentrated in certain areas; consequently the design effects calculated for these variables in a clustered sample are greater than the design effects calculated for variables less strongly associated with area, such as attitudinal variables.

		% (p)	Complex standard error of p (%)	95 per cent confidence interval	DEFT
Classification variables					
DV*	**Party identification**				
	Conservative	27.9	0.9	26.1 - 29.7	1.23
	Liberal Democrat	10.7	0.6	9.5 - 11.9	1.17
	Labour	41.7	1.2	39.4 - 44.0	1.42
DV*	**Housing tenure**				
	Owns	69.9	1.4	67.1 - 72.7	1.87
	Rents from local authority	16.6	1.3	14.1 - 19.1	2.06
	Rents privately	11.8	1.0	9.8 - 13.8	1.86
DV*	**Religion**				
	No religion	42.6	1.0	40.7 - 44.6	1.17
	Church of England	29.3	0.9	27.4 - 31.2	1.26
	Roman Catholic	8.9	0.6	7.8 - 10.0	1.19
Q.795	**Age of completing continuous full-time education**				
	16 or under	63.3	1.3	60.7 - 65.8	1.59
	17 or 18	16.4	0.8	14.8 - 18.1	1.34
	19 or over	16.1	1.0	14.0 - 18.1	1.70

* DV = Derived variable

		% (p)	Complex standard error of p (%)	95 per cent confidence interval	DEFT
Attitudinal variables					
Q.216	**Benefits for the unemployed are ...**				
	... too low	47.6	1.2	45.3 - 50.0	1.42
	... too high	31.6	1.0	29.6 - 33.6	1.29

		% (p)	Complex standard error of p (%)	95 per cent confidence interval	DEFT
A.527	Importance of continuing to have a monarchy				
	Very important	32.0	1.6	28.7 - 35.2	1.20
	Quite important	34.6	1.3	32.0 - 37.1	0.93
	Not very important	16.9	1.2	14.5 - 19.3	1.09
	Not at all important	4.6	0.7	3.3 - 5.9	1.09
	Abolish monarchy	10.7	1.1	8.4 - 12.9	1.24
B.611	The countryside generally has changed for the worse	60.9	1.7	57.4 - 64.3	1.09
C.719	Helping homeless people in Britain is a very good way of spending National Lottery money	32.5	1.6	29.3 - 35.6	1.81
A2.30 B2.05 C2.05	Hospital waiting lists for non-emergency operations are in need of a lot of improvement	34.4	1.1	32.2 - 36.5	1.28
A2.07	The government has a lot of different pieces of information about people which computers can bring together very quickly				
	A very serious threat	25.8	1.7	22.5 - 29.1	1.20
	A fairly serious threat	34.6	1.5	31.6 - 37.5	0.98
	Not a serious threat	28.2	1.7	24.8 - 31.7	1.21
	Not a threat at all	4.9	0.8	3.3 - 6.6	1.18
	Can't choose	5.3	0.9	3.4 - 7.1	1.31
B2.32	Strongly support or support cutting in half spending on new roads	16.0	1.1	13.7 - 18.2	1.01
C2.11	How well do state secondary schools nowadays prepare young people for work				
	Very well	3.8	0.6	2.6 - 4.9	0.98
	Quite well	34.0	1.5	31.0 - 37.1	1.04
	Not very well	51.0	1.8	47.5 - 54.5	1.14
	Not at all well	7.9	0.9	6.0 - 9.8	1.13

These calculations are based on the 3,620 respondents (aged 18 or above) to the main questionnaire and 3,103 returning self-completion questionnaires; on the A version respondents (1171 for the main questionnaire and 993 for the self-completion); on the B version respondents (1235 and 1075 respectively); or on the C version respondents (1214 and 1035 respectively). As the examples above show, sampling errors for proportions based only on respondents to just one of the three versions of the questionnaire, or on subgroups within the sample, are somewhat larger than they would have been had the questions been asked of everyone.

Analysis techniques

Regression

Regression analysis aims to summarise the relationship between a 'dependent' variable and one or more 'independent' variables. It shows how well we can estimate a respondent's score on the dependent variable from knowledge of their scores on the independent variables. It is often undertaken to support a claim that the phenomena measured by the independent variables cause the phenomenon measured by the dependent variable. However, the causal ordering, if any, between the variables cannot be verified or falsified by the technique. Causality can only be inferred through special experimental designs or through assumptions made by the analyst.

All regression analysis assumes that the relationship between the dependent and each of the independent variables takes a particular form. In *linear regression*, the most common form of regression analysis, it is assumed that the relationship can be adequately summarised by a straight line. This means that a one point increase in the value of an independent variable is assumed to have the same impact on the value of the dependent variable on average irrespective of the previous values of those variables.

Strictly speaking the technique assumes that both the dependent and the independent variables are measured on an interval-level scale, although it may sometimes still be applied even where this is not the case. For example, one can use an ordinal variable (e.g. a Likert scale) as a *dependent* variable if one is willing to assume that there is an underlying interval level scale and the difference between the observed ordinal scale and the underlying interval scale is due to random measurement error. Categorical or nominal data can be used as *independent* variables by converting them into dummy or binary variables; these are variables where the only valid scores are 0 and 1, with 1 signifying membership of a particular category and 0 otherwise.

The assumptions of linear regression can cause particular difficulties where the *dependent* variable is binary. The assumption that the relationship between the dependent and the independent variables is a straight line means that it can produce estimated values for the dependent variable of less than 0

or greater than 1. In this case it may be more appropriate to assume that the relationship between the dependent and the independent variables takes the form of an S-curve, where the impact on the dependent variable of a one-point increase in an independent variable becomes progressively less the closer the value of the dependent variable approaches 0 or 1. *Logistic regression* is an alternative form of regression which fits such an S-curve rather than a straight line. The technique can also be adapted to analyse multinomial non-interval level dependent variables, that is, variables which classify respondents into more than two categories.

The two statistical scores most commonly reported from the results of regression analyses are:

A measure of variance explained: This summarises how well all the independent variables combined can account for the variation in respondent's scores in the dependent variable. The higher the measure, the more accurately we are able in general to estimate the correct value of each respondent's score on the dependent variable from knowledge of their scores on the independent variables.

A parameter estimate: This shows how much the dependent variable will change on average, given a one unit change in the independent variable (while holding all other independent variables in the model constant). The parameter estimate has a positive sign if an increase in the value of the independent variable results in an increase in the value of the dependent variable. It has a negative sign if an increase in the value of the independent variable results in a decrease in the value of the dependent variable. If the parameter estimates are standardised, it is possible to compare the relative impact of different independent variables; those variables with the largest standardised estimates can be said to have the biggest impact on the value of the dependent variable.

Regression also tests for the statistical significance of parameter estimates. A parameter estimate is said to be significant at the five per cent level, if the range of the values encompassed by its 95 per cent confidence interval (see also section on sampling errors) are either all positive or all negative. This means that there is less than a five per cent chance that the association we have found between the dependent variable and the independent variable is simply the result of sampling error and does not reflect a relationship that actually exists in the general population.

Factor analysis

Factor analysis is a statistical technique which aims to identify whether there are one or more apparent sources of commonality to the answers given by respondents to a set of questions. It ascertains the smallest number of *factors* (or dimensions) which can most economically summarise all of the variation found in the set of questions being analysed. Factors are established where respondents who give a particular answer to one question in the set, tend to

give the same answer as each other to one or more of the other questions in the set. The technique is most useful when a relatively small number of factors is able to account for a relatively large proportion of the variance in all of the questions in the set.

The technique produces a *factor loading* for each question (or variable) on each factor. Where questions have a high loading on the same factor then it will be the case that respondents who give a particular answer to one of these questions tend to give a similar answer to the other questions. The technique is most commonly used in attitudinal research to try to identify the underlying ideological dimensions which apparently structure attitudes towards the subject in question.

International Social Survey Programme

The *International Social Survey Programme (ISSP)* is run by a group of research organisations, each of which undertakes to field annually an agreed module of questions on a chosen topic area. Since 1985, an *International Social Survey Programme* module has been included in one of the *British Social Attitudes* self-completion questionnaires. Each module is chosen for repetition at intervals to allow comparisons both between countries (membership is currently standing at 27) and over time. In 1996, the chosen subject was the Role of Government[8], and the module was carried on the A version of the self-completion questionnaire (Qs. 2.01-2.12).

Notes

1. Until 1991 all *British Social Attitudes* samples were drawn from the Electoral Register (ER). However, following concern that this sampling frame might be deficient in its coverage of certain population subgroups, a 'splicing' experiment was conducted in 1991. We are grateful to the Market Research Development Fund for contributing towards the costs of this experiment. Its purpose was to investigate whether a switch to PAF would disrupt the time-series - for instance, by lowering response rates or affecting the distribution of responses to particular questions. In the event, it was concluded that the change from ER to PAF was unlikely to affect time trends in any noticeable ways, and that no adjustment factors were necessary. Since significant differences in efficiency exist between PAF and ER, and because we considered it untenable to continue to use a frame that is known to be biased, we decided to adopt PAF as the sampling frame for future British Social Attitudes surveys. For details of the PAF/ER 'splicing' experiment, see Lynn and Taylor (1995).

2. In 1993 it was decided to mount a split-sample experiment designed to test the applicability of Computer-Assisted Personal Interviewing (CAPI) to the *British Social Attitudes* survey series. CAPI has been used increasingly over the past decade as an alternative to traditional interviewing techniques. As the name implies, CAPI involves the use of lap-top computers during the interview, with interviewers entering responses directly into the computer. One of the advantages of CAPI is that it significantly reduces both the amount of time spent on data processing and the number of coding and editing errors. Over a longer period, there could also be significant cost savings. There was,

however, concern that a different interviewing technique might alter the distribution of responses and so affect the year-on-year consistency of *British Social Attitudes* data.
Following the experiment, it was decided to change over to CAPI completely in 1994 (the self-completion questionnaire still being administered in the conventional way). The results of the experiment are discussed in the *11th Report* (Lynn and Purdon, 1994).

3. An experiment was conducted on the 1991 *British Social Attitudes* survey, which showed that sending advance letters to sampled addresses before fieldwork begins has very little impact on response rates. However, interviewers do find that an advance letter helps them to introduce the survey on the doorstep, and a majority of respondents have said that they preferred some advance notice. For these reasons, advance letters have been used on the *British Social Attitudes* surveys since 1991.

4. Before 1991, occupational coding was carried out according to the OPCS *Classification of Occupations 1980* (CO80). However, analysts can be confident that the change to SOC does not affect year-on-year comparability of Social Class variables in the *British Social Attitudes* survey. For further details see Appendix I in Jowell *et al.* (1992).

5. Because of methodological experiments on scale development, the exact items detailed below have not been asked on all versions of the questionnaire each year. However, in 1996, these items were asked on all three versions.

6. In 1994, this item was replaced by: Ordinary people get their fair share of the nation's wealth. *[Wealth1]*

7. In constructing the scale, a decision had to be taken on how to treat missing values ("Don't knows" and refused/not answered). Respondents who had more than two missing values on the left-right scale and more than three missing values on the libertarian-authoritarian and welfare scale were excluded for that scale. For respondents with just a few missing values, "Don't knows" were recoded to the midpoint of the scale and not answered or 'refused' were recoded to the scale mean for that respondent on their valid items.

8. The Role of Government module was a part-replication of modules fielded in 1985 and 1990.

References

DeVellis, R.F. (1991), 'Scale development: theory and applications', *Applied Social Research Methods Series*, **26**, Newbury Park: Sage.

Jowell, R., Brook, L., Prior, G. and Taylor, B. (1992), *British Social Attitudes: the 9th Report*, Aldershot: Dartmouth.

Lilley, S.J., Brook, L., Park, A. and Thomson, K. (1997), *British Social Attitudes 1995 Survey: Technical Report*, London: SCPR.

Lynn, P. and Purdon, S. (1994), 'Time-series and lap-tops: the change to computer- assisted interviewing', in Jowell, R., Curtice, J., Brook, L. and Ahrendt, D. (eds.) *British Social Attitudes: the 11th Report*, Aldershot: Dartmouth.

Lynn, P. and Taylor, B. (1995), 'On the bias and variance of samples of individuals: a comparison of the Electoral Registers and Postcode Address File as sampling frames', *The Statistician*, **44**, 173-94.

Spector, P.E (1992), 'Summated rating scale construction: an introduction', *Quantitative Applications in the Social Sciences*, **82**, Newbury Park: Sage.

Appendix II
Notes on the tabulations

1. Figures in the tables are from the 1996 *British Social Attitudes* survey unless otherwise indicated. Those aged 17 at the time of the survey have been excluded.
2. Tables are percentaged as indicated.
3. In tables, '*' indicates less than 0.5 per cent but greater than zero, and '-' indicates zero.
4. When findings based on the responses of fewer than 100 respondents are reported in the text, reference is generally made to the small base size.
5. Percentages equal to or greater than 0.5 have been rounded up in all tables (e.g. 0.5 per cent = one per cent, 36.5 per cent = 37 per cent).
6. In many tables the proportions of respondents answering "Don't know" or not giving an answer are omitted. This, together with the effects of rounding and weighting, means that percentages will not always add to 100 per cent.
7. The self-completion questionnaire was not completed by all respondents to the main questionnaire (see Appendix I). Percentage responses to the self-completion questionnaire are based on all those who completed it.
8. Where tables show the base (the number of respondents who answered the question), this is printed in small italics. The bases are *un*weighted, unless otherwise stated.

Appendix III
The questionnaires

As explained in Appendix I, three different versions of the questionnaire (A, B and C) were administered, each with its own self-completion supplement. The diagram that follows shows the structure of the questionnaires and the topics covered (not all of which are reported on in this volume).

The three interview questionnaires reproduced on the following pages are derived from the Blaise program in which they were written. For ease of reference, each item has been allocated a question number. Gaps in the numbering system indicate items that are essential components of the Blaise program but which are not themselves questions, and so have been omitted. In addition, on all six questionnaires we have removed the keying codes and inserted instead the percentage distribution of answers to each question. We have also included the SPSS variable name, bracketed and in italics, beside each question. Above the questions we have included filter instructions. A filter instruction should be considered as staying in force until the next filter instruction. Percentages for the core questions are based on the total weighted sample, while those for questions in versions A, B or C are based on the appropriate weighted subsamples. Respondents aged 17 are excluded. We reproduce first version A of the interview questionnaire in full; then those parts of version B and version C that differ. The three versions of the self-completion questionnaire follow, with those parts fielded in more than one version reproduced in one version only.

The percentage distributions do not necessarily add up to 100 because of weighting and rounding, or for one or more of the following reasons:

(i)   Some sub-questions are filtered - that is, they are asked of only a proportion of respondents. In these cases the percentages add up

(approximately) to the proportions who were asked them. Where, however, a series of questions is filtered, we have indicated the weighted base at the beginning of that series (for example, all employees), and throughout have derived percentages from that base.

(ii) If fewer than 50 respondents (unweighted) are asked a question, frequencies (the number of people giving each response) are shown, rather than percentages.

(iii) At a few questions, respondents were invited to give more than one answer and so percentages may add to well over 100 per cent. These are clearly marked by interviewer instructions on the questionnaires.

As reported in Appendix I, the *British Social Attitudes* self-completion questionnaire was not completed by 14 per cent of respondents who were successfully interviewed. To allow for comparisons over time, the answers in the supplement have been repercentaged on the base of those respondents who returned it (for version A:993 weighted; for version B:1,075 weighted; and for version C:1,035 weighted). This means that the distribution of responses to questions asked in earlier years are comparable with those given in Appendix III of all earlier reports in this series except in *The 1984 Report*, where the percentages for the self-completion questionnaire need to be recalculated if comparisons are to be made.

BRITISH SOCIAL ATTITUDES: 1996 SURVEY

Main questionnaire plan

A	B	C

1. Household grid

2. Newspaper readership

3. Party identification

4. Housing

5. Electoral registration, politics and political knowledge

6. Public spending, welfare benefits and health care

7. Economic activity, labour market and learning

8. Gambling, the National Lottery and Scratchcards.

A	B	C
9. Social divisions		9. Education
10. Political Trust and Europe	10. Countryside	10. Local authority spending
11. Northern Ireland	11. Transport	11. Charitable giving
		12. Welfare/Social Security
13. Taste and decency	13. Public understanding of science	
14. Religion and classification		

....

Self-completion questionnaire

A	B	C

1. ISSP Role of government

2. Political Trust

3. Housing

4. Health care

A	B	C
	5. Public understanding of science	
6. Social divisions		6. Education
	7. Countryside	7. Charitable giving
8. Northern Ireland	8. Transport	8. Welfare/Social Security
9. Taste and decency		9. Taxation

10. Politics and political knowledge

11. Attitude scales

BRITISH SOCIAL ATTITUDES: 1996 FACE-TO-FACE INTERVIEW

Documentation

Contents page

INTRODUCTION

ASK ALL **(NOT ON SCREEN)**

Q1 *[Serial]* **(NOT ON SCREEN)**
Serial number
Range: 80001 ... 89200

Q3 *[Version]* **(NOT ON SCREEN)**
Version (A=1, B=2, C=3)
%
32.4 A
34.1 B
33.5 C

Q6 *[StRegion]* **(NOT ON SCREEN)**
Standard region
%
9.4 Scotland
5.8 Northern
10.2 North West
9.9 Yorkshire & Humberside
9.4 West Midlands
6.8 East Midlands
3.4 East Anglia
8.6 South West
18.7 South East (excl Greater London)
12.3 Greater London
5.6 Wales

[First]

INTERVIEWER: FOR YOUR INFORMATION ... you are in the
Questionnaire for -
Serial number: *(serial number)*
You should have a *(green/blue/orange)*coloured ARF and
self-completion questionnaire

- TO RETURN TO THE MENU, PRESS <Esc>
- TO GO DIRECTLY TO 'ADMIN', PRESS <Ctrl + Enter>
- OTHERWISE TO CONTINUE WITH THE INTERVIEW PRESS '1' AND
  <Enter>

1

HOUSEHOLD GRID

ASK ALL

Q26 *[Household]*
(You have just been telling me about the adults that
live in this household. Thinking of **everyone** living in
the household, **now including children**:)
Including yourself, how many people live here regularly
as members of this household?
CHECK INTERVIEWER MANUAL FOR DEFINITION OF HOUSEHOLD IF
NECESSARY.
IF YOU DISCOVER THAT YOU WERE GIVEN THE WRONG
INFORMATION FOR THE RESPONDENT SELECTION ON THE ARF:
DO NOT REDO THE ARF SELECTION PRODECURE
DO ENTER THE CORRECT INFORMATION HERE
DO USE <CTRL + F4> TO MAKE A NOTE OF WHAT HAPPENED.

**HOUSEHOLD GRID: QUESTIONS *[Name]* TO *[RelResp]* ARE ASKED
ONCE FOR EACH HOUSEHOLD MEMBER.**

[Name] **(NOT ON DATA FILE)**
FOR RESPONDENT: (Can I just check, what is your first
name?) PLEASE TYPE IN THE FIRST NAME (OR INITIALS) OF
RESPONDENT
FOR OTHER HOUSEHOLD MEMBERS: PLEASE TYPE IN THE FIRST
NAME (OR INITIALS) OF PERSON NUMBER *(number)*
Open Question (Maximum of 10 characters)

[RSex], *[P2Sex]*-*[P12Sex]*
PLEASE CODE SEX OF *(Name)* (figures refer to *[Rsex]*)
%
45.7 Male
54.3 Female

[RAge], *[P2Age]*-*[P12Age]*
FOR RESPONDENT: I would like to ask you a few details
about each person in your household. Starting with
yourself, what was your **age** last birthday?
FOR OTHER HOUSEHOLD MEMBERS: PLEASE ENTER AGE OF *(Name)*
Range: 1 ... 97
%
Median: 45 years (figures refer to *[RAge]*)
0.1 Don't know
0.4 Refusal/NA

2

IF NOT RESPONDENT

N=3620

[P2Rel]-[P12Rel]
PLEASE ENTER RELATIONSHIP OF (Name) TO RESPONDENT
Partner/spouse/cohabitee
Son/daughter (inc step/adopted)
Parent/parent-in-law
Other relative
Other non-relative
(Don't Know)
(Refusal/NA)

END OF HOUSEHOLD GRID

Q90   [MarStat2]
CARD
Can I just check, which of these applies to you at present?
%   **CODE FIRST TO APPLY**
58.7 Married
7.0 Living as married
1.9 Separated (after being married)
5.3 Divorced
8.0 Widowed
19.0 Single (never married)
- (Don't Know)
0.1 (Refusal/NA)

NEWSPAPER READERSHIP

N=3620

ASK ALL

Q96   [ReadPap]
Do you normally read any daily **morning** newspaper at least 3 times a week?
%
58.7 Yes
41.3 No
- (Don't Know)
- (Refusal/NA)

IF 'Yes' AT [ReadPap]

Q97   [WhPaper]
Which one do you normally read?
IF MORE THAN ONE: Which one do you read **most** frequently?
%
5.2 (Scottish) Daily Express
9.1 (Scottish) Daily Mail
13.2 Daily Mirror/Record
1.9 Daily Star
14.2 The Sun
3.8 Daily Telegraph
0.6 Financial Times
2.2 The Guardian
0.9 The Independent
2.8 The Times
0.1 Morning Star
3.8 Other Irish/Northern Irish/Scottish regional or local daily morning paper (**WRITE IN**)
0.4 Other (**WRITE IN**)
0.3 (More than one paper)
0.0 (Don't Know)
0.0 (Refusal/NA)

ASK ALL

Q100   [NwConYst]
And did you read any **daily** morning newspaper yesterday (**IF INTERVIEWED ON MONDAY**: on Saturday)?
%
49.9 Yes
50.1 No
0.0 (Don't Know)
- (Refusal/NA)

IF 'No' AT [ReadPap] AND 'Yes' AT [NwConYst] N=3620

Q101 *[WhPapYst]*
Which one did you read?
% **IF MORE THAN ONE ASK**: Which one did you read **most** of?
0.3 (Scottish) Daily Express
0.9 (Scottish) Daily Mail
0.7 Daily Mirror/Record
0.1 Daily Star
0.7 The Sun
0.4 Daily Telegraph
0.0 Financial Times
0.3 The Guardian
0.3 The Independent
0.2 The Times
0.1 Morning Star
0.3 Other Irish/Northern Irish/Scottish regional or local
     daily morning paper **(WRITE IN)**
0.0 Other **(WRITE IN)**
 -   (Don't Know)
0.1 (Refusal/NA)

IF 'Yes' AT [NwConYst]

Q104 *[NwAttEcn]*
When you read the newspaper yesterday **(IF INTERVIEWED ON MONDAY**: on Saturday), how much attention did you pay to
% stories about the **economy** .. **READ OUT** ..
2.6 ...a great deal,
6.1 quite a bit,
9.5 some,
14.8 a little,
16.4 or, none?
0.6 (No stories about the economy)
 -   (Don't Know)
0.0 (Refusal/NA)

Q105 *[NwAttPol]*
And how much attention did you pay to stories about
% **politics** .. **READ OUT** ..
2.9 ...a great deal,
6.7 quite a bit,
10.1 some,
15.1 a little,
14.8 or, none?
0.3 (No stories about politics)
 -   (Don't Know)
0.0 (Refusal/NA)

VERSION A: ASK ALL N=3620

Q106 *[TVHrsWk]*
How many hours of television do you normally watch on an
ordinary day or evening **during the week**, that is, Monday
to Friday?
INTERVIEWER: ROUND UP TO NEAREST HOUR
IF DOES NOT WATCH TELEVISION ON WEEKDAYS, CODE 0
IF NEVER WATCHES TELEVISION AT ALL, CODE 97
Range: 0 ... 97
% **Median: 3 hours**
0.0 (Never watches television)

**IF WATCHES TELEVISION (I.E. NOT 'Never watches
television at all/DK/Refusal') AT [TVHrsWk]**
Q107 *[TVHrsWke]*
How many hours of television do you normally watch on an
ordinary day or evening **at the weekend**?
INTERVIEWER: ROUND UP TO NEAREST HOUR
IF DOES NOT WATCH TELEVISION AT WEEKENDS, CODE 0
Range: 0 ... 24
% **Median: 3 hours**

VERSION A: ASK ALL N=1171

Q108 *[Satellit]*
Do you have a satellite dish or are you connected to a
cable network in your own home?
**INTERVIEWER: PROMPT FOR CORRECT PRECODE
EXCLUDE DISHES NO LONGER WORKING OR NO LONGER CONNECTED**
%
18.2 Yes, satellite
8.3 Yes, cable
0.4 Yes, both
73.1 No
0.0 (Don't Know)
 -   (Refusal/NA)

Q109 *[Video]*
% Do you have a video recorder in your own home?
86.4 Yes
13.6 No
 -   (Don't Know)
 -   (Refusal/NA)

IF 'Yes' AT [Video]
Q110 *[VidFilm]*
CARD
How often nowadays do you personally watch a rented or
bought video?

VERSION A: ASK ALL

Q111 [CineOft]
CARD AGAIN
How often do you go to the cinema nowadays?

	[VidFilm]	[CineOft]
	%	%
Once a week or more	10.4	1.0
Once a month	16.4	9.0
Once a year	28.0	30.8
LT once a year	31.6	59.2
Don't know	0.1	-
Refusal/NA	-	-

PARTY IDENTIFICATION

Q113 [SupParty]
Generally speaking, do you think of yourself as a supporter of any one political party?

%	
43.9	Yes
55.9	No
0.1	(Don't Know)
0.1	(Refusal/NA)

IF 'No/DK' AT [SupParty]

Q114 [ClosePty]
Do you think of yourself as a little closer to one political party than to the others?

%	
25.6	Yes
30.2	No
0.1	(Don't Know)
0.2	(Refusal/NA)

IF 'Yes' AT [SupParty] OR 'Yes/No/DK' AT [ClosePty]

Q118 [PartyID1]
IF 'Yes' AT [SupParty] OR AT [ClosePty]: Which one?
IF 'No/DK' AT [ClosePty]: If there were a general election tomorrow, which political party do you think you would be most likely to support?
DO NOT PROMPT

%	
27.9	Conservative
41.7	Labour
10.7	Liberal Democrat
1.7	Scottish Nationalist
0.3	Plaid Cymru
0.3	Other party
0.5	Other answer
10.0	None
1.0	Green Party
4.0	(Don't Know)
1.8	(Refusal/NA)

IF ANY PARTY AT [PartyFW]

Q121 [IDStrng]
Would you call yourself very strong (party given at [PartyID1]), fairly strong, or not very strong?

%	
9.0	Very strong (party at [PartyID1])
28.0	Fairly strong
46.6	Not very strong
0.1	(Don't Know)
6.3	(Refusal/NA)

ASK ALL

Q122 *[Politics]*
How much interest do you generally have in what is going on in politics .. **READ OUT** ..

%	
9.0	... a great deal,
21.6	quite a lot,
32.7	some,
25.5	not very much,
11.2	or, none at all?
0.0	(Don't Know)
-	(Refusal/NA)

N=3620

N=3620

HOUSING

ASK ALL

Q124 *[AreaChng]*
Now some questions about the area in which you live. Taking everything into account, would you say this area has got better, worse or remained about the same as a place to live during the last two years?
IF NECESSARY: By 'your area' I mean whatever you feel is your local area.

Q125 *[AreaFut]*
And what do you think will happen during the next two years: will this area get better, worse or remain about the same as a place to live?

	[AreaChng]	*[AreaFut]*
	%	%
Better	12.1	13.2
Worse	29.6	25.7
About the same	55.8	57.4
(Don't Know)	2.4	3.6
(Refusal/NA)	0.0	-

Q126 *[NoisyNgb]*
CARD
Please use this card to say how common or uncommon each of the following things is in your area.
Noisy neighbours or loud parties?

Q127 *[Graffiti]*
CARD AGAIN
(How common or uncommon is this **in your area**?)
Graffiti on walls and buildings?

Q128 *[TeenOnSt]*
CARD AGAIN
(How common or uncommon is this **in your area**?)
Teenagers hanging around on the streets?

Q129 *[Drunks]*
CARD AGAIN
(How common or uncommon is this **in your area**?)
Drunks or tramps on the streets?

Q130 *[Rubbish]*
CARD AGAIN
(How common or uncommon is this **in your area**?)
Rubbish and litter lying about?

Q131 [HmGdBad]
CARD AGAIN
(How common or uncommon is this **in your area**?)
Homes and gardens in bad condition?

Q132 [Vandals]
CARD AGAIN
(How common or uncommon is this **in your area**?)
Vandalism and deliberate damage to property?

Q133 [RaceTens]
CARD AGAIN
(How common or uncommon is this **in your area**?)
Insults or attacks to do with someone's race or colour?

Q134 [Burglary]
CARD AGAIN
(How common or uncommon is this **in your area**?)
Homes broken into?

Q135 [VehTheft]
CARD AGAIN
(How common or uncommon is this **in your area**?)
Cars broken into or stolen?

Q136 [Attacks]
CARD AGAIN
(How common or uncommon is this **in your area**?)
People attacked in the streets?

	[NoisyNgb]	[Graffiti]	[TeenOnSt]
	%	%	%
Very common	4.6	3.3	17.2
Fairly common	7.9	12.3	29.9
Not very common	36.4	37.0	29.1
Not at all common	51.0	47.2	23.6
(Don't Know)	0.0	0.1	0.2
(Refusal/NA)	-	-	-

	[Drunks]	[Rubbish]	[HmGdBad]
	%	%	%
Very common	3.6	14.2	3.7
Fairly common	9.0	26.5	12.1
Not very common	32.0	37.4	53.0
Not at all common	55.1	21.9	30.7
(Don't Know)	0.3	0.0	0.4
(Refusal/NA)	-	-	-

N=3620

	[Vandals]	[RaceTens]	[Burglary]
	%	%	%
Very common	8.0	1.3	8.7
Fairly common	18.6	4.4	29.4
Not very common	46.3	28.3	45.2
Not at all common	26.8	64.3	15.2
(Don't Know)	0.3	1.7	1.6
(Refusal/NA)	-	-	-

	[VehTheft]	[Attacks]
	%	%
Very common	12.8	1.9
Fairly common	30.0	6.9
Not very common	39.6	35.8
Not at all common	15.2	54.5
(Don't Know)	2.4	1.0
(Refusal/NA)	-	-

Q137 [LocTrans]
Generally speaking, would you say that compared to other areas the public transport around here is better, worse or about average?
IF 'BETTER' OR 'WORSE': Is that much (better/worse), or just a bit (better/worse)?

Q138 [LocEduc]
Now thinking about schools around here. Generally speaking, would you say that compared to other areas the schools around here are better, worse or about average?
IF 'BETTER' OR 'WORSE': Is that much (better/worse), or just a bit (better/worse)?

N=3620

Q139 *[LocJobs]*
What about someone from around here applying for a job? Generally speaking, would you say that compared to people in other areas the person's chance of being given an interview are *better*, *worse* or *about average*?
IF 'BETTER' OR 'WORSE': Is that much *(better/worse)*, or just a bit *(better/worse)*?

	[LocTrans] %	*[LocEduc]* %	*[LocJobs]* %
Much better than average	9.1	10.9	2.5
A bit better than average	15.3	21.0	12.5
About average	49.6	47.1	58.5
A bit worse than average	9.1	3.7	9.5
Much worse than average	7.8	1.8	3.8
Depends	0.5	0.6	1.7
(Don't Know)	8.6	14.8	11.4
(Refusal/NA)	0.0	0.0	0.1

Q140 *[NghBrHd]*
Can I just check, how long have you lived in your present neighbourhood?
ENTER YEARS. ROUND TO NEAREST YEAR.
PROBE FOR BEST ESTIMATE.
IF LESS THAN ONE YEAR, CODE 0.
Range: 0 ... 97
% **Median: 13 years**
\- (Don't know)
0.0 (Refusal/NA)

N=1214

VERSION C: ASK ALL
Q141 *[MoveLast]*
When did you last move home?
% **PROBE FOR CORRECT CODE.**
9.3 Less than a year ago
12.4 One or two years ago
11.8 Three or four years ago
6.5 Five or six years ago
55.9 More than six years ago
4.1 Never moved
\- (Don't Know)
\- (Refusal/NA)

N=1214

IF MOVED IN LAST SIX YEARS AT [MoveLast]
Q142 *[WhereMov]*
When you last moved, did you move into this area or were
% you already living here?
22.8 Moved into area
17.2 Already living in area
\- (Don't Know)
\- (Refusal/NA)

Q143 -151 **CARD**
People move home for lots of reasons. On this card are just some of them.
IF 'Already living in area' AT [WhereMov]: When you last moved, did any of the things on this card matter to you in deciding to stay in this area?
IF 'Moved into area/DK/Refusal' AT [WhereMov]: When you were deciding where to move to, did any of the things on this card matter to you in choosing this area?
IF RESPONDENT HAS MOVED SEVERAL TIMES, ASK ABOUT MOST RECENT MOVE.
% Multicoded (Maximum of 7 codes)
1.1 The level of the Council Tax or Poll Tax *[WhyM1]*
5.9 The local schools *[WhyM2]*
1.0 The services for the elderly, such as home helps and old people's homes *[WhyM3]*
2.3 The services for children, such as nurseries *[WhyM4]*
0.7 Street cleaning and rubbish collection *[WhyM5]*
3.4 Local parks, sports centres or libraries *[WhyM6]*
2.0 The standard and availability of council housing *[WhyM7]*
29.1 None of these *[WhyM8]*
\- (Don't Know)
\- (Refusal/NA)

ASK ALL

Q153 *[HomeType]*

N=3620

CODE FROM OBSERVATION AND CHECK WITH RESPONDENT.
Would I be right in describing this accommodation as a ...
READ OUT ONE YOU THINK APPLIES ...

%
22.4 ...detached house or bungalow
35.2 ...semi-detached house or bungalow
26.6 ...terraced house or bungalow
10.9 ...self-contained, purpose-built flat/maisonette (inc. tenement block)
3.8 ...self-contained converted flat/maisonette
0.6 ...room(s), not self-contained
0.5 Other answer (WRITE IN)
- (Don't Know)
- (Refusal/NA)

Q155 *[NoRooms]*

How many rooms does your household have for its own use?
Please exclude kitchens under 2 metres (6 feet 6 inches) wide, bathrooms, toilets and hallways.
PROMPT ON HOUSEHOLD DEFINITION IF NECESSARY
Range: 1 ... 97
Median: 5 rooms

%
- (Don't Know)
0.1 (Refusal/NA)

Q156 *[HomeEst]*

May I just check, is your home part of a housing estate?
NOTE: MAY BE PUBLIC OR PRIVATE, BUT IT IS THE
RESPONDENT'S VIEW WE WANT

%
41.5 Yes, part of estate
58.3 No
0.1 (Don't Know)
- (Refusal/NA)

Q157 *[HomeMove]*

If you had a free choice, would you choose to stay in your present home, or would you choose to move out?

%
57.8 Would choose to stay
41.4 Would choose to move out
0.8 (Don't Know)
- (Refusal/NA)

Q158 *[HsePExpt]*

N=3620

In a year from now, do you expect house prices in your area to have gone up, to have stayed the same, or to have gone down?
IF 'GONE UP' OR 'GONE DOWN': By a lot or a little?

%
3.6 To have gone up by a lot
38.2 To have gone up by a little
44.7 To have stayed the same
5.9 To have gone down by a little
1.4 To have gone down by a lot
6.2 (Don't Know)
0.0 (Refusal/NA)

Q159 *[HsePChng]*

And compared to five years ago, would you say that house prices in your area have gone up, have stayed the same, or have gone down?
IF 'GONE UP' OR 'GONE DOWN': By a lot or a little?

%
5.5 Have gone up by a lot
21.1 Have gone up by a little
20.3 Have stayed the same
25.0 Have gone down by a little
18.5 Have gone down by a lot
9.5 (Don't Know)
0.1 (Refusal/NA)

Q160 *[Tenure5]*

Does your household own or rent this accommodation?
PROBE IF OWNS: Outright or on a mortgage?
PROBE IF RENTS: From whom?

%
27.4 OWNS: Own (leasehold/freehold) outright
42.5 OWNS: Buying (leasehold/freehold) on mortgage
16.6 RENTS: Local authority/council
3.0 RENTS: Housing Association/Housing Trust
1.5 RENTS: Property company
0.4 RENTS: Employer
0.9 RENTS: Other organisation
0.4 RENTS: Relative
5.4 RENTS: Other individual
0.2 RENTS: Housing Action Trust
1.2 Rent free (other than squatting)
- Squatting
0.4 Other answer (WRITE IN)
0.1 (Don't Know)
0.0 (Refusal/NA)

Q164 [LegalRes]   N=3620

IF 'OWNS: Owns outright' AT [Tenure5]: Are the deeds for the (house/flat) in your name or are they in someone else's? IF IN RESPONDENT'S NAME: Are they in your name only or jointly with someone else?
IF 'OWNS: Buying on a mortgage' AT [Tenure5]: Is the mortgage in your name or is it in someone else's? IF IN RESPONDENT'S NAME: Is it in your name only or jointly with someone else?
IF 'RENTS' AT [Tenure5]: Is the rent book in your name or is it in someone else's? IF IN RESPONDENT'S NAME: Is it in your name only or jointly with someone else?
IF 'Rent free/Squatting/Other/DK/Refusal' AT [Tenure5]: Are you legally responsible for the accommodation or is someone else? IF LEGALLY RESPONSIBLE: Is that on your own or jointly with someone else?

%
28.3 (Deeds/Mortgage/Rent book) in respondent's name only/ Yes, respondent solely responsible
53.5 Jointly with someone else
17.5 (Deeds/Mortgage/Rent book) in someone else's name/ No responsibility
0.5 (Don't Know)
0.2 (Refusal/NA)

Q165 [CTaxBand]
CARD
What is the council tax band of this (house/flat)?
HOUSE VALUES ON CARD ARE FOR 1991 - ASSUME LITTLE/NO CHANGE IN HOUSE PRICES SINCE 1991
IF RESPONDENT IS NOT SURE OF BAND, ACCEPT GUESS IF POSSIBLE

%	Band	(England)	(Scotland)	(Wales)
17.2	A	£40,000 or less	£27,000 or less	£30,000 or less
18.6	B	£40,001-£52,000	£27,001-£35,000	£30,001-39,000
19.0	C	£52,001-£68,000	£35,001-£45,000	£39,001-£51,000
15.3	D	£68,001-£88,000	£45,001-£58,000	£51,001-£66,000
9.6	E	£88,001-£120,000	£58,001-£80,000	£66,001-£90,000
5.4	F	£120,001-£160,000	£80,001-£106,000	£90,001-£120,000
3.8	G	£160,001-£320,000	£106,001-£212,000	£120,001-£240,000
0.5	H	£320,001 and over	£212,001 and over	£240,001 and over

10.5 (Don't Know)
0.1 (Refusal/NA)

17

Q166 [BuyFrmLA]   N=2548
ASK ALL WHO OWN OUTRIGHT OR ARE BUYING ON A MORTGAGE
Did you, or the person responsible for the mortgage, buy your present home from the local authority as a tenant?
% 'LOCAL AUTHORITY' INCLUDES GLC, LONDON RESIDUARY BODY AND NEW TOWN DEVELOPMENT CORPORATION
11.1 Yes
87.8 No
0.3 (Don't Know)
0.0 (Refusal/NA)

Q167 [CopeMorg]   N=1555
ASK ALL WHO ARE BUYING ON A MORTGAGE
How are you and your household coping with the cost of your mortgage these days? Does it make things
... READ OUT ...
%
6.4 ... very difficult,
19.9 a bit difficult,
70.0 or, not really difficult?
2.5 (Don't Know)
1.2 (Refusal/NA)

Q168 [EasySell]   N=2548
ASK ALL WHO OWN OUTRIGHT OR ARE BUYING ON A MORTGAGE
CARD
If you were to put your home on the market, how easy or difficult do you think it would be to sell under present market conditions?
%
7.5 Very easy
30.7 Fairly easy
19.1 Neither easy nor difficult
28.2 Fairly difficult
10.7 Very difficult
3.0 (Don't Know)
0.9 (Refusal/NA)

18

Q169 **ASK ALL WHO RENT**   N=1046
[RentLev1]
How would you describe the rent for this accommodation?
Would you say it was .. **READ OUT** ..
%
32.1 ... on the high side,
53.0 reasonable,
7.3 or, on the low side?
2.2 (Living rent free)
3.5 (Don't Know)
2.0 (Refusal/NA)

Q170 **ASK ALL**   N=3620
[RentPrf1]
If you had a free choice would you choose to rent accommodation, or would you choose to buy?
%
15.2 Would choose to rent
83.9 Would choose to buy
0.9 (Don't Know)
0.0 (Refusal/NA)

Q171 **ASK ALL WHO RENT**   N=1046
[RentExpt]
And apart from what you would **like**, do you **expect** to buy a house or a flat in the next two years, or not?
IF EXPECTS TO BUY PRESENT HOUSE/FLAT, CODE 1.
%
18.8 Yes, expect to buy
78.5 No, do not expect to buy
0.7 (Don't Know)
2.0 (Refusal/NA)

Q172 Here are some reasons people might give for not wanting to buy a home. As I read out each one, please tell me whether or not it applies to you at present.
[NotBuy1]
I could not afford the deposit

Q173 [NotBuy2]
(And does this apply or not apply to you **at present**)
I would not be able to get a mortgage

Q174 [NotBuy3]
(And does this apply or not apply to you **at present**)
It might be difficult to keep up the repayments

Q175 [NotBuy4]
(And does this apply or not apply to you **at present**)
I can't afford any of the properties I'd want to buy

Q176 [NotBuy5]   N=1046
(And does this apply or not apply to you **at present**)
I do not have a secure enough job

Q177 [NotBuy8]
(And does this apply or not apply to you **at present**)
I might not be able to resell the property when I wanted to

	[NotBuy1]	[NotBuy2]	[NotBuy3]
	%	%	%
Applies	70.6	57.1	62.4
Does not apply	27.2	37.8	34.4
(Don't Know)	0.2	3.1	1.2
(Refusal/NA)	2.0	2.0	2.0

	[NotBuy4]	[NotBuy5]	[NotBuy8]
	%	%	%
Applies	67.3	59.3	40.1
Does not apply	29.4	38.3	54.7
(Don't Know)	1.3	0.4	3.2
(Refusal/NA)	2.0	2.0	2.0

ELECTORAL REGISTRATION, POLITICS AND POLITICAL KNOWLEDGE   N=3620

ASK ALL

Q179   [Citizen]
%   Are you ... **READ OUT** ...
96.8   a British citizen,
2.3   or, a citizen of another country?
0.9   (Both)
-    (Don't Know)
-    (Refusal/NA)

IF 'citizen of another country' OR 'Both' AT [Citizen]

Q180   [OthCit]
Of which (other) country are you a citizen?
    PROBE FOR FULL DETAILS
%
0.8   Irish Republic/Eire
1.3   Commonwealth
0.4   European Union (exc. Ireland)
0.7   Other
-    (Don't Know)
-    (Refusal/NA)

ASK ALL

Q181   [ElRegOn]
As far as you know, is your name on the electoral
register, that is the official list of people entitled
to vote, either at this address or somewhere else?
IF 'YES': At this address, another or both at this
%   address and another?
90.8   Yes, at this address
4.6   Yes, at another address
0.3   Yes, both at this address and another
0.2   Yes, don't know address
3.1   No
1.0   (Don't Know)
-    (Refusal/NA)

21

IF 'No' AT [ElRegOn]

Q182   [ElRegNot]
    CARD
    Which of the following best describes why your name is
%   not on the Electoral Register?
0.8   I'm not entitled to vote
0.1   I got left off by mistake
0.0   I didn't know how to register
0.2   I didn't want other people knowing about me
0.2   I'm not interested in elections
0.5   I never received the application form
0.7   I have recently moved
0.2   I just couldn't be bothered
0.3   Some other reason (WRITE IN)
0.0   (Don't Know)
1.0   (Refusal/NA)

**IF 'Yes, at another address' OR 'Yes, both at this
address and another' AT [ElRegOn]**

Q184   [ElRegAd1]
At which (other) address is that?
**PLEASE WRITE IN FULL ADDRESS AND POSTCODE AT Q40 ON THE
BACK PAGE OF THE ARF.**
%
4.1   Address given
0.8   Address not given
-    (Don't Know)
1.0   (Refusal/NA)

ASK ALL

Q185   [ElRegOct]
**IF REGISTERED 'at another address' OR 'both at this
address and another' AT [ElRegOn] AND 'Address
given/DK/Refusal' AT [ElRegAd1]**: Were you living at this
address you have just given me in October 1995?
**IF REGISTERED 'at another address' OR 'both at this
address and another' AT [ElRegOn], BUT 'Address not
given' AT [ElRegAd1]**: Were you living there in October
1995 ?
ALL OTHERS: Were you living at this address in October
1995?
%
95.3   Yes
4.7   No
-    (Don't Know)
-    (Refusal/NA)

IF MOVED DURING OCTOBER 1995, CODE 'No'.

N=3620

22

N=3620

IF NOT REGISTERED AT PRESENT ADDRESS AT [ElRegOn] AND NOT LIVING AT PRESENT ADDRESS IN OCTOBER 1995 AT [ElRegOct]

[ElRegAd2]

Q186   Where were you living in October 1995?
%
1.4   At current address
2.1   At other address
-      (Don't Know)
0.0   (Refusal/NA)

IF 'At another address' AT [ElRegAd2] OR IF REGISTERED AT PRESENT ADDRESS BUT NOT LIVING AT PRESENT ADDRESS IN OCTOBER 1995

[ElRegAd3]

IF REGISTERED AT PRESENT ADDRESS AT [ElRegOn] BUT NOT LIVING AT PRESENT ADDRESS IN OCTOBER 1995 AT [ElRegOct]:
Where were you living in October 1995?
WRITE IN FULL OCTOBER 1995 ADDRESS AND POSTCODE AT Q41 ON THE BACK PAGE OF ARF.
%
2.1   Address given
1.2   Address not given
-      (Don't Know)
0.0   (Refusal/NA)

ASK ALL

[TVConWk]

Q188   On about how many days in the past week, that is, the seven days from last (same day of week as interview) until yesterday, did you watch all or part of the news on any television channel?
IF 'NONE', CODE AS 0.
ENTER NUMBER OF DAYS ON WHICH NEWS WATCHED
%
9.4   None
3.6   One day
7.1   Two days
7.7   Three days
5.6   Four days
7.0   Five days
4.9   Six days
54.7   Seven days
0.1   (Don't Know)
-      (Refusal/NA)

23

N=3620

IF WATCHED THE NEWS LAST WEEK OR DK AT [TVConWk] (I.E. NOT 'NONE')

[TVConYst]

Q189   And did you watch all or part of the news on any television channel yesterday?
%
68.1   Yes
22.4   No
0.1   (Don't Know)
-      (Refusal/NA)

IF 'Yes' AT [TVConYst]

[TVAttEcn]

Q190   People pay attention to different parts of the television news.
When you watched the television news yesterday, how much attention did you play to stories about the **economy**
... READ OUT ...
%
5.4   ...a great deal,
10.7   quite a bit,
14.9   some,
16.6   a little,
15.7   or, none?
4.6   (No stories about the economy)
0.3   (Don't Know)
0.1   (Refusal/NA)

[TVAttPol]

Q191   And how much attention did you pay to stories about **politics ... READ OUT ...**
%
6.0   ...a great deal,
11.8   quite a bit,
17.1   some,
18.2   a little,
14.0   or, none?
1.0   (No stories about politics)
0.0   (Don't Know)
0.1   (Refusal/NA)

ASK ALL

[ConFeel5]
CARD

Q192   Now some questions about different political parties. Please choose a phrase from this card to say how you feel about ... **READ OUT ...**
...the Conservative Party

24

Q193 [LabFeel15]
CARD AGAIN
(Please choose a phrase from this card to say how you feel about ...)
...the Labour Party

N=3620

Q194 [LdFeel15]
CARD AGAIN
(Please choose a phrase from this card to say how you feel about ...)
...the Liberal Democrats

ASK IN SCOTLAND
Q195 [SNPFeel15]
CARD AGAIN
(Please choose a phrase from this card to say how you feel about ...)
...the Scottish National Party

N=339

ASK IN WALES
Q196 [PCFeel15]
CARD AGAIN
(Please choose a phrase from this card to say how you feel about ...)
...Plaid Cymru

N=203

	[ConFeel15]	[LabFeel15]	[LdFeel15]
	%	%	%
Strongly in favour	2.7	9.0	1.9
In favour	18.4	30.6	16.7
Neither in favour nor against	31.3	36.4	57.1
Against	24.0	17.1	17.9
Strongly against	22.6	5.6	4.1
(Don't Know)	0.9	1.0	2.1
(Refusal/NA)	0.2	0.2	0.2

	[SNPFeel15]	[PCFeel15]
	%	%
Strongly in favour	8.2	0.5
In favour	24.7	19.3
Neither in favour nor against	37.6	41.1
Against	20.5	27.6
Strongly against	6.2	9.4
(Don't Know)	2.8	2.1
(Refusal/NA)	-	-

25

ASK ALL
Q197 [KnowPR]
These next questions are about things that different parties are in favour of.
If you feel you don't know, just tell me and we'll go to the next question.
Firstly, which party would you say is ... **READ OUT** ...
... **most in favour of** changing the voting system to a form of proportional representation?
DO NOT PROMPT

N=3620

Q198 [KnowCtTx]
(And which party would you say is ...)
... **most in favour of** reducing government spending in order to cut taxes?
DO NOT PROMPT

Q199 [KnowOptO]
(And which party would you say is ...)
...**most in favour of** schools being under local authority control?
DO NOT PROMPT

Q200 [KnowScot]
(And which party would you say is ...)
... **most in favour of** independence for Scotland?
DO NOT PROMPT

Q201 [KnowRail]
(And which party would you say is ...)
... **most in favour of** letting private industry run the railways?
DO NOT PROMPT

Q202 [KnowMnWg]
(And which party would you say is ...)
... **most in favour of** setting a minimum wage level, below which no-one can be paid?
DO NOT PROMPT

26

N=3620

	[KnowPR]	[KnowCtTx]	[KnowOptO]
	%	%	%
Conservative	2.9	48.0	14.7
Labour	18.0	26.0	54.6
Liberal Democrat	36.2	2.4	2.1
Scottish National Party	0.6	0.1	0.2
Plaid Cymru	0.0	-	0.0
Other party	0.1	0.1	0.1
None	1.1	2.8	0.9
(Don't Know)	40.9	20.4	27.3
(Refusal/NA)	0.3	0.1	0.2

	[KnowScot]	[KnowRail]	[KnowMnWg]
	%	%	%
Conservative	2.5	78.6	6.7
Labour	21.3	4.4	72.2
Liberal Democrat	5.9	0.3	1.5
Scottish National Party	31.9	0.1	0.0
Plaid Cymru	0.1	0.0	0.0
Other party	-	0.0	0.1
None	1.5	0.3	0.8
(Don't Know)	36.7	16.2	18.5
(Refusal/NA)	0.1	0.1	0.2

Q203   [EconPast]
Looking back over the last year or so, would you say that Britain's economy has got stronger, got weaker or has stayed about the same?
% IF 'STRONGER' OR 'WEAKER': By a lot or a little?
2.4 Got a lot stronger
21.9 Got a little stronger
41.3 Stayed about the same
19.1 Got a little weaker
9.4 Got a lot weaker
5.9 (Don't Know)
- (Refusal/NA)

Q204   [EconXpct]   N=3620
And looking forward to the **year ahead**, do you think Britain's economy will get stronger, get weaker or stay about the same?
% IF 'STRONGER' OR 'WEAKER': By a lot or a little?
2.0 Get a lot stronger
21.4 Get a little stronger
51.4 Stay about the same
12.9 Get a little weaker
3.5 Get a lot weaker
8.9 (Don't Know)
0.0 (Refusal/NA)

Q205   [HIncPst5]
Looking back over the **last year** or so, would you say your household's income has fallen behind prices, kept up with prices or gone up by more than prices?
% IF 'FALLEN' OR 'GONE UP': By a lot or a little?
16.1 Fallen behind prices a lot
28.3 Fallen behind prices a little
39.5 Kept up with prices
9.2 Gone up by a little more than prices
4.2 Gone up by a lot more than prices
2.6 (Don't Know)
0.1 (Refusal/NA)

Q207 [HIncXpc5]   N=3620
And looking forward to the **year ahead**, do you expect your household's income will fall behind prices, keep up with prices or go up by more than prices?
IF 'FALL BEHIND' OR 'GO UP': By a lot or a little?

%
9.2 Fall behind prices a lot
25.8 Fall behind prices a little
46.8 Keep up with prices
10.7 Go up by a little more than prices
2.8 Go up by a lot more than prices
4.6 (Don't Know)
0.1 (Refusal/NA)

Q209 [FuturVot]
Now, thinking of the next General Election in a year or so's time, which party do you think you are most likely to vote for then?

DO NOT PROMPT
%
22.0 Conservative
42.2 Labour
10.6 Liberal Democrat
1.7 Scottish Nationalist Party
0.3 Plaid Cymru
0.8 Green Party
0.8 Other **(WRITE IN)**
1.9 Refused to say
11.1 (Probably) would not vote
8.6 (Don't Know)
- (Refusal/NA)

PUBLIC SPENDING, WELFARE BENEFITS AND HEALTH CARE   N=3620

Q212 [Spend1]
CARD
Here are some items of government spending. Which of them, if any, would be your highest priority for **extra** spending? Please read through the whole list before deciding.
ENTER ONE CODE ONLY FOR HIGHEST PRIORITY

IF ANSWER GIVEN AT [Spend1] (I.E. NOT 'None of these/DK/Refusal')
Q213 [Spend2]
CARD AGAIN
And which next?
ENTER ONE CODE ONLY FOR NEXT HIGHEST

	[Spend1]	[Spend2]
	%	%
Education	27.6	38.7
Defence	0.5	1.9
Health	54.4	25.6
Housing	3.8	8.5
Public transport	2.0	3.7
Roads	1.1	2.0
Police and prisons	3.4	7.4
Social security benefits	2.9	5.1
Help for industry	3.5	5.8
Overseas aid	0.2	0.3
(None of these)	0.1	0.3
(Don't Know)	0.3	0.2
(Refusal/NA)	0.1	0.5

ASK ALL
Q214 [SocBen1]
CARD
Thinking now only of the government's spending on **social benefits** like those on the card. Which, if any, of these would be your highest priority for **extra** spending?
ENTER ONE CODE ONLY FOR HIGHEST PRIORITY

IF ANSWER GIVEN AT [SocBen1] (I.E. NOT 'None of these/DK/Refusal')
Q215 [SocBen2]
CARD AGAIN
And which next?
ENTER ONE CODE ONLY FOR NEXT HIGHEST

N=3620

	[SocBen1]	[SocBen2]
	%	%
Retirement pensions	49.8	21.2
Child benefits	12.1	18.1
Benefits for the unemployed	11.1	14.7
Benefits for disabled people	19.3	35.2
Benefits for single parents	5.5	6.6
(None of these)	1.4	1.5
(Don't Know)	0.7	0.6
(Refusal/NA)	0.1	2.2

ASK ALL

Q216 [Dole]

Opinions differ about the level of benefits for unemployed people.
Which of these two statements comes closest to your own view ... **READ OUT** ...

%
47.6 ...benefits for unemployed people are **too low** and cause hardship,
31.6 or, benefits for unemployed people are **too high** and discourage them from finding jobs?
13.7 (Neither)
2.0 Other answer **(WRITE IN)**
0.5 (Both: Unemployment Benefit causes hardship but can't be higher or there would be no incentive to work)
1.3 (Both: Unemployment Benefit causes hardship to some, while others do well out of it)
0.4 (About right/in between)
2.9 (Don't Know)
0.0 (Refusal/NA)

Q218 [TaxSpend]
CARD

Suppose the government had to choose between the three options on this card. Which do you think it should choose?

%
3.9 Reduce taxes and spend less on health, education and social benefits
33.6 Keep taxes and spending on these services at the same level as now
59.3 Increase taxes and spend more on health, education and social benefits
2.0 (None)
1.2 (Don't Know)
0.0 (Refusal/NA)

N=1214

VERSION C: ASK ALL

Q219 [LTaxServ]
CARD

Suppose your local council had to choose between the three options on this card. Which do you think it should choose?

%
14.4 Reduce the level of Council Tax and spend **less** on local services
62.4 Keep the Council Tax and spending on local services at the **same** level as now
20.6 Increase the Council Tax and spend **more** on local services
2.4 (Don't Know)
0.1 (Refusal/NA)

Q220 [CntlCncl]

Do you think that **local councils** ought to be controlled by **central government** more, less or about the same amount as now?

%
15.6 More
35.1 Less
41.0 About the same
8.3 (Don't Know)
0.0 (Refusal/NA)

Q221 [Rates]

Do you think the **level of the council tax** should be up to the local council to decide, or should central government have the final say?

%
63.4 Local council
29.4 Central government
7.0 (Don't Know)
0.2 (Refusal/NA)

Q222 [CTaxVal]
CARD

And thinking about the level of the council tax in your area, do you think it gives good value or poor value for money?
Please choose a phrase from this card.

%
2.5 Very good value for money
38.9 Good value
25.8 Neither good value nor poor value
24.1 Poor value
4.9 Very poor value for money
3.8 (Don't Know)
- (Refusal/NA)

Q223 [LGMoney] N=1214

The two **main** sources of local government money are **the council tax and the grant from central government.** Do you think that in total your local council(s) get(s) more money from the council tax, or more from central government, or about the same amount from each?

IF 'MORE FROM COUNCIL TAX' OR 'MORE FROM CENTRAL GOVERNMENT': A lot more or a little more?

11.0 A lot more from the council tax
18.9 A little more from the council tax
23.0 About the same amount from each
8.3 A little more from central government
7.0 A lot more from central government
31.6 (Don't Know)
0.2 (Refusal/NA)

ASK ALL

Q224 [NHSSat] N=3620
CARD
All in all, how satisfied or dissatisfied would you say you are with the way in which the National Health Service is run nowadays?
Choose a phrase from this card.

Q225 [GPSat]
CARD AGAIN
From your own experience or from what you have heard, please say how satisfied or dissatisfied you are with the way in which each of these parts of the National Health Service runs nowadays.
'First, local doctors or GPs?

Q226 [DentSat]
CARD AGAIN
(And how satisfied or dissatisfied are you with the NHS as regards..)
... National Health Service dentists?

Q227 [InPatSat]
CARD AGAIN
(And how satisfied or dissatisfied are you with the NHS as regards..)
... Being in hospital as an in-patient?

33

Q228 [OutPaSat] N=3620
CARD AGAIN
(And how satisfied or dissatisfied are you with the NHS as regards...)
... Attending hospital as an out-patient?

	[NHSSat]	[GPSat]	[DentSat]
	%	%	%
Very satisfied	7.2	29.0	14.2
Quite satisfied	28.8	48.4	37.4
Neither satisfied nor dissatisfied	13.5	9.3	16.2
Quite dissatisfied	27.9	9.7	15.8
Very dissatisfied	22.2	3.2	9.6
(Don't Know)	0.3	0.4	6.7
(Refusal/NA)	-	-	0.0

	[InPatSat]	[OutPaSat]
	%	%
Very satisfied	18.0	13.4
Quite satisfied	34.5	38.6
Neither satisfied nor dissatisfied	17.1	17.6
Quite dissatisfied	14.9	16.7
Very dissatisfied	6.7	8.1
(Don't Know)	8.8	5.6
(Refusal/NA)	-	0.1

Q229 [PrivMed]
Are **you yourself** covered by a private health insurance scheme, that is an insurance scheme that allows you to get private medical **treatment**?
ADD IF NECESSARY: 'For example, BUPA or PPP.'
IF INSURANCE COVERS DENTISTRY ONLY, CODE 'No'
%
17.0 Yes
82.9 No
0.1 (Don't Know)
- (Refusal/NA)

IF 'Yes' AT [PrivMed]
Q230 [PrivPaid]
Does your employer (or your partner's employer) pay the majority of the cost of membership of this scheme?
%
8.2 Yes
8.7 No
0.1 (Don't Know)
0.1 (Refusal/NA)

34

Q231 **ASK ALL**
[*NHSLimit*]
It has been suggested that the National Health Service should be available **only to those with lower incomes**. This would mean that contributions and taxes could be lower and most people would then take out medical insurance or pay for health care.
Do you support or oppose this idea?
IF 'SUPPORT' OR 'OPPOSE': A lot or a little?

%
7.4 Support a lot
13.4 Support a little
15.9 Oppose a little
61.2 Oppose a lot
2.1 (Don't Know)
0.0 (Refusal/NA)

Q232 [*WhchHosp*]
CARD
Now suppose you needed to go into hospital for an operation.
Do you think you would have a say about which hospital you went to?

%
12.6 Definitely would
20.9 Probably would
41.7 Probably would not
22.1 Definitely would not
2.7 (Don't Know)
0.0 (Refusal/NA)

Q233 [*GPChange*]
Suppose you wanted to change your GP and go to a different practice, how difficult or easy do you think this would be to arrange?
Would it be ...**READ OUT** ...

%
5.6 ...very difficult,
17.0 fairly difficult,
36.1 not very difficult,
33.0 or, not at all difficult?
8.1 (Don't Know)
0.1 (Refusal/NA)

N=3620

Q234 [*DentLimt*]
Many dentists now provide NHS treatment only to those with lower incomes. This means that other people have to pay the full amount for their dental treatment, or take out private insurance to cover their treatment. Do you support or oppose this happening?
IF 'SUPPORT' OR 'OPPOSE': A lot or a little?

%
5.5 Support a lot
14.6 Support a little
18.6 Oppose a little
58.2 Oppose a lot
3.1 (Don't Know)
0.0 (Refusal/NA)

IF 'Yes' AT [PrivMed]
Q235 [*DentInsu*]
Does the private medical insurance scheme you belong to cover your treatment **at the dentist**?

%
3.3 Yes
12.7 No
0.2 (Don't go to the dentist)
0.8 (Don't Know)
0.1 (Refusal/NA)

IF 'No' AT [PrivMed] OR 'No' AT [DentInsu]
Q236 [*DentOthr*]
Is your **dental** treatment covered by any (other) private insurance scheme?

%
4.1 Yes
88.1 No
3.2 (Don't go to the dentist)
0.3 (Don't Know)
1.0 (Refusal/NA)

N=3620

ECONOMIC ACTIVITY, LABOUR MARKET AND LEARNING

ASK ALL N=3620

Q240 [REconAct]
% Priority coded
3.5 In full-time education (not paid for by employer, including on vacation)
0.2 On government training/employment programme (eg. Youth Training, Training for Work etc)
54.3 In paid work (or away temporarily) for at least 10 hours in week
0.3 Waiting to take up paid work already accepted
4.1 Unemployed and registered at a benefit office
0.7 Unemployed, not registered, but actively looking for a job (of at least 10 hrs a week)
0.4 Unemployed, wanting a job (of at least 10 hrs per week) but not actively looking for a job
4.8 Permanently sick or disabled
18.6 Wholly retired from work
12.7 Looking after the home
0.2 (Doing something else) **(WRITE IN)**
- (Don't Know)
0.1 (Refusal/NA)

ASK ALL NOT IN PAID WORK/WAITING TO TAKE UP WORK N=1641

Q241 [RLastJob]
How long ago did you last have a paid job of at least 10 hours a week?
GOVERNMENT PROGRAMS/SCHEMES DO NOT COUNT AS 'PAID JOBS'.
%
12.9 Within past 12 months
23.1 Over 1, up to 5 years ago
17.6 Over 5, up to 10 years ago
23.9 Over 10, up to 20 years ago
14.1 Over 20 years ago
8.1 Never had a paid job of 10+ hours a week
0.2 (Don't Know)
0.2 (Refusal/NA)

ASK ALL WHO HAVE EVER WORKED N=3486

Q242 [RTitle]
IF 'in paid work' AT [EconAct]: Now I want to ask you about your present job. What is your job? **PROBE IF NECESSARY:** What is the name or title of the job?
IF 'waiting to take up paid work' AT [EconAct]: Now I want to ask you about your future job. What is your job? **PROBE IF NECESSARY:** What is the name or title of the job?
IF EVER HAD A JOB AT [LastJob]: Now I want to ask you about your last job. What was your job? **PROBE IF NECESSARY:** What was the name or title of the job?
Open Question (Maximum of 80 characters)

Q243 [RTypeWk]
What kind of work (do/will/did) you do most of the time? **IF RELEVANT:** What materials/machinery (do/will/did) you use?
Open Question (Maximum of 80 characters)

Q244 [RTrain]
What training or qualifications (are/were) needed for that job?
Open Question (Maximum of 80 characters)

Q245 [RSuper2]
(Do/Will/Did) you directly supervise or (are you/will you be/were you) directly responsible for the work of any other people?
%
35.8 Yes
63.9 No
0.0 (Don't Know)
0.3 (Refusal/NA)

IF 'Yes' AT [Super2]
Q246 [RMany]
How many?
Range: 0 ... 9997
% **Median (of those supervising any): 5**
0.1 (Don't Know)
0.3 (Refusal/NA)

Q248   **ASK ALL WHO HAVE EVER WORKED**   N=3486
[RSupMan]
Can I just check, (are you/will you be/were you) ...
READ OUT ...
%
18.2 ...a manager,
13.4 a foreman or supervisor,
68.1 or not?
0.0 (Don't Know)
0.3 (Refusal/NA)

Q249   [REmplyee]
In your (main) job (are you/will you be/were you) ...
READ OUT ...
%
87.0 ... an employee,
12.7 or self-employed?
0.0 (Don't Know)
0.3 (Refusal/NA)

Q251   **ASK ALL EMPLOYEES IN CURRENT OR LAST JOB**   N=3042
[ROcSect]
CARD
Which of the types of organisation on this card (do you work/will you be working/did you work) for?
%
65.2 Private sector firm or company (including limited companies and PLCs)
4.1 Nationalised industry/public corporation
15.1 Local authority/Local Education Authority (including 'opted out' schools)
5.9 Health authority/NHS hospital/NHS Hospital Trust (including GP surgeries)
5.1 Central government/Civil service/Government Agency
2.5 Charity/Voluntary sector (including charitable companies)
1.7 Other answer (**WRITE IN**)
0.1 (Don't Know)
0.3 (Refusal/NA)

Q253   **ASK ALL WHO HAVE EVER WORKED**   N=3486
[REmpMake]
What (does/did) your employer (**IF SELF-EMPLOYED:** you) make or do at the place where you (work/will work/worked) (from)?
Open Question (Maximum of 80 characters)

Q254   **ASK ALL CURRENTLY SELF-EMPLOYED**   N=305
[SPartnrs]
In your work or business, do you have any partners or other self-employed colleagues?
READ OUT ...
NOTE: DOES NOT INCLUDE EMPLOYEES
%
42.0 Yes, has partner(s)
57.8 No
0.2 (Don't Know)
- (Refusal/NA)

Q256   **ASK ALL SELF-EMPLOYED IN CURRENT OR LAST JOB**   N=3486
[SEmpNum]
In your work or business, (do/did) you have any employees, or not?
IF YES: How many?
IF 'NO EMPLOYEES', CODE 0.
FOR 500+ EMPLOYEES, CODE 500.
NOTE: FAMILY MEMBERS MAY BE EMPLOYEES ONLY IF THEY RECEIVE A REGULAR WAGE OR SALARY.
Range: 0 ... 500
Median: 0 employees

Q257   **ASK WHO HAVE EVER WORKED (ASKED OF EMPLOYEES DERIVED FROM [SEmgNum] FOR SELF-EMPLOYED)**   N=3486
[REmpWht]
Including yourself, how many people (are/were) employed at the place where you usually (work/will work/worked) (from)?
IF YES: PROBE FOR CORRECT PRECODE.
%
8.5 None
18.3 Under 10
13.9 10-24
21.7 25-99
20.4 100-499
15.9 500 or more
1.1 (Don't Know)
0.3 (Refusal/NA)

Q260   **ASK ALL IN PAID WORK**   N=1967
[WkJbTrim]
In your present job, are you working ... **READ OUT** ...
RESPONDENT'S OWN DEFINITION
%
78.4 ... full-time,
21.3 or, part-time?
0.4 (Don't Know)
- (Refusal/NA)

Q263 [WkJbHrsI]

N=1967

How many hours do you normally work a week in your main job - including any paid or unpaid overtime?
ROUND TO NEAREST HOUR.
IF RESPONDENT CANNOT ANSWER, ASK ABOUT LAST WEEK.
IF RESPONDENT DOES NOT KNOW EXACTLY, ACCEPT AN ESTIMATE.
FOR 95+ HOURS, CODE 95.
FOR 'VARIES TOO MUCH TO SAY', CODE 96.
Range: 10 ... 96
% **Median: 40 hours**
1.3 (Varies too much to say)
0.2 (Don't Know)
0.4 (Refusal/NA)

ASK ALL CURRENT EMPLOYEE

N=1663

Q264 [EJbHrsX]
What are your basic or contractual hours each week in your main job - excluding any paid and unpaid overtime?
ROUND TO NEAREST HOUR.
IF RESPONDENT CANNOT ANSWER, ASK ABOUT LAST WEEK.
IF RESPONDENT DOES NOT KNOW EXACTLY, ACCEPT AN ESTIMATE.
FOR 95+ HOURS, CODE 95.
FOR 'VARIES TOO MUCH TO SAY', CODE 96.
Range: 0 ... 96
% **Median: 37 hours**
2.0 (Varies too much to say)
1.3 (Don't Know)
0.5 (Refusal/NA)

ASK THOSE WAITING TO TAKE UP WORK OR EVER HAD A JOB (BUT NOT WORKING NOW)

N=1519

Q265 [ExPrtFul]
(Is/Was) the job ... **READ OUT** ...
%
71.5 ... full-time - that is, 30 or more hours per week,
27.9 or, part-time?
0.1 (Don't Know)
0.6 (Refusal/NA)

ASK ALL WHO HAVE EVER WORKED

N=3486

Q295 [UnionSA]
(May I just check) are you **now** a member of a trade union or staff association?
CODE FIRST TO APPLY
%
20.4 Yes, trade union
3.6 Yes, staff association
75.5 No
0.2 (Don't Know)
0.3 (Refusal/NA)

41

N=3486

Q296 **IF 'No'/DK AT [UnionSA]**
[UnionEvr]
Have you **ever** been a member of a trade union or staff association?
CODE FIRST TO APPLY
%
25.7 Yes, trade union
3.6 Yes, staff association
46.3 No
0.2 (Don't Know)
0.3 (Refusal/NA)

ASK ALL CURRENT EMPLOYEES

N=1663

Q299 [EmploydT]
For how long have you been continuously employed by your present employer?
ENTER NUMBER. THEN SPECIFY MONTHS OR YEARS
Range: 1 ... 60
% **Median: 60 months**
0.6 (Refusal/NA)

ASK ALL NOT IN PAID WORK

N=1653

Q300 [NPWork10]
In the seven days ending last Sunday, did you have any paid work of less than 10 hours a week?
%
4.5 Yes
95.2 No
0.0 (Don't Know)
0.3 (Refusal/NA)

ASK ALL CURRENT EMPLOYEES

N=1663

Q301 [WageNow]
How would you describe the wages or salary you are paid for the job you do - on the low side, reasonable, or on the high side?
IF LOW: Very low or a bit low?
%
12.9 Very low
25.6 A bit low
54.4 Reasonable
6.6 On the high side
- Other answer (**WRITE IN**)
0.1 (Don't Know)
0.4 (Refusal/NA)

42

Q303 [PayGap]
CARD
Thinking of the **highest** and the **lowest** paid people at your place of work, how would you describe the **gap** between their pay, as far as you know?
Please choose a phrase from this card.
%
19.4 Much too big a gap
25.5 Too big
43.4 About right
2.0 Too small
0.5 Much too small a gap
8.7 (Don't Know)
0.5 (Refusal/NA)

Q304 [WageXpct]
If you stay in this job, would you **expect** your wages or salary over the coming year to ... **READ OUT** ...
%
17.7 ... rise by **more** than the cost of living,
42.6 rise by the **same** as the cost of living,
23.8 rise by **less** than the cost of living,
12.3 or, **not** to rise at all?
1.9 (Will not stay in job)
1.3 (Don't Know)
0.4 (Refusal/NA)

IF 'not rise at all' AT [WageXpct]

Q305 [WageDrop]
Would you expect your wages or salary to stay the same, or in fact to go down?
%
11.6 Stay the same
0.8 Go down
- (Do-n't Know)
1.7 (Refusal/NA)

ASK ALL CURRENT EMPLOYEE

Q306 [NumEmp]
Over the coming year do you expect your workplace to be ... **READ OUT** ...
%
24.5 ... increasing its number of employees,
21.0 reducing its number of employees,
51.8 or, will the number of employees stay about the same?
0.6 Other answer **(WRITE IN)**
1.7 (Don't Know)
0.4 (Refusal/NA)

Q308 [LeaveJob]
Thinking now about your own job. How likely or unlikely is it that you will leave this employer over the next year for any reason?
Is it ... **READ OUT** ...
%
13.6 ... very likely,
12.6 quite likely,
28.2 not very likely,
43.8 or, not at all likely?
1.2 (Don't Know)
0.5 (Refusal/NA)

IF 'very likely' OR 'quite likely' AT [LeaveJob]

Q311- CARD
319 Why do you think you will leave? Please choose a phrase from this card or tell me what other reason there is.
% Multicoded (Maximum of 9 codes)
1.0 Firm will close down [WhyGo1]
3.1 I will be declared redundant [WhyGo2]
0.7 I will reach normal retirement age [WhyGo3]
1.8 My contract of employment will expire [WhyGo4]
1.0 I will take early retirement [WhyGo5]
15.3 I will decide to leave and work for another employer [WhyGo6]
1.9 I will decide to leave and work for myself, as self-employed [WhyGo7]
0.9 I will leave to look after home/children/relative [WhyGo10]
2.2 Other answer **(WRITE IN)** [WhyGo8]
0.9 (I will return to education) [WhyGo11]
- (Don't Know)
0.5 (Refusal/NA)

ASK ALL CURRENT EMPLOYEES

Q321 [ELookJob]
Suppose you lost your job for one reason or another - would you start looking for another job, would you wait for several months or longer before you started looking, or would you decide **not** to look for another job?
%
87.1 Start looking
5.5 Wait several months or longer
6.1 Decide not to look
0.9 (Don't Know)
0.4 (Refusal/NA)

N-1663

IF 'Start looking' AT [ELookJob]

Q322 [EFindJob]
How long do you think it would take you to find an acceptable replacement job?
IF LESS THAN ONE MONTH, CODE AS ONE MONTH
IF 'NEVER' PLEASE CODE 96
ENTER NUMBER. THEN SPECIFY MONTHS OR YEARS
Range: 1 ... 96
Median: 2 months
1.8 (Never)
8.0 (Don't Know)
1.3 (Refusal/NA)

IF 3 MONTHS OR MORE/NEVER/DK AT [EFindJob]

Q325 [ERetrain]
How willing do you think you would be in these circumstances to retrain for a different job ... **READ OUT** ...
%
21.5 ...very willing,
15.0 quite willing,
7.2 or - not very willing?
0.2 (Don't Know)
1.3 (Refusal/NA)

ASK ALL CURRENT EMPLOYEES

Q326 [ESelfEm]
For any period during the last five years, have you worked as a self-employed person as your main job?
%
5.0 No
94.6 No
-    (Don't Know)
0.4 (Refusal/NA)

Q327 [JbReview]
In your present job, is there a system for reviewing or reporting on your work performance?
%
61.2 Yes
37.1 No
1.3 (Don't Know)
0.4 (Refusal/NA)

45

N=1047

ASK THOSE WITH JOB REVIEWS

Q328 [OftRev]
How often do these reviews or reports take place? Is it ... **READ OUT** ...
CODE FIRST TO APPLY
%
12.8 ..about once a month
12.1 about once every three months,
16.1 about twice a year
46.2 about once a year
6.1 or, less often than that?
3.1 (Varies/depends)
0.8 (Don't Know)
2.7 (Refusal/NA)

Q329 [WritRev]
%   And is this usually a written report?
72.1 Yes
23.0 No
2.1 (Don't Know)
2.7 (Refusal/NA)

Q330 [RevPay]
Are the results of reports like these used in helping to decide your pay?
%
37.2 Yes
57.0 No
3.1 (Don't Know)
2.7 (Refusal/NA)

IF 'Yes' AT [RevPay]

Q331 [RevPayUp]
Has your pay ever gone up as a result of one of these reports?
%
26.3 Yes
9.5 No
1.3 (Don't Know)
5.8 (Refusal/NA)

ASK THOSE WITH JOB REVIEWS

Q332 [RevWorks]
And, in general, how well do you think this system works in your workplace ... **READ OUT** ...
%
15.3 ... very well,
46.6 quite well,
23.2 not very well,
9.3 or, not at all well?
2.9 (Don't Know)
2.7 (Refusal/NA)

46

Q340-
345
ASK ALL CURRENT EMPLOYEES   [N=1663]

CARD

Some organisations have schemes which link pay or employee benefits to the financial performance of the organisation. As far as you know, does your organisation have any of the schemes on this card?

Multicoded (Maximum of 5 codes)

%
15.7 Productivity-linked bonus scheme   [Payb1]
17.3 Annual bonus (at organisation's discretion) [Payb2]
11.8 Share ownership or share option scheme [PayB3]
13.9 Profit-sharing scheme [PayB4]
2.1 Other similar scheme (WRITE IN) [PayB7]
57.0 None of these [PayB8]
1.4 (Don't Know)
0.4 (Refusal/NA)

Q335
IF 'Productivity-linked bonus scheme' AT [PayBens]
[PayBen1]
Have you personally received any payments or benefits under the productivity-linked bonus scheme, in the last 12 months?

Q336
IF 'Annual bonus' AT [PayBens]
[PayBen2]
Have you personally received any payments or benefits under the annual bonus scheme, in the last 12 months?

Q337
IF 'Share ownership/option scheme' AT [PayBens]
[PayBen3]
Have you personally received any payments or benefits under the share ownership or share option scheme, in the last 12 months?

Q338
IF 'Profit-sharing scheme' AT [PayBens]
[PayBen4]
Have you personally received any payments or benefits under the profit-sharing scheme, in the last 12 months?
IF 'Other similar scheme' AT [PayBens]

Q339
[PayBen7]
Have you personally received any payments or benefits under this other scheme you mentioned, in the last 12 months?

[N=1663]

	[PayBen1]	[PayBen2]	[PayBen3]
	%	%	%
Yes - received	10.2	11.5	4.5
No - hasn't received	5.0	5.7	7.3
(Don't Know)	-	-	-
(Refusal/NA)	2.3	1.9	1.8

	[PayBen4]	[PayBen7]
	%	%
Yes - received	8.8	1.5
No - hasn't received	5.1	0.6
(Don't Know)	-	-
(Refusal/NA)	1.8	1.8

ASK ALL WHO ARE NOT UNEMPLOYED, PERMANENTLY SICK OR RETIRED   [N=2583]

Q347 [NwUnemp]
During the last **five** years - that is since May 1991 - have you been unemployed and seeking work for any period?
%
20.4 Yes
79.3 No
0.1 (Don't Know)
0.3 (Refusal/NA)

ASK THOSE CURRENTLY OR AT ANY TIME IN THE LAST FIVE YEARS UNEMPLOYED   [N=722]

Q348 [NwUnempT]
For how many *months* in total during the last five years, (that is, since May 1991, have you been unemployed and seeking work)?
INTERVIEWER: IF LESS THAN ONE MONTH, CODE AS 1.
Range: 1 ... 60
Median: 7 months
%
1.9 (Don't Know)
- (Refusal/NA)

ASK ALL CURRENTLY UNEMPLOYED   [N=190]

Q352 [CurUnemp]
How long has this **present** period of unemployment and seeking work lasted so far?
ENTER NUMBER. THEN SPECIFY MONTHS OR YEARS
Range: 1 ... 60
Median: 11 months
%
1.9 (Don't Know)
1.4 (Refusal/NA)

N=190

Q353 *[JobQual]*
How confident are you that you will find a job to match your qualifications ... **READ OUT** ...
%
10.8   ... very confident,
30.8   quite confident,
33.8   not very confident,
23.5   or, not at all confident?
1.1   (Don't Know)
-      (Refusal/NA)

Q356 *[UFindJob]*
Although it may be difficult to judge, how long **from now** do you think it will be before you find an acceptable job?
ENTER NUMBER. THEN SPECIFY MONTHS OR YEARS
CODE 96 FOR NEVER
Range: 1 ... 96
Median: 4 months
%
10.0   (Never)
23.2   (Don't Know)
-      (Refusal/NA)

IF MORE THAN 2 YEARS AT [UFindJob]

Q357 *[Uretrain]*
How willing do you think you would be in these circumstances to retrain for a different job ... **READ OUT** ...

Q358 *[UJobMove]*
How willing would you be to move to a different area to find an acceptable job ... **READ OUT** ...

Q359 *[UBadJob]*
And how willing do you think you would be in these circumstances to take what you now consider to be an unacceptable job ... **READ OUT** ...

	Uretrain	UJobMove	UBadJob
	%	%	%
... very willing,	30.0	12.7	8.9
quite willing,	27.4	20.2	18.2
or, not very willing?	17.9	43.9	49.1
(Don't Know)	2.2	0.7	1.4
(Refusal/NA)	-	-	-

ASK ALL CURRENTLY UNEMPLOYED   **N=190**

Q360 *[ConMove]*
Have you ever **actually** considered moving to a different area - an area other than the one you live in now - to try to find work?
%
34.4   Yes
65.6   No
-      (Don't Know)
-      (Refusal/NA)

Q361 *[UJobChnc]*
Do you think that there is a real chance nowadays that you will get a job in this area, or is there **no** real chance nowadays?
%
43.0   Real chance
49.8   No real chance
2.2   (Don't Know)
-      (Refusal/NA)

Q362 *[FPtWork]*
Would you prefer full- or part-time work, if you had the choice?
%
68.1   Full-time
27.7   Part-time
4.2   Not looking for work
-      (Don't Know)
-      (Refusal/NA)

IF 'Part-time' AT [FptWork]

Q363 *[PartTime]*
About how many hours per week would you like to work?
PROBE FOR BEST ESTIMATE
Range: 1 ... 30
Median: 20 hours
%
1.1   (Don't Know)
0.8   (Refusal/NA)

ASK ALL LOOKING AFTER THE HOME   **N=459**

Q364 *[EverJob]*
Have you, during **the last five years**, ever had a full- or part-time job of 10 hours or more a week?
%
27.3   Yes
72.3   No
-      (Don't Know)
0.3   (Refusal/NA)

N=459

IF 'NO' AT [EverJob]
Q365 *[FtJobSer]*
How seriously in the past five years have you considered getting a **full-time job**
PROMPT, IF NECESSARY: Full-time is 30 or more hours a week
... **READ OUT** ...

IF 'not very seriously', 'not at all seriously' OR DK AT [FtJobSer]
Q366 *[PtJobSer]*
How seriously, in the past five years, have you considered getting a **part-time** job ... **READ OUT** ...

	FtJobSer	PtJobSer
	%	%
... very seriously,	2.0	1.1
quite seriously,	3.1	6.4
not very seriously,	6.7	8.5
or, not at all seriously?	60.6	51.2
(Don't Know)	-	-
(Refusal/NA)	0.3	0.3

ASK ALL CURRENTLY SELF-EMPLOYED

N=305

Q367 *[SEmplee]*
Have you, for any period in the last five years, worked as an **employee** as your main job rather than as self-employed?
%
28.4 Yes
71.6 No
- (Don't Know)
- (Refusal/NA)

IF 'Yes' AT [SEmplee]
Q368 *[SEmpleeT]*
In total for how many months during the last five years have you been an employee?
ENTER NUMBER OF MONTHS
Range: 1 ... 60
%
Median: 24 months

N=305

IF 'No'/DK AT [SEmplee]
Q369 *[SEmplSer]*
How seriously in the last five years have you considered getting a job as an **employee** ... **READ OUT** ...
%
3.1 ... very seriously,
7.4 quite seriously,
6.6 not very seriously,
54.4 or, not at all seriously?
- (Don't Know)
- (Refusal/NA)

ASK ALL CURRENTLY SELF-EMPLOYED
Q370 *[Bus1OK]*
Compared with **a year ago**, would you say your business is doing ... **READ OUT** ...
%
16.1 ... very well,
19.7 quite well,
44.2 about the same,
12.2 not very well,
1.0 or, not at all well?
6.4 (Business not in existence then)
0.3 (Don't Know)
- (Refusal/NA)

Q371 *[Bus1Fut]*
And over **the coming year**, do you think your business will do ... **READ OUT** ...
%
36.4 ... better,
51.1 about the same,
9.7 or, worse than this year?
0.5 Other answer **(WRITE IN)**
2.3 (Don't Know)
- (Refusal/NA)

ASK ALL CURRENT EMPLOYEES

N=1663

Q373 *[WpUnions]*
At your place of work are there unions, staff associations, or groups of unions recognised by the management for negotiating pay and conditions of employment?
IF YES, PROBE FOR UNION OR STAFF ASSOCIATION
IF 'BOTH', CODE '1'
%
45.6 Yes : trade union(s)
4.1 Yes : staff association
47.0 No, none
2.8 (Don't Know)
0.4 (Refusal/NA)

N=1663

IF 'Yes: trade unions/staff association' AT [WpUnions]

Q374 [WpUnsure]
Can I just check: does management recognise these unions or staff associations for the purposes of negotiating pay and conditions of employment?

%
46.4 Yes
2.3 No
1.0 (Don't Know)
3.3 (Refusal/NA)

Q375 [WpUnionW]
On the whole, do you think (these unions do their/this staff association does its) job well or not?

%
29.2 Yes
16.2 No
4.2 (Don't Know)
3.3 (Refusal/NA)

Q376 [TUShould]
CARD
Listed on the card are a number of things trade unions or staff associations can do. Which, if any, do you think is the most important thing they should try to do at your workplace?

UNIONS OR STAFF ASSOCIATIONS SHOULD TRY TO:
%
11.8 Improve working conditions
11.0 Improve pay
17.4 Protect existing jobs
1.3 Have more say over how work is done day-to-day
3.7 Have more say over management's long-term plans
0.8 Work for equal opportunities for women
0.1 Work for equal opportunities for ethnic minorities
1.9 Reduce pay differences at the workplace
1.1 (None of these)
0.5 (Don't Know)
3.3 (Refusal/NA)

N=1663

ASK ALL CURRENT EMPLOYEES

Q377 [IndRel]
In general how would you describe relations between management and other employees at your workplace ...
READ OUT ...
%
28.2 ... very good,
51.0 quite good,
13.4 not very good,
6.2 or, not at all good?
0.7 (Don't Know)
0.5 (Refusal/NA)

Q378 [WorkRun]
And in general, would you say your workplace was ...
READ OUT ...
%
23.7 ... very well managed,
54.0 quite well managed,
21.6 or, not well managed?
0.2 (Don't Know)
0.4 (Refusal/NA)

N=2773

ASK ALL EXCEPT THOSE WHO ARE WHOLLY RETIRED OR PERMANENTLY SICK OR DISABLED

Q379 [NwEmpErn]
IF IN PAID WORK: Now for some more general questions about your work. For some people their job is simply something they do in order to earn a living. For others it is much more than that. On balance, is your present job ... **READ OUT ...**
IF NOT IN PAID WORK: For some people work is simply something they do in order to earn a living. For others it means much more than that. In general, do you think of work as ... **READ OUT ...**
%
32.7 ...just a means of earning a living,
66.2 or, does it mean much more to you than that?
1.0 (Don't Know)
0.1 (Refusal/NA)

Q380 [NwEmpLiv]
IF 'just a means of earning a living' AT [NwEmpErn]
Is that because ... **READ OUT** ....
%
8.7 ...there are no (good) jobs around here,
7.4 you don't have the right skills to get a (good) job
13.9 or, because you would feel the same about any job you had?
2.4 (Don't Know)
1.4 (Refusal/NA)

ASK ALL IN PAID WORK

N=1967

CARD

Q383- Now I'd like you to look at the statements on the card
391 and tell me which ones best describe your own reasons
for working at present.
PROBE: Which others?

% Multicoded (Maximum of 9 codes)
27.6 Working is the normal thing to do   [WkWork1]
68.8 Need money for basic essentials such as
     food, rent or mortgage   [WkWork2]
43.6 To earn money to buy extras   [WkWork3]
29.6 To earn money of my own   [WkWork4]
29.7 For the company of other people   [WkWork5]
56.8 I enjoy working   [WkWork6]
32.1 To follow my career   [WkWork7]
8.9 For a change from my children or housework [WkWork8]
2.7 Other answer **(WRITE IN)**   [WkWork9]
-   (Don't Know)
0.4 (Refusal/NA)

IF MORE THAN ONE ANSWER GIVEN AT [WkWork]

Q393 *[WkWkMain]*
CARD AGAIN
And which one of these would you say is your *main* reason
for working?

%
3.2 Working is the normal thing to do
45.9 Need money for basic essentials such as food, rent or
     mortgage
6.5 To earn money to buy extras
6.9 To earn money of my own
1.3 For the company of other people
12.0 I enjoy working
6.8 To follow my career
0.4 For a change from my children or housework
0.8 Other answer **(WRITE IN)**
0.1 (Don't Know)
0.4 (Refusal/NA)

ASK ALL CURRENT EMPLOYEES

N=1663

[SayJob]

Q394 Suppose there was going to be some decision made at your
place of work that changed the way you do your job. Do
you think that you *personally* would have any say in the
decision about the change, or not?
IF 'DEPENDS': Code as 'Don't Know'

%
55.3 Yes
42.5 No
1.7 (Don't Know)
0.5 (Refusal/NA)

IF 'Yes' AT [SayJob]

Q395 *[MuchSay]*
How much say or chance to influence the decision do you
think you would have ... **READ OUT** ...

%
11.6 ...a great deal,
23.1 quite a lot,
20.6 or, just a little?
-   (Don't Know)
2.2 (Refusal/NA)

ASK ALL CURRENT EMPLOYEES

[MoreSay]

Q396 Do you think you should have *more* say in decisions
affecting your work, or are you satisfied with the way
things are?

%
46.1 Should have more say
53.0 Satisfied with way things are
0.4 (Don't Know)
0.4 (Refusal/NA)

ASK ALL IN PAID WORK

N=1967

[WkPrefJb]

Q397 If without having to work, you had what you would regard
as a reasonable living income, do you think you would
still prefer to have a paid job (**IF SELF-EMPLOYED:** do
paid work) or wouldn't you bother?

%
68.2 Still prefer paid job (work)
29.1 Wouldn't bother
1.9 Other answer **(WRITE IN)**
0.4 (Don't Know)
0.4 (Refusal/NA)

ASK ALL CURRENT EMPLOYEES [N=1663]

Q399 [PrefHour]
Thinking about the number of hours you work each week including regular overtime, would you prefer a job where you worked ... **READ OUT** ...

%
4.6 ...more hours per week,
38.0 fewer hours per week,
57.0 or, are you happy with the number of hours you work at present?
- (Don't Know)
0.5 (Refusal/NA)

IF 'more hours' AT [PrefHour]

Q400 [MoreHour]
Is the reason why you don't work more hours because ... **READ OUT** ...

%
3.4 ..your employer can't offer you more hours,
0.9 or, your personal circumstances don't allow it?
0.1 (Both)
0.2 Other answer **(WRITE IN)**
- (Don't Know)
0.5 (Refusal/NA)

IF 'fewer hours' AT [PrefHour]

Q402 [FewHour]
In which of these ways would you like your working hours to be shortened ... **READ OUT** ...

%
12.0 ... shorter hours each day,
25.0 or, fewer days each week?
0.8 Other answer **(WRITE IN)**
0.1 (Don't Know)
0.5 (Refusal/NA)

IF 'fewer hours' AT [PrefHour]

Q404 [EarnHour]
Would you still like to work fewer hours, if it meant earning less money as a result?

%
9.9 Yes
26.2 No
1.9 It depends
- (Don't Know)
0.5 (Refusal/NA)

ASK ALL IN PAID WORK [N=1967]

Q405 [WkWkHrd]
CARD
Which of these statements best describes your feelings about your job?
In my job:

%
7.6 I only work as hard as I have to
40.1 I work hard, but not so that it interferes with the rest of my life
51.7 I make a point of doing the best I can, even if it sometimes does interfere with the rest of my life
0.2 (Don't Know)
0.4 (Refusal/NA)

ASK ALL WHO ARE WHOLLY RETIRED [N=672]

Q406 [REmplPen]
Do you receive a pension from any past employer?

%
48.5 Yes
50.8 No
- (Don't Know)
0.7 (Refusal/NA)

IF WHOLLY RETIRED AND MARRIED

Q407 [SEmplPen]
Does your (**husband/wife/partner**) receive a pension from any past employer?

%
19.2 Yes
19.5 No
- (Don't Know)
0.2 (Refusal/NA)

ASK ALL WHOLLY RETIRED

Q408 [PrPenGet]
And do you receive a pension from any **private** arrangements you have made in the past, that is **apart** from the state pension or one arranged through an employer?

%
8.4 Yes
90.7 No
- (Don't Know)
0.9 (Refusal/NA)

IF WHOLLY RETIRED AND MARRIED

N=672

Q409   [SPrPnGet]
And does your (husband/wife/partner) receive a pension from any private arrangements (he/she) has made in the past, that is apart from the state pension or one arranged through an employer?

%
3.1   Yes
35.7   No
-   (Don't Know)
0.2   (Refusal/NA)

IF WHOLLY RETIRED AND MALE AGED 61 OR OVER OR FEMALE AGED 66 OR OVER

N=582

Q411   [RPension]
On the whole would you say the present **state** pension is on the low side, reasonable, or on the high side?
IF 'ON THE LOW SIDE': Very low or a bit low?

%
42.9   Very low
31.5   A bit low
23.3   Reasonable
0.1   On the high side
0.8   (Don't Know)
1.4   (Refusal/NA)

Q412   [RPenInYr]
Do you expect your state pension in a year's time to purchase **more** than it does now, **less**, or about the **same**?

%
3.1   More
56.7   Less
36.6   About the same
2.3   (Don't Know)
1.4   (Refusal/NA)

ASK ALL WHOLLY RETIRED

N=672

Q413   [RetirAg2]
At what age did you retire from work?
NEVER WORKED, CODE: 00
Range: 0 ... 80
Median: 60 years

%
2.2   (Never worked)
1.1   (Don't Know)
0.9   (Refusal/NA)

59

ASK IF NOT WHOLLY RETIRED

N=2948

Q414   [Learner]
In the past two years have you done any learning, training or education to do with a job or getting a job? This could have been done either at home, at work, or at college or another educational institution.

%
40.7   Yes
59.1   No
0.0   (Don't Know)
0.2   (Refusal/NA)

ALL DOING LEARNING, TRAINING OR EDUCATION

N=1206

Q415   [OpnLearn]
Was any of this 'open learning' - that is, learning, training or education that you do at a time, place and speed that is convenient to you?

%
36.6   Yes
62.8   No
0.1   (Don't Know)
0.5   (Refusal/NA)

ALL WHO HAVE DONE OPEN LEARNING

N=448

Q416   [WhnLearn]
And are you still doing this 'open learning'?
IF MORE THAN ONE EXAMPLE OF OPEN LEARNING DONE IN LAST TWO YEARS, WE ARE INTERESTED IN THE MOST RECENT.
IF 'NOT SURE': Code as 'Don't know'

%
50.4   Yes
48.1   No
-   (Don't Know)
1.5   (Refusal/NA)

Q417   [LearnQul]
(Is/was) this learning designed to lead directly to a qualification, to part of a qualification or to no qualification?
IF MORE THAN ONE EXAMPLE OF OPEN LEARNING, ASK ABOUT MOST RECENT.
WE ARE INTERESTED IN WHETHER LEARNING *DESIGNED* TO LEAD TO A QUALIFICATION - NOT WHETHER RESPONDENT OBTAINED ONE.

%
42.0   Yes, to whole qualification
15.5   Yes, to part of qualification (including 'module')
40.9   No
0.1   (Don't Know)
1.5   (Refusal/NA)

60

N=448

Q448 [LearnTim]
CARD
I am now going to read out some things people say about learning in general. Thinking of the learning you (are doing/have done), please tell me whether each applies to you wholly, partly, or does not apply at all. Firstly,
... it (suits/suited) the time I (have/had) available

Q449 [LearnHrd]
CARD AGAIN
... I (find/found) it difficult to motivate myself to do the work

Q450 [LearnSut]
CARD AGAIN
... I (can/could) do the learning at a place that (suits/suited) me

Q451 [LearnSup]
CARD AGAIN
... I (do/did) not have good enough support from others

ALL WHO HAVE DONE OPEN LEARNING

	[LearnTim]	[LearnHrd]
	%	%
Wholly applies	55.8	5.4
Partly applies	31.8	29.4
Does not apply at all	10.9	63.7
(Don't Know)	-	-
(Refusal/NA)	1.5	1.5

	[LearnSut]	[LearnSup]
	%	%
Wholly applies	66.0	6.4
Partly applies	19.9	17.3
Does not apply at all	12.6	74.8
(Don't Know)	-	-
(Refusal/NA)	1.5	1.5

62

Q420-425
CARD
Which of the ways on this card (are/were) used to pay any fees for your 'open learning'?
PROBE: Which others?
Multicoded (Maximum of 6 codes)

%		
34.5	No fees	[Fee1]
26.6	Self/family/relative	[Fee2]
31.1	Employer or potential employer	[Fee3]
4.7	Training for Work, Youth Training, Employment Training (or through a TEC)	[Fee4]
0.7	Training Credit	[Fee5]
4.1	Other answer (WRITE IN)	[Fee6]
-	(Don't Know)	
1.5	(Refusal/NA)	

Q429-436
CARD
And which of the materials on this card (are/were) used to do your learning?
PROBE: Which others?
Multicoded (Maximum of 7 codes)

%		
7.2	No materials used	[LMat1]
76.6	Work books/magazines/other printed materials	[LMat2]
16.8	Audio cassette	[LMat3]
24.0	Video cassette	[LMat4]
12.6	Radio or television	[LMat5]
51.4	Computer(s)	[LMat6]
12.4	CD Rom	[LMat7]
5.5	Other answer (WRITE IN)	[LMat8]
-	(Don't Know)	
-	(Refusal/NA)	

N=448

IF MATERIALS USED AT [LearnMat]
[WhereMat]
Q438
CARD
And where did you get these materials from? Again, please choose your answers from this card.
Multicoded (Maximum of 7 codes)

%		
41.1	Your employer	[WMat1]
33.6	College	[WMat2]
10.7	Public library	[WMat3]
2.2	School	[WMat4]
25.4	Shop or independent supplier	[WMat5]
3.4	The Internet	[WMat6]
8.7	Other answer (WRITE IN)	[WMat7]
0.1	(Don't Know)	
1.5	(Refusal/NA)	

61

SCRATCHCARDS

ASK ALL

Q452 *[LottPrt]*
Now some questions on the National Lottery
Have you personally ever taken part in the National
Lottery draw, either directly or with other people?
IF 'Yes': Is that directly, or with others?
IF 'Both': Code 1
%
74.3 Yes, directly
12.1 Yes, with others
13.6 No
- (Don't Know)
- (Refusal/NA)

IF 'Yes, directly' OR 'Yes, with others' AT [LottPrt]

Q453 *[LottWon]*
Do you happen to have won anything ever on the National
Lottery? I'm not interested in the amount.
%
61.7 Yes
24.7 No
- (Don't Know)
- (Refusal/NA)

Q454 *[LottFreq]*
Do you take part ... **READ OUT** ...
%
58.7 ...every week if you can,
7.7 around 2 or 3 times a month,
5.0 around once a month,
15.0 or, less often than that?
- (Don't Know)
- (Refusal/NA)

Q455 *[LottLast]*
Did you take part, either directly or with other people,
in the latest draw, that is the one held on (date of
previous Saturday)?
IF 'Yes': Is that directly, or with others?
IF 'Both': Code 1
%
49.3 Yes, directly
13.7 Yes, with others
23.3 No
- (Don't Know)
- (Refusal/NA)

IF 'Yes, directly' OR 'Yes, with others' AT [LottLast]

Q456 *[LottSpnd]*
How much did **you yourself** spend in the **latest** National
Lottery draw?
IF LESS THAN 50 PENCE, CODE 0
IF BETWEEN 50 PENCE AND £1, CODE 1
CODE TO NEAREST POUND (IF £x.50, ROUND UP)
Range: 0 ... 997
%
- **Median: £2**
- (Don't Know)
0.1 (Refusal/NA)

ASK ALL

Q457 *[Pools]*
And have you personally, or with others, done the
football pools **in the last week**?

Q458 *[Horses]*
And what about horse- or dog-racing? Have you
personally, or with others, placed a bet **in the last
week**?

Q459 *[Bingo]*
And how about bingo? Have you played bingo **in the last
week**?

Q460 *[FruitMac]*
And fruit machines in pubs, clubs or arcades? Have you
played fruit machines **in the last week**?

Q461 *[ScratEvr]*
Have you **ever** used one of the scratchcards people **buy** to
try to win a money prize? I don't mean those given away
by newspapers, petrol stations and so on.

	[Pools]	[Horses]	[Bingo]
	%	%	%
Yes	16.9	3.9	5.3
No	83.1	96.1	94.7
(Don't know)	-	-	-
(Refusal/NA)	-	-	-

	[FruitMac]	[ScratEvr]
	%	%
Yes	5.8	45.5
No	94.2	54.5
(Don't Know)	-	-
(Refusal/NA)	-	-

IF 'Yes' AT [ScratEvr]

Q462 [ScratRec]
How many of these cards have you personally scratched in the last week, that is, since last (day of interview)? Again, please don't include any give-aways.
IF 'NONE', CODE 0
Range: 0 ... 997
Median: 0 cards
%
- (Don't Know)
- (Refusal/NA)

IF BOUGHT ANY SCRATCHCARDS LAST WEEK AT [ScratRec]

Q463 [ScratWon]
And in the last week, how many of these happened to be winning scratchcards? (Again,) I am not interested in how much you actually won.
IF 'NONE', CODE 0
Range: 0 ... 997
Median: 0 cards
%
0.0 (Don't know)
- (Refusal/NA)

IF 'Yes' AT [ScratEvr]

Q464 [ScraAvWk]
About how many cards would you say you scratch in an average week?
IF 'NONE', CODE 0
IF 'VARIES TOO MUCH TO SAY', CODE 997
Range: 0 ... 997
Median: 0 cards
%
1.6 (Varies too much to say)
0.1 (Don't Know)

N=3620

Q465 [ScraXcsl]
And has there ever been a time when you felt that you were buying more scratchcards than you could really afford?
IF 'Yes', PROBE: 'Is that often or just occasionally?'
%
0.4 Yes, often
1.6 Yes, occasionally
43.5 No
(Don't Know)
(Refusal/NA)

ASK ALL

Q466 [SizePriz]
CARD
Thinking again of the National Lottery draw.
If you could have a say in what the biggest prize should be for any winning ticket, what amount would you choose, or do you think that there should be no limit at all?
Please choose your answer from this card.
%
9.9 No more than a hundred thousand pounds
9.4 No more than half a million pounds
35.8 No more than a million pounds
14.1 No more than five million pounds
3.9 No more than ten million pounds
1.5 No more than twenty million pounds
21.5 There should be no limit at all
0.1 (No more than ten thousand pounds)
0.2 (No more than fifty thousand pounds)
0.5 (No more than two million)
0.4 (Other limit mentioned)
1.1 (Shouldn't be a lottery)
0.3 (Prizes should be shared more equally/more smaller prizes/more winners)
0.0 (Not interested/wouldn't take part)
0.2 Other answer (WRITE IN)
1.1 (Don't Know)
0.0 (Refusal/NA)

N=3620

SOCIAL DIVISIONS (VERSION A AND B)

VERSIONS A AND B: ASK ALL　　　　　　　　　　　N=2406

Q469 [SCOpport]
Now moving on to the subject of social class in Britain.
To what extent do you think a person's social class
affects his or her opportunities in Britain today? ...
READ OUT ...

%	
26.1	... a great deal
42.8	quite a lot
23.2	not very much
3.8	or - not at all?
0.6	Other answer (WRITE IN)
3.3	(Don't Know)
0.2	(Refusal/NA)

Q471 [SCImpAgo]
Do you think social class is **more** or **less** important now
in affecting a person's opportunities than it was 10
years ago, or has there been no real change?

%	
22.4	**More** important now
30.0	**Less** important now
43.6	No change
3.9	(Don't Know)
0.2	(Refusal/NA)

Q472 [SCImpFut]
Do you think that in 10 years time social class will be
more or **less** important than it is now in affecting a
person's opportunities, or will there be no real change?

%	
19.7	**More** important in 10 years' time
30.4	**Less** important in 10 years' time
44.3	No change
5.5	(Don't Know)
0.2	(Refusal/NA)

Q473 [SRSocCl]
CARD
Most people see themselves as belonging to a particular
social class. Please look at this card and tell me which
social class you would say **you** belong to?

Q474 [PrSocCl]　　　　　　　　　　　　　　　　　　N=2406
CARD AGAIN
And which social class would you say your **parents**
belonged to when you started at primary school?

	[SRSocCl]	[PrSocCl]
	%	%
Upper middle	2.5	2.9
Middle	27.2	16.9
Upper working	22.8	14.1
Working	41.5	57.4
Poor	3.5	7.0
(Don't Know)	1.8	1.4
(Refusal/NA)	0.7	0.4

VERSION A: ASK ALL　　　　　　　　　　　　　N=1171

Q475 CARD
Please say which, if any, of the words on this card
describes the way you think of yourself. Please choose
as many or as few as apply.
PROBE: Any other?
Multicoded (Maximum of 8 codes)

%		
66.9	British	[NatBrit]
44.9	English	[NatEng]
10.0	European	[NatEuro]
2.5	Irish	[NatIrish]
0.6	Northern Irish	[NatNI]
9.6	Scottish	[NatScot]
5.9	Welsh	[NatWelsh]
3.2	Other answer (WRITE IN)	[NatOth]
0.3	(None of these)	[NatNone]
-	(Don't Know)	
-	(Refusal/NA)	

Q477 **IF MORE THAN ONE ANSWER AT [National]**
[ENation]
CARD AGAIN
And if you had to choose, which one best describes the way you think of yourself?
%
19.2 British
10.8 English
0.9 European
0.3 Irish
0.1 Northern Irish
2.3 Scottish
1.8 Welsh
0.4 Other answer (**WRITE IN**)
0.3 (None of these)
- (Don't Know)
0.5 (Refusal/NA)

VERSIONS A AND B: ASK ALL
ASKED AT Q814 ON VERSION C

Q479 [RaceOri2]
CARD
% To which of these groups do you consider you belong?
0.5 **BLACK:** of African origin
6.9 **BLACK:** of Caribbean origin
0.0 **BLACK:** of other origin (**WRITE IN**)
1.5 **ASIAN:** of Indian origin
0.8 **ASIAN:** of Pakistani origin
0.2 **ASIAN:** of Bangladeshi origin
0.2 **ASIAN:** of Chinese origin
0.6 **ASIAN:** of other origin (**WRITE IN**)
93.7 **WHITE:** of any European origin
0.6 **WHITE:** of other origin (**WRITE IN**)
0.3 **MIXED ORIGIN (WRITE IN)**
0.3 **OTHER (WRITE IN)**
- (Don't Know)
0.4 (Refusal/NA)

VERSIONS A AND B: ASK ALL

Q485 [PrejAs]
Now I would like to ask you some questions about racial prejudice in Britain. First, thinking of **Asians** - that is, people whose families were originally from India, Pakistan or Bangladesh - who now live in Britain.
Do you think there is a lot of prejudice against them in Britain nowadays, a little or hardly any?

Q486 [PrejBlk]
And black people - that is people whose families were originally from the West Indies or Africa - who now live in Britain. Do you think there is a lot of prejudice against them in Britain nowadays, a little, or hardly any?

	[PrejAS]	[PrejBlk]
	%	%
A lot	59.6	49.4
A little	33.6	42.2
Hardly any	4.8	6.5
(Don't Know)	1.7	1.7
(Refusal/NA)	0.2	0.2

Q487 [PrejNow]
Do you think there is generally **more** racial prejudice in Britain now than there was 5 years ago, **less**, or about the same amount?
%
28.8 More now
19.8 Less now
48.2 About the same
0.2 Other answer (**WRITE IN**)
2.9 (Don't Know)
0.2 (Refusal/NA)

Q489 [PrejFut]
Do you think there will be **more**, **less** or about the **same** amount of racial prejudice in Britain in 5 years time compared with now?
%
31.7 More in 5 years
19.5 Less
43.5 About the same
0.7 Other answer (**WRITE IN**)
4.4 (Don't Know)
0.2 (Refusal/NA)

Q491 [SRPrej]
How would you describe yourself ... **READ OUT** ...
2.3 ... as very prejudiced against people of other races,
26.8 a little prejudiced,
70.0 or, not prejudiced at all?
0.5 Other answer (**WRITE IN**)
0.1 (Don't Know)
0.2 (Refusal/NA)

Q493 [AsJob]
On the whole, do you think people of Asian origin in Britain are **not** given jobs these days **because** of their race ...**READ OUT** ...

N=2406

Q494 [WIJob]
And on the whole, do you think people of West Indian origin in Britain are **not** given jobs these days **because** of their race ...**READ OUT** ...

	[AsJob]	[WIJob]
	%	%
... a lot,	19.4	24.2
a little,	40.5	40.8
or, hardly at all?	31.6	26.9
(Don't Know)	8.3	8.0
(Refusal/NA)	0.2	0.2

Q495 [RaceLaw]
There is a law in Britain **against** racial discrimination, that is against giving unfair preference to a particular race in housing, jobs and so on. Do you generally **support** or oppose the idea of a law for this purpose?

%
74.5 Support
20.6 Oppose
4.6 (Don't Know)
0.2 (Refusal/NA)

VERSION A AND B: ASK WHITE RESPONDENTS WITH ODD SERIAL NUMBER

N=1090

Q496 [OBossAs]
Do you think **most** white people in Britain would mind or not mind if a suitably qualified person of **Asian** origin were appointed as their boss?
IF 'WOULD MIND': A lot or a little?

%
18.8 Mind a lot
35.1 Mind a little
38.1 Not mind
1.2 Other answer (WRITE IN)
5.9 (Don't Know)
0.9 (Refusal/NA)

Q498 [SBossAs]
And you personally? Would you mind or not mind?
IF 'WOULD MIND': A lot or a little?

%
6.3 Mind a lot
6.1 Mind a little
84.2 Not mind
1.1 Other answer (WRITE IN)
1.4 (Don't Know)
0.8 (Refusal/NA)

Q500 [OMarAs]
Do you think that **most** white people in Britain would mind or not mind if one of their close relatives were to marry a person of **Asian** origin?
IF 'WOULD MIND': A lot or a little?

%
32.0 Mind a lot
40.0 Mind a little
21.4 Not mind
1.1 Other answer (WRITE IN)
4.7 (Don't Know)
0.8 (Refusal/NA)

Q502 [SMarAs]
And you personally? Would you mind or not mind?
IF 'WOULD MIND': A lot or a little?

%
14.7 Mind a lot
17.2 Mind a little
64.3 Not mind
1.0 Other answer (WRITE IN)
2.0 (Don't Know)
0.8 (Refusal/NA)

VERSION A AND B: ASK WHITE RESPONDENTS WITH EVEN SERIAL NUMBER

N=1178

Q504 [OBossWI]
Do you think **most** white people in Britain would mind or not mind if a suitably qualified person of **black or West Indian** origin were appointed as their boss?
IF 'WOULD MIND': A lot or a little?

%
17.1 Mind a lot
33.1 Mind a little
42.8 Not mind
0.6 Other answer (WRITE IN)
5.5 (Don't Know)
0.9 (Refusal/NA)

N=1178

Q506 [SBossWI]
And you personally? Would you mind or not mind?
IF 'WOULD MIND': A lot or a little?
%
4.3 Mind a lot
6.5 Mind a little
86.8 Not mind
0.4 Other answer (WRITE IN)
0.9 (Don't Know)
1.0 (Refusal/NA)

Q508 [OMarWI]
Do you think that **most** white people in Britain would mind or not mind if one of their close relatives were to marry a person of **black or West Indian** origin?
IF 'WOULD MIND': A lot or a little?
%
29.9 Mind a lot
42.4 Mind a little
22.1 Not mind
0.6 Other answer (WRITE IN)
4.1 (Don't Know)
0.9 (Refusal/NA)

Q510 [SMarWI]
And you personally? Would you mind or not mind?
IF 'WOULD MIND': A lot or a little?
%
15.0 Mind a lot
19.8 Mind a little
62.7 Not mind
0.4 Other answer (WRITE IN)
1.3 (Don't Know)
0.9 (Refusal/NA)

VERSIONS A AND B: ASK ALL

N=2406

Q512 [StifrSnt]
CARD
Here are some possible ways of helping to prevent crime in Britain. How effective do you think each one is?
Stiffer sentences generally

Q513 [LsViolTv]
CARD AGAIN
Less violence and crime on television
(How effective do you think this would be to help prevent crime?)

N=2406

Q514 [CareProp]
CARD AGAIN
People taking more care of their property
(How effective do you think this would be to help prevent crime?)

Q515 [MorRelig]
CARD AGAIN
People taking religion more seriously
(How effective do you think this would be to help prevent crime?)

Q516 [NghWatch]
CARD AGAIN
More schemes like Neighbourhood Watch
(How effective do you think this would be to help prevent crime?)

Q517 [PrisnMor]
CARD AGAIN
Sending **more** people to prison
(How effective do you think this would be to help prevent crime?)

Q518 [PrisnLss]
CARD AGAIN
Sending **fewer** people to prison
(How effective do you think this would be to help prevent crime?)

Q519 [FamDiscp]
CARD AGAIN
Firmer discipline in families
(How effective do you think this would be to help prevent crime?)

Q520 [SchDiscp]
CARD AGAIN
Firmer discipline in schools
(How effective do you think this would be to help prevent crime?)

Q521 [MorPolic]
CARD AGAIN
More police on the beat
(How effective do you think this would be to help prevent crime?)

N=2406

Q522 *[ReducPov]*
CARD AGAIN
Reducing poverty
(How effective do you think this would be to help prevent crime?)

	[StifrSnt]	*[LsViolTV]*	*[CaveProp]*
	%	%	%
Very effective	30.4	27.4	23.8
Quite effective	39.7	35.0	53.0
Not very effective	24.7	29.8	18.8
Not at all effective	4.2	6.9	3.6
(Don't Know)	0.7	0.7	0.5
(Refusal/NA)	0.2	0.2	0.2

	[MorRelig]	*[NghWatch]*	*[PrisnMor]*
	%	%	%
Very effective	9.6	24.3	16.8
Quite effective	20.7	58.5	31.2
Not very effective	38.8	13.2	39.7
Not at all effective	28.8	2.6	9.2
(Don't Know)	1.9	1.1	2.9
(Refusal/NA)	0.2	0.2	0.2

	[PrisnLss]	*[FamDiscp]*	*[SchDiscp]*
	%	%	%
Very effective	1.4	63.6	62.8
Quite effective	16.3	29.8	29.8
Not very effective	47.8	5.1	5.7
Not at all effective	28.1	0.8	0.7
(Don't Know)	6.2	0.5	0.6
(Refusal/NA)	0.2	0.2	0.2

	[MorPolic]	*[ReducPov]*
	%	%
Very effective	58.1	40.5
Quite effective	34.6	42.8
Not very effective	5.9	12.8
Not at all effective	0.7	2.6
(Don't Know)	0.5	1.1
(Refusal/NA)	0.2	0.2

POLITICAL TRUST AND EUROPE (VERSION A)

N=1171

VERSION A: ASK ALL
Q524 *[GovtWork]* **(NOT ON SCREEN)**
CARD
Which of these statements best describes your opinion on the present system of governing in Britain?

%	
1.9	Works extremely well and could not be improved
33.2	Could be improved in small ways but mainly works well
44.3	Could be improved quite a lot
18.5	Needs a great deal of improvement
1.7	(Don't Know)
0.5	(Refusal/NA)

Q525 *[Lords]*
Do you think that the House of Lords should remain as it is or is some change needed?

%	
28.7	Remain as it is
56.6	Change needed
14.3	(Don't Know)
0.5	(Refusal/NA)

IF 'Change needed' AT [Lords]
Q526 *[LordsHow]*
Do you think the House of Lords should be ... **READ OUT** ...

%	
15.5	.....replaced by a different body
10.8	abolished and replaced by nothing
28.3	or, should there be some other kind of change?
2.0	(Don't Know)
14.7	(Refusal/NA)

VERSION A: ASK ALL
Q527 *[Monarchy]*
How about the monarchy or the Royal Family in Britain. How important or unimportant do you think it is for Britain to continue to have a monarchy ... **READ OUT** ...

%	
32.0	....very important
34.6	quite important
16.9	not very important
4.6	not at all important
10.7	or, do you think the monarchy should be abolished?
0.8	(Don't Know)
0.5	(Refusal/NA)

N=1171

	[GovNoSayt]	[LoseTch]	[VoteIntr]
	%	%	%
Agree strongly	24.2	26.0	28.0
Agree	37.4	50.3	47.0
Neither agree or disagree	13.3	10.9	12.0
Disagree	20.4	10.9	11.3
Disagree strongly	3.2	0.2	0.6
(Don't Know)	0.9	1.4	0.5
(Refusal/NA)	0.5	0.5	0.5

	[VoteOnly]	[GovComp]	[PtyNtMatr]
	%	%	%
Agree strongly	15.3	21.7	15.6
Agree	51.6	44.4	43.9
Neither agree or disagree	11.8	9.7	8.4
Disagree	18.2	20.1	26.9
Disagree strongly	1.4	2.7	3.9
(Don't Know)	1.1	0.7	0.8
(Refusal/NA)	0.5	0.6	0.5

	[InfPolit]	[MPsCare]
	%	%
Agree strongly	1.4	15.1
Agree	18.4	44.6
Neither agree or disagree	26.6	18.4
Disagree	41.5	19.4
Disagree strongly	10.6	0.9
(Don't Know)	0.9	0.9
(Refusal/NA)	0.5	0.5

Q548 [VoteIntr]
CARD AGAIN
(Please choose a phrase from this card to say how much you agree or disagree with this statement)
Parties are only interested in people's votes, not in their opinions

Q549 [VoteOnly]
CARD AGAIN
(Please choose a phrase from this card to say how much you agree or disagree with this statement)
Voting is the only way people like me can have any say about how the government runs things

Q550 [GovComp]
CARD AGAIN
(Please choose a phrase from this card to say how much you agree or disagree with this statement)
Sometimes politics and government seem so complicated that a person like me cannot really understand what is going on.

Q551 [PtyNtMat]
CARD AGAIN
(Please choose a phrase from this card to say how much you agree or disagree with this statement)
It doesn't really matter which party is in power, in the end things go on much the same.

Q552 [InfPolit]
CARD AGAIN
(Please choose a phrase from this card to say how much you agree or disagree with this statement)
I think I am better informed than most people about politics and government

Q553 [MPsCare]
CARD AGAIN
(Please choose a phrase from this card to say how much you agree or disagree with this statement)
MPs don't care much about what people like me think.

Q554 [GovTrust]
CARD
How much do you trust British governments of any party to place the needs of the nation above the interests of their own political party?
Please choose a phrase from this card.

Q555 [ClrTrust]
CARD AGAIN
And how much do you trust local councillors of any party to place the needs of their area above the interests of their own political party?

Q556 [PolTrust]   N=1171
CARD AGAIN
And how much do you trust British police not to bend the rules in trying to get a conviction?

Q557 [CSTrust]
CARD AGAIN
And how much do you trust top civil servants to stand firm against a minister who wants to provide false information to parliament?

Q558 [MPsTrust]
CARD AGAIN
And how much do you trust politicians of any party in Britain to tell the truth when they are in a tight corner?

Q559 [JugTrust]
CARD AGAIN
And how much do you trust high court judges to stand up to a government which wishes them to reach a particular verdict?

Q554-559	[GovTrust]	[ClrTrust]	[PolTrust]
	%	%	%
Just about always	2.0	2.7	7.2
Most of the time	20.0	25.7	43.4
Only some of the time	52.5	49.0	35.4
Almost never	22.9	19.8	10.0
(Don't Know)	1.8	2.2	3.4
(Refusal/NA)	0.6	0.5	0.6

	[CSTrust]	[MPsTrust]	[JugTrust]
	%	%	%
Just about always	4.2	0.7	10.9
Most of the time	23.9	8.3	36.9
Only some of the time	41.6	38.4	34.2
Almost never	19.6	49.4	10.2
(Don't Know)	10.0	2.7	7.2
(Refusal/NA)	0.7	0.6	0.6

Q560 **CARD**   N=1171
Now thinking of MPs, which of the following qualities shown on this card would you say are important for an MP to have? You may choose more than one, none, or suggest others.

%
% Multicoded (Maximum of 9 codes)
59.5 To be well educated   [MPEd]
45.9 To know what being poor means   [MPPoor]
33.7 To have business experience   [MPBus]
14.3 To have trade union experience   [MPUnion]
61.3 To have been brought up in the area he or she represents   [MPLocal]
43.8 To be loyal to the party he or she represents   [MPLoyal]
51.0 To be independent minded   [MPInd]
3.0 (To be honest/trustworthy/open)   [MPOth8]
0.9 (To be caring/compassionate)   [MPOth9]
1.0 (To be loyal to their constituents)   [MPOth10]
0.1 (To be upright/moral)   [MPOth11]
0.5 (To be courageous)   [MPOth12]
1.2 (To be prepared to listen/keep in touch)   [MPOth13]
0.1 None of these qualities   [MPNone]
1.7 Other important qualities **(PLEASE SPECIFY)**   [MPOth2]
7.9 (Don't Know)
– (Refusal/NA)

NORTHERN IRELAND (VERSION A)

N=1171

Q563 *[PrejRC]*
Now I would like to ask some questions about religious prejudice against both Catholics and Protestants in Northern Ireland.
First thinking of **Catholics** - do you think there is a lot of prejudice against them in Northern Ireland nowadays, a little, or hardly any?

Q564 *[PrejProt]*
And now thinking of **Protestants** - do you think there is a lot of prejudice against them in Northern Ireland nowadays, a little, or hardly any?

	[PrejRC]	*[PrejProt]*
	%	%
A lot	45.8	40.6
A little	32.3	34.8
Hardly any	5.2	7.9
(Don't Know)	15.8	15.8
(Refusal/NA)	0.9	0.9

Q565 *[SrRlPrej]*
%   How would you describe yourself ... **READ OUT** ...
0.9   ... as very prejudiced against people of other religions,
10.0   a little prejudiced,
87.5   or, not prejudiced at all?
0.2   Other answer **(WRITE IN)**
0.7   (Don't Know)
0.7   (Refusal/NA)

Q567 *[RlRelAgo]*
What about **relations** between Protestants and Catholics in Northern Ireland? Would you say they are **better** than they were 5 years ago, **worse**, or about the **same** now as then?
%   **IF 'IT DEPENDS', PROBE BEFORE CODING 'other'**
49.0   Better
5.5   Worse
36.4   About the same
0.0   Other answer **(WRITE IN)**
7.9   (Don't Know)
1.0   (Refusal/NA)

85

VERSION A: ASK ALL

N=1171

Q569 *[RlRelFut]*
And what about in 5 year's time? Do you think relations between Protestants and Catholics will be **better** than now, **worse** than now, or about the **same** as now?
%   **IF 'IT DEPENDS', PROBE BEFORE CODING 'other'**
40.1   Better than now
5.4   Worse than now
42.0   About the same
0.6   Other answer **(WRITE IN)**
10.8   (Don't Know)
1.0   (Refusal/NA)

Q571 *[RelgAlwy]*
Do you think that religion will **always** make a difference to the way people feel about each other in Northern Ireland?
%
84.3   Yes
10.0   No
1.0   Other answer **(WRITE IN)**
3.7   (Don't Know)
0.9   (Refusal/NA)

Q573 *[UntdIrel]*
At any time in the next 20 years, do you think it is likely or unlikely that there will be a united Ireland? **PROBE:** Very likely/unlikely or quite likely/unlikely?
%
7.2   Very likely
33.5   Quite likely
28.6   Quite unlikely
18.2   Very unlikely
3.2   (Even chance)
8.3   (Don't Know)
0.9   (Refusal/NA)

Q574 *[GovIntNI]*
CARD
Under direct rule from Britain, as now, how much do you generally trust **British governments** of **any** party to act in the best interests of Northern Ireland?

Q575 *[StrIntNI]*
CARD AGAIN
If there was self-rule, how much do you think you would trust a **Belfast government** to act in the best interests of Northern Ireland?

86

Q576 [IreIntNI]
CARD AGAIN
And if there was a united Ireland, how much do you think you would generally trust an **Irish government** to act in the best interests of Northern Ireland?

N=1171

	[GovIntNI]	[StrIntNI]	[IreIntNI]
	%	%	%
Just about always	4.1	8.2	7.1
Most of the time	32.9	43.4	44.0
Only some of the time	43.1	26.0	30.2
Rarely	9.6	7.1	6.4
Never	3.1	2.8	2.0
(Don't Know)	6.5	11.7	9.5
(Refusal/NA)	0.8	0.8	0.8

TASTE AND DECENCY (VERSION A)

N=1171

VERSION A: ASK ALL

Q578 [StbMCine]
CARD
I am now going to ask what you think should be allowed or not allowed to be shown on television or at the cinema. Thinking first about a film which contains a scene, filmed in close-up, of someone **being repeatedly stabbed and cut**. I have in mind a scene where you can see a lot of blood. Using this card, please say what you feel about a **film at the cinema** which includes a scene like that.

%
42.8　Should not be shown at all
8.0　Only at special film clubs
42.8　At ordinary cinemas but only to people of 18 or over
3.0　At ordinary cinemas but only to people of 15 or over
0.3　At ordinary cinemas but only to people of 12 or over
1.6　Should be allowed to be shown to anyone
0.8　(Don't Know)
0.7　(Refusal/NA)

Q579 [StbMRgTV]
CARD
How about the same scene in a film on one of the **regular television channels**, that is, BBC1 and 2, ITV and (Channel4/S4C)?
Using this card, please say what you would feel about that.

%
50.5　Should not be shown at all
14.7　Only after midnight
24.9　Only after 10 o'clock in the evening
6.2　Only after 9 o'clock in the evening
0.2　Only after 8 o'clock in the evening
2.0　Should be allowed to be shown at any time
0.8　(Don't Know)
0.7　(Refusal/NA)

N=1171

Q580 *[StbMCbTV]*
CARD
And the same scene in a film on a paid satellite or cable channel?
%
42.4 Should not be shown at all
12.5 Only on special channels
10.3 On any satellite or cable channel but only after midnight
24.3 On any satellite or cable channel but only after 10 o'clock in the evening
5.7 On any satellite or cable channel but only after 9 o'clock in the evening
0.9 On any satellite or cable channel but only after 8 o'clock in the evening
1.6 On any satellite or cable channel at any time
1.7 (Don't Know)
0.7 (Refusal/NA)

Q581 *[StbMVide]*
CARD
Now suppose the **same** film, including the close-up scene of someone being repeatedly stabbed and cut - showing a lot of blood, was available on a **video for sale or rent.** Using this card, please say how widely you think the video should be available.
%
45.6 Should be banned altogether
10.0 Only in special shops
40.0 In any shop but only to people of 18 or over
2.0 In any shop but only to people of 15 or over
0.2 In any shop but only to people of 12 or over
0.8 Available to anyone
0.8 (Don't Know)
0.7 (Refusal/NA)

Q582 *[StbMSee]*
If you heard of a film that contained a scene like this, would **you** try to avoid seeing the film, or would you be quite interested to see it, or would you treat it just like any other film?
%
61.5 Try to avoid
2.5 Quite interested to see
34.7 Treat like any other film
0.6 (Don't Know)
0.7 (Refusal/NA)

N=1171

Q583 *[StbDCine]*
CARD AGAIN
Now how about a film with the scene of someone being stabbed or cut, but this time filmed **from a distance** so that you could not see any blood.
Using this card, please say what you feel about **a film at the cinema** which includes a scene like that.
%
23.1 Should not be shown at all
4.6 Only at special film clubs
51.4 At ordinary cinemas but only to people of 18 or over
14.4 At ordinary cinemas but only to people of 15 or over
3.0 At ordinary cinemas but only to people of 12 or over
2.3 Should be allowed to be shown to anyone
0.6 (Don't Know)
0.7 (Refusal/NA)

Q584 *[StbDRgTV]*
CARD AGAIN
How about this scene in a film on one of the **regular television channels**?
(Using this card, please say what you would feel about that.)
REGULAR TV CHANNELS = BBC1 AND 2, ITV AND CHANNEL 4/S4C.
%
27.0 Should not be shown at all
15.9 Only after midnight
35.5 Only after 10 o'clock in the evening
14.9 Only after 9 o'clock in the evening
3.2 Only after 8 o'clock in the evening
2.0 Should be allowed to be shown at any time
0.7 (Don't Know)
0.7 (Refusal/NA)

Q585 *[StbDCbTV]*
CARD AGAIN
And this scene in a film on a **paid satellite or cable channel**?

N=1171

```
 %
26.0  Should not be shown at all
 8.0  Only on special channels
10.7  On any satellite or cable channel but only after
      midnight
33.8  On any satellite or cable channel but only after 10
      o'clock in the evening
13.3  On any satellite or cable channel but only after 9
      o'clock in the evening
 3.7  On any satellite or cable channel but only after 8
      o'clock in the evening
 2.5  On any satellite or cable channel at any time
 1.4  (Don't Know)
 0.7  (Refusal/NA)
```

Q586 *[StbDVide]*
CARD AGAIN
Now suppose the same film, including the scene with the stabbing, filmed from a distance, was available on a **video for sale or rent.**
Using this card, please say how widely you think the video should be available.

```
 %
26.5  Should be banned altogether
 8.8  Only in special shops
44.9  In any shop but only to people of 18 or over
14.4  In any shop but only to people of 15 or over
 2.1  In any shop but only to people of 12 or over
 1.8  Available to anyone
 0.9  (Don't Know)
 0.7  (Refusal/NA)
```

Q587 *[FantCine]*
CARD AGAIN
Now think again of a film with a scene of someone being repeatedly stabbed and cut, filmed **in close-up**, but this time the stabbing is done, not by another human being, but by a **fantasy monster.**
Using this card, please say what you feel about a **film at the cinema** which includes a scene like that.

N=1171

```
 %
36.0  Should not be shown at all
 6.1  Only at special film clubs
40.4  At ordinary cinemas but only to people of 18 or over
11.7  At ordinary cinemas but only to people of 15 or over
 2.1  At ordinary cinemas but only to people of 12 or over
 1.4  Should be allowed to be shown to anyone
 1.6  (Don't Know)
 0.7  (Refusal/NA)
```

Q588 *[FantRgTV]*
CARD AGAIN
How about this scene in a film on one of the **regular television channels**?
Using this card, please say what you would feel about that.

```
 %     REGULAR TV CHANNELS = BBC1 AND 2, ITV AND CHANNEL4/S4C.
38.9  Should not be shown at all
12.5  Only after midnight
30.1  Only after 10 o'clock in the evening
12.3  Only after 9 o'clock in the evening
 3.2  Only after 8 o'clock in the evening
 1.4  Should be allowed to be shown at any time
 0.9  (Don't Know)
 0.7  (Refusal/NA)
```

N=1171

Q589 [FantCbTV]
CARD AGAIN
And this scene in a film on a **paid satellite or cable channel**?

%
35.5 Should not be shown at all
8.1 Only on special channels
11.9 On any satellite or cable channel but only after midnight
26.0 On any satellite or cable channel but only after 10 o'clock in the evening
11.3 On any satellite or cable channel but only after 9 o'clock in the evening
3.1 On any satellite or cable channel but only after 8 o'clock in the evening
1.8 On any satellite or cable channel at any time
1.5 (Don't Know)
0.7 (Refusal/NA)

Q590 [FantVide]
CARD AGAIN
Now suppose the same film, including the scene with someone being stabbed and cut by a fantasy monster, was available on a **video for sale or rent**.
Using this card, please say how widely you think the video should be available.

%
35.1 Should be banned altogether
8.4 Only in special shops
38.9 In any shop but only to people of 18 or over
12.5 In any shop but only to people of 15 or over
2.0 In any shop but only to people of 12 or over
1.4 Available to anyone
1.0 (Don't Know)
0.7 (Refusal/NA)

Q591 [FantGame]
CARD AGAIN
What if it was not a film but a **computer game** where someone was stabbed and cut by a fantasy monster. How widely do you think that this should be available?

%
41.0 Should be banned altogether
9.5 Only in special shops
24.5 In any shop but only to people of 18 or over
14.4 In any shop but only to people of 15 or over
4.5 In any shop but only to people of 12 or over
3.2 Available to anyone
2.2 (Don't Know)
0.7 (Refusal/NA)

N=1171

Q592 [KickCine]
CARD AGAIN
Now think of a film where there was a realistic scene of a someone being severely beaten or kicked by another person.
Using this card, please say what you feel about **a film at the cinema** which includes a scene like that?

%
38.1 Should not be shown at all
4.2 Only at special film clubs
45.3 At ordinary cinemas but only to people of 18 or over
8.4 At ordinary cinemas but only to people of 15 or over
1.3 At ordinary cinemas but only to people of 12 or over
1.2 Should be allowed to be shown to anyone
0.8 (Don't Know)
0.7 (Refusal/NA)

Q593 [KickRgtTV]
CARD AGAIN
How about this scene in a film on one of the **regular television channels**?
(Using this card, please say what you would feel about that.)

%
REGULAR TV CHANNELS = BBC1 AND 2, ITV AND CHANNEL4/S4C.
38.2 Should not be shown at all
13.8 Only after midnight
30.9 Only after 10 o'clock in the evening
12.2 Only after 9 o'clock in the evening
1.9 Only after 8 o'clock in the evening
1.4 Should be allowed to be shown at any time
0.9 (Don't Know)
0.7 (Refusal/NA)

Q594 [KickCbTV]   N=1171
CARD AGAIN
And this scene in a film on a **paid satellite or cable channel**?
%
34.4 Should not be shown at all
8.1 Only on special channels
10.9 On any satellite or cable channel but only after midnight
29.5 On any satellite or cable channel but only after 10 o'clock in the evening
11.2 On any satellite or cable channel but only after 9 o'clock in the evening
2.0 On any satellite or cable channel but only after 8 o'clock in the evening
1.6 On any satellite or cable channel at any time
1.6 (Don't Know)
0.7 (Refusal/NA)

Q595 [KickVide]
CARD AGAIN
Now suppose the same film, including the scene with someone being severely beaten or kicked, was available on a **video for sale or rent**.
Using this card, please say how widely you think the video should be available.
%
36.7 Should be banned altogether
7.4 Only in special shops
42.1 In any shop but only to people of 18 or over
9.0 In any shop but only to people of 15 or over
1.8 In any shop but only to people of 12 or over
1.2 Available to anyone
1.0 (Don't Know)
0.7 (Refusal/NA)

Q596 [KickReal]
CARD AGAIN
What if the scene of someone being severely beaten or kicked was not in a fictional film, but was **documentary film footage** being shown in a **television news broadcast**? What would your opinion be?
%
21.1 Should not be shown at all
5.6 Only after midnight
34.3 Only after 10 o'clock in the evening
22.1 Only after 9 o'clock in the evening
5.0 Only after 8 o'clock in the evening
9.8 Should be allowed to be shown at any time
1.4 (Don't Know)
0.7 (Refusal/NA)

Q597 [VioGra12]   N=1171
We have been talking about films and videos containing violence, but there are, of course, different ways of handling violence within a film. Some films contain violent scenes which are part of a developing story. Others show violent scenes which don't seem to be essential to the plot.
Think first of a film containing a scene of someone being repeatedly stabbed and cut, filmed in close-up, that does **not** seem to be essential to the plot. Should it **ever**, in your view be allowed to be...
...seen by **12** year olds?

IF 'No'/DK AT [VioGra12]
Q598 [VioGra15]
(Thinking of a film containing a scene of someone being repeatedly stabbed and cut, filmed in close-up, that does **not** seem to be essential to the plot. Should it **ever**, in your view be ...)
...allowed to be seen by **15** year olds?

IF 'No'/DK AT [VioGra15]
Q599 [VioGra18]
(Thinking of a film containing a scene of someone being repeatedly stabbed and cut, filmed in close-up, that does **not** seem to be essential to the plot. Should it **ever**, in your view be ...)
...allowed to be seen by **18** year olds?

IF 'No'/DK AT [VioGra18]
Q600 [VioGraAn]
(Thinking of a film containing a scene of someone being repeatedly stabbed and cut, filmed in close-up, that does **not** seem to be essential to the plot. Should it **ever**, in your view be ...)
...allowed to be seen by anyone at all?

N=1171

	[VioGra12]	[VioGra15]	[VioGra18]
	%	%	%
Yes	1.4	8.1	43.3
No	96.8	88.7	45.3
(Don't Know)	1.1	1.1	1.3
(Refusal/NA)	0.7	0.7	0.7

	[VioGraAn]
	%
Yes	4.3
No	41.5
(Don't Know)	0.8
(Refusal/NA)	0.7

VERSION A: ASK ALL

Q601 [VioPlt12]
And how about a film containing a scene of someone being repeatedly stabbed or cut, filmed in close-up, that **is** a **central** part of the plot. Should it **ever**, in your view, be...

...allowed to be seen by **12** year olds?

IF 'No'/DK AT [VioPlt12]
Q602 [VioPlt15]
(Thinking of a film containing a scene of someone being repeatedly stabbed, filmed in close-up, that **is** a **central** part of the plot. Should it **ever**, in your view be...)

...allowed to be seen by **15** year olds?

IF 'No'/DK AT [VioPlt15]
Q603 [VioPlt18]
(Thinking of a film containing a scene of someone being repeatedly stabbed, filmed in close-up, that **is** a **central** part of the plot. Should it **ever**, in your view be...)

...allowed to be seen by **18** year olds?

N=1171

IF 'No'/DK AT [VioPlt18]
Q604 [VioPltAn]
(Thinking of a film containing a scene of someone being repeatedly stabbed, filmed in close-up, that **is** a **central** part of the plot. Should it **ever**, in your view be...)

...allowed to be seen by anyone at all?

	[VioPlt12]	[VioPltAn]
	%	%
Yes	3.8	14.0
No	94.5	80.3
(Don't Know)	1.0	1.1
(Refusal/NA)	0.7	0.8

	[VioPlt18]	[VioPltAn]
	%	%
Yes	50.2	4.1
No	30.7	26.4
(Don't Know)	0.6	0.8
(Refusal/NA)	0.8	0.8

IF ('No'/DK AT [VioGraAn] AND AT [VioPltAn]) **AND**
('Should not be allowed to be shown at all' AT ALL OF
[StbMCine], [StbMRgTV], [StbMCbTV], [StbMVide],
[StbDCine], [StbDRgTV], [StbDCbTV], [StbDVide],
[FantCine], [FantRgTV], [FantCbTV], [FantVide],
[KickCine], [KickRgTV], [KickCbTV] AND [KickVide])

Q605 [VioNever]
Do you believe that scenes showing violence on film or video should never be seen by anyone at all, or can you imagine circumstances in which they might be acceptable?

	%
Never be seen	10.4
Can imagine acceptable circumstances	2.5
(Don't Know)	0.2
(Refusal/NA)	-

IF 'Can imagine acceptable circumstances' AT [VioNever]
Q606 [VioCer]
Are you able to say what those circumstances might be?
Open Question (Maximum of 80 characters)

CLASSIFICATION

N=3620

ASK ALL

Q802 *[Religion]*
Do you regard yourself as belonging to any particular religion?

IF YES: Which?

CODE ONE ONLY - DO NOT PROMPT

%	
42.6	No religion
4.7	Christian - no denomination
8.9	Roman Catholic
29.3	Church of England/Anglican
0.8	Baptist
2.2	Methodist
3.7	Presbyterian/Church of Scotland
0.5	Other Christian
0.6	Hindu
0.3	Jewish
1.8	Islam/Muslim
0.2	Sikh
0.5	Buddhist
0.4	Other non-Christian
0.1	Free Presbyterian
0.1	Brethren
0.8	United Reform Church (URC)/Congregational
1.7	Other Protestant
0.1	(Don't Know)
0.7	(Refusal/NA)

IF NOT 'Refusal/NA' AT [Religion]

N=3620

Q808 *[FamRelig]*
Derived variable
In what religion, if any, were you brought up?
PROBE IF NECESSARY: What was your family's religion?
CODE ONE ONLY - DO NOT PROMPT

%	
9.8	No religion
4.8	Christian - no denomination
13.0	Roman Catholic
51.7	Church of England/Anglican
1.6	Baptist
5.1	Methodist
6.4	Presbyterian/Church of Scotland
0.4	Other Christian
0.7	Hindu
0.4	Jewish
1.9	Islam/Muslim
0.3	Sikh
0.2	Buddhist
0.1	Other non-Christian
0.2	Free Presbyterian
0.2	Brethren
0.9	United Reform Church (URC)/Congregational
1.4	Other Protestant
0.3	(Don't Know)
0.7	(Refusal/NA)

IF RELIGION GIVEN AT EITHER [Religion] OR AT [FamRelig]

Q813 *[ChAttend]*
Apart from such special occasions as weddings, funerals and baptisms, how often nowadays do you attend services or meetings connected with your religion?
PROBE AS NECESSARY.

%	
11.2	Once a week or more
1.9	Less often but at least once in two weeks
5.9	Less often but at least once a month
9.1	Less often but at least twice a year
5.1	Less often but at least once a year
3.6	Less often
52.7	Never or practically never
0.4	Varies too much to say
0.0	(Don't Know)
0.8	(Refusal/NA)

N=3620

VERSION C: ASK ALL (ASKED AT Q479 ON VERSIONS A AND B)

Q814 [RaceOri2]
CARD
% To which of these groups do you consider you belong?
0.5 BLACK: of African origin
0.9 BLACK: of Caribbean origin
0.0 BLACK: of other origin (WRITE IN)
1.5 ASIAN: of Indian origin
0.8 ASIAN: of Pakistani origin
0.2 ASIAN: of Bangladeshi origin
0.2 ASIAN: of Chinese origin
0.6 ASIAN: of other origin (WRITE IN)
93.7 WHITE: of any European origin
0.6 WHITE: of other origin (WRITE IN)
0.3 MIXED ORIGIN (WRITE IN)
0.3 OTHER (WRITE IN)
0.4 (Don't Know)
- (Refusal/NA)

ASK ALL
Q820 [RPrivEd]
Have you ever attended a fee-paying, private primary or secondary school in the United Kingdom?
'PRIVATE' PRIMARY OR SECONDARY SCHOOLS INCLUDE:
INDEPENDENT SCHOOLS
SCHOLARSHIPS AND ASSISTED PLACES AT FEE-PAYING SCHOOLS
THEY EXCLUDE:
DIRECT GRANT SCHOOLS (UNLESS FEE-PAYING)
VOLUNTARY-AIDED SCHOOLS
GRANT-MAINTAINED ('OPTED OUT') SCHOOLS
NURSERY SCHOOLS
%
11.1 Yes
88.3 No
- (Don't Know)
0.6 (Refusal/NA)

N=3620

IF 'Married' OR 'living as married' AT [MarStat2]
Q821 [SPrivEd]
Has you (husband/wife/partner) ever attended a fee-paying, private primary or secondary school in the United Kingdom?
'PRIVATE' PRIMARY OR SECONDARY SCHOOLS INCLUDE:
INDEPENDENT SCHOOLS
SCHOLARSHIPS AND ASSISTED PLACES AT FEE-PAYING SCHOOLS
THEY EXCLUDE:
DIRECT GRANT SCHOOLS (UNLESS FEE-PAYING)
VOLUNTARY-AIDED SCHOOLS
GRANT-MAINTAINED ('OPTED OUT') SCHOOLS
NURSERY SCHOOLS
%
6.3 Yes
58.8 No
0.1 (Don't Know)
0.4 (Refusal/NA)

IF NO CHILDREN IN HOUSEHOLD AT [NumChild]
Q822 [OthChld3]
Have you ever been responsible for bringing up any children of school age, including stepchildren?
%
31.9 Yes
36.5 No
- (Don't Know)
0.5 (Refusal/NA)

IF RESPONDENT HAS CHILDREN AGED 5 OR OVER (AS GIVEN IN HOUSEHOLD GRID) OR ANSWERED 'Yes' AT [OthChld3]
Q823 [ChPrivEd]
And (have any of your children/has your child) ever attended a fee-paying, private primary or secondary school in the United Kingdom?
'PRIVATE' PRIMARY OR SECONDARY SCHOOLS INCLUDE:
INDEPENDENT SCHOOLS
SCHOLARSHIPS AND ASSISTED PLACES AT FEE-PAYING SCHOOLS
THEY EXCLUDE:
DIRECT GRANT SCHOOLS (UNLESS FEE-PAYING)
VOLUNTARY-AIDED SCHOOLS
GRANT-MAINTAINED ('OPTED OUT') SCHOOLS
NURSERY SCHOOLS
%
7.9 Yes
54.9 No
- (Don't Know)
0.7 (Refusal/NA)

Q824 VERSION C: IF 'Yes' AT [ChPrivEd]   N=1214
[ChPEdNow]
(Are any of your children/Is your child) attending a fee-paying, private primary or secondary school in the United Kingdom at present?
'PRIVATE' PRIMARY OR SECONDAY SCHOOLS INCLUDE:
INDEPENDENT SCHOOLS
SCHOLARSHIPS AND ASSISTED PLACES AT FEE-PAYING SCHOOLS
THEY EXCLUDE:
DIRECT GRANT SCHOOLS (UNLESS FEE-PAYING)
VOLUNTARY-AIDED SCHOOLS
GRANT-MAINTAINED ('OPTED OUT') SCHOOLS
NURSERY SCHOOLS
%
1.8 Yes
6.5 No
  - (Don't Know)
0.8 (Refusal/NA)

ASK ALL   N=3620
Q826 [TEA2]/[TEA]
How old were you when you completed your continuous full-time education?
PROBE IF NECESSARY
'STILL AT SCHOOL' - CODE 95
'STILL AT COLLEGE OR UNIVERSITY' - CODE 96
'OTHER ANSWER' - CODE 97 AND WRITE IN
%
36.3 15 or under
27.0 16
8.0 17
8.5 18
16.1 19 or over
0.4 Still at school
2.7 Still at college or university
0.4 Other answer (WRITE IN)
0.0 (Don't Know)
0.7 (Refusal/NA)

Q829 [SchQual]
CARD
Have you passed any of the examinations on this card?
%
57.2 Yes
42.0 No
0.1 (Don't Know)
0.7 (Refusal/NA)

IF 'Yes' AT [SchQual]   N=3620
Q830 [SchQFW]
CARD AGAIN
Which ones? PROBE: Any others?
  Multicoded (Maximum of 15 codes)
%
17.2 CSE Grades 2-5   [EdQual1]
      GCSE Grades D-G
46.6 CSE Grade 1   [EdQual2]
      GCE 'O'level
      GCSE Grades A-C
      School certificate or matriculation
      Scottish (SCE) Ordinary
      Scottish School-leaving Certificate lower grade
      SUPE Ordinary
      Northern Ireland Junior Certificate
20.7 GCE 'A'level/'S'level   [EdQual3]
      Higher school certificate
      Scottish SCE/SLC/SUPE at Higher grade
      Northern Ireland Senior Certificate
1.6 Overseas school leaving exam or certificate [EdQual4]
0.1 (Don't Know)
0.8 (Refusal/NA)

ASK ALL
Q835 [PSchQual] CARD
And have you passed any of the exams or got any of the qualifications on this card?
%
53.1 Yes
46.2 No
0.0 (Don't Know)
0.7 (Refusal/NA)

N=3620

IF 'Yes' AT [PSchQual]

Q837-
854 **CARD AGAIN**
Which ones? **PROBE:** Any others?
% Multicoded (Maximum of 17 codes)
7.6 Recognised trade apprenticeship completed [EdQual5]
12.4 RSA/other clerical, commercial qualification [EdQual6]
9.3 City & Guilds Certificate - Craft/Intermediate/Ordinary/Part I [EdQual7]
5.2 City & Guilds Certificate - Advanced/Final/Part II or Part III [EdQual8]
1.9 City & Guilds Certificate - Full technological [EdQual9]
5.3 BEC/TEC General/Ordinary National Certificate (ONC) or Diploma (OND) [EdQual10]
3.9 BEC/TEC Higher/Higher National Certificate (HNC) or Diploma (HND) [EdQual11]
1.9 NVQ/SVQ Level 1/GNVQ Foundation level [EdQual17]
2.7 NVQ/SVQ Level 2/GNVQ Intermediate level [EdQual18]
1.5 NVQ/SVQ Level 3/GNVQ Advanced level [EdQual19]
0.2 NVQ/SVQ Level 4 [EdQual20]
0.1 NVQ/SVQ Level 5 [EdQual21]
4.8 Teacher training qualification [EdQual12]
3.7 Nursing qualification [EdQual13]
5.8 Other technical or business qualification/certificate [EdQual14]
11.1 University or CNAA degree or diploma [EdQual15]
5.9 Other recognised academic or vocational qualification (WRITE IN) [EdQual16]
- (Don't Know)
0.7 (Refusal/NA)

ASK ALL

Q855 [HEdQual] **(NOT ON SCREEN)**
% Highest Educational Qualification - Derived variable
11.1 Degree
14.5 Higher education below degree
13.6 A level or equivalent
18.9 O level or equivalent
9.4 CSE or equivalent
1.4 Foreign or other
30.4 No qualification
0.8 DK/Refusal/NA

N=2449

VERSIONS B AND C: ASK ALL

Q856 [SciQual]
Have you passed any exams, or got any qualifications in physics, chemistry or biology?
%
30.9 Yes
68.4 No
0.1 (Don't Know)
0.6 (Refusal/NA)

IF 'Yes' AT [SciQual]

Q857 [HSciQual]
What is your highest qualification in these subjects?
PROBE FOR CORRECT PRECODE
%
4.5 CSE grade 2-5/GCSE grades D-G or equivalent
15.9 CSE Grade 1/O-level/GCSE grades A-C or equivalent
6.6 A-level or equivalent
1.9 Degree/Postgraduate qualification or equivalent
0.1 Other answer (WRITE IN)
0.1 (Don't Know)
0.7 (Refusal/NA)

N=3620

ASK ALL

Q859 [PastVot]
Thinking back to the last **general election** in 1992 - do you remember which party you voted for then, or perhaps you didn't vote in that election?
IF NECESSARY, SAY: The one where John Major won against Neil Kinnock
DO NOT PROMPT
% **Yes, voted:**
30.3 - Conservative
30.9 - Labour
9.2 - Liberal Democrat
1.2 - Scottish National Party
0.3 - Plaid Cymru
0.5 - Green Party
0.1 - Other (WRITE IN)
1.9 **Refused to say**
23.6 **Did not vote**
1.9 (Can't remember/Don't know)
0.1 (Don't Know)
- (Refusal/NA)

Q861   **VERSION A: IF 'Did not vote' AT [PastVot]**   N=1171
        [WhNtVot]
        CARD
        Which of the reasons on this card comes closest to
        explaining why you did not manage to vote in the last
        general election in 1992?
    %
    5.6   I was not eligible or not registered to vote
    2.2   I wanted to vote but was not able to get to the polling
           station
    2.2   I didn't understand enough about politics
    4.3   I was not interested enough in the election
    0.4   I wanted to vote but forgot to
    1.1   I never vote for reasons of conscience
    1.3   I couldn't decide who to vote for
    2.7   There was no one I wanted to vote for
    1.2   Other reason **(WRITE IN)**
    0.1   (Don't Know)
    0.2   (Refusal/NA)

ASK ALL   N=3620

Q863   *[VoteNow]*
        Now what if there were a general election tomorrow?
        Which political party do you think you would be most
        likely to vote for, or do you think you would not vote?
        DO NOT PROMPT
    %
    21.2   Conservative
    41.7   Labour
    10.5   Liberal Democrat
    1.5   Scottish National Party
    0.4   Plaid Cymru
    0.9   Green Party
    1.0   Other answer **(WRITE IN)**
    14.1   None/would not vote
    2.7   Refused to say
    5.9   (Don't Know)
    -      (Refusal/NA)

Q867   **ASK ALL WHO ARE MARRIED OR LIVING AS MARRIED**   N=2378
        [SEconAct]
        CARD
        Which of these descriptions applied to what your partner
        was doing last week, that is the seven days ending last
        Sunday?
        PROBE: Any others?
        CODE ALL THAT APPLY
        (Figures refer to first answer on the list)
    %
    0.5   Priority coded
    0.5   In full-time education (not paid for by employer,
           including on vacation)
    0.2   On government training/employment programme (eg. Youth
           Training, Training for Work etc)
    61.5   In paid work (or away temporarily) for at least 10 hours
           in week
    0.1   Waiting to take up paid work already accepted
    2.1   Unemployed and registered at a benefit office
    0.6   Unemployed, not registered, but actively looking for a
           job (of at least 10 hrs a week)
    0.5   Unemployed, wanting a job (of at least 10 hrs per week)
           but not actively looking for a job
    3.9   Permanently sick or disabled
    16.0   Wholly retired from work
    13.5   Looking after the home
    0.3   (Doing something else) **(WRITE IN)**
    -      (Don't Know)
    0.7   (Refusal/NA)

        **ASK ALL WHOSE PARTNER IS NOT IN PAID WORK/WAITING
        TO TAKE UP WORK]**

Q868   *[SLastJob]*
        How long ago did your partner last have a paid job of at
        least 10 hours a week?
        GOVERNMENT PROGRAMS/SCHEMES DO NOT COUNT AS 'PAID JOBS'.
    %
    4.5   Within past 12 months
    8.7   Over 1, up to 5 years ago
    7.2   Over 5, up to 10 years ago
    9.1   Over 10, up to 20 years ago
    5.0   Over 20 years ago
    2.7   Never had a paid job of 10+ hours a week
    0.4   (Don't Know)
    0.7   (Refusal/NA)

ASK ALL WHOSE PARTNER HAS EVER WORKED   N=2313

Q869 [STitle]
IF IN PAID WORK: Now I want to ask you about your
partner's present job. What is (his/her) job? **PROBE IF
NECESSARY:** What is the name or title of the job?
IF WAITING TO TAKE UP PAID WORK: Now I want to ask you
about your partner's future job. What is (his/her) job?
PROBE IF NECESSARY: What is the name or title of the
job?
IF EVER HAD A JOB: Now I want to ask you about your
partner's last job. What was (his/her) job? **PROBE IF
NECESSARY:** What was the name or title of the job?
Open Question (Maximum of 80 characters)

Q870 [STypeWk]
What kind of work (does/will/did) (he/she) do most of
the time?
IF RELEVANT: What materials/machinery (does/will/did)
(he/she) use?
Open Question (Maximum of 80 characters)

Q871 [STrain]
What training or qualifications (are/were) needed for
that job?
Open Question (Maximum of 80 characters)

Q872 [Ssuper2]
(Does/Will/Did) your partner directly supervise or (does
he/she/will he/she be/was he/she) directly responsible
for the work of any other people?
%
37.8 Yes
60.4 No
0.4 (Don't Know)
1.3 (Refusal/NA)

IF 'Yes' AT [Super2]
Q873 [SMany]
How many?
Range: 0 ... 9997
% **Median (of those who supervise any): 6**
2.8 (Don't Know)
1.8 (Refusal/NA)

ASK ALL WHOSE PARTNER HAS EVER WORKED   N=2313

Q875 [SSupMan]
Can I just check, (is he/she/will he/she be/was he/she)
... **READ OUT** ...
%
21.0 ...a manager,
13.9 a foreman or supervisor,
63.4 or not?
0.3 (Don't Know)
1.3 (Refusal/NA)

Q876 [SEmploye]
In (his/her) (main) job (is he/she/will he/she be/was
he/she) ... **READ OUT** ...
%
84.8 ... an employee,
13.7 or self-employed?
0.2 (Don't Know)
1.3 (Refusal/NA)

ASK ALL WHOSE PARTNER IS/WAS EMPLOYEE   N=1997

Q878 [SOcSect]
CARD
Which of the types of organisation on this card (does
he/she work/will he/she be working/did he/she work) for?
%
63.8 Private sector firm or company (including limited
companies and PLCs)
3.5 Nationalised industry/public corporation
16.7 Local authority/Local Education Authority (including
'opted out' schools)
6.0 Health authority/NHS hospital/NHS Hospital Trust
(including GP surgeries)
5.0 Central government/Civil service/Government Agency
1.6 Charity/Voluntary sector (including charitable
companies)
1.3 Other answer (WRITE IN)
0.4 (Don't Know)
1.8 (Refusal/NA)

ASK ALL WHOSE PARTNER HAS EVER WORKED   N=2313

Q880 [SEmpMake]
What (does/did) (his/her) employer (IF SELF-EMPLOYED:
(he/she)) make or do at the place where (he/she)
(works/will work/worked) (from)?
Open Question (Maximum of 80 characters)

Q885   [SEmpWork]   N=2313
Including (himself/herself), how many people (are/were) employed at the place where (he/she) usually (works/will work/worked) (from)? (IF SELF-EMPLOYED: (works/will (he/she) have any employees?
IF YES: PROBE FOR CORRECT PRECODE.
%
8.0 None
18.2 Under 10
13.8 10-24
20.6 25-99
19.1 100-499
14.2 500 or more
4.8 (Don't Know)
1.3 (Refusal/NA)

Q896   [SPartFul]
(Is the job/Was the job/Will the job be) ... READ OUT
%
77.1 ... full-time - that is, 30 or more hours per week,
21.4 or, part-time
0.2 (Don't Know)
1.3 (Refusal/NA)

VERSION A AND C: ASK ALL (On Version B derived from [TransCar] Q627]
N=3620

Q925   [CarOwn]
Do you, or does anyone else in your household, own or have the regular use of a car or van?
%
77.5 Yes
21.9 No
0.0 (Don't Know)
0.6 (Refusal/NA)

ASK ALL
Q926   [AnyBn2]
CARD
Do you (or your husband/wife/partner) receive any of the state benefits on this card at present?
%
61.8 Yes
37.3 No
0.0 (Don't Know)
0.9 (Refusal/NA)

111

N=3620

IF 'Yes' AT [AnyBn2]

Q927   [BenftNFW]
CARD AGAIN
Which ones? PROBE: Any others?
% Multicoded (Maximum of 16 codes)
21.6 Retirement pension (National Insurance)   [BenefOAP]
1.0 War Pension (War Disablement Pension or War Widow's Pension)   [BenefWar]
1.3 Widow's Benefits (Widow's Pension and Widowed Mother's Allowance)   [BenefWid]
3.5 Unemployment Benefit/Income Support for the Unemployed (Jobseekers Allowance)   [BenefUB]
8.2 Income Support (other than for unemployment)   [BenefIS]
28.7 Child Benefit (formerly Family Allowance)   [BenefCB]
2.3 One Parent Benefit   [BenefOP]
2.1 Family Credit   [BenefFC]
9.6 Housing Benefit (Rent Rebate)   [BenefHB]
11.3 Council Tax Benefit (or Rebate) (formerly Community Charge/Poll Tax Benefit)   [BenefCT]
6.4 Incapacity Benefit/Sickness Benefit/Invalidity Benefit   [BenefInc]
3.7 Disability Living Allowance   [BenefDLA]
1.9 Attendance Allowance   [BenefAtA]
0.8 Severe Disablement Allowance   [BenefSev]
1.0 Invalid Care Allowance   [BenefICA]
0.4 Other state benefit (WRITE IN)   [BenefOth]
0.0 (Don't Know)
0.9 (Refusal/NA)

ASK ALL
Q930   [MainInc]
CARD
Which of these is the main source of income for you (and your husband/wife/partner) at present?
%
60.8 Earnings from employment (own or spouse/partner's)
7.9 Occupational pension(s) - from previous employer(s)
13.8 State retirement or widow's pension(s)
1.6 Unemployment benefit
6.5 Income Support
0.4 Family Credit
3.7 Invalidity, sickness or disabled pension or benefit(s)
0.0 Other state benefit (WRITE IN)
1.1 Interest from savings or investments
1.2 Student grant
1.5 Dependent on parents/other relatives
0.5 Other main source (WRITE IN)
0.1 (Don't Know)
1.0 (Refusal/NA)

112

ASK ALL

Q933 [HHIncome]
CARD   N=3620

Which of the letters on this card represents the total income of your household from all sources **before tax**? Please just tell me the letter.

NOTE: INCLUDES INCOME FROM BENEFITS, SAVINGS, ETC.

ASK ALL IN PAID WORK

Q934 [REarn]   N=1967
CARD AGAIN

Which of the letters on this card represents your **own** gross or total **earnings**, before deduction of income tax and national insurance.

	[HHIncome]	[REarn]
	%	%
Q Less than £3,999	5.2	8.3
T £4,000-£5,000	8.9	7.3
O £6,000-£7,999	7.5	8.5
K £8,000-£9,999	5.2	9.1
L £10,000-£11,999	6.2	9.6
B £12,000-£14,999	6.8	10.4
Z £15,000-£17,999	6.4	11.2
M £18,000-£19,999	4.8	5.6
F £20,000-£22,999	5.5	6.5
J £23,000-£25,999	4.9	4.7
D £26,000-£28,999	4.7	3.2
H £29,000-£31,999	3.7	2.3
C £32,000-£34,999	3.2	1.3
G £35,000-£37,999	2.4	0.9
P £38,000-£40,999	2.1	0.8
N £41,000 or more	8.5	3.6
(Don't Know)	9.9	2.8
(Refusal/NA)	4.0	3.9

ASK ALL

Q935 [OwnShare]   N=3620

Do you (or does your husband/wife/partner) own any shares quoted on the Stock Exchange, including unit trusts?

%
24.0 Yes
74.8 No
0.3 (Don't Know)
0.9 (Refusal/NA)

Q936 [FagsNow2]   N=3620

% Do you yourself ever smoke cigarettes?
29.8 Yes
69.4 No
0.0 (Don't Know)
0.7 (Refusal/NA)

IF 'Yes' AT [FagsNow2]

Q937 [SmokDay]

About how many cigarettes a day do you usually smoke?
IF 'CAN'T SAY', CODE 997
Range: 0 ... 997
Median: 15 cigarettes
%
0.6 (Don't know/Can't say)
0.8 (Refusal/NA)

N=3620

ADMINISTRATION

ASK ALL

Q939 [PhoneX]
Is there a telephone in (your part of) this accommodation?

%
94.4 Yes
5.1 No
- (Don't Know)
0.6 (Refusal/NA)

IF 'Yes' AT [PhoneX]

Q940 [PhoneBck]
Some of my interviews are checked. May I take your 'phone number for that purpose?
ADD IF NECESSARY: Your 'phone number will **not** be passed to anyone outside SCPR.
IF NUMBER GIVEN, WRITE ON ARF – DO NOT KEY IT IN!

%
85.6 Number given
8.8 Number refused
- (Don't Know)
0.6 (Refusal/NA)

ASK ALL

Q941 [ComBacPh]
Sometime in the next year, we may be doing a short follow up survey (**if on the telephone:**on the telephone) and might wish to contact you again. Would this be all right?
DO NOT PROMPT ABOUT USE OF TELEPHONE. USE CODE 2 ONLY IF ANSWER VOLUNTEERED BY RESPONDENT.

%
81.2 Yes
5.7 (Yes – but not on the telephone)
12.2 No
0.2 (Don't Know)
0.7 (Refusal/NA)

N=3620

IF 'Yes' OR 'Yes – but not on the telephone' AT [ComBacPh]

Q942 [Stable]
Suppose we call (**if not on the telephone:** on) you again and for some reason cannot get in touch with you. Is there another address or 'phone number you could give us of someone who would know your whereabouts?
IF NECESSARY, PROMPT: Perhaps the address of a relative or friend who is unlikely to move.
IF GIVEN, RECORD ALL INFORMATION ON BACK PAGE OF ARF AT Q.42
IF RESPONDENT SAYS THEY WILL BE MOVING, RECORD FUTURE ADDRESS IN BOX ON ARF FOR ADDITIONAL INFORMATION.

%
27.5 Information given
59.3 Information not given
- (Don't Know)
0.9 (Refusal/NA)

ASK ALL

Q943 [SCXplain]
INTERVIEWER: THANK RESPONDENT FOR (HIS/HER) HELP AND EXPLAIN ABOUT THE SELF-COMPLETION QUESTIONNAIRE.
PLEASE MAKE SURE YOU GIVE THE RESPONDENT THE (GREEN VERSION A/BLUE VERSION B/ORANGE VERSION C) QUESTIONNAIRE
THEN TELL US WHETHER IT IS TO BE ...

%
14.3 ... filled in immediately after interview in your presence,
77.9 or, left behind to be filled in later,
7.2 or, if the respondent refused.
- (Don't Know)
0.7 (Refusal/NA)

Q944 [SelfComp] (NOT ON SCREEN)
Status of self-completion
Range: 0 ... 97

%
14.3 Not returned
85.7 Returned

Q947 [DateInt]
PLEASE TYPE IN DATE OF INTERVIEW
Date

N=1235

COUNTRYSIDE (VERSION B)

VERSION B: ASK ALL

Q608 *[Outing]*
Now some questions about the countryside.
Have you yourself visited the countryside or coast **in the past year**, for an outing of some sort, like a drive, a walk or a picnic, or to do something else?
IF 'Yes', PROBE: Was that just once, or twice or more?

%
9.6 Yes, once
76.2 Yes, twice or more
14.0 No
- (Don't Know)
0.2 (Refusal/NA)

IF 'Yes, once' OR 'Yes, twice or more' AT [Outing]

Q609 *[OutInCar]*
When you visited the countryside in the past year, did you **usually** spend... **READ OUT** ...

%
1.5 ...all the time in the car,
3.3 almost all of the time,
28.3 only some of the time,
41.6 very little of the time,
10.7 or, did you not use a car at all?
0.3 (Depends)
- (Don't Know)
0.3 (Refusal/NA)

VERSION B: ASK ALL

Q610 *[CtrySame]*
Do you think the countryside **generally** is much the same as it was twenty years ago, or do you think it has changed?
IF CHANGED: Has it changed a bit or a lot?

%
22.3 Much the same
26.5 Changed a bit
44.6 Changed a lot
6.3 (Don't Know)
0.3 (Refusal/NA)

N=1235

IF 'Changed a bit' OR 'Changed a lot' AT [CtrySame]

Q611 *[CtryBetr]*
Do you think the countryside *generally* has changed for the better or worse?

%
12.3 Better
47.3 Worse
10.5 (Better in some ways/worse in others)
0.9 (Don't Know)
6.6 (Refusal/NA)

VERSION B: ASK ALL

Q612 *[CtryConc]*
Are you personally concerned about things that may happen to the countryside, or does it not concern you particularly?
IF CONCERNED: Are you very concerned, or just a bit concerned?

%
42.8 Very concerned
34.7 A bit concerned
22.1 Does not concern me particularly
0.2 (Don't Know)
0.2 (Refusal/NA)

Q613 *[CThtNew1]*
CARD
Which, if any, of the things on this card do you think is the **greatest threat** to the countryside; if you think none of them is a threat, please say so.

IF ANSWER GIVEN AT [CThtNew1]

Q615 *[CThtNew2]*
CARD AGAIN
And which do you think is the **next greatest** threat?

N=1235

	[AreaChng]	[AreaFut]
	%	%
Litter and fly-tipping of rubbish	14.4	10.1
New housing and urban sprawl	15.0	12.9
Superstores and out-of-town shopping centres	5.3	9.0
Building new roads and motorways	17.1	16.0
Industrial development like factories, quarries and power stations	10.0	13.4
Land and air pollution, or discharges into rivers and lakes	27.9	21.9
Changes to traditional ways of farming and of using farmland	2.6	6.3
Changes to the ordinary natural appearance of the countryside, including plants and wildlife	2.4	3.9
The number of tourists and visitors in the countryside	2.1	1.8
Other answer	0.6	0.4
(None of these)	1.3	0.7
(Don't Know)	1.2	0.7
(Refusal/NA)	0.2	2.8

VERSION B: ASK ALL

Q617 [FactWste]
Suppose it is discovered that some of a factory's waste has begun leaking into a nearby river. Should the factory ... **READ OUT** ...

%
5.7 ...just be asked to do something about it,
40.6 or, should it be *heavily fined for every week it continues,*
53.1 or, should it be shut down unless it does something about it?

0.3 (Don't Know)
0.3 (Refusal/NA)

Q618 [PollPays]
Do you think the government should ... **READ OUT** ...

%
20.2 ...help factories meet the cost of preventing pollution,
77.9 or, should those factories that cause pollution be made to pay the bills themselves?

1.6 (Don't Know)
0.3 (Refusal/NA)

N=1235

Q619 [CtryPay1]
CARD
Looking after the countryside costs a great deal of money.
From the groups on this card, please say which should have the **most** responsibility for footing the bill, and which the **next most**.
First, the **most** responsibility.

IF ANSWER GIVEN AT [CtryPay1]
Q620 [CtryPay2]
CARD AGAIN
And which one do you feel should have the *next most* responsibility?

	[CtryPay1]	[CtryPay2t]
	%	%
General public	44.3	14.4
Everyone who lives in	10.9	11.2
Visitors and holiday	8.3	21.1
The farming community	5.6	12.1
Other businesses	25.4	31.5
None of these	2.2	3.5
(Don't Know)	3.0	0.9
(Refusal/NA)	0.3	5.5

Q621 [EnvirPty]
VERSION B: ASK ALL
Which political party's views on the environment would you say comes *closest* to your own views?
DO NOT PROMPT

%
11.2 Conservative
14.0 Labour
11.0 Liberal Democrat
14.2 Green Party
8.9 (None)
0.9 Other answer **(WRITE IN)**
39.5 (Don't Know)
0.4 (Refusal/NA)

N=1235

Q623 [ResPres]
Can I just check, would you describe the place where you live as ... **READ OUT** ...
%
6.8 ...a big city,
26.5 the suburbs or outskirts of a big city,
44.8 a small city or town,
17.9 a country village,
3.6 or, a farm or home in the country?
0.1 (Other answer (**WRITE IN**))
.0.1 (Don't Know)
0.3 (Refusal/NA)

N=1235

TRANSPORT (VERSION B)

VERSION B: ASK ALL

Q626 [MotorVPT]
If over the next few years the government **had to** choose, to which should it give greater priority ...**READ OUT** ...
%
15.1 ...the needs of motorists,
73.4 or, the needs of public transport users?
3.2 (Neither)
6.8 (Both)
1.3 (Don't Know)
0.3 (Refusal/NA)

Q627 [TransCar]
(May I just check...) ... do you, or does anyone in your household, own or have the regular use of a car or a van?
IF 'YES' PROBE FOR WHETHER RESPONDENT, OR OTHER PERSON(S) ONLY, OR BOTH
%
25.9 Yes, respondent only
19.2 Yes, other(s) only
33.0 Yes, both
21.7 No
- (Don't Know)
0.2 (Refusal/NA)

IF YES AT [TransCar]
Q628 [NumbCars]
How many vehicles in all?
%
44.0 One
27.5 Two
4.7 Three
1.3 Four
0.6 Five or more
- (Don't Know)
0.2 (Refusal/NA)

Q629 [CompCar]
Is the vehicle (Are any of these vehicles) provided by an employer or run as a business expense?
%
61.1 No
15.0 Yes, one (of them)
1.5 Yes, two (of them)
0.6 Yes, three or more (of them)
- (Don't Know)
0.2 (Refusal/NA)

N=1235

Q630 **IF 'Yes, respondent only' OR 'Yes, both' AT [TransCar]**
[NCarIncv]
If for some reason you could no longer have the use of a car (or a van), would you find it **really** inconvenient

%   ... **READ OUT** ...
34.6 ... more or less every day of your life,
14.0 several times a week,
3.9   several times a month,
4.3   only occasionally,
2.2   or - would you never **really** find it inconvenient?
-     (Don't Know)
0.2   (Refusal/NA)

IF WOULD EVER FIND IT INCONVENIENT AT [NCarIncv]
Q631 [NCarPtr]
Now, suppose that public transport in your area were better or less expensive. Do you think you would then use a car (or a van) as much as now, or might you use it less?

IF 'LESS': Would that be much less or a bit less?
%
30.5 Use it as much as now
18.1 Use it a bit less
7.7   Use it much less
0.4   (Don't Know)
0.2   (Refusal/NA)

IF YES AT [TransCar]
Q632 [GetAbou1]
CARD
I am going to read out some of the things that might get people to **cut down** on the number of car journeys they take.

For each one, please tell me what effect, if any, this might have on how much **you yourself** use the car to get about.

...gradually doubling the cost of petrol over the next ten years?

Q633 [GetAbou2]
CARD AGAIN
(What effect, if any, might this have on how much you yourself use the car?)
...greatly improving **long distance** rail and coach services?

N=1235

Q634 [GetAbou3]
CARD AGAIN
(What effect, if any, might this have on how much you yourself use the car?)
...greatly improving the reliability of **local** public transport?

Q635 [GetAbou4]
CARD AGAIN
(What effect, if any, might this have on how much you yourself use the car?)
...charging all motorists around £2 each time they enter or drive through a city or town centre at peak times?

Q636 [GetAbou5]
CARD AGAIN
(What effect, if any, might this have on how much you yourself use the car?)
...charging £1 for every 50 miles motorists travel on motorways?

Q637 [GetAbou6]
CARD AGAIN
(What effect, if any, might this have on how much you yourself use the car?)
...making parking penalties and restrictions much more severe?

Q638 [GetAbou7]
CARD AGAIN
(What effect, if any, might this have on how much you yourself use the car?)
...special cycle lanes on roads around here?

IF YES AT [TransCar] AND RESPONDENT HAS CHILDREN AGED BETWEEN 4 AND 15
Q639 [GetAbou8]
CARD AGAIN
(What effect, if any, might this have on how much you yourself use the car?)
...a free school bus service for your children?

N=1235

	[GetAbou1] %	[GetAbou2] %	[GetAbou3] %	[GetAbou4] %	[GetAbou5] %	[GetAbou6] %	[GetAbou7] %	[GetAbou8] %
Might use cars even more	1.3	0.8	0.8	0.4	-	0.4	0.4	0.1
Might use car little less	23.2	18.5	20.5	14.9	16.5	12.5	9.5	1.4
Might use car quite bit less	18.4	14.8	17.1	20.6	12.0	12.7	7.8	2.3
Might give up using car	5.0	3.2	5.0	6.8	5.2	3.6	2.6	1.3
It would make no difference	30.0	40.7	34.5	35.0	43.9	48.4	57.6	10.9
(Don't Know)	0.2	0.1	0.1	0.4	0.5	0.5	0.2	0.1
(Refusal/NA)	0.2	0.2	0.2	0.2	0.2	0.2	0.2	0.3

N=1235

IF YES AT [TransCar]

Q640   [TraNear1]
CARD

Suppose you had to get somewhere in this neighbourhood, say within a mile or two of your home, how would you **normally** get there?

IF 2+ WAYS GIVEN, PROBE FOR THE ONE USED FOR THE LONGEST DISTANCE

%
1.8 By taxi or mini-cab
41.4 By car on my own
5.4 By car as a passenger
0.2 By motorbike, moped or motor scooter
0.5 By train, tube or metro
4.5 By bus
3.9 By cycle
19.8 By foot
0.1 By another way (**PLEASE SAY WHAT**)
0.3 (Varies too much to say)
0.2 I never go out these days
- (Don't Know)
0.2 (Refusal/NA)

IF MODE OF TRANSPORT GIVEN AT [TraNear1]

Q642   [TraNear2]
CARD AGAIN

Just suppose you could not go (answer given at [TraNear1] how do you think you would have got there?

%
9.9 By taxi or mini-cab
10.8 By car on my own
10.2 By car as a passenger
0.6 By motorbike, moped or motor scooter
0.5 By train, tube or metro
12.5 By bus
9.0 By cycle
22.9 By foot
0.4 By another way (**PLEASE SAY WHAT**)
0.8 (Don't Know)
0.7 (Refusal/NA)

VERSION B: ASK ALL

Q644   [Drive]

May I just check, do **you yourself** drive a car at all these days?

%
65.4 Yes
34.4 No
- (Don't Know)
0.2 (Refusal/NA)

N=1235

N=1235

IF 'Yes' AT [Drive]

Q645 [Travel1]
CARD
How often nowadays do you **usually** travel
..by car as a driver?

VERSION B: ASK ALL

Q646 [Travel2]
CARD AGAIN
(How often nowadays do you **usually**...)
..travel by car as a passenger?

Q647 [Travel3]
CARD AGAIN
(How often nowadays do you **usually**...)
..travel by local bus?

Q648 [Travel4]
CARD AGAIN
(How often nowadays do you **usually**...)
..travel by train?

Q649 [Travel6]
CARD AGAIN
(How often nowadays do you **usually**...)
..travel by bicycle?

Q650 [Travel9]
CARD AGAIN
(How often nowadays do you **usually**...)
..go somewhere on foot at least 15 minutes' walk away?

	Travel1	2	3	4	6	9
	%	%	%	%	%	%
Everyday or nearly every day	41.8	9.1	7.4	3.2	3.7	34.0
2-5 days a week	14.4	23.8	10.7	2.4	3.7	24.4
Once a week	5.9	23.5	10.5	2.3	4.7	15.7
Less often than that but at least once a month	1.0	16.0	9.7	9.4	4.2	6.5
Less often than that	1.5	13.6	16.0	31.5	7.5	5.1
Never nowadays	0.9	13.7	45.5	51.0	75.9	14.1
(Don't Know)	-	-	-	-	-	-
(Refusal/NA)	0.2	0.3	0.3	0.3	0.3	0.3

PUBLIC UNDERSTANDING OF SCIENCE (VERSION B AND C)

N=2449

VERSIONS B AND C: ASK ALL

Q753 [SportNw]
I am going to ask about which issues in the news interest you. For each issue I read out, please tell me whether you are very interested, moderately interested, or not at all interested in it?
Sports in the news - are you very interested, moderately interested, or not at all interested in it?

Q754 [PolitNw]
Politics (- are you very interested, moderately interested, or not at all interested in it)?

Q755 [MedicNw]
New medical discoveries - are you very interested, moderately interested, or not at all interested in them?

Q756 [FilmNw]
New films - are you very interested, moderately interested, or not at all interested in them?

Q757 [InvenNw]
New inventions and technologies - are you very interested, moderately interested, or not at all interested in them?

Q758 [DiscNw]
New scientific discoveries - are you very interested, moderately interested, or not at all interested in them?

Q753-758	[SportNw]	[PolitNw]	[MedicNw]
	%	%	%
Very interested	29.0	15.7	43.8
Moderately interested	37.2	52.2	45.8
Not at all interested	33.5	31.7	10.0
(Don't Know)	0.1	0.1	0.2
(Refusal/NA)	0.3	0.3	0.3

	[FilmNw]	[InvenNw]	[DiscNw]
	%	%	%
Very interested	16.4	34.6	35.7
Moderately interested	43.2	47.8	45.8
Not at all interested	40.0	17.2	18.0
(Don't Know)	0.1	0.2	0.3
(Refusal/NA)	0.3	0.3	0.3

N=2449

Q759 [NaturTV]
If there was a nature programme on television about **animals and wildlife**, would you ... **READ OUT** ...

Q760 [StarTV]
And how about a programme about **stars and planets**, would you ... **READ OUT** ...

Q761 [InvenTV]
And how about a programme about **new inventions and technology**, would you ... **READ OUT** ...

Q762 [MedicTV]
And how about a programme about **advances in medicine**, would you ... **READ OUT** ...

	[NaturTV]	[StarTV]
	%	%
Special watch it	53.3	20.2
Nothing better	34.2	28.1
Tend not to watch it	11.2	50.4
Never watches TV	0.8	0.9
(Don't Know)	0.2	0.1
(Refusal/NA)	0.3	0.3

	[InvenTV]	[MedicTV]
	%	%
Special watch it	32.7	46.6
Nothing better	41.3	34.7
Tend not to watch it	24.7	17.3
Never watches TV	0.8	0.8
(Don't Know)	0.2	0.4
(Refusal/NA)	0.3	0.3

N=2449

Q763 **CARD**
Suppose you were advising a 16 year old who had just got good grades in their GCSEs and was considering what to study for A-level. Which **three** subjects on this card would you advise them to study for A-levels to give them the best career prospects?
PROBE: Any others?
CODE UP TO THREE

%		
54.4	Multicoded (Maximum of 3 codes)	
	English	[ALevEngl]
66.9	Mathematics	[ALevMath]
3.2	History	[ALevHist]
3.4	Geography	[ALevGeog]
15.1	French	[ALevFren]
9.2	German	[ALevGerm]
24.3	Economics	[ALevEcon]
4.9	Biology	[ALevBiol]
13.4	Physics	[ALevPhys]
8.3	Chemistry	[ALevChem]
63.0	Computer studies	[ALevComp]
17.6	Design and technology	[ALevDesi]
0.1	(Would not advise them to study for A-levels)	[ALevNone]
3.0	(Other answer/other subject(s)) **(WRITE IN)**	[ALevOth]
2.9	(Don't Know)	
0.3	(Refusal/NA)	

Q766 [ZooVst]
In the last 12 months, how many times have you done each of the following ...
... visited a zoo, aquarium, safari park or wildlife park?
INCLUDE BOTH EVENTS ATTENDED AS LEISURE PURSUITS AND EVENTS ATTENDED FOR WORK.
PROBE FOR CORRECT PRECODE

Q767 [MuseVst]
(In the last 12 months, how many times have you ...)
... visited a science, technology or natural history museum or science centre?
INCLUDE BOTH EVENTS ATTENDED AS LEISURE PURSUITS AND EVENTS ATTENDED FOR WORK.
PROBE FOR CORRECT PRECODE

N=2449

Q768 [LectVst]
(In the last 12 months, how many times have you ...)
...attended a science festival or a lecture or evening
class on a scientific subject?
INCLUDE BOTH EVENTS ATTENDED AS LEISURE PURSUITS AND
EVENTS ATTENDED FOR WORK.
PROBE FOR CORRECT PRECODE

Q769 [FairVst]
(In the last 12 months, how many times have you ...)
... attended a technological, computer or electronic
show or fair?
INCLUDE BOTH EVENTS ATTENDED AS LEISURE PURSUITS AND
EVENTS ATTENDED FOR WORK.
PROBE FOR CORRECT PRECODE

	[ZooVst]	[MuseVst]
	%	%
Never	67.0	75.6
Once or twice	25.6	20.8
Three or more times	7.0	3.2
(Don't Know)	0.1	0.1
(Refusal/NA)	0.3	0.3

	[LectVst]	[FairVst]
	%	%
Never	91.1	87.8
Once or twice	5.2	9.4
Three or more times	3.3	2.4
(Don't Know)	0.1	0.1
(Refusal/NA)	0.3	0.3

N=2449

Q770 [WhatSci]
Some news stories talk about the results of a
'scientific study'. When you read or hear this term,
can you tell me in your own words what you think it
means to study something scientifically?
RECORD FULLY.
PROBE IF NECESSARY: Could you explain more about that?
IF NECESSARY, USE <CTRL + F4> TO OPEN A NOTE TO CONTINUE
THE ANSWER

% Open Question (Maximum of 120 characters) coded as -
2.8 Theory construction and testing
15.3 To undertake tests/experiments
13.4 Open-minded, rational in-depth explorations of
phenomena/problem to be examined
4.0 To measure or classify but no mention of any rigour in
process
38.9 Other answers
25.0 (Don't know)
0.6 (Refusal/NA)

Q772 [LifeBet]
CARD
I have here a list of statements. For each one, use
this card to tell me how much you agree or disagree with
it.
Science and technology are making our lives healthier,
easier and more comfortable.

Q773 [DepSci]
CARD AGAIN
(Please tell me how much you agree or disagree with this
statement)
We depend too much on science and not enough on faith.

Q774 [BenfSci]
CARD AGAIN
(Please tell me how much you agree or disagree with this
statement)
The benefits of science are greater than any harmful
effects.

Q775 [TooFast]
CARD AGAIN
(Please tell me how much you agree or disagree with this
statement)
Science makes our way of life change too fast.

N=2449

Q776 [SciNImp]
CARD AGAIN
(Please tell me how much you agree or disagree with this statement)
It is **not** important for me to know about science in my daily life.

	[LifeBet]	[DepSciI]	[BenfSci]
	%	%	%
Agree strongly	27.7	11.1	12.5
Agree slightly	45.1	29.1	32.3
Neither	17.7	25.5	25.7
Disagree slightly	5.8	19.8	20.0
Disagree strongly	1.7	12.1	5.5
(Don't Know)	1.4	1.9	3.5
(Refusal/NA)	0.5	0.5	0.5

	[Toofast]	[SciNImp]
	%	%
Agree strongly	16.5	10.2
Agree slightly	36.0	21.7
Neither	20.5	14.8
Disagree slightly	18.9	31.4
Disagree strongly	5.7	20.4
(Don't Know)	2.6	1.0
(Refusal/NA)	0.5	0.5

Q777 [Horoscop]
Do you read a horoscope or a personal astrology report ... **READ OUT** ....
%
15.9 ...often,
17.1 fairly often,
28.4 rarely,
38.0 or, never?
0.2 (Don't Know)
0.5 (Refusal/NA)

IF EVER READ A HOROSCOPE
Q778 [HoroSer]
How seriously do you take what they say ... **READ OUT** ....
%
0.9 ...very seriously,
3.0 seriously,
57.4 or, not very seriously?
- (Don't Know)
0.6 (Refusal/NA)

N=2449

VERSIONS B AND C: ASK ALL
Q779 [DrugTest]
CARD
Suppose a drug used to treat high blood pressure is suspected of not working well. On this card are three different ways scientists might use to investigate the problem. Which **one** do you think scientists would be most likely to use?
%
15.6 Talk to patients to get their opinions
23.5 Use their knowledge of medicine to decide how good the drug is
57.0 Give the drug to some patients but not to others. Then compare what happens to each group.
3.3 (Don't Know)
0.5 (Refusal/NA)

Q780 [SciQuiz1]
Here is a quick quiz. For each thing I say, tell me if it is **true** or **false**. If you don't know, say so and we will skip to the next.
The centre of the earth is very hot.

Q781 [SciQuiz2]
Lasers work by focusing sound waves.
(Is that true or false - or don't you know?)

Q782 [SciQuiz3]
It is the father's gene which decides whether the baby is a boy or a girl.
(Is that true or false - or don't you know?)

Q783 [SciQuiz4]
Antibiotics kill viruses as well as bacteria.
(Is that true or false - or don't you know?)

	[SciQuiz1]	[SciQuiz2]
	%	%
True	87.0	21.8
False	5.6	53.4
(Don't Know)	6.9	24.2
(Refusal/NA)	0.5	0.6

	[SciQuiz3]	[SciQuiz4]
	%	%
True	53.4	42.6
False	27.8	45.7
(Don't Know)	18.3	11.1
(Refusal/NA)	0.5	0.6

N=2449

Q784 [SciQuiz5] Does the ... **READ OUT** ...
%
66.3 ...earth go round the sun
24.1 or, the sun around the earth?
9.1 (Don't Know)
0.5 (Refusal/NA)

Q785 [SciQuiz6]
Here is a statement about which people disagree.
Human beings as we know them today developed from
earlier species of animals - would you say this was
... **READ OUT** ...
%
31.4 ...definitely true,
50.1 probably true,
8.1 probably untrue,
7.7 or, definitely untrue?
2.3 (Don't Know)
0.5 (Refusal/NA)

Q786 [SciQuiz7]
When scientists use the term DNA, do you think it is to
do with the study of ... **READ OUT** ...
%
0.5 ...stars,
0.9 rocks,
83.0 living things,
4.0 or, computers?
11.1 (Don't Know)
0.5 (Refusal/NA)

Q787 [SciSpend]
Who do you think spends most on scientific research in
this country ... **READ OUT** ...
%
19.7 ... the government,
52.4 industry,
19.2 or, charities and foundations?
8.2 (Don't Know)
0.7 (Refusal/NA)

Q788 [Probab1]
CARD
Doctors tell a couple that their genetic make-up means
that they've got a one in four chance of having a child
with an inherited illness. Does this mean that ... **READ
OUT** ...
...If they have only three children, none will have the
illness?

N=2449

Q789 [Probab2]
CARD AGAIN
(Doctors tell a couple that their genetic make-up means
that they've got a one in four chance of having a child
with an inherited illness. Does this mean that ... **READ
OUT** ...)
If their first child has the illness, the next three
will not?

Q790 [Probab3]
CARD AGAIN
(Doctors tell a couple that their genetic make-up means
that they've got a one in four chance of having a child
with an inherited illness. Does this mean that ... **READ
OUT** ...)
Each of the couple's children has the same risk of
suffering from the illness?

Q791 [Probab4]
CARD AGAIN
(Doctors tell a couple that their genetic make-up means
that they've got a one in four chance of having a child
with an inherited illness. Does this mean that ... **READ
OUT** ...)
If their first three children are healthy, the fourth
will have the illness?

	[Probab1]	[Probab2]
	%	%
Yes	4.6	7.2
No	87.5	85.5
(Don't Know)	7.4	6.8
(Refusal/NA)	0.5	0.6

	[Probab3]	[Probab4]
	%	%
Yes	83.4	7.9
No	9.6	84.6
(Don't Know)	6.6	7.0
(Refusal/NA)	0.5	0.5

N=2449

Q792 [BSEDisag]
CARD
Scientists disagree about whether the presence of 'mad cow disease' - BSE - makes it dangerous for people to eat British beef. Which of the reasons on this card do you think is the most likely reason why they disagree?

%
59.6 No one has all the facts
26.9 Scientists interpret the facts using different theories
5.0 Scientists have different political beliefs
5.5 Scientists have different personal and career interests
2.4 (Don't Know)
0.6 (Refusal/NA)

Q793 [BSEConfM]
CARD
If each of the people on this card made a statement about mad cow disease - BSE - who would you have **most** confidence in?

Q794 **IF ANSWER GIVEN AT [BSEConfM] (I.E. NOT 'None of these')**
[BSEConfN]
CARD AGAIN
(And if each of the people on this card made a statement about mad cow disease - BSE - ....)
...who would you have **next most** confidence in?

VERSIONS B AND C: ASK ALL
Q795 [BSEConfL]
CARD AGAIN
(And if each of the people on this card made a statement about mad cow disease - BSE - ....)
...who would you have **least** confidence in?

N=2449

	[BSEConfM]	[BSEConfN]	[BSEConfL]
	%	%	%
A scientist in a government department	4.6	11.3	26.4
A scientist in a consumer organisation	18.0	35.4	1.5
A scientist in a university	42.0	23.0	0.5
A scientist in the meat industry	26.7	8.8	13.5
A scientist writing in a newspaper	0.9	10.1	2.4
A journalist writing in a newspaper	0.4	1.1	52.0
(None of these)	4.5	2.0	1.0
(Don't Know)	2.3	3.0	2.1
(Refusal/NA)	0.6	5.2	0.6

Q796 [NucDisag]
CARD
Scientists also disagree about whether nuclear power stations pose a threat to the people living around them. Which of the reasons on this card do you think is the most likely reason why they disagree?

%
40.7 No one has all the facts
33.9 Scientists interpret the facts using different theories
8.8 Scientists have different political beliefs
12.4 Scientists have different personal and career interests
3.6 (Don't Know)
0.6 (Refusal/NA)

Q797 [NucConfM]
CARD
If each of the people on this card made a statement about the safety of nuclear power stations, who would you have **most** confidence in?

Q798 **IF ANSWER GIVEN AT [NucConfM] (I.E. NOT 'None of these')**
[NucConfN]
CARD AGAIN
(And if each of the people on this card made a statement about the safety of nuclear power stations ....)
...who would you have **next most** confidence in?

VERSIONS B AND C: ASK ALL   N=2449

Q799 [NucConfL]
CARD AGAIN
(And if each of the people on this card made a statement about the saftey of nuclear power stations ...)
...who would you have **least** confidence in?

	[NucConfM]	[NucConfN]	[NucConfL]
	%	%	%
A scientist in a government department	4.5	13.6	20.6
A scientist in an environ-mental campaign group	21.0	26.9	2.8
A scientist in a university	43.2	23.7	0.3
A scientist in the nuclear power industry	22.9	12.7	16.4
A scientist writing in a newspaper	1.4	11.6	2.0
A journalist writing in a newspaper	0.3	1.1	53.2
(None of these)	3.1	2.3	1.0
(Don't Know)	3.0	4.3	3.0
(Refusal/NA)	0.6	3.7	0.6

EDUCATION (VERSION C)   N=1214

VERSION C: ASK ALL

Q652 [EdSpend1]
CARD
Now some questions about education.
Which of the groups on this card, if any, would be your highest priority for extra government spending on education?

IF ANSWER GIVEN AT [EdSpend1]
Q653 [EdSpend2]
CARD AGAIN
And which is your next highest priority?

	[EdSpend1]	[EdSpend2]
	%	%
Nursery or pre-school children	17.4	11.0
Primary school children	21.4	24.5
Secondary school choldren	25.4	25.7
Less able children with special needs	21.2	20.7
Students at colleges or universities	10.6	13.1
(None of these)	1.3	0.5
(Don't Know)	2.8	0.3
(Refusal/NA)	-	4.1

VERSION C: ASK ALL

Q654 *[PrimImp1]*

CARD

Here are a number of things that some people think would improve education in our schools.

Which do you think would be the *most* useful one for improving the education of children in *primary* schools - aged 5-11 years? Please look at the whole list before deciding.

IF ANSWER GIVEN AT [PrimImp1]

Q656 *[PrimImp2]*

CARD AGAIN

And which do you think would be the *next* most useful one for children in *primary* schools?

	[PrimImp1] %	[PrimImp2] %
More information available about individual schools	1.1	0.7
More links between parents and schools	6.5	9.9
More resources for buildings, books and equipment	20.6	23.8
Better quality teachers	19.0	13.5
Smaller class sizes	34.6	19.3
More emphasis on exams and tests	1.1	2.7
More emphasis on developing the child's skills and interests	11.7	23.2
Better leadership within individual schools	1.7	3.3
Other **(WRITE IN)**	1.1	0.2
(Don't Know)	2.5	0.7
(Refusal/NA)	0.1	2.7

VERSION C: ASK ALL

Q658 *[SecImp1]*

CARD

And which do you think would be the *most* useful thing for improving the education of children in *secondary* schools - aged 11-18 years?

IF ANSWER GIVEN AT [SecImp1]

Q660 *[SecImp2]*

CARD AGAIN

And which do you think would be the *next* most useful one for children in *secondary* schools?

	[SecImp1] %	[Sec Imp2] %
More information available about individual schools	1.0	0.5
More links between parents and schools	3.3	5.3
More resources for buildings, books and equipment	20.8	16.4
Better quality teachers	21.0	14.8
Smaller class sizes	21.0	14.6
More emphasis on exams and tests	5.0	5.4
More emphasis on developing the child's skills and interests	9.8	15.2
More training and preparation for jobs	13.1	21.7
Better leadership within individual schools	2.0	2.7
Other **(WRITE IN)**	0.4	0.3
(Don't Know)	2.6	0.4
(Refusal/NA)	0.1	2.7

VERSION C: ASK ALL

Q662 *[SchSelec]*

CARD

Which of the following statements comes closest to your views about what kind of *secondary* school children should go to?

%

50.5 Children should go to a different kind of secondary school, according to how well they do at primary school

45.9 All children should go to the same kind of secondary school, no matter how well or badly they do at primary school

3.5 (Don't Know)

0.1 (Refusal/NA)

LOCAL AUTHORITY SPENDING (VERSION C)   `N=1214`

Q668   **VERSION C: ASK ALL**
       [HIncDiff]
       CARD
       Which of the phrases on this card would you say comes
       closest to your feelings about your household's income
       these days?
%
29.9   Living comfortably on present income
50.6   Coping on present income
13.9   Finding it difficult on present income
 4.9   Finding it very difficult on present income
 0.0   (Other answer **(WRITE IN)**)
 0.4   (Don't Know)
 0.2   (Refusal/NA)

Q670   *[SizeCTax]*
       CARD
       About how much do you think that a ten per cent increase
       in Council Tax would cost your household?
       **IF RESPONDENT DOES NOT KNOW, ENCOURAGE THEM TO GIVE AN
       ESTIMATE.**
       IF THEY CAN'T, CODE DON'T KNOW.
%
 4.2   A   Nothing
           Per week   Per year
 8.7   B   <50p   <£25
24.5   C   50p-£1   £25-£50
30.7   D   £1-£2   £50-£100
12.3   E   £2+   £100+
19.3   (Don't Know)
 0.3   (Refusal/NA)

Q673   **VERSION C: ASK ALL WITH ODD SERIAL NUMBERS**
       [LSpdPr2a]
       HAND OVER LILAC ANSWER SHEET.
       Here are seven areas of local authority spending.
       POINT TO THE SEVEN SPENDING AREAS.
       Suppose that the local authority had to choose between
       these three options ... **READ OUT** ...
       ...increasing spending and putting up the Council Tax by
       ten per cent,
       keeping spending and the Council Tax about the same as
       now, and
       cutting spending and reducing the Council Tax by ten per
       cent.
       POINT TO THE THREE TAX/SPENDING OPTIONS.

Q663   *[ChoicePS]*
       From what you know or have heard, do you think parents
       in your area have enough choice about which *primary*
       school their children attend, or would you like to see
       more choice?
       IF MORE: A bit more or a lot more?

Q664   *[ChoiceSS]*
       And do you think parents in your area have enough choice
       about which *secondary school* their children attend, or
       would you like to see more choice?
       IF MORE: A bit more or a lot more?

	[ChoicePS]	*[ChoiceSS]*
	%	%
Enough choice	46.1	41.4
A bit more choice	18.8	23.1
A lot more choice	14.6	17.3
(Don't Know)	20.3	18.1
(Refusal/NA)	0.1	0.1

Q665   *[PubRes]*
       It is now compulsory for state *secondary schools* to
       publish their exam results. How useful do you think
       this information is for parents of present or future
       pupils. Is it ... **READ OUT** ...

Q666   *[PSTests]*
       And how useful do you think it is for parents of present
       or future pupils to have results of tests for 7 and 11
       year olds at primary *school?* Is it ... **READ OUT** ...

	[PubRes]	*[PSTests]*
	%	%
very useful,	34.3	27.3
quite useful,	40.1	38.6
or, not very useful?	21.2	29.2
(Don't Know)	4.4	4.6
(Refusal/NA)	0.1	0.3

`N=1214`

143

N=1214

Q675 *[LSpdPre3]*
For each of these seven areas of local authority spending, which option do you think would be best for **people in this area generally**? Please tick **one** box on each line.
If you change your mind as you go through, just cross your old answer out.
Please tell me when you are ready.

Q676 *[SchSpdA1]*
Now I'd just like to make a note of your answers.
RETRIEVE LILAC ANSWER SHEET FROM RESPONDENT.
(Which of these would be best for **people in this area generally**?)
LOCAL SCHOOLS:

Q677 *[EldSpdA1]*
(Which of these would be best for **people in this area generally**?)
SERVICES FOR THE ELDERLY, SUCH AS HOME HELPS AND OLD PEOPLE'S HOMES:

Q678 *[ChdSpdA1]*
(Which of these would be best for **people in this area generally**?)
SERVICES FOR CHILDREN SUCH AS NURSERIES:

Q679 *[StrSpdA1]*
(Which of these would be best for **people in this area generally**?)
STREET CLEANING AND RUBBISH COLLECTION:

Q680 *[LeiSpdA1]*
(Which of these would be best for **people in this area generally**?)
LOCAL PARKS, SPORTS CENTRES AND LIBRARIES:

Q681 *[HouSpdA1]*
(Which of these would be best for **people in this area generally**?)
LOCAL HOUSING NEEDS:

Q682 *[LPoSpdA1]*
(Which of these would be best for **people in this area generally**?)
LOCAL POLICE:

N=1214

	[SchSpdA1]	[EldSpdA1]
	%	%
Increase spending and taxes	18.5	20.3
Keep spending and taxes the same	26.3	24.7
Cut spending and taxes	2.5	2.5
None of these	0.7	0.3
(Don't Know)	1.2	1.5
(Refusal/NA)	0.1	0.1

	[ChdSpdA1]	[StrSpdA1]	[LeiSpdA1]
	%	%	%
Increase spending and taxes	13.6	6.0	9.7
Keep spending and taxes the same	29.6	38.1	32.7
Cut spending and taxes	4.1	4.2	5.6
None of these	0.4	0.2	0.3
(Don't Know)	1.5	0.8	0.9
(Refusal/NA)	0.1	0.1	0.1

	[HouSpdA1]	[LPoSpdA1]
	%	%
Increase spending and taxes	13.5	19.0
Keep spending and taxes the same	29.5	25.2
Cut spending and taxes	4.1	3.5
None of these	0.6	0.4
(Don't Know)	1.5	1.1
(Refusal/NA)	0.1	0.1

Q690 *[LSpdPre4]*
HAND OVER WHITE ANSWER SHEET.
Now I want to ask you which options you think would be best for **you and your household**. Again suppose that, for each of these seven areas of local authority spending, the local authority had to choose between these three options.
POINT TO THE THREE TAX/SPENDING OPTIONS.
Please tick one box per line
If you change your mind as you go through, just cross your old answer out. Please tell me when you are ready.

N=1214

	[SchSpdR1]	[EldSpdR1]
	%	%
Increase spending and taxes	13.2	15.6
Keep spending and taxes the same	25.7	24.5
Cut spending and taxes	8.1	7.3
None of these	1.1	0.9
(Don't Know)	1.1	0.9
(Refusal/NA)	0.1	0.2

	[ChdSpdR1]	[StrSpdR1]	[LeiSpdR1]
	%	%	%
Increase spending and taxes	9.3	7.8	11.5
Keep spending and taxes the same	26.5	34.7	28.8
Cut spending and taxes	10.8	5.6	7.6
None of these	1.1	0.3	0.4
(Don't Know)	1.5	0.9	0.9
(Refusal/NA)	0.1	0.1	0.1

	[HouSpdR1]	[LPoSpdR1]
	%	%
Increase spending and taxes	8.8	18.3
Keep spending and taxes the same	27.7	24.9
Cut spending and taxes	10.6	4.6
None of these	1.0	0.5
(Don't Know)	1.2	1.0
(Refusal/NA)	0.1	0.1

N=1214

Q691 [SchSpdR1]
Now I'd just like to make a note of your answers.
RETRIEVE WHITE ANSWER SHEET FROM RESPONDENT.
(Which of these would be best for **you and your household?**)
LOCAL SCHOOLS:

Q692 [EldSpdR1]
(Which of these would be best for **you and your household?**)
SERVICES FOR THE ELDERLY, SUCH AS HOME HELPS AND OLD PEOPLE'S HOMES:

Q693 [ChdSpdR1]
(Which of these would be best for **you and your household?**)
SERVICES FOR CHILDREN SUCH AS NURSERIES:

Q694 [StrSpdR1]
(Which of these would be best for **you and your household?**)
STREET CLEANING AND RUBBISH COLLECTION:

Q695 [LeiSpdR1]
(Which of these would be best for **you and your household?**)
LOCAL PARKS, SPORTS CENTRES AND LIBRARIES:

Q696 [HouSpdR1]
(Which of these would be best for **you and your household?**)
LOCAL HOUSING NEEDS:

Q697 [LPoSpdR1]
(Which of these would be best for **you and your household?**)
LOCAL POLICE:

Q674 [LSpdPr2b]
VERSION C: ASK ALL WITH EVEN SERIAL NUMBERS
HAND OVER LIME GREEN ANSWER SHEET.
Here are seven areas of local authority spending.
POINT TO THE SEVEN SPENDING AREAS.
Suppose that the local authority had to choose between **these** three options ... **READ OUT** ...
...increasing spending and putting up local taxes **for every adult in this area** by £25 a year,
keeping spending and local taxes about the same as now, and
cutting spending and reducing local taxes for **every adult in this area** by £25 a year.
POINT TO THE THREE TAX/SPENDING OPTIONS.

N=1214

Q675 [LSpdPre3]
For each of these seven areas of local authority spending, which option do you think would be best for people in this area generally? Please tick one box on each line.
If you change your mind as you go through, just cross your old answer out.
Please tell me when you are ready.

Q683 [SchSpdA2]
Now I'd just like to make a note of your answers.
RETRIEVE LIME GREEN ANSWER SHEET FROM RESPONDENT.
(Which of these would be best for people in this area generally?)
LOCAL SCHOOLS:

Q684 [EldSpdA2]
(Which of these would be best for people in this area generally?)
SERVICES FOR THE ELDERLY, SUCH AS HOME HELPS AND OLD PEOPLE'S HOMES:

Q685 [ChdSpdA2]
(Which of these would be best for people in this area generally?)
SERVICES FOR CHILDREN SUCH AS NURSERIES:

Q686 [StrSpdA2]
(Which of these would be best for people in this area generally?)
STREET CLEANING AND RUBBISH COLLECTION:

Q687 [LeiSpdA2]
(Which of these would be best for people in this area generally?)
LOCAL PARKS, SPORTS CENTRES AND LIBRARIES:

Q688 [HouSpdA2]
(Which of these would be best for people in this area generally?)
LOCAL HOUSING NEEDS:

149

N=1214

Q689 [LPoSpdA2]
(Which of these would be best for people in this area generally?)
LOCAL POLICE:

	[SchSpdA2]]	[EldSpdA2]
	%	%
Increase spending and taxes	19.9	22.1
Keep spending and taxes the same	25.9	24.4
Cut spending and taxes	2.3	2.3
None of these	0.5	0.2
(Don't Know)	1.5	1.2
(Refusal/NA)	0.4	0.4

	[ChdSpdA2]	[StrSpdA2]
	%	%
Increase spending and taxes	15.8	7.1
Keep spending and taxes the same	28.3	38.8
Cut spending and taxes	3.8	3.2
None of these	0.5	0.3
(Don't Know)	1.9	0.9
(Refusal/NA)	0.4	0.4

	[LeiSpdA2]	[HouspdA2]	[LPoSpdA2]
	%	%	%
Increase spending and taxes	10.1	13.3	19.4
Keep spending and taxes the same	34.1	30.1	26.4
Cut spending and taxes	4.6	4.9	3.1
None of these	0.2	0.4	0.2
(Don't Know)	1.2	1.5	1.2
(Refusal/NA)	0.4	0.4	0.4

Q690 [LSpdPre4]
HAND OVER BEIGE ANSWER SHEET.
Now I want to ask you which options you think would be best for you and your household. Again suppose that, for each of these seven areas of local authority spending, the local authority had to choose between these three options.
POINT TO THE THREE TAX/SPENDING OPTIONS.
Please tick one box per line
If you change your mind as you go through, just cross your old answer out. Please tell me when you are ready.

150

N=1214

Q698 [SchSpdR2]
Now I'd just like to make a note of your answers.
RETRIEVE BEIGE ANSWER SHEET FROM RESPONDENT.
(Which of these would be best for you and your household?)
LOCAL SCHOOLS:

Q699 [EldSpdR2]
(Which of these would be best for you and your household?)
SERVICES FOR THE ELDERLY, SUCH AS HOME HELPS AND OLD PEOPLE'S HOMES:

Q700 [ChdSpdR2]
(Which of these would be best for you and your household?)
SERVICES FOR CHILDREN SUCH AS NURSERIES:

Q701 [StrSpdR2]
(Which of these would be best for you and your household?)
STREET CLEANING AND RUBBISH COLLECTION:

Q702 [LeiSpdR2]
(Which of these would be best for you and your household?)
LOCAL PARKS, SPORTS CENTRES AND LIBRARIES:

Q703 [HouSpdR2]
(Which of these would be best for you and your household?)
LOCAL HOUSING NEEDS:

Q704 [LPoSpdR2]
(Which of these would be best for you and your household?)
LOCAL POLICE:

N=1214

	[SchSpdR2]	[EldSpdR2]
	%	%
Increase spending and taxes	13.1	15.1
Keep spending and taxes the same	24.8	26.0
Cut spending and taxes	9.4	7.3
None of these	1.2	0.4
(Don't Know)	1.7	1.4
(Refusal/NA)	0.4	0.4

	[ChdSpdR2]	[StrSpdR2]	[LeiSpdR2]
	%	%	%
Increase spending and taxes	10.0	7.2	12.4
Keep spending and taxes the same	27.3	37.4	29.8
Cut spending and taxes	10.2	4.2	6.7
None of these	1.2	0.4	0.3
(Don't Know)	1.5	1.1	1.1
(Refusal/NA)	0.4	0.4	0.4

	[HouSpdR2]	[LPoSpdR2]
	%	%
Increase spending and taxes	9.6	18.1
Keep spending and taxes the same	29.9	27.0
Cut spending and taxes	9.1	3.7
None of these	0.2	0.6
(Don't Know)	1.3	0.9
(Refusal/NA)	0.4	0.4

N=975

Q705 IF INTERVIEW TOOK PLACE AFTER 2 MAY 1996
[VtMay96]
Did people in your neighbourhood have the chance to vote in local elections this May (1996)?

N=1214

Q706 IF INTERVIEW TOOK PLACE UP TO 2 MAY 1996
OR 'NO'/DK AT [VtMay96]
[VtMay95]
(And) did people in your neighbourhood have the chance to vote in local elections in May last year (1995)?
IF 'NO'/DK AT [VtMay95]

Q707 [VtMay94]
And did people in your neighbourhood have the chance to vote in local elections in May 1994?

N=1214

	[VtMay96]	[VtMay95]	[VtMay94]
	%	%	%
Yes	44.0	39.4	6.5
No	50.4	10.3	2.2
(Don't Know)	5.4	12.4	14.0
(Refusal/NA)	0.2	2.6	2.6

IF 'Yes' AT [VtMay96], [VtMay95] OR [VtMay94]

Q708 *[LocVoted]*

A lot of people don't manage to vote in the local elections.

How about you? Did you manage to vote in the last local elections in your area?

%
2.2 (No election)
45.2 Yes
33.6 No
0.7 Too young to vote
1.5 Not eligible/Not on register
0.3 (Don't Know)
16.6 (Refusal/NA)

IF 'Yes' AT [LocVoted]

Q709 *[LocPtyVt]*

Which party did you vote for, or perhaps you voted for an independent candidate?

DO NOT PROMPT

%
11.3 Conservative
19.1 Labour
8.6 Liberal Democrats
0.6 Scottish Nationalist Party
- Plaid Cymru
2.7 Independent
0.6 Green
0.1 Other party (WRITE IN)
- More than one (WRITE IN)
0.2 Other answer (WRITE IN)
1.5 Refused to say
0.6 (Don't Know)
16.8 (Refusal/NA)

N=1214

IF 'No'/DK AT [LocVoted]

Q713 *[LocPtyIf]*

Which party would you have voted for, if you had voted, or perhaps you would have voted for an independent candidate?

DO NOT PROMPT

%
4.6 Conservative
12.8 Labour
4.6 Liberal Democrats
0.3 Scottish Nationalist
0.1 Plaid Cymru
2.2 Independent
0.4 Green
0.1 Other party (WRITE IN)
- More than one (WRITE IN)
3.8 Other answer (WRITE IN)
3.0 (Don't Know)
18.6 (Refusal/NA)

CHARITABLE GIVING (VERSION C)

N=1214

Q719 VERSION C: ASK ALL
[Lottr1]
CARD
Money raised by the National Lottery is spent on many kinds of causes. Please use this card to say what you think about spending the extra money on helping homeless people in Britain

Q720 [Lottr2]
CARD AGAIN
(And extra money raised by the National Lottery ...)
... helping disabled people in Britain?

Q721 [Lottr3]
CARD AGAIN
And what about money from the National Lottery being spent on helping starving people in poor countries?

Q722 [Lottr4]
CARD AGAIN
(And extra money raised by the National Lottery ...)
... helping ex-prisoners to find homes and jobs?

Q723 [Lottr5]
CARD AGAIN
(And extra money raised by the National Lottery ...)
... helping to restore historic buildings in Britain?

Q724 [Lottr6]
CARD AGAIN
And what about it being spent on supporting art galleries, theatres and orchestras in Britain?

Q725 [Lottr7]
CARD AGAIN
(And extra money raised by the National Lottery ...)
... helping to protect the environment?

Q726 [Lottr8]
CARD AGAIN
(And extra money raised by the National Lottery ...)
... providing sports facilities in Britain?

N=1214

Q727 [Lottr9]
CARD AGAIN
And National Lottery money spent on helping to prevent cruelty to animals in Britain?

Q728 [Lottr10]
CARD AGAIN
(And extra money raised by the National Lottery ...)
... helping to protect children in need in Britain?

Q729 [Lottr11]
CARD AGAIN
And National Lottery money spent on medical research in Britain?

	[Lottr1] %	[Lottr2] %	[Lottr3] %
An excellent way to spend it	24.8	35.7	10.3
A very good way	32.5	40.8	16.6
Quite a good way	28.1	19.1	28.4
Not a very good way	9.0	2.4	27.1
Should not be spent on this	4.5	1.0	16.5
(Don't Know)	0.9	0.6	0.8
(Refusal/NA)	0.3	0.3	0.3

	[Lottr4] %	[Lottr5] %	[Lottr6] %
An excellent way to spend it	3.0	2.7	2.2
A very good way	10.5	15.1	6.7
Quite a good way	36.2	42.9	28.6
Not a very good way	30.9	26.0	33.3
Should not be spent on this	17.3	12.2	28.1
(Don't Know)	1.8	0.9	0.8
(Refusal/NA)	0.3	0.3	0.3

	[Lottr7] %	[Lottr8] %	[Lottr9] %
An excellent way to spend it	14.7	10.2	15.2
A very good way	37.8	29.1	25.2
Quite a good way	40.0	42.5	41.0
Not a very good way	4.6	13.6	13.1
Should not be spent on this	2.0	3.7	4.5
(Don't Know)	0.6	0.6	0.8
(Refusal/NA)	0.3	0.3	0.3

N=1214

	[Lottrl0]	[Lottrl1]
	%	%
An excellent way to spend it	38.9	37.2
A very good way	39.6	34.3
Quite a good way	15.6	18.6
Not a very good way	3.0	5.7
Should not be spent on this	2.2	3.1
(Don't Know)	0.6	0.8
(Refusal/NA)	0.3	0.3

WELFARE/SOCIAL SECURITY (VERSION C)

VERSION C: ASK ALL WITH ODD SERIAL NUMBERS   N=600

Q731 [UBPoor1]
Now for a few questions on state benefits.
Think of a married couple living only on unemployment benefit.
Would you say that they are ... **READ OUT** ...

Q732 [PensPool]
Now thinking of a married couple living only on the state pension.
Would you say that they are ... **READ OUT** ...

Q733 [PoorUB41]
Now thinking of a married couple without children living on £78 per week
Would you say that they are ... **READ OUT** ...

Q734 [PoorSPn1]
And what about a pensioner couple living on £98 per week.
Would you say that they are ... **READ OUT** ...

	[UBPoor1]	[PensPool]	[PoorUB41]	[PoorSPn1]
	%	%	%	%
... really poor,	15.4	23.0	36.9	18.5
hard up,	50.2	55.9	49.6	53.3
have enough to live on,	24.0	16.2	10.9	25.4
or, have more than enough?	1.7	-	0.3	1.1
(Don't Know)	8.3	4.5	1.8	1.3
(Refusal/NA)	0.5	0.4	0.4	0.4

VERSION C: ASK ALL WITH EVEN SERIAL NUMBERS   N=615

Q735 [PensPoo2]
Now for a few questions on state benefits.
Now thinking of a married couple living only on the state pension.
Would you say that they are ... **READ OUT** ...

Q736 [UB\Poo2]
Think of a married couple without children living only on unemployment benefit.
Would you say that they are ... **READ OUT** ...

Q737   [PoorSPn2]   N=615
And what about a pensioner couple living on £98 per week.
Would you say that they are ... **READ OUT** ...

Q738   [PoorUB42]
Now thinking of a married couple without children living on £78 per week.
Would you say that they are ... **READ OUT** ...

	[UBPoor2]	[PensPoo2]	[PoorSPn2]	[PoorUB42]
	%	%	%	%
.. really poor,	21.1	18.7	27.8	46.3
hard up,	58.8	51.0	51.7	44.3
have enough to live on,	15.5	21.8	17.6	7.8
or, have more than enough?	0.3	0.8	0.4	0.1
(Don't Know)	3.9	7.5	1.8	0.1
(Refusal/NA)	0.3	0.3	0.7	0.3

VERSION C: ASK ALL   N=1214

Q743   [SameHlth]
Do you think that health care should be the same for everyone, or should people who can afford it be able to pay for better health care?

Q744   [SameEduc]
Should the quality of education be the same for all children, or should parents who can afford it be able to pay for better education?

Q745   [SamePens]
And do you think that pensions should be the same for everyone, or should people who can afford it be able to pay for better pensions?

	[SameHlth]	[SameEduc]	[SamePens]
	%	%	%
Same for everyone	59.8	58.9	35.5
Able to pay for better	38.9	39.2	61.5
(Don't Know)	1.0	1.7	2.6
(Refusal/NA)	0.3	0.3	0.3

Q746   [MstUnemp]   N=1214
Suppose two people working for a large firm each became unemployed through no fault of their own. One had a very high income, one had a very low income.
Do you think the very high earner should be entitled to ... **READ OUT** ...
%
10.4   ...more unemployment benefit than the very low earner,
74.8   the same amount,
9.1   less benefit,
2.2   or, no unemployment benefit at all?
0.6   Other answer **(WRITE IN)**
0.1   (It depends)
2.5   (Don't Know)
0.3   (Refusal/NA)

Q748   [MstRetir]
Now suppose a very high earner and a very low earner in a large firm retired.
Do you think the very high earner should be entitled to ... **READ OUT** ...
%
10.2   ...a bigger state retirement pension than the very low earner,
75.7   the same amount,
8.8   a lower state pension,
3.0   or, no state pension at all?
0.3   Other answer **(WRITE IN)**
1.8   (Don't Know)
0.3   (Refusal/NA)

Q750   [MstChild]
Now what about child benefit. Should very high earners be entitled to ... **READ OUT** ...
%
1.3   ...more child benefit than very low earners,
50.2   the same amount,
20.7   less,
25.5   or, no child benefit at all?
0.5   Other answer **(WRITE IN)**
0.0   (It depends)
1.5   (Don't Know)
0.3   (Refusal/NA)

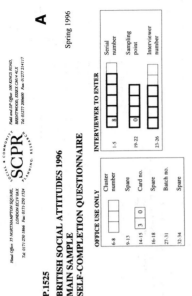

Head Office: 35 NORTHAMPTON SQUARE,
LONDON EC1V 0AX
Tel. 0171-250 1866 Fax: 0171-250 1524

Field and DP Office: 100 KINGS ROAD,
BRENTWOOD, ESSEX CM14 4LX
Tel. 01277 200600 Fax: 01277 214117

SCPR
SOCIAL & COMMUNITY PLANNING RESEARCH

A

Spring 1996

P.1525

BRITISH SOCIAL ATTITUDES 1996
MAIN SAMPLE
SELF-COMPLETION QUESTIONNAIRE

OFFICE USE ONLY		INTERVIEWER TO ENTER	
6-8	Cluster number	1-5 [8]	Serial number
9-13	Spare		
14-15 [3] [0]	Card no.	19-22 [0]	Sampling point
16-18	Spare		
27-31	Batch no.	23-26	Interviewer number
32-34	Spare		

To the selected respondent:

Thank you very much for agreeing to take part in this important study - the twelfth in this annual series. The study consists of this self-completion questionnaire, and the interview you have already completed. The results of the survey are published in a book each autumn; some of the questions are also being asked in twenty-four other countries, as part of an international survey.

Completing the questionnaire:

The questions inside cover a wide range of subjects, but most can be answered simply by placing a tick (✓) in one or more of the boxes. No special knowledge is required: we are confident that everyone will be able to take part, not just those with strong views or particular viewpoints. The questionnaire should not take very long to complete, and we hope you will find it interesting and enjoyable. **Only you should fill it in, and not anyone else at your address.** The answers you give will be treated as confidential and anonymous.

Returning the questionnaire:

Your interviewer will arrange with you the most convenient way of returning the questionnaire. If the interviewer has arranged to call back for it, please fill it in and keep it safely until then. If not, please complete it and post it back in the pre-paid, addressed envelope, AS SOON AS YOU POSSIBLY CAN.

THANK YOU AGAIN FOR YOUR HELP.

Social and Community Planning Research is an independent social research institute registered as a charitable trust. Its projects are funded by government departments, local authorities, universities and foundations to provide information on social issues in Britain. The British Social Attitudes survey series is funded mainly by one of the Sainsbury Family

A01

N=993

2.01 [SCOBEYLW]
In general, would you say that people should obey the law without exception, or are there exceptional occasions on which people should follow their consciences even if it means breaking the law?

PLEASE TICK ONE BOX ONLY
%
Obey the law without exception	36.2
OR	
Follow conscience on occasions	59.1
Can't choose	3.3
(NA)	1.4

2.02 There are many ways people or organisations can protest against a government action they strongly oppose. Please show which you think should be allowed and which should not be allowed by ticking a box on each line.

PLEASE TICK ONE BOX ON EACH LINE

		Should it be allowed?				
	Definitely	Probably	Probably not	Definitely not	Can't choose	(NA)
[PROTEST1] a. Organising public meetings to protest against the government	% 53.9	30.6	4.5	5.0	4.0	2.0
[PROTEST3] b. Organising protest marches and demonstrations	% 31.3	36.6	12.1	10.9	4.3	4.7
[PROTEST6] c. Organising a nationwide strike of all workers against the government	% 12.4	17.3	25.8	34.7	5.2	4.6

2.03 Would you or would you not do any of the following to protest against a government action you strongly opposed?

PLEASE TICK ONE BOX ON EACH LINE

	Definitely would	Probably would	Probably would not	Definitely would not	Can't choose	(NA)
[PROTWLD1] a. Attend a public meeting organised to protest against the government	% 22.8	38.1	22.1	12.3	3.3	1.4
[PROTWLD2] b. Go on a protest march or demonstration	% 10.2	20.8	30.6	31.2	2.4	4.7

2.04 And in the past five years how many times have you done each of the following to protest against a government action you strongly oppose?

PLEASE TICK ONE BOX ON EACH LINE

	Never	Once	More than once	(NA)
[PROTDON1] a. Attended a public meeting organised to protest against the government	% 87.5	8.8	2.5	1.2
[PROTDON2] b. Gone on a protest march or demonstration	% 90.5	3.1	2.4	4.0

A02

N=993

2.05 There are some people whose views are considered extreme by the majority. Consider people who want to overthrow the government by revolution. Do you think such people should be allowed to ...

PLEASE TICK ONE BOX ON EACH LINE

	Definitely	Probably	Probably not	Definitely not	Can't choose	(NA)
[REVMEET] a. ... hold public meetings to express their views?	% 18.4	28.6	15.9	29.7	5.7	1.6
[REVPUB] b. ... publish books expressing their views?	% 21.0	37.0	16.4	17.2	5.0	3.4

2.06 [JUSTICE]
All systems of justice make mistakes, but which do you think is worse?

PLEASE TICK ONE BOX ONLY
%
... to convict an innocent person,	55.6
OR to let a guilty person go free?	27.3
Can't choose	16.0
(NA)	1.2

2.07 [GOVINFO]
The government has a lot of different pieces of information about people which computers can bring together very quickly. Is this ...

PLEASE TICK ONE BOX ONLY
%
... a very serious threat to individual privacy,	25.8
a fairly serious threat,	34.6
not a serious threat,	28.2
or, not a threat at all to individual privacy?	4.9
Can't choose	5.3
(NA)	1.2

2.08 [INCDIFF]
What is your opinion of the following statement:
"It is the responsibility of the government to reduce the differences in income between people with high incomes and those with low incomes."

PLEASE TICK ONE BOX ONLY
%
Agree strongly	19.5
Agree	31.2
Neither agree nor disagree	19.5
Disagree	17.5
Disagree strongly	6.1
Can't choose	5.2
(NA)	1.0

A03

N=993

2.09 Here are some things the government might do for the economy. Please show which actions you are in favour of and which you are against.

PLEASE TICK ONE BOX ON EACH LINE

		Strongly in favour of	In favour of	Neither in favour of nor against	Against	Strongly against	(DK)	(NA)
a.	Control of wages by law [GOVECON1]	% 10.3	25.7	19.8	32.1	8.7	0.1	3.3
b.	Control of prices by law [GOVECON2]	% 13.9	35.4	21.3	21.5	5.0	0.1	2.7
c.	Cuts in government spending [GOVECON3]	% 12.1	30.9	27.5	21.1	4.7	0.1	3.6
d.	Government financing of projects to create new jobs [GOVECON4]	% 30.3	53.3	11.2	2.3	0.4	0.1	2.4
e.	Less government regulation of business [GOVECON5]	% 8.0	32.2	42.1	11.8	1.8	0.1	3.9
f.	Support for industry to develop new products and technology [GOVECON6]	% 33.8	52.1	10.0	1.0	0.3	0.1	2.7
g.	Support for declining industries to protect jobs [GOVECON7]	% 22.0	40.0	22.3	11.8	1.4	0.1	2.4
h.	Reducing the working week to create more jobs [GOVECON8]	% 10.8	26.1	30.6	23.8	6.0	0.1	2.6

2.10 Listed below are various areas of government spending. Please show whether you would like to see more or less government spending in each area. Remember that if you say "much more", it might require a tax increase to pay for it.

PLEASE TICK ONE BOX ON EACH LINE

		Spend much more	Spend more	Spend the same as now	Spend less	Spend much less	Can't choose	(NA)
a.	The environment [GVSPEND1]	% 8.0	33.0	47.5	4.3	0.7	2.0	4.4
b.	Health [GVSPEND2]	% 41.9	47.6	8.1	0.3	0.1	0.2	1.8
c.	The police and law enforcement [GVSPEND3]	% 20.0	50.2	24.4	1.2	0.5	1.1	2.7
d.	Education [GVSPEND4]	% 31.1	51.2	14.5	0.8	0.1	0.5	1.9
e.	The military and defence [GVSPEND5]	% 3.1	13.9	46.3	23.3	7.9	2.0	3.4
f.	Old age pensions [GVSPEND6]	% 26.0	50.2	20.5	0.7	0.3	0.4	1.9
g.	Unemployment benefits [GVSPEND7]	% 6.6	26.7	41.9	14.9	4.4	2.2	3.3
h.	Culture and the arts [GVSPEND8]	% 0.5	5.2	27.6	32.0	29.4	2.4	2.7

OFFICE USE ONLY

A04

N=993

2.11a [TUPOWER] Do you think that trade unions in this country have too much power or too little power?

PLEASE TICK ONE BOX ONLY

	%
Far too much power	4.6
Too much power	13.6
About the right amount of power	48.3
Too little power	18.2
Far too little power	3.8
Can't choose	10.6
(NA)	0.9

b. [BUSPOWER] How about business and industry? Do they have too much power or too little power?

PLEASE TICK ONE BOX ONLY

	%
Far too much power	6.3
Too much power	25.4
About the right amount of power	45.2
Too little power	8.3
Far too little power	0.5
Can't choose	13.4
(NA)	0.9

c. [GOVPOWER] And what about the government, does it have too much power or too little power?

PLEASE TICK ONE BOX ONLY

	%
Far too much power	14.6
Too much power	32.3
About the right amount of power	39.5
Too little power	4.6
Far too little power	0.3
Can't choose	7.8
(NA)	0.9

OFFICE USE ONLY

A05

N=993

2.12 On the whole, do you think it should or should not be the government's responsibility to …

PLEASE TICK ONE BOX ON EACH LINE

		Definitely should be	Probably should be	Probably should not be	Definitely should not be	Can't choose	(NA)
a.	…provide a job for everyone who wants one [GOVRESP1]	% 26.4	38.6	18.7	10.7	3.2	2.3
b.	…keep prices under control [GOVRESP2]	% 40.4	41.3	9.7	4.6	2.3	1.8
c.	…provide health care for the sick [GOVRESP3]	% 80.6	16.2	1.2	0.3	0.6	1.2
d.	…provide a decent standard of living for the old [GOVRESP4]	% 69.5	25.7	2.2	0.4	1.0	1.3
e.	…provide industry with the help it needs to grow [GOVRESP5]	% 37.8	49.9	6.6	0.3	3.2	2.1
f.	…provide a decent standard of living for the unemployed [GOVRESP6]	% 26.5	46.0	14.2	6.6	4.7	2.0
g.	…reduce income differences between the rich and the poor [GOVRESP7]	% 32.2	30.3	20.5	9.8	5.4	1.8
h.	…give financial help to university students from low-income families [GOVRESP8]	% 35.2	50.5	7.2	2.4	3.1	1.6
i.	…provide decent housing for those who can't afford it [GOVRESP9]	% 33.9	49.9	8.0	2.3	4.1	1.7
j.	…impose strict laws to make industry do less damage to the environment [GOVRESP0]	% 58.3	31.5	3.8	1.1	3.7	1.6

Now some questions about politics.

2.13 How interested would you say you personally are in politics?
[POLINRST]

PLEASE TICK ONE BOX ONLY

	%
Very interested	8.2
Fairly interested	28.7
Somewhat interested	25.9
Not very interested	23.6
Not at all interested	11.7
Can't choose	1.0
(NA)	0.8

A06

N=993

2.14 Please tick one box on each line to show how much you agree or disagree with each of the following statements.

PLEASE TICK ONE BOX ON EACH LINE

		Strongly agree	Agree	Neither agree nor disagree	Disagree	Strongly disagree	Can't choose	(NA)
a.	People like me don't have any say about what the government does [GOVNOSA2]	% 23.9	40.3	15.2	16.0	1.8	1.2	1.6
b.	The average citizen has considerable influence on politics [POLITIC3]	% 1.3	11.2	18.4	50.0	13.9	2.9	2.3
c.	Even the best politician cannot have much impact because of the way government works [APATHY4]	% 8.2	36.9	26.0	19.8	2.8	4.3	2.0
d.	I feel that I have a pretty good understanding of the important political issues facing our country [USTNDPOL]	% 4.5	36.4	24.2	20.9	5.7	5.9	2.5
e.	Elections are a good way of making governments pay attention to what the people think [ELECATTN]	% 17.1	51.0	15.0	10.3	2.7	1.8	2.1
f.	I think most people are better informed about politics and government than I am [INFPOLI2]	% 3.4	23.2	33.0	29.9	4.1	4.3	2.2
g.	People we elect as MPs try to keep the promises they have made during the election [IMPPROMIS]	% 3.2	17.8	27.3	37.8	8.5	2.8	2.4
h.	Most civil servants can be trusted to do what is best for the country [CSTRUST2]	% 1.6	20.7	33.1	29.7	7.4	5.4	2.3

2.15 All in all, how well or badly do you think the system of democracy in Britain works these days?
[GBDMCRCY]

PLEASE TICK ONE BOX ONLY

	%
It works well and needs no changes	5.7
It works well but needs some changes	57.2
It does not work well and needs a lot of changes	22.0
It does not work well and needs to be completely changed	4.2
Can't choose	9.8
(NA)	1.1

And now some questions about taxes. [TAXSOC]

2.16 If the government had a choice between reducing taxes or spending more on social services which do you think it should do? (We mean all taxes together, including Income Tax, National Insurance, VAT and all the rest.)

PLEASE TICK ONE BOX ONLY

	%
Reduce taxes, even if this means spending less on social services	21.9
OR Spend more on social services, even if this means higher taxes?	53.6
Can't choose	23.3
(NA)	1.2

OFFICE USE ONLY

A07

N=993

[TAXHISC]
2.17a Generally, how would you describe taxes in Britain today?
First, for those with high incomes, are taxes ...

PLEASE TICK ONE BOX ONLY

	%
... much too high,	3.7
too high,	13.0
about right,	31.6
too low,	35.5
or, are they much too low?	6.3
Can't choose	7.8
(NA)	2.1

[TAXMIDSC]
b. Next, for those with middle incomes, are taxes ...

PLEASE TICK ONE BOX ONLY

	%
... much too high,	4.4
too high,	25.1
about right,	55.6
too low,	6.9
or, are they much too low?	0.6
Can't choose	5.6
(NA)	1.8

[TAXLOWSC]
c. Lastly, for those with low incomes, are taxes ...

PLEASE TICK ONE BOX ONLY

	%
... much too high,	23.0
too high,	46.1
about right,	22.5
too low,	0.9
or, are they much too low?	0.1
Can't choose	5.1
(NA)	2.4

2.18 Please tick one box on each line to show whether you think each of the following should mainly be run by private organisations or companies, or by government?

PLEASE TICK ONE BOX ON EACH LINE

		Mainly run by private organisations or companies	Mainly run by government	Can't choose	(NA)
[GOVRUN1]	Electricity %	38.8	49.7	10.1	1.5
[GOVRUN2]	Hospitals %	10.0	81.2	7.2	1.6
[GOVRUN3]	Banks %	67.2	17.5	13.8	1.5

A08

N=993

[LAWDECID]
2.19 Which of these statements comes closest to your view?

PLEASE TICK ONE BOX ONLY

	%
British courts should be allowed to overrule parliament on any law which denies people their basic rights	60.4
OR Britain's democratically elected parliament should always have the final say on what the law should be	22.3
Can't choose	15.9
(NA)	1.4

[PROPREP]
2.20 How much do you agree or disagree with this statement?

"Britain should introduce proportional representation, so that the number of MPs each party gets matches more closely the number of votes each party gets."

PLEASE TICK ONE BOX ONLY

	%
Strongly agree	14.6
Agree	30.9
Neither agree nor disagree	20.3
Disagree	12.2
Strongly disagree	3.8
Can't choose	16.9
(NA)	1.2

2.21 Here are some more ways people or organisations can protest against a government action they strongly oppose. Please show which you think should be allowed and which should not be allowed by ticking a box on each line.

PLEASE TICK ONE BOX ON EACH LINE

		Should it be allowed?					
		Definitely	Probably	Probably not	Definitely not	Can't choose	(NA)
[PROTEST2] a. Publishing pamphlets to protest against the government	%	37.5	39.6	7.8	5.4	7.3	2.5
[PROTEST4] b. Occupying a government office and stopping work there for several days	%	2.1	6.1	33.1	46.7	7.4	4.6
[PROTEST5] c. Seriously damaging government buildings	%	0.5	1.0	5.1	82.8	6.0	4.5

A09

N=993

[VOTEWRTH]
2.22 Which of these statements comes closest to your view about general elections?

PLEASE TICK ONE BOX ONLY
%

In a general election ...

It's not really worth voting,	8.3
People should vote only if they care who wins	26.4
It is everyone's duty to vote	64.0
(NA)	1.2

2.23 Here are some decisions that could be made either by the MPs we elect to parliament or by everyone having a say in a special vote or referendum.

[REFECU]
a. First, who do you think should make the decision about whether or not Britain should replace the pound with a single European currency? Should the decision be made ....
%

PLEASE TICK ONE BOX ONLY

	... by elected MPs in parliament	13.1
OR	by everyone in a referendum?	76.8
	Can't choose	8.9
	(NA)	1.2

[REFHANG]
b. And who do you think should make the decision about whether or not we should reintroduce the death penalty for some crimes? Should the decision be made.....
%

PLEASE TICK ONE BOX ONLY

	... by elected MPs in parliament	18.2
OR	by everyone in a referendum?	70.8
	Can't choose	9.8
	(NA)	1.1

[REFPR]
c. And who do you think should decide whether or not Britain should introduce proportional representation so that the number of MPs each party gets matches more closely the number of votes each party gets? Should that decision be made ...
%

PLEASE TICK ONE BOX ONLY

	... by elected MPs in parliament	15.4
OR	by everyone in a referendum?	65.2
	Can't choose	18.3
	(NA)	1.1

A10

N=993

[MPOTHJOB]
2.24 Which of these statements about MPs comes closest to your view?

PLEASE TICK ONE BOX ONLY
%

It is a bad thing for MPs to have another paid job because being an MP is a full-time job in itself	65.3
It is a good thing for MPs to have another paid job because it keeps them in touch with the outside world	22.1
Can't choose	11.5
(NA)	1.0

2.25 Please tick one box for each statement below to show how much you agree or disagree with it.

PLEASE TICK ONE BOX ON EACH LINE

	Strongly agree	Agree	Neither agree nor disagree	Disagree	Strongly disagree	Can't choose	(NA)
[POLGIFT] a. Any individual who gives money to a political party should be allowed to keep their gift private if they wish %	11.5	37.5	14.8	20.0	8.5	4.9	2.8
[POLLIMIT] b. There should be a limit on how much money a single individual can give to a political party %	8.8	27.5	25.1	23.3	6.5	6.3	2.6
[POLFUND] c. Political parties need to be funded by the government to do their job properly %	7.1	26.2	26.3	22.7	6.0	9.1	2.5

N=3103

[AREAHELP]
Now a few questions about the area where you live.

2.26 In some areas people do things together and try to help each other, while in other areas people mostly go their own way. In general, would you say you live in an area where ...
%

PLEASE TICK ONE BOX ONLY

	... people help each other,	26.5
OR	people go their own way?	25.4
	Mixture	46.7
	Can't choose	1.0
	(NA)	0.4

[BURGHELP]
2.27a Do you think you live in the sort of area where people who thought a house was being broken into would ....
%

PLEASE TICK ONE BOX ONLY

	... do something about it,	66.0
OR	just turn a blind eye?	4.9
	Mixture	24.3
	No burglaries in this area	2.9
	Can't choose	1.4
	(NA)	0.4

A12

OFFICE USE ONLY

N=3103

2.30 From what you know or have heard, please tick a box for each of the items below to show whether you think the National Health Service in your area is, on the whole, satisfactory or in need of improvement.

PLEASE TICK ONE BOX ON EACH LINE

	In need of a lot of improvement	In need of some improvement	Satisfactory	Very good	(DK)	(NA)
a. GPs' appointment systems [HSAREA1]	% 12.8	30.3	43.1	12.6	0.1	1.2
b. Amount of time GP gives to each patient [HSAREA2]	% 7.6	22.9	54.1	14.0	0.1	1.4
c. Being able to choose which GP to see [HSAREA3]	% 7.4	19.6	54.5	16.4	0.2	2.0
d. Quality of medical treatment by GPs [HSAREA4]	% 4.8	17.0	51.6	24.3	0.1	2.2
e. Hospital waiting lists for non-emergency operations [HSAREA5]	34.4	42.1	19.2	1.7	0.5	2.1
f. Waiting time before getting appointments with hospital consultants [HSAREA6]	38.6	40.2	17.0	1.8	0.4	2.0
g. General condition of hospital buildings [HSAREA7]	14.5	35.1	38.1	10.0	0.2	2.1
h. Staffing level of nurses in hospitals [HSAREA9]	33.7	37.4	22.6	3.7	0.4	2.2
i. Staffing level of doctors in hospitals [HSAREA10]	31.6	37.9	24.7	3.1	0.5	2.2
j. Quality of medical treatment in hospitals [HSAREA11]	% 7.0	24.6	47.7	18.5	0.3	1.9
k. Quality of nursing care in hospitals [HSAREA12]	6.9	19.6	43.7	27.4	0.2	2.2
l. Waiting areas in accident and emergency departments in hospitals [HSAREA13]	% 20.8	34.9	36.1	5.3	0.4	2.5
m. Waiting areas for out-patients in hospitals [HSAREA14]	% 15.2	33.5	43.6	5.0	0.4	2.3
n. Waiting areas at GPs' surgeries [HSAREA15]	% 4.9	16.0	60.1	17.3	0.1	1.6
o. Time spent waiting in out-patient departments [HSAREA16]	24.5	43.6	27.0	2.0	0.4	2.6
p. Time spent waiting in accident and emergency departments before being seen by a doctor [HSAREA17]	33.2	39.5	21.3	2.3	0.8	2.9
q. Time spent waiting for an ambulance after a 999 call [HSAREA18]	8.3	27.6	47.4	10.9	1.7	4.0

A11

OFFICE USE ONLY

N=3103

[BURGAREA]

2.27b And do you think burglaries in this area are ...

PLEASE TICK ONE BOX ONLY

	%
... mostly done by people from other areas, OR	33.2
... mostly done by people from around here?	17.9
Mixture	31.2
No burglaries in this area	7.9
Can't choose	9.4
(NA)	0.5

[RENTBUY]

2.28 Suppose a newly-married young couple, both with steady jobs, asked your advice about whether to buy or rent a home. If they had the choice, what would you advise them to do?

PLEASE TICK ONE BOX ONLY

	%
To buy a home as soon as possible OR	54.2
To wait a bit, then try to buy a home	35.3
Not to plan to buy a home at all	2.7
Can't choose	7.1
(NA)	0.8

2.29 Still thinking of what you might say to this young couple, please tick one box for each statement below to show how much you agree or disagree with it.

PLEASE TICK ONE BOX ON EACH LINE

	Agree strongly	Just agree	Neither agree nor disagree	Just disagree	Disagree strongly	(DK)	(NA)
a. Owning your home can be a risky investment [HOMERISK]	% 13.4	36.9	22.0	18.9	7.1	0.0	1.7
b. Over time, buying a home works out less expensive than paying rent [BUYCHEAP]	% 43.6	38.5	11.3	4.0	1.2	0.1	1.3
c. Owning your home makes it easier to move when you want to [MOVEHOME]	% 12.1	21.8	29.6	23.0	12.0	0.0	1.5
d. Owning a home ties up money you may need urgently for other things [MONEYTIE]	% 6.1	26.6	33.4	25.2	7.0	0.0	1.7
e. Owning a home gives you the freedom to do what you want to it [FREEDOM]	% 31.7	39.1	16.4	8.8	2.4	0.1	1.5
f. Owning a home is a big financial burden to repair and maintain [FINBURDN]	% 17.1	37.6	27.5	13.4	2.6	0.0	1.7
g. Your own home will be something to leave your family [LEAVEFAM]	% 37.5	38.6	15.5	4.9	1.9	0.0	1.7
h. Owning a home is just too much of a responsibility [HOMERESP]	% 3.1	8.9	24.8	35.8	25.1	0.1	2.2
i. Owning a home is too much of a risk for couples without secure jobs [RISKJOB]	% 34.0	34.5	15.0	11.6	3.5	0.0	1.3
j. Couples who buy their own homes would be wise to wait before starting a family [WAITFAM]	% 19.7	30.0	32.8	11.9	4.6	0.0	1.2

A13

OFFICE USE ONLY

N=3103

2.31 In the last two years, have you or a close family member ....

PLEASE TICK ONE BOX ON EACH LINE

	% Yes	% No	% (NA)
a. ... visited an NHS GP? [NHSDOC]	95.0	3.8	1.1
b. ... been an out-patient in an NHS hospital? [NHSOUTP]	70.9	27.4	1.7
c. ... been an in-patient in an NHS hospital? [NHSINP]	46.7	51.2	2.1
d. ... visited a patient in an NHS hospital? [NHSVISIT]	70.8	26.7	2.5
e. ... had any medical treatment as a private patient? [PRIVPAT]	12.2	85.6	2.2
f. ... had any dental treatment as a private patient? [PRIVDENT]	23.1	74.9	2.1

2.32a [SMOKOPWD] Suppose two men with a heart condition go on a hospital waiting list at the same time. Both would benefit from an operation. One man does not smoke and the other smokes heavily. Who do you think would get the operation first....

PLEASE TICK ONE BOX ONLY

	%
... the non-smoker,	52.9
the heavy smoker,	2.9
or, would their smoking habits make no difference?	33.1
Can't choose	10.1
(NA)	1.0

b. [SMOKOPSD] And in your view, who do you think should get the operation first ...

PLEASE TICK ONE BOX ONLY

	%
... the non-smoker,	38.6
the heavy smoker,	1.7
or, should their smoking habits make no difference?	49.4
Can't choose	9.4
(Not answered)	0.8

c. [SMOKOPTR] If decisions like this had to be made, who would you trust most to decide whether non-smokers or smokers should get the operation first?

PLEASE TICK ONE BOX ONLY

	%
The government	2.2
Managers working for local health authorities	2.0
Managers in hospitals	3.7
Hospital doctors	75.4
Can't choose	15.9
(NA)	0.9

A14

OFFICE USE ONLY

N=3103

2.33a [AGEOPWLD] Now suppose another two men with a heart condition go on a hospital waiting list at the same time. Both would benefit from an operation. One man is aged 40 and other aged 60. Who do you think would get the operation first....

PLEASE TICK ONE BOX ONLY

	%
... the younger man,	34.8
the older man,	5.9
or, would their ages make no difference?	47.8
Can't choose	10.5
(NA)	1.0

b. [AGEOPSHD] And in your view, who do you think should get the operation first....

PLEASE TICK ONE BOX ONLY

	%
... the younger man,	19.5
the older man,	5.1
or, would their ages make no difference?	64.8
Can't choose	9.3
(NA)	1.2

2.34a [WGTOPWLD] Again suppose there are two men with a heart condition. One man is of average weight and eats healthily, whilst the other is very overweight and eats unhealthily. Again, both would benefit from an operation. Who do you think would get the operation first....

PLEASE TICK ONE BOX ONLY

	%
... the man whose weight is average and eats healthily,	41.5
the man who is very overweight and eats unhealthily,	3.7
or, would their weights make no difference?	41.4
Can't choose	12.3
(NA)	1.1

b. [WGTOPSHD] And in your view, who do you think should get the operation first...

PLEASE TICK ONE BOX ONLY

	%
... the man whose weight is average and eats healthily,	29.4
the man who is very overweight and eats unhealthily,	2.7
or, would their weights make no difference?	55.1
Can't choose	11.8
(NA)	1.0

A15

Now some questions on different topics.

2.35 As long as there is no threat to security, should prisoners be allowed to ...

PLEASE TICK *ONE BOX ON EACH LINE*

OFFICE USE ONLY

N=2068

		Definitely	Probably	Probably not	Definitely not	Can't choose	(NA)
[PRISBKS] a. ... have as many books as they wish to read?	%	49.5	35.6	4.2	7.0	1.6	2.1
[PRISVIST] b. ... visit home occasionally, say one weekend a month?	%	3.8	14.9	23.5	51.9	3.9	2.1
[PRISCONG] c. ... have their wife or husband occasionally stay overnight with them at the prison?	%	4.2	13.4	16.7	60.1	3.4	2.3
[PRISJOB] d. ... earn a little money in prison?	%	18.8	46.7	9.2	20.7	2.8	1.8

2.36 And please tick one box for each statement below to show how much you agree or disagree with it.

PLEASE TICK *ONE BOX ON EACH LINE*

		Agree strongly	Agree	Neither agree nor disagree	Disagree	Disagree strongly	(DK)	(NA)
[PCNOSOLC] a. The police should be allowed to question suspects for up to a week without letting them see a solicitor	%	3.4	9.1	12.6	42.6	30.0	0.0	2.2
[REFUGEES] b. Refugees who are in danger because of their political beliefs should always be welcome in Britain	%	6.5	20.5	31.1	29.1	10.8	0.0	2.0
[PCCOMPLN] c. Serious complaints against the police should be investigated by an independent body, not by the police themselves	%	44.1	45.4	5.3	2.6	0.7	0.0	1.9
[IDCARDS] d. Every adult in Britain should have to carry an identity card	%	24.2	33.2	21.0	12.4	7.3	-	1.9

[IMMEXCLU]
2.37 How much do you agree or disagree with the following statement?

"Britain should take stronger measures to exclude illegal immigrants."

PLEASE TICK *ONE BOX ONLY*

	%
Strongly agree	45.5
Agree	28.2
Neither agree nor disagree	14.6
Disagree	5.0
Strongly disagree	2.2
Can't choose	3.2
(NA)	1.4

A16

OFFICE USE ONLY

N=2068

2.38 Britain controls the numbers of people from abroad that are allowed to settle in this country. Please say, for each of the groups below, whether you think Britain should allow more settlement, less settlement, or about the same amount as now.

PLEASE TICK *ONE BOX ON EACH LINE*

		More settlement	Less settlement	About the same as now	(DK)	(NA)
a. *[AUSIEIMM]* Australians and New Zealanders	%	8.3	29.0	59.5	0.3	3.0
b. *[ASIANIMM]* Indians and Pakistanis	%	1.7	52.9	42.2	0.2	2.9
c. *[EECIMM]* People from European Union countries	%	6.2	39.2	51.3	0.3	3.1
d. *[WIIMM]* West Indians	%	2.0	49.3	45.3	0.2	3.2
e. *[EEUROIMM]* People from Eastern Europe	%	3.6	45.4	47.4	0.2	3.4
f. *[HKONGIMM]* People from Hong Kong	%	9.9	43.1	43.5	0.2	3.2
g. *[AFRICIMM]* Africans	%	2.9	49.0	44.7	0.2	3.3

[RELCONTL]
2.39 Now thinking about the families (husbands, wives, children, parents) of people who have already settled in Britain, would you say in general that Britain should ...

PLEASE TICK *ONE BOX ONLY*

	%
... be stricter in controlling the settlement of close relatives,	49.5
OR ... be less strict in controlling the settlement of close relatives,	10.5
OR keep the controls about the same as now?	38.1
(DK)	0.2
(NA)	1.8

2.40 Here are some ideas about sending people to prison. Please tick one box on each line to show how much you agree or disagree with each of these statements.

PLEASE TICK *ONE BOX ON EACH LINE*

		Strongly agree	Agree	Neither agree nor disagree	Disagree	Strongly disagree	Can't choose	(NA)
[PRISSEN1] a. People who get sent to prison have much too easy a time	%	23.9	37.2	22.8	8.1	1.9	4.1	2.0
[PRISSEN2] b. Prisons should try harder to reform prisoners, rather than just punishing them	%	25.3	54.0	10.3	5.3	1.4	1.5	2.2
[PRISSEN3] c. Prisoners who behave well should usually be released before the end of their sentence	%	3.9	30.8	20.7	30.1	9.6	3.0	2.0
[PRISSEN4] d. Courts should give longer sentences to criminals	%	23.2	37.9	23.6	7.9	1.8	4.0	1.7
[PRISSEN5] e. Only hardened criminals, or those who are a danger to society, should be sent to prison	%	13.4	17.8	12.5	38.1	14.1	2.1	2.0
[PRISSEN6] f. Life sentences should mean life	%	57.9	29.1	4.5	3.8	1.2	1.9	1.6

OFFICE USE ONLY

A17

N=993

[PROTRCMX]

2.41 Some people think that better relations between Protestants and Catholics in Northern Ireland will only come about through more mixing of the two communities. Others think that better relations will only come about through more separation. Which comes closest to your views?

PLEASE TICK **ONE** BOX ONLY

	%
Better relations will come about through more mixing	89.3
Better relations will come about through more separation	5.5
(DK)	1.0
(NA)	4.3

2.42 People feel closer to some groups than to others. For you personally, how close would you say you feel towards...

PLEASE TICK **ONE** BOX ON EACH LINE

		Very close	Fairly close	A little close	Not very close	Not at all close	(DK)	(NA)
a.	...people born in the same area as you? [CLSEBORN]	% 6.4	40.3	25.4	17.3	6.9	0.2	3.5
b.	...people who have the same social class background as yours? [CLSECLAS]	% 8.0	45.4	30.1	10.1	3.4	0.3	2.8
c.	...people who have the same religious background as yours? [CLSERELG]	% 6.5	26.9	25.6	23.9	12.0	0.4	4.8
d.	...people of the same race as you? [CLSERACE]	% 9.3	38.3	29.6	13.9	4.4	0.3	4.2
e.	...people who live in the same area as you do now? [CLSELIVE]	% 7.1	37.9	32.4	13.8	4.7	0.3	3.9
f.	...people who have the same political beliefs as you? [CLSEPOL]	% 3.3	25.8	29.1	23.6	13.5	0.5	4.2

[NIBRITRN]

2.43a How much say do you think a British government of any party should have in the way Northern Ireland is run? Do you think it should have ...

PLEASE TICK **ONE** BOX ONLY

	%
...a great deal of say,	14.2
some say,	33.4
a little say,	19.3
or, no say at all?	17.5
Can't choose	13.6
(NA)	2.0

A18

N=993

[NIEIRERN]

2.43b And how much say do you think an Irish government of any party should have in the way Northern Ireland is run? Do you think it should have ...

PLEASE TICK **ONE** BOX ONLY

	%
...a great deal of say,	30.4
some say,	32.1
a little say,	14.2
or, no say at all?	8.4
Can't choose	12.6
(NA)	2.3

[ADALLSE2]

2.44 Which one of these two statements comes closer to your own view?

PLEASE TICK **ONE** BOX ONLY

	%
Adults should be allowed to see whatever films they like, even if the film shows a lot of violence or pornography	31.5
OR	
... films are too violent or pornographic to be available even to adults	59.2
Can't choose	7.2
(NA)	2.2

[PORNCRI2]

2.45 Which one of these two statements comes closer to your own view?

PLEASE TICK **ONE** BOX ONLY

	%
The easy availability of pornography will lead to more sex crimes	60.3
OR	
Pornography does not lead to sex crimes	18.3
Can't choose	19.1
(NA)	2.3

[VIOLTV2]

2.46 Which one of these two statements comes closer to your own view?

PLEASE TICK **ONE** BOX ONLY

	%
We should worry more about violence on TV than about sex on TV	63.2
OR	
We should worry more about sex on TV than about violence on TV	4.0
can't choose	30.7
(NA)	2.0

OFFICE USE ONLY

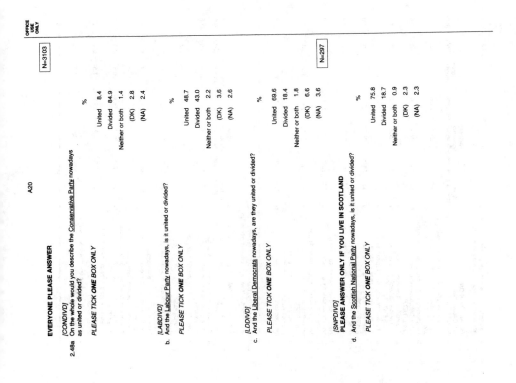

A19

2.47a [CONXTRME]
On the whole would you describe the Conservative Party nowadays as extreme or moderate?

PLEASE TICK *ONE* BOX ONLY

N=3103

OFFICE USE ONLY

	%
Extreme	35.4
Moderate	49.6
Neither or both	7.4
(DK)	3.8
(NA)	3.8

b. [LABXTRME]
And the Labour Party nowadays, is it extreme or moderate?

PLEASE TICK *ONE* BOX ONLY

	%
Extreme	17.8
Moderate	69.4
Neither or both	4.6
(DK)	4.4
(NA)	3.8

c. [LDXTRME]
And the Liberal Democrats nowadays, are they extreme or moderate?

PLEASE TICK *ONE* BOX ONLY

	%
Extreme	7.7
Moderate	77.5
Neither or both	4.4
(DK)	6.2
(NA)	4.2

N=297

d. [SNPXTRME]
PLEASE ANSWER ONLY IF YOU LIVE IN SCOTLAND
And the Scottish National Party nowadays, is it extreme or moderate?

PLEASE TICK *ONE* BOX ONLY

	%
Extreme	42.8
Moderate	48.0
Neither or both	2.5
(DK)	2.7
(NA)	4.1

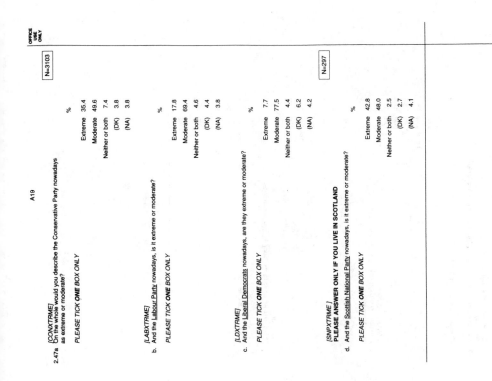

A20

EVERYONE PLEASE ANSWER

[CONDIVD]
2.48a On the whole would you describe the Conservative Party nowadays as united or divided?

PLEASE TICK *ONE* BOX ONLY

N=3103

OFFICE USE ONLY

	%
United	8.4
Divided	84.9
Neither or both	1.4
(DK)	2.8
(NA)	2.4

b. [LABDIVD]
And the Labour Party nowadays, is it united or divided?

PLEASE TICK *ONE* BOX ONLY

	%
United	48.7
Divided	43.0
Neither or both	2.2
(DK)	3.6
(NA)	2.6

c. [LDDIVD]
And the Liberal Democrats nowadays, are they united or divided?

PLEASE TICK *ONE* BOX ONLY

	%
United	69.6
Divided	18.4
Neither or both	1.8
(DK)	6.6
(NA)	3.6

N=297

d. [SNPDIVD]
PLEASE ANSWER ONLY IF YOU LIVE IN SCOTLAND
And the Scottish National Party nowadays, is it united or divided?

PLEASE TICK *ONE* BOX ONLY

	%
United	75.8
Divided	18.7
Neither or both	0.9
(DK)	2.3
(NA)	2.3

A21

EVERYONE PLEASE ANSWER

[MAJPM]

2.49a How good a job do you think John Major is doing as Prime Minister?

PLEASE TICK ONE BOX ONLY

	%
Very good	3.9
Quite good	25.9
Not very good	36.3
Not at all good	28.0
Can't choose	4.5
(NA)	1.4

[BLRPM]

b. How good a job do you think Tony Blair would do as Prime Minister?

PLEASE TICK ONE BOX ONLY

	%
Very good	12.2
Quite good	41.9
Not very good	22.8
Not at all good	8.3
Can't choose	13.2
(NA)	1.5

[ASHPM]

c. How good a job do you think Paddy Ashdown would do as Prime Minister?

PLEASE TICK ONE BOX ONLY

	%
Very good	6.6
Quite good	36.7
Not very good	28.1
Not at all good	12.1
Can't choose	15.1
(NA)	1.5

A22

2.50 Please tick one box for each statement to show how much you agree or disagree with it.

PLEASE TICK ONE BOX ON EACH LINE

[WELFRESP]

		Agree strongly	Agree	Neither agree nor disagree	Disagree	Disagree strongly	(DK)	(NA)
a.	The welfare state makes people nowadays less willing to look after themselves [WELFSTIG]	% 10.7	33.4	24.3	24.8	4.8	0.0	1.9
b.	People receiving social security are made to feel like second class citizens [WELFHELP]	% 11.6	38.2	24.8	21.8	1.7	0.0	1.9
c.	The welfare state encourages people to stop helping each other [MOREWELF]	% 4.8	26.5	33.2	30.4	3.3	0.0	1.8
d.	The government should spend more money on welfare benefits for the poor, even if it leads to higher taxes [UNEMPJOB]	% 10.2	33.0	28.5	23.1	3.3	0.0	1.8
e.	Around here, most unemployed people could find a job if they really wanted one [SOCHELP]	% 8.4	30.7	22.1	30.4	6.6	0.1	1.9
f.	Many people who get social security don't really deserve any help [DOLEFIDL]	% 5.7	22.7	28.0	32.8	8.9	0.1	1.9
g.	Most people on the dole are fiddling in one way or another [WELFFEET]	% 9.1	25.7	32.1	25.1	6.2	0.0	1.8
h.	If welfare benefits weren't so generous, people would learn to stand on their own two feet	% 8.3	24.9	23.5	29.7	11.9	0.0	1.6

2.51 Please tick one box for each statement below to show how much you agree or disagree with it.

PLEASE TICK ONE BOX ON EACH LINE

[WEALTH1]

		Agree strongly	Agree	Neither agree nor disagree	Disagree	Disagree strongly	(DK)	(NA)
a.	Ordinary working people get their fair share of the nation's wealth [RICHLAW]	% 1.3	13.5	21.8	50.3	11.2	0.1	1.8
b.	There is one law for the rich and one for the poor [TRADVALS]	% 26.7	44.6	15.5	10.5	1.3	0.0	1.4
c.	Young people today don't have enough respect for traditional British values [CENSOR]	% 19.8	46.2	22.5	8.4	1.6	0.0	1.4
d.	Censorship of films and magazines is necessary to uphold moral standards [NOTRUNS]	% 20.6	45.4	15.2	13.1	3.9	0.1	1.7
e.	There is no need for strong trade unions to protect employees' working conditions and wages [PRENTBST]	% 2.9	12.9	22.7	43.3	16.5	0.0	1.7
f.	Private enterprise is the best way to solve Britain's economic problems [PUBOWNST]	% 4.1	20.9	40.6	25.1	7.5	0.1	1.7
g.	Major public services and industries ought to be in state ownership	% 12.6	30.2	32.4	18.6	4.4	0.0	1.7

A23

N=3103

2.52 Please tick one box for **each** statement below to show how much you agree or disagree with it.

PLEASE TICK ONE BOX ON EACH LINE

		Agree strongly	Agree	Neither agree nor disagree	Disagree	Disagree strongly	(DK)	(NA)
a.	*[GOVJOB]* It is the government's responsibility to provide a job for everyone who wants one	12.0	33.7	24.4	25.6	2.9	0.0	1.4
b.	*[PROTMEET]* People should be allowed to organise public meetings to protest against the government	15.2	53.5	21.6	7.1	0.7	0.1	1.8
c.	*[GAYSEX]* Homosexual relations are always wrong	11.6	12.7	33.6	27.3	13.0	0.0	1.7
d.	*[TOLERANT]* People in Britain should be more tolerant of those who lead unconventional lives	9.8	39.1	35.5	11.7	2.0	0.1	1.8
e.	*[BANPARTY]* Political parties which wish to overthrow democracy should be allowed to stand in general elections	2.8	16.9	30.9	30.9	16.1	0.1	2.3

(All rows shown as %)

2.53 Please tick one box for **each** statement below to show how much you agree or disagree with it.

PLEASE TICK ONE BOX ON EACH LINE

		Agree strongly	Agree	Neither agree nor disagree	Disagree	Disagree strongly	(DK)	(NA)
a.	*[REDISTRB]* Government should redistribute income from the better-off to those who are less well off	11.9	32.4	25.8	24.0	4.1	0.0	1.8
b.	*[BIGBUSNN]* Big business benefits owners at the expense of workers	14.5	44.0	24.9	12.9	1.5	0.0	2.2
c.	*[WEALTH]* Ordinary working people do not get their fair share of the nation's wealth	16.1	50.1	21.7	10.0	0.6	0.0	1.5
d.	*[INDUST4]* Management will always try to get the better of employees if it gets the chance	16.6	45.0	20.8	15.0	0.8	0.0	1.8
e.	*[STIFSENT]* People who break the law should be given stiffer sentences	28.4	42.5	19.6	7.1	0.6	0.0	1.7
f.	*[DEATHAPP]* For some crimes, the death penalty is the most appropriate sentence	35.1	30.1	12.7	12.0	8.5	0.0	1.6
g.	*[OBEY]* Schools should teach children to obey authority	32.5	48.9	12.4	3.7	0.7	0.0	1.6
h.	*[WRONGLAW]* The law should always be obeyed, even if a particular law is wrong	8.0	29.2	28.6	29.2	3.3	0.1	1.6

(All rows shown as %)

A24

N=3103

[QTIME]
2.54a To help us plan better in future, please tell us about how long it took you to complete this questionnaire.

PLEASE TICK ONE BOX ONLY

	%
Less than 15 minutes	11.9
Between 15 and 20 minutes	27.4
Between 21 and 30 minutes	29.7
Between 31 and 45 minutes	16.6
Between 46 and 60 minutes	7.2
Over one hour	5.4
(NA)	1.8

[SQDATE2]
b. And on what date did you fill in the questionnaire?

PLEASE WRITE IN: DATE [ ] [0] MONTH 1996

Thank you very much for your help

Please keep the completed questionnaire for the interviewer if he or she has arranged to call for it. Otherwise, please post it as soon as possible in the pre-paid envelope provided.

B

SOCIAL & COMMUNITY

SCPR

PLANNING RESEARCH

Head Office: 35 NORTHAMPTON SQUARE,
LONDON EC1V 0AX
Tel. 0171/250 1866 Fax: 0171/250 1524

Field and DP Office: 100 KINGS ROAD,
BRENTWOOD, ESSEX CM14 4LX
Tel. 01277 200600 Fax: 01277 214117

Spring 1996

P.1525

BRITISH SOCIAL ATTITUDES 1996
MAIN SAMPLE
SELF-COMPLETION QUESTIONNAIRE

OFFICE USE ONLY		
6-8		Cluster number
9-13		Spare
14-15	3 2	Card no.
16-18		Spare
27-31		Batch no.
32-34		Spare

INTERVIEWER TO ENTER		
1-5	8	Serial number
19-22	0	Sampling point
23-26		Interviewer number

To the selected respondent:

Thank you very much for agreeing to take part in this important study - the twelfth in this annual series. The study consists of this self-completion questionnaire, and the interview you have already completed. The results of the survey are published in a book each autumn; some of the questions are also being asked in twenty-four other countries, as part of an international survey.

Completing the questionnaire:

The questions inside cover a wide range of subjects, but most can be answered simply by placing a tick (✓) in one or more of the boxes. No special knowledge is required: we are confident that everyone will be able to take part, not just those with strong views or particular viewpoints. The questionnaire should not take very long to complete, and we hope you will find it interesting and enjoyable. **Only you should fill it in, and not anyone else at your address.** The answers you give will be treated as confidential and anonymous.

Returning the questionnaire:

Your interviewer will arrange with you the most convenient way of returning the questionnaire. If the interviewer has arranged to call back for it, please fill it in and keep it safely until then. If not, please complete it and post it back in the pre-paid, addressed envelope, AS SOON AS YOU POSSIBLY CAN.

THANK YOU AGAIN FOR YOUR HELP.

Social and Community Planning Research is an independent social research institute registered as a charitable trust. Its projects are funded by government departments, local authorities, universities and foundations to provide information on social issues in Britain. The British Social Attitudes survey series is funded mainly by one of the Sainsbury Family

B10

Note: questions B2.01-2.09 are the same as questions A2.26-A2.34 of version A of the questionnaire.

N=1075

2.10 How likely or unlikely do you think it is <u>within the next 25 years</u> that genetic information will be used to judge a person's suitability for getting ...

PLEASE TICK ONE BOX ON EACH LINE

		Very likely	Quite likely	Not very likely	Not at all likely	Can't choose	(NA)
	[DNAINSUR]	%					
a.	... health or life insurance?	30.9	41.5	13.2	3.2	9.3	1.9
	[DNAJOB]	%					
b.	... a job they've applied for?	13.4	29.4	33.7	10.2	10.2	3.2
	[DNACREDT]	%					
c.	... credit at the bank?	11.5	21.4	34.5	18.5	10.8	3.2

B11

Note: questions B2.11-2.16 are the same as questions A2.35-A2.40 of version A of the questionnaire.

N=1075

Now some questions about the countryside.
[DAMAGE]

2.17a Which one of these two statements comes <u>closest</u> to your own views?

PLEASE TICK ONE BOX ONLY

%

Industry should be prevented from causing damage to the countryside, even if this sometimes leads to higher prices   91.6

OR

Industry should keep prices down, even if this sometimes causes damage to the countryside   6.3

(DK) 0.2

(NA) 1.9

[CTRYJOBS]

b. And which of these two statements comes <u>closest</u> to your own views?

PLEASE TICK ONE BOX ONLY

%

The countryside should be protected from development, even if this sometimes leads to fewer jobs   75.8

OR

New jobs should be created, even if this sometimes causes damage to the countryside   21.7

(DK) 0.1

(NA) 2.4

B12

N=1075

2.18 Please tick one box on each line to show how you feel about ...

PLEASE TICK ONE BOX ON EACH LINE
[CTRYFARM]

	It should be stopped altogether	It should be discouraged	Don't mind one way or the other	It should be encouraged	(DK)	(NA)
a. ... increasing the amount of countryside being farmed [CTRYFARM] %	4.3	27.5	47.7	18.5	0.0	2.1
b. ... building new housing in country areas [CTRYHSNG] %	11.1	58.7	22.0	6.5	-	1.7
c. ... putting the needs of farmers before protection of wildlife [WILDLIFE] %	15.7	54.2	22.5	5.5	0.0	2.0
d. ... providing more roads in country areas [CTRYROAD] %	14.6	52.7	22.8	8.0	-	1.8
e. ... increasing the number of picnic areas and camping sites in the countryside [PICNIC] %	2.6	16.9	32.1	46.8	-	1.5

2.19a [CLOSEHOM]
The new owner of a stately home containing historic paintings and furniture wishes to close it to the public. Should he or should he not have the right to do this?

PLEASE TICK ONE BOX ONLY
%

Definitely should have the right	30.9
Probably should have the right	29.9
Probably should not have the right	10.3
Definitely should not have the right	5.3
It depends	18.6
Can't choose	3.9
(NA)	1.0

b. [CLOSEEST]
A new landowner of a large estate in a beautiful part of Britain decides to fence off a remote part of his land to stop people visiting it. Should he or should he not have the right to do this?

PLEASE TICK ONE BOX ONLY
%

Definitely should have the right	25.9
Probably should have the right	31.7
Probably should not have the right	13.0
Definitely should not have the right	10.6
It depends	15.4
Can't choose	2.5
(NA)	0.9

B13

N=1075

c. [CLOSEPTH]
Suppose a rarely-used public footpath runs through farming land. Should the farmer be able to get it closed without a lot of fuss and bother?

PLEASE TICK ONE BOX ONLY
%

Definitely should have the right	10.1
Probably should have the right	18.6
Probably should not have the right	20.6
Definitely should not have the right	32.7
It depends	16.0
Can't choose	1.4
(NA)	0.5

And now some questions about the environment.

2.20 How much do you agree or disagree with each of these statements?

PLEASE TICK ONE BOX ON EACH LINE
[ENVIRDIF]

	Strongly agree	Agree	Neither agree nor disagree	Disagree	Strongly disagree	Can't choose	(NA)
a. It is just too difficult for someone like me to do much about the environment [ENVIRRGT] %	6.9	26.9	20.3	30.4	7.9	4.5	3.1
b. I do what is right for the environment, even when it costs more money or takes more time %	6.5	44.3	30.1	8.0	0.8	7.1	3.2

2.21a [CARSPOL1]
In general, do you think that air pollution caused by cars is ...

PLEASE TICK ONE BOX ONLY
%

... extremely dangerous for the environment,	25.1
very dangerous,	23.8
somewhat dangerous,	41.7
not very dangerous,	6.0
or, not dangerous at all for the environment?	0.3
Can't choose	2.7
(NA)	0.4

OFFICE USE ONLY

B14

N=1075

OFFICE USE ONLY

[CARSPOL2]

2.21b And do you think that air pollution caused by cars is ...

PLEASE TICK *ONE BOX ONLY*

	%
... extremely dangerous for you and your family,	20.7
very dangerous,	21.5
somewhat dangerous,	46.1
not very dangerous,	7.9
or, not dangerous at all for you and your family?	0.8
Can't choose	2.6
(NA)	0.4

[CARSPOL3]

c. Within the next ten years, how likely do you think it is that there will be a large increase in ill-health in Britain's cities as a result of air pollution caused by cars?

PLEASE TICK *ONE BOX ONLY*

	%
Certain to happen	25.4
Very likely to happen	29.2
Fairly likely to happen	29.6
Not very likely to happen	11.0
Certain not to happen	-
Can't choose	4.5
(NA)	0.4

[CARSPOL1]

2.22 Please tick the box that comes closest to your opinion of how true this statement is.

"Cars are not really an important cause of air pollution in Britain."

PLEASE TICK *ONE BOX ONLY*

	%
Definitely true	5.0
Probably true	21.6
Probably not true	27.3
Definitely not true	40.8
Can't choose	4.8
(NA)	0.6

B15

N=1075

OFFICE USE ONLY

[PROTENVP]

2.23 If you had to chose, which one of the following would be closest to your views?

PLEASE TICK *ONE BOX ONLY*

	%
Government should let ordinary people decide for themselves how to protect the environment, even if it means they don't always do the right thing	23.7
OR	
Government should pass laws to make ordinary people protect the environment, even if it interferes with people's rights to make their own decisions	47.7
Can't choose	26.7
(NA)	1.8

[PROTENVB]

2.24 And which one of the following would be closest to your own views?

PLEASE TICK *ONE BOX ONLY*

	%
Government should let businesses decide for themselves how to protect the environment, even if it means they don't always do the right thing	4.4
OR	
Government should pass laws to make businesses protect the environment, even if it interferes with business' rights to make their own decisions	83.1
Can't choose	11.1
(NA)	1.4

[ENVPRTCT]

2.25 On the whole, which of these statements comes closest to your own views?

PLEASE TICK *ONE BOX ONLY*

	%
It's mainly up to the government to protect the environment - ordinary people can't do much on their own	54.3
OR	
It's mainly up to ordinary people to do what they can to protect the environment - the government can do only a limited amount	42.8
(Can't choose)	0.2
(NA)	2.7

2.26 Please tick one box for each statement below to show how much you agree or disagree with it.

PLEASE TICK *ONE BOX ON EACH LINE*

	Agree strongly	Agree	Neither agree nor disagree	Disagree	Disagree strongly	(DK)	(NA)
[GOVENVIR] a. The government should do more to protect the environment, even if it leads to higher taxes	11.8	45.4	28.9	11.0	0.9	0.1	1.8
[INDENVIR] b. Industry should do more to protect the environment, even if it leads to lower profits and fewer jobs	16.7	49.9	23.8	6.7	0.5	0.1	2.3
[PLENVIR] c. Ordinary people should do more to protect the environment, even if it means paying higher prices	9.3	50.6	26.0	10.9	0.7	0.1	2.3
[CARALLOW] d. People should be allowed to use their cars as much as they like, even if it causes damage to the environment	2.0	13.8	34.6	37.2	9.8	0.1	2.5

B16

[TOWNTRAN]

Now, two questions on towns and public transport.

2.27a Thinking first about *towns and cities*. If the government *had* to choose …

PLEASE TICK *ONE BOX ONLY*

	%
It should improve roads	25.8
It should improve public transport	72.3
(DK)	0.1
(NA)	1.8

[CTRYTRAN]

b. And in *country areas*, if the government *had* to choose …

PLEASE TICK *ONE BOX ONLY*

	%
It should improve roads	29.4
It should improve public transport	68.4
(DK)	0.2
(NA)	2.1

2.28 How much trust do you have in each of the following groups to help Britain make the right decisions about the environment?

PLEASE TICK *ONE BOX* ON EACH LINE

		A lot of trust	Some trust	Very little trust	No trust at all	Can't choose	(NA)
[SCIENENV] a.	Scientists	% 18.1	59.4	11.3	2.9	4.6	3.6
[BUSENV] b.	Business and industry	% 1.7	24.7	47.3	17.4	5.0	3.9
[ENVENV] c.	Environmental groups	% 30.8	50.4	9.3	2.7	3.8	3.0
[GOVTENV] d.	The government	% 2.9	33.5	37.5	17.4	4.6	4.0
[PEOPENV] e.	Ordinary people	% 9.3	55.0	22.4	3.6	6.5	3.1

[CARWALK]

2.29 How much do you agree or disagree with this statement?

"Many of the short journeys I now make by car I could just as easily walk."

PLEASE TICK *ONE BOX ONLY*

	%
Agree strongly	22.5
Agree	33.3
Neither agree nor disagree	11.0
Disagree	17.7
Disagree strongly	6.4
I never travel by car	5.1
Can't choose	2.4
(NA)	1.6

N=1075

B17

2.30 Please tick *one* box for *each* statement to show how much you agree or disagree.

PLEASE TICK *ONE BOX* ON EACH LINE

		Agree strongly	Agree	Neither agree nor disagree	Disagree	Disagree strongly	Can't choose	(NA)
[CARTAXHI] a.	For the sake of the environment, car users should pay higher taxes	% 3.3	15.9	22.8	39.2	14.7	2.6	1.4
[MOTORWAY] b.	The government should build more motorways to reduce traffic congestion	% 4.5	20.6	21.0	34.2	14.4	3.8	1.5
[CARECON] c.	A thriving car industry is essential to Britain's economy	% 6.0	34.5	30.6	17.8	5.3	4.3	1.5
[CARCONV] d.	Driving one's own car is too convenient to give up for the sake of the environment	% 3.1	31.7	29.8	24.2	4.8	4.6	1.7
[BUILDTRA] e.	Building more roads just encourages more traffic	% 18.6	38.3	18.9	17.6	2.2	2.8	1.6

[CUTCARS]

2.31a How important do you think it is to *cut down the number of cars* on Britain's roads?

PLEASE TICK *ONE BOX ONLY*

	%
Very important	28.2
Fairly important	43.3
Not very important	17.8
Not at all important	3.4
Can't choose	6.6
(NA)	0.8

[PTIMPRIM]

b. And how important is it to *improve public transport* in Britain?

PLEASE TICK *ONE BOX ONLY*

	%
Very important	67.9
Fairly important	27.1
Not very important	2.7
Not at all important	0.0
Can't choose	1.5
(NA)	0.7

N=1075

OFFICE USE ONLY

B18

N=1075

2.32 Many people feel that public transport <u>should</u> be improved. Here are some ways of finding the money to do it. How much would you support or oppose each one, as a way of raising money to improve public transport?

PLEASE TICK ONE BOX ON EACH LINE [PTIMPR1]		Strongly support	Support	Neither support nor oppose	Oppose	Strongly oppose	Can't choose	OFFICE USE ONLY (NA)
a. Gradually doubling the cost of petrol over the next ten years [PTIMPR2]	%	3.2	12.8	18.0	40.1	20.8	2.8	2.4
b. Charging all motorists around £2 each time they enter or drive through a city or town centre at peak times [PTIMPR3]	%	6.7	23.5	14.4	32.9	17.9	2.1	2.4
c. Cutting in half spending on new roads [PTIMPR4]	%	8.7	27.2	23.2	23.3	11.0	4.3	2.3
d. Cutting in half spending on maintenance of the roads we have already [PTIMPR5]	%	1.2	4.9	15.8	46.5	25.6	3.4	2.6
e. Charging £1 for every 50 miles motorists travel on motorways [PTIMPR6]	%	6.1	23.7	17.1	29.8	17.6	3.2	2.4
f. Increasing taxes like VAT that we all pay on goods and services	%	1.7	9.9	15.1	39.9	28.2	3.1	2.0

Note: questions B2.33-2.41 are the same as questions A2.47-2.54 of Version A of the questionnaire.

C

Spring 1996

Head Office: 35 NORTHAMPTON SQUARE,
LONDON EC1V 0AX
Tel: 0171-250 1866 Fax: 0171-250 1524

Field and DP Office: 100 KINGS ROAD,
BRENTWOOD, ESSEX CM14 4LX
Tel: 01277 200600 Fax: 01277 214117

SCPR

P.1525

BRITISH SOCIAL ATTITUDES 1996
MAIN SAMPLE
SELF-COMPLETION QUESTIONNAIRE

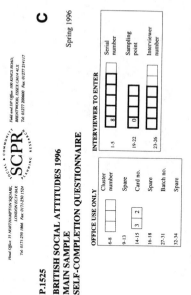

OFFICE USE ONLY	
6-8	Cluster number
9-13	Spare
14-15	Card no. [3][2]
16-18	Spare
27-31	Batch no.
32-34	Spare

INTERVIEWER TO ENTER	
1-5 [8]	Serial number
19-22 [0]	Sampling point
23-26	Interviewer number

To the selected respondent:

Thank you very much for agreeing to take part in this important study - the twelfth in this annual series. The study consists of this self-completion questionnaire, and the interview you have already completed. The results of the survey are published in a book each autumn; some of the questions are also being asked in twenty-four other countries, as part of an international survey.

Completing the questionnaire:

The questions inside cover a wide range of subjects, but most can be answered simply by placing a tick (✓) in one or more of the boxes. No special knowledge is required: we are confident that everyone will be able to take part, not just those with strong views or particular viewpoints. The questionnaire should not take very long to complete, and we hope you will find it interesting and enjoyable. **Only you should fill it in, and not anyone else at your address.** The answers you give will be treated as confidential and anonymous.

Returning the questionnaire:

Your interviewer will arrange with you the most convenient way of returning the questionnaire. If the interviewer has arranged to call back for it, please fill it in and keep it safely until then. If not, please complete it and post it back in the pre-paid, addressed envelope, AS SOON AS YOU POSSIBLY CAN.

THANK YOU AGAIN FOR YOUR HELP.

Social and Community Planning Research is an independent social research institute registered as a charitable trust. Its projects are funded by government departments, local authorities, universities and foundations to provide information on social issues in Britain. The British Social Attitudes survey series is funded mainly by one of the Sainsbury Family

C10

Note: question C2.01-2.09 are the same as questions A2.26-2.34 of Version A of the questionnaire. Question C2.10 is the same as question B2.10 of version B of the questionnaire.

N=1035

2.11 From what you know or have heard, please tick one box on each line to show how well you think state secondary schools nowadays ...

PLEASE TICK ONE BOX ON EACH LINE		Very well	Quite well	Not very well	Not at all well	(DK)	(NA)
[STATSEC1] a. ... prepare young people for work?	%	3.8	34.0	51.0	7.9	0.3	2.9
[STATSEC2] b. ... teach young people basic skills such as reading, writing and maths?	%	9.5	46.4	33.5	7.9	0.3	2.4
[STATSEC3] c. ... bring out young people's natural abilities?	%	5.2	35.3	45.7	10.9	0.4	2.5

2.12 Please tick one box to show how much you agree or disagree with each of these statements.

PLEASE TICK ONE BOX ON EACH LINE		Agree strongly	Agree	Neither agree nor disagree	Disagree	Disagree strongly	Can't choose	(NA)
[MORALTH1] a. Teaching children the difference between right and wrong should be left to the family and kept out of schools	%	12.5	11.0	13.5	33.4	26.3	1.6	1.6
[MORALTH2] b. Schools should spend more time teaching children right from wrong, even if it means less time is spent on basic subjects like reading and arithmetic	%	6.6	19.4	20.7	36.3	13.1	2.6	1.3

C11

2.13 Now please tick one box for each statement to show how much you agree or disagree.

N=1035

PLEASE TICK ONE BOX ON EACH LINE		Agree strongly	Agree	Neither agree nor disagree	Disagree	Disagree strongly	Can't choose	(NA)
[VOLUNT1] a. As a society, we rely too much on volunteers	%	14.2	43.1	24.2	12.6	1.5	2.5	1.9
[VOLUNT2] b. Everyone has a duty to do voluntary work at some time in their lives	%	4.0	25.6	30.1	31.8	4.3	2.0	2.1
[VOLUNT3] c. I would rather donate money to a charity than give up my time for it	%	2.8	21.8	33.2	28.9	5.9	5.6	1.9

2.14 Please tick one box for each statement to show how much you agree or disagree.

PLEASE TICK ONE BOX ON EACH LINE		Agree strongly	Agree	Neither agree nor disagree	Disagree	Disagree strongly	Can't choose	(NA)
[CHARMANY] a. There are so many charities that it is difficult to decide which to give to	%	22.4	51.2	12.6	10.5	0.8	1.4	1.1
[CHARWAST] b. Most charities are wasteful in their use of funds	%	6.8	27.1	30.4	25.3	4.0	5.2	1.2
[CHARITY1] c. The smaller the charity, the more likely it is to put its money to good use	%	6.7	27.3	38.1	19.8	2.2	4.3	1.5
[CHARITY2] d. Nowadays charities can only do their job properly if they are run by paid professionals, not volunteers	%	3.6	17.3	25.6	40.4	7.5	4.1	1.5
[CHARITY3] e. The more money people give to British charities, the less the government will spend on people in need	%	20.8	44.0	16.4	12.6	2.3	2.8	1.1
[CHARITY4] f. Too often charities don't bother to say how the money they get is being spent	%	16.3	52.8	17.6	8.6	1.1	2.4	1.1
[CHARITY5] g. The bigger a charity becomes, the more out of touch it gets with those it is trying to help	%	12.3	31.2	31.6	18.9	1.4	3.4	1.3
[CHARITY6] h. Doing voluntary work is a good thing for volunteers because it makes them feel they are contributing to society	%	17.2	60.4	15.9	3.0	0.2	2.2	1.1

C12

2.15 For each statement please tick one box to show how much you agree or disagree with it.

PLEASE TICK ONE BOX ON EACH LINE

[SAVFRRET]

N=1035

	Agree strongly	Agree	Neither agree nor disagree	Disagree	Disagree strongly	(DK)	(NA)
a. The government should encourage people to provide something for their own retirement instead of relying only on the state pension [PNGYABAN] %	11.2	42.1	19.2	18.7	7.2	-	1.7
b. The government is gradually abandoning its responsibility to provide adequate old age pensions [STPENWOR] %	37.8	45.0	8.1	5.5	2.0	-	1.6
c. State pensions used to provide a better standard of living than they do nowadays %	24.7	37.5	24.0	10.1	1.5	0.4	1.8

2.16 [HHTAX] Do you consider the amount of income tax that your household has to pay is …

PLEASE TICK ONE BOX ONLY

	%
… much too high,	14.0
too high,	30.9
about right,	31.4
too low,	4.6
or, much too low?	0.2
Can't choose	4.3
Does not apply	13.6
(NA)	1.0

2.17 [COUNTAX] Do you consider the amount of council tax that your household has to pay is …

PLEASE TICK ONE BOX ONLY

	%
… much too high,	20.4
too high,	31.8
about right,	34.8
too low,	1.5
or, much too low?	0.2
Can't choose	3.0
Does not apply	7.6
(NA)	0.8

C13

N=1035

2.18 [INDTAX] Do you consider the amount of tax that business and industry have to pay is …

PLEASE TICK ONE BOX ONLY

	%
… much too high,	8.6
too high,	22.7
about right,	29.9
too low,	13.1
or, much too low?	1.5
Can't choose	23.2
(NA)	0.9

2.19 [HILOWTAX] Do you think that people with high incomes should pay a larger share of their income in taxes than those with low incomes, the same share, or a smaller share?

PLEASE TICK ONE BOX ONLY

	%
Much larger share	13.9
Larger	55.8
The same share	23.6
Smaller	0.9
Much smaller share	0.4
Can't choose	4.8
(NA)	0.7

C14

N=1035

2.21a **[VAT500]**
Consider this situation:

A householder is having a job done by a builder. He is told that if he pays cash, he will not be charged VAT. So he pays cash and saves £500. Do you feel this is wrong or not wrong?

*PLEASE TICK **ONE BOX** ONLY*

	%
Not wrong	27.8
A bit wrong	26.8
Wrong	36.7
Seriously wrong	6.7
Can't choose	7.2
(NA)	0.8

b. **[VAT500 DO]**
And how likely do you think it is that you would do this, if you found yourself in this situation?

*PLEASE TICK **ONE BOX** ONLY*

	%
Very likely	33.7
Fairly likely	29.2
Not very likely	18.3
Not at all likely	9.6
Can't choose	8.3
(NA)	0.9

C15

N=1035

2.22a **[BEN500]**
Now consider this situation:

An unemployed person on benefit takes a casual job and is paid in cash. He does not report it to the benefit office and is £500 in pocket. Do you feel this is wrong or not wrong?

*PLEASE TICK **ONE BOX** ONLY*

	%
Not wrong	7.2
A bit wrong	17.2
Wrong	48.5
Seriously wrong	23.3
Can't choose	2.9
(NA)	0.9

b. **[BEN500DO]**
And how likely do you think it is that you would do this, if you found yourself in this situation?

*PLEASE TICK **ONE BOX** ONLY*

	%
Very likely	9.3
Fairly likely	14.4
Not very likely	30.8
Not at all likely	39.4
Can't choose	5.2
(NA)	0.9

2.23a **[PAY500]**
A person in paid work takes on an extra weekend job and is paid in cash. He does not declare it for tax and so is £500 in pocket. Do you feel this is wrong or not wrong?

*PLEASE TICK **ONE BOX** ONLY*

	%
Not wrong	15.9
A bit wrong	28.9
Wrong	41.7
Seriously wrong	8.2
Can't choose	4.5
(NA)	0.9

b. **[PAY500DO]**
And how likely do you think it is that you would do this, if you found yourself in this situation?

*PLEASE TICK **ONE BOX** ONLY*

	%
Very likely	14.4
Fairly likely	25.1
Not very likely	27.4
Not at all likely	26.7
Can't choose	5.5
(NA)	0.9

Note: questions C2.24-C2.31 are the same as questions A2.47-A2.54 of Version A of the questionnaire.

Subject index